De Vere as Shakespeare

De Vere as Shakespeare

An Oxfordian Reading of the Canon

WILLIAM FARINA

Foreword by Felicia Hardison Londré

McFarland & Company, Inc., Publishers
Jefferson, North Carolina, and London

Portions of the chapter on *Twelfth Night* are reprinted from William Farina, "Twelfth Night in Siena," *The Shakespeare Oxford Newsletter* (Shakespeare-Oxford Society), Winter 2003, pp. 5–6.

Portions of the chapter on *Venus and Adonis* are reprinted from William Farina, "Edward de Vere and the Courtesan Culture of Venice," *The Shakespeare Oxford Newsletter* (Shakespeare-Oxford Society), Winter 2004, pp. 6–8.

LIBRARY OF CONGRESS CATALOGUING-IN-PUBLICATION DATA

Farina, William, 1955–
De Vere as Shakespeare : an Oxfordian reading of the canon /
William Farina ; foreword by Felicia Hardison Londré.
p.   cm.
Includes bibliographical references and index.

ISBN 0-7864-2383-8 (softcover : 50# alkaline paper) ∞

1. Shakespeare, William, 1564–1616—Authorship—Oxford theory.
2. Oxford, Edward De Vere, Earl of, 1550–1604—Authorship.
I. Title
PR2947.O9F37   2006   822.'3—dc22   2005034171

British Library cataloguing data are available

On the cover: Edward de Vere, 17th Earl of Oxford, unkown artist,
oil on canvas 29¼" × 25", 1575 (*National Portrait Gallery, London*)

Manufactured in the United States of America

*McFarland & Company, Inc., Publishers
Box 611, Jefferson, North Carolina 28640
www.mcfarlandpub.com*

To my partner in life, Marion Buckley,
who first conceived of the idea,
and without whose continuing encouragement
and feedback this project would
never have come to fruition

Acknowledgments

Thanks to Robert and Norma Howe for their unwavering personal and professional support; Richard Whalen for his cool-headedness and prophetic instincts; Daniel L. Wright for his incredible patience and consistently good advice; Felicia Hardison Londré for lending me a very small part of her vast credibility; Jerome Bloom for his numerous helpful suggestions; Philip and Kathleen Farina for their keen, down-to-earth perceptiveness; and Robert L. Wolf, for getting me started on this kick. Special thanks to the staffs at the Harold Washington Library Center and Newberry Library in Chicago. You guys are the best.

Table of Contents

Part Three: Tragedies and Poems

Foreword

by Felicia Hardison Londré

It is exciting when works of literature written over 400 years ago still generate debate and controversy. Shakespeare's plays are so rich in ideas and in the language that expresses them, so insightful in the portrayal of characters with conflicting views, so provocative in challenging presumptions and evocative in conjuring the mysteries of existence that there is and will be endless fodder for interpretation.

The best works of art rightly give rise to variety of interpretation. In turn, our understanding of a work of art says something about us. As Gary Taylor noted in *Reinventing Shakespeare* (411): "We find in Shakespeare only what we bring to him or what others have left behind; he gives us back our own values." Shakespeare's plays speak to us and through us both as literary works and as dramas embodied by living actors engaged in a collaborative process of interpreting and communicating. Multiple meanings ripple outward through audiences.

While latitude for interpretation surely contributes to the appeal of Shakespeare's plays, ambiguities in the biography of the author are not so welcome. Biography is supposed to rest on documented facts, as many as can be mustered from baptismal records, contracts, account books, letters, diaries, wills, tombstones. Only after establishing that foundation of primary-source documentation does a biographer proceed to fill in the blanks using common sense, knowledge of the era, and what can be inferred from the subject's creative writing. The problem with Shakespeare biography is how few documented facts we have to start with. If we weed out the conjectures connecting the dots of what is actually on the record and keep our focus on the man from Stratford himself without reference to the world around him, we can scarcely fill a page. What is on that page will show no direct link to the theater in London or to the Earl of Southampton or to many of the other tenets of Shakespearean biographies. Yet we cannot make assumptions based upon what is not there. What is on that page can neither prove nor disprove the Stratford man's authorship of the plays and sonnets we love.

It is not enough to use the circular reasoning employed by the judge in a Houston trial on the authorship question: Shakespeare wrote Shakespeare because Shakespeare's name is on the published work. What we seek is not the conflation of pen name and real name, but the identity of the person who wrote the works, many of which were originally published with no author's name on them. And so we begin to sift the contextual evidence to see how it might fit with the documented facts that we do have. At this point the plays may well serve as resources for conjecture about their author.

What is surprising is how vehemently Shakespeare scholarship hardens into intransigence when it moves from analyzing the works to relating them to their authorship. I say this is surprising because it is contrary to everything we expect of academia. Those who devote their lives to the pursuit of knowledge are supposed to be open-minded enough to follow the clues even when they do not like where the trail is taking them. Scholars whose interests take them along other paths should be honest enough to acknowledge that until we have absolute proof of authorship one way of another, it must remain an open question; and those who choose to direct their research toward uncovering the facts of authorship are entitled to as much respect as those who theorize about the dramatic literature.

I have wondered why the minds of otherwise intelligent people often snap shut when it comes to the Shakespeare authorship question. One possibility is concern that allowing any opening would admit a wedge and the ensuing debate could lead outside the comfort zone of English professors who specialize in Shakespeare. The very real problem is that examining the evidence for the authorship quickly demands familiarity with a whole slew of Elizabethan personalities and with chronologies of public and court events from the 1550s, if not much earlier. Most Shakespeare scholars teach in English departments, and they didn't sign up to be historians.

When I am asked what I consider to be the single most compelling evidence in favor of Edward de Vere, 17th Earl of Oxford, as a candidate for the Shakespeare authorship, my answer usually is the dates of the plays. But this answer requires some explanation. We all know that the dates traditionally assigned to the plays are conjectural, based upon the publication date as a *terminus ad quem* and on the fact that the young man from Stratford could not have left his family and come to London earlier than the latter 1580s. Thus, to consider the Stratford man as the author, one has to squeeze a lot of plays into scarcely two decades, with no years for apprenticeship. My focus on the dates, however, derives not from the negative evidence against the Stratford man, but from the positive evidence in the plays that often links them topically to events of the 1570s and 1580s: to people, places, and specific incidents with which Edward de Vere was associated during those years. Moreover, all of Geoffrey Bullough's careful scholarship turned up no topical reference (other than one speculative "probable source") in the plays later than 1604, the year de Vere died.

Bullough's exception pertains to *The Tempest*, which some scholars persist in citing as evidence of work written after de Vere's death. I mention this only because it often serves as the big gun they haul out to clinch the argument in favor of the man from Stratford. Their point is that the phrase "the still-vexed Bermoothes" relates to a storm and shipwreck off Bermuda in 1609. My response is that there were expeditions that lost ships off Bermuda as early as 1593. More pertinently, "Bermoothes" does not refer to Bermuda at all, but to a section of London where the making of alcohol was unregulated, so it was vexed by stills.

Most scholars who see the evidence stacking up more meaningfully in favor of Edward de Vere cite the sonnets as the compelling factor. The deeply personal sonnets afford us glimpses of the author's own emotional life unmediated by dramatic characterization. We find the same themes emerging repeatedly—the pain of being misrepresented or slandered, the author's lameness, his aging, his doting on a younger man—and we can tie these concerns to documented facts in the life of Edward de Vere. Of course, this does not prove that he wrote the plays. Yet in my recent rereading of *Othello*, for example, there was for me an added poignancy about the seriousness of Cassio's leg wound, because I know that de Vere's lameness (as mentioned in Sonnets 37, 66, and 189) was caused by a similar ambush in the street.

William Farina's book wonderfully pulls together hundreds, perhaps thousands, of such insights, no one of which can be said to prove the case for de Vere as Shakespeare. But when we look at the overwhelming mass of correlations that he has presented, the least we can do is keep an open mind. If open-mindedness is too much to ask, then one can surely admit that it is refreshing to read work like this: that finds the fun in *funda-*mentals, that elicits the *hola!* from *scholarship*.

Felicia Hardison Londré
Kansas City

Dr. Londré is Curators' Professor of Theatre, University of Missouri–Kansas City. She was named Outstanding Teacher of the Year in 2001 by the Association for Theatre in Higher Education.

Introduction

Merely human opinions become accepted when derived from ancient beliefs, and are taken on authority and trust like religion or law! We parrot whatever opinions are commonly held, accepting them, as truths, with all the paraphernalia of supporting arguments and proofs, as though they were something firm and solid; nobody tries to shake them; nobody tries to refute them. On the contrary, everybody vies with each other to plaster over the cracks and prop up received beliefs with all his powers of reason—a supple instrument which can be turned on the lathe into any shape at all. Thus the world is pickled in stupidity and brimming over with lies.
—Montaigne, *An Apology for Raymond Sebond* (1580)[1]

The traditional biography of William Shakespeare is widely viewed as the greatest "poor boy makes good" story ever told; consequently, doubters and skeptics stand accused of snobbery or worse. It is wrongly assumed that anyone who questions the orthodox Shakespeare must in fact believe that born commoners are incapable of great writing; however, as the legendary George Greenwood wrote, "That a man [or woman] of humble birth and very imperfect education may rise to the highest ranks of literature is one of the notorious facts of history."[2] The true question is whether Shakespeare belonged to this same group, or was he different—a renegade nobleman, perhaps? Either way, we maintain that yes, in theory at least, the actor Will Shakspere of Stratford-upon-Avon (for so shall we call him) *could* have been Shakespeare the writer. We suggest, though, that he probably was *not*, based upon the record. Furthermore, Edward de Vere, 17th Earl of Oxford, seems a more likely candidate, given what we know about him.

The Stratfordian tradition has become the Horatio Alger story of all literary biography; to question this holy relic invites hostility. It is far easier to be a true believer—all a great writer needs is genius and "will" power. One ridiculous theory on how the Bard acquired his education is that he absorbed it all hanging out at the Mermaid Tavern—as depicted in the fanciful Victorian painting by John Faed titled *Shakespeare and His Friends*. More later on this "human sponge" notion of genius (see Chapter 9). Dr. Jack Shuttleworth, Chairman Emeritus of the U.S. Air Force Academy English Department in Colorado Springs, has spoken out against the insidiously destructive nature of the traditional biography, from an educational standpoint. After all, who needs education when one has the "tavern of universal knowledge"?[3]

Elitism, for most people, is a dirty word and rightfully so; however, class prejudice can work both ways. This was recently underscored during an authorship discussion at the Goodman Theatre in Chicago by Felicia Hardison Londré of the University of Missouri–Kansas City. Dr. Londré, a recognized authority in both Shakespeare and Russian theater studies, said she doubted whether Shakespeare would have been taught in Soviet-era Russia had it been seriously suspected the Bard may have been a nobleman with bourgeois instincts. Fortunately, this was not the Soviet perception, and the Russians have always had a keen appreciation for Shakespeare. In England, things are only slightly better. A successful British politician (one with working-class roots) once told us that any sea change in popular opinion over Shakespeare's identity will have to originate in America, rather than England. He added that Shakespeare is *the* hero of the English middle class—who also comprise most of British academia—and that any discussion becomes hopelessly bogged down with all of the historical baggage that England carries with respect to class and economic issues.[4] Americans are perhaps less encumbered than the English and the Soviets, but that is not saying much.[5]

For those who stubbornly maintain that snobbery lies at the root of this problem, a shadowy figure such as Christopher Marlowe can be instructive. What little we know about him makes perfect sense. We know his genius was recognized as a child in Canterbury because he was sent to Cambridge on scholarship, though he came from an unprivileged background. We know that he had patrons—this is documented, unlike the case of Shakespeare, where it is merely inferred; that he was engaged in espionage; that he was gay; that he was a reputed atheist; and that he had a temper. And all this seems in keeping with the fiery style and controversial subject matter of his writing, not to mention the way he lived and died. The 1955 best-seller *Murder of the Man Who Was Shakespeare* by Calvin Hoffman advanced the theory that Marlowe faked his own death and then wrote Shakespeare's works in exile. Improbable to be sure, yet no one has ever questioned that Marlowe was a brilliant writer, commoner or not.

To give a somewhat more modern example, the *Personal Memoirs* of Ulysses S. Grant are by any standard a literary classic. How could this son of a tanner who failed at everything—except Civil War generalship and marital relations—have produced such an extraordinary masterpiece?[6] Many wondered and doubted, claiming that the true author may have been Grant's publisher, Mark Twain. Closer inspection, however, revealed Grant's innate genius. For starters, there were manuscripts in Grant's handwriting. Recollections from subordinate officers during the war reflected a pattern—he excelled at issuing clear and concise written orders, far more so than other commanders. In fact, his first major commission after the rebellion resulted (by Grant's own admission) from his facility with paperwork. On the surface, skeptics only saw an undistinguished student at West Point; but Grant sheepishly explained this was partly the result of his addiction to reading novels as a junior cadet. As for his humble tanner of a father, Jesse Grant was a dedicated newspaper reader who announced to his rather disappointed and alarmed son that everything in their lives was subservient to the son's future education. We recite this litany only because every detail stands in stark contrast to the official biography of Will Shakspere, another alleged author suspected of having written nothing.

Today Will Shakspere's claim to authorship is questioned more than ever, especially given that another compelling Elizabethan personality has come to light. Edward de Vere was perhaps the most flamboyant of the courtier poets, a three-time jousting champion, man of the theater, and literary patron, and during the 20th century he became the leading candidate for an alternative Shakespeare.[7] The Oxfordian theory proposes that "William Shakespeare" the writer was in reality a pen name, while the actor Will Shakspere of Stratford-upon-Avon was hired as a front man. One of the most appealing aspects of the Oxfordian theory is that de Vere lived a very Shakespearean life; that is, there appear to be hundreds of parallels between his biography and Shakespeare's story lines, some of them very unusual.

The Traditional Biography

This study will not devote much space to attacking Will Shakspere's credentials as Shakespeare the writer. That has already been done by others many times over. At the very least, the actor from Stratford-upon-Avon remains an essential part of the story, an ambitious and energetic man who overcame poverty and a bad marriage to achieve fame, wealth and respectability—no one will ever take that away from him. Some may argue that Will Shakspere's claim must be first disproved before that of another can be put forth, that Shakspere absolutely could not have written the canon, and that they never, ever believed in the Stratford myth. The author makes none of these claims. A small part of him still wants to believe in the traditional biography; a bigger part is glad not to, since his enthusiasm for Shakespeare has grown to proportions never anticipated.

Most biographies, issued at frequent and regular intervals, add little or nothing to our understanding of history's greatest writer. These must fill in the blanks regarding the crucial details, at least insofar as these relate to his life as an artist. As Mark Twain memorably quipped, Shakespearean biographies are like dinosaur skeletons that are "nine bones and six hundred barrels of plaster of Paris."[8] Information solemnly presented as if documented, factual detail reveals itself upon close examination to be the purest conjecture and speculation. This scarcity of data by itself does not necessarily refute the traditional biography; in fact, it probably adds mystique, an attractive feature for those who may be concerned about confronting the awful truth. Yet the lack of information is puzzling given that Shakespeare had been proclaimed king of the poet-playwright hill as early as 1598 by Francis Meres.[9] The traditional biography has us first seeing Shakespeare the writer with the publication of *Venus and Adonis* in 1593 when Will Shakspere was 29 years old; then five years later, at age 34, he is acknowledged as having reached the pinnacle of his profession, an impressive career trajectory indeed.

We assume Will Shakspere was a student at the Stratford grammar school, although there are no records or anecdotes of such. Prior to 1592, Stratford marriage and baptism records provide the only known documentation for his first 28 years. When written biographies began to appear during the 18th century, they repeated legends regarding Shakspere's penchant for doggerel, such as one claiming he made speeches while butchering calves for his father's glovemaking business. These may or may not be true, although Samuel Schoenbaum was especially skeptical of the latter. In any event, this kind of posthumous oral tradition cannot be given the same amount of weight as tradition from Shakespeare's own time, of which there is none. Worse, these legends are only one step above the admitted fictions that began to appear around the same period, such as the notorious forgeries by William Henry Ireland.[10]

We must also account for the "lost years" of 1585–1592, for which there have been a host of speculations regarding activities that would have provided the prodigious learning displayed by the author of the canon: teaching, law clerking, soldiering, foreign travel and more. These lost years provide a perfect canvas for biographers, eager to fill it out in any manner their fancy dictates, without the annoyance of contradictory documentation. George Greenwood summed up the situation almost a hundred years ago in a statement that still holds true: "such are the methods of Stratfordian controversy. Tradition is to be scouted [mocked] when it is found inconvenient, but cited as irrefragable truth when it suits the case."[11]

After an indirect but hostile notice in 1592 from *Greene's Groatsworth of Wit*, Shakespeare's first credited poems and anonymous plays were published in 1593–1594, followed by the Meres tribute and credited play quartos of 1598. Shakespearean quartos continued to appear through 1604 and then more sporadically after that.[12] With the death of Queen Elizabeth and the accession of King James in 1603, Will Shakspere presumably prospered. James took control over the Lord Chamberlain's Men, rechristening them the King's Men, and sponsored what appears to have been the first festival of Shakespeare's works at court during the 1604–1605 holiday season. Orthodox scholars generally maintain that the first decade of the 17th century would have been a period of intense activity and high creativity for the Bard.

One arguable connection between Shakespeare the writer and Shakespeare the actor is found in a 1610 poem by John Davies of Hereford, titled "To our English Terence, Mr. William Shake-speare." Davies only remarks that Shakespeare "played some Kingly parts in sport" and beyond this is teasingly vague, like all other contemporaries who dared to mention the Bard's name in print. The very title of the poem, referring to the Roman playwright Terence, would have suggested to many readers that "Shake-speare"[13] the writer had a front man, since Terence was himself accused of being a front man. We also know that Edward de Vere acted on at least one occasion,[14] so were these "Kingly parts" played by de Vere or Shakspere? Schoenbaum declared the Davies poem "cryptic" and understandably puzzled over its true meaning.[15]

Sometime soon after this, Shakspere retired to his native Stratford, dying in 1616. Afterward (precisely when is not known) a monument to Shakespeare was erected in Trinity Church. The earliest known rendering is from 1653, in which the effigy appears to be holding a grain sack. Drawings of the monument as we know it today, with the icon holding a quill and paper, first appeared about a century after Shakspere's death.[16] As to his handwriting, the only certified examples we have are six tortured signatures, three from his last will and testament, all appearing to be spelled "Shakspere."[17] Though these are often cited as evidence of illiteracy, bad penmanship proves nothing and can be the result of illness or just bad handwriting. Seven years after Shakspere's death, the First Folio was published in 1623, containing ringing tributes by Ben Jonson and others confirming Shakespeare's exalted status among English writers.

At a glance, this thumbnail sketch of Shakspere's life has been accepted, at one time or another, by most Bardolators. Nevertheless, as many have discovered, minimal reflection can lead to doubt. For example, what happened to Shakespeare's letters, manuscripts and books? Why is there not more of a paper trail? Why did no one talk about the Bard's education? In fact, why did third parties, such as patrons and fellow artists, talk and write about him so little, and on the celebrated occasions when they did, why were they so guarded and vague? *And how did he accumulate his wealth?* Why did Will Shakspere prosper so much more than his fellow artists? Was he just more popular, smarter, or both?[18] As for posthumous tributes, these can be charitably described as muted and circumspect. Even Ben Jonson's First Folio eulogy, usually considered the most extravagant of its genre, has left more than a few readers scratching their heads in bewilderment. Options for biographers are stark: fill in a blank canvas (which many are more than happy to do), or look for another Shakespeare.

The sketchiness of Shakespeare's biography appears, if nothing else, to make him relatively unique among the great writers. The following are just a few examples:

- *Among Will Shakspere's parents, wife, and three children, posterity has handed down a grand total of one written signature, that from his daughter Susanna.* Even Susanna's literacy must be viewed skeptically, given other known details of her life; for example, her failure to recognize her own husband's handwriting when presenting his journals to Dr. James Cooke in 1642.[19] As hard as it is to imagine the parents and wife of Shakespeare could not read or write (this is rarely contested), it is nearly unthinkable that the children of Shakespeare the writer were illiterate.

- *No manuscripts, no journals, no books, and incredibly, no letters from Shakespeare have ever been found, or rumored to exist*[20]—hard to explain at best. For example, there is no evidence the Richard Quiney letter, written to "Wm. Shackespere" regarding money-lending, was ever sent or received.[21]

- *There are no records or anecdotes regarding the genius, talent or exceptional qualities of the young Will Shakspere when he was in Stratford-upon-Avon, or from his first years in London.* This lack of notice would appear to be nearly without precedent in the history of the arts. Shakespeare is often compared to the composer Mozart, who was also a genius, but quite unlike Will Shakspere. For example, we know Mozart had the best music teacher in Europe—his father. We know Mozart was composing as a child and producing masterpieces by the time he was a teenager. We know that, in recognition of his accomplishments, Mozart was knighted by the Pope when he was 14 years old! For Shakspere, there was no evidence of his literary talent until he was more than twice that age, assuming he was in fact the author of *Venus and Adonis.* Shakespeare's contemporary Montaigne, writing about human genius in his essay *On the Length of Life,* quotes the French proverb "If a thorn pricks not at its birth, it will hardly prick at all."[22] In other words, if a person has outstanding qualities, then they will be noticed early on. Montaigne even goes so far as to say that by age 20 these qualities will be apparent. Thus ends Book I of his *Essays.*

- *Little (if anything) connects Shakespeare the writer with Stratford-upon-Avon until the First Folio of 1623, seven years after Will Shakspere's death, and only then in a very ambiguous and equivocal manner.*[23] That a man acknowledged during his lifetime (and 18 years before his death) as the greatest English playwright should not be widely associated with the provincial town where he came of age and retired until seven years after his death is a source of wonder. An undated poem by the Oxford student William Basse recites that Shakespeare died in April 1616, and proposes that he should be buried in Westminster Abbey, but Ben Jonson sneered at this idea in the First Folio preface.[24] Was Basse knowledgeable, or just repeating what he had heard?

- *As a successful playwright, Shakespeare is surprisingly invisible among his contemporaries.* Everybody one thinks would have written about Shakespeare did not. William Camden, one of the most prolific chroniclers of the era and a name-dropper of poets, mentions Shakespeare only once in passing (during 1605) but then fails to mention Shakespeare in 1607 when listing famous people from Warwickshire and Stratford. Nor is there any mention of Shakespeare in the diaries of theatrical colleague Philip Henslowe or Shakspere's own son-in-law Dr. John Hall (who did see fit to mention the poet Michael Drayton), to name just a few.[25] Perhaps the pages with Shakespeare's name had been torn out. Perhaps Shakespeare was working so hard that he was able to keep a low profile. In any event, silence is another form of testimony, and in the case of Shakespeare, there is a disturbing amount of silence.

- *Shakespeare, according to the standard chronology, wrote several of his greatest masterpieces during the first decade of the 17th century, then supposedly retired at the height of his fame to Stratford-upon-Avon; yet he left no mark of his physical presence in London during that period.* Will Shakspere purchased Stratford New Place in 1597 and by 1612 made it his domicile. The problem is that there is no recorded mention of his presence in London between 1605 and 1612,[26] despite this supposedly being the period of his greatest renown and productivity. This seven-year interval rivals Shakspere's earlier "lost years" in terms of mysteriousness, except this time he was not lost—he was at the top of his game, at least according to the standard biography.[27]

- *The text of the Shakespearean canon itself suggests attitudes and a world view completely at odds with Will Shakspere's documented life.* A small sampling of these attitudes includes a profound contempt for money and commerce, a feudalistic political outlook favoring the aristocracy, and an enthusiastic love of travel. If Will Shakspere was the true author, we are forced to conclude that he used his writing to express feelings and ideas in direct contradiction to the way he lived his life. This is not what creative writers tend to do; again, we must assume Shakespeare was unique.

This list continues, but our sole purpose is to give a hint as to why the Stratford biography has provoked skepticism from disbelievers, as well as frustration among staunch defenders. To repeat, these points do not refute Will Shakspere's claim, but the traditional assignment of authorship is merely suggested rather than proved by the record. As Schoenbaum wrote, "Perhaps we should despair of ever bridging the vertiginous expanse between the sublimity of the subject and the mundane inconsequence of the documentary record."[28] His life story, or at least what is known of it, serves more to increase our awareness of Schoenbaum's "vertiginous expanse" rather than to conclusively prove Will Shakspere's claim to authorship.

The traditional biography of Shakespeare has over the years raised many an eyebrow because, apart from generic references to Shakespeare the writer, the quantity and quality of verified, biographical data is comparatively scarce.[29] Once the compelling figure of Edward de Vere steps into the spotlight, however, wonder turns into doubt. De Vere's candidacy as an alternative Shakespeare is bolstered by an imposing cumulative weight of circumstantial evidence that demands serious evaluation. De Vere's one-of-a-kind (and often horrific) biography forces us to confront layer upon layer of seemingly endless parallels with the sources and storylines of the Shakespearean canon. Anyone with a shred of intellectual honesty can only pause, and then either embrace the brave new world of Oxfordian interpretation or scramble hard to refute it.

Why an Authorship Hoax?

Much has been written concerning the social stigma attached to noblemen authors during Shakespeare's era, and this factor certainly would have been a deterrent for anyone other than a commoner taking credit for the Bard's works. The phenomenon is discussed by period writers such as Montaigne[30] and by the anonymous author of *The Arte of English Poesie*. Social stigma was especially applicable to popular drama, considered to be a highly disreputable art form. On the other hand, the barrier was beginning to break down and many courtier poets (including de Vere himself) were starting to push the envelope. The question then becomes why such a hoax would have been perpetuated indefinitely, long after the death of the true author.

Less frequently discussed, perhaps because of the embarrassing implications to our national heritage, is the troubled relationship between Shakespeare and our Puritan forefathers. In short, English Puritans during the late 16th and early 17th centuries wanted to do away with Shakespeare and briefly succeeded in doing so between 1642 and 1660. In this respect, the documentary record is voluminous and unequivocal; yet we do not like to talk about anything that goes against our perceived past. Occasionally, some aspiring apologist will try to smooth over the edges or deny that it really happened—but it did. After two generations of heated tensions and bitter invective, a civil war was fought, the king executed, and the acting profession outlawed. The playhouses were then closed and demolished. Most of what we know about Shakespeare was gathered long after these events had transpired and eyewitnesses disappeared.

In her best-selling memoir *Reading Lolita in Tehran*, Azar Nafisi recalled teaching English novels to her Iranian students. Of all the "scandalous" western writers that were assigned, it was the unassuming Henry James that caused the most outrage. In the eyes of religious fundamentalists, James was offensive because his novels offered no clear-cut moral judgments. James was all about ambiguity; for this he was considered degenerate by an intolerant, ayatollah-ruled society. Like the novels of Henry James,[31] Shakespeare's works are often viewed as unsatisfactory by those who insist on black and white answers to the moral dilemmas of life. Unambiguous interpretations are oftentimes artificially imposed on these "open" works; however, as Oxfordian dramaturg Merilee Karr has noted:

> The reader has to work a lot harder to interpret an open work, but they arrive at the finish line, panting, with a pearl of great price. The reader owns their interpretation . . . This level of involvement in a work of literature can change a reader's life.[32]

It was precisely this kind of open literature (i.e., Shakespeare) that infuriated English Puritans and to this day angers religious hard-liners everywhere. Adding injury to insult, the Bard's history plays may have been the most effective political propaganda ever created, aimed at unifying an English society threatening to split apart over religious and social issues, which it would in fact soon do so. For "Shakespeare" to have been someone unlike Will Shakspere would have been a difficult sell to the groundlings.

How Could It Happen?

Not long ago the *New York Times* revealed that the inglorious 1967 best-seller *Coffee, Tea or Me?* had not in fact been written by two airline flight attendants, Trudy Baker and Rachel Jones, to whom it had originally been credited. Not only were the names of the flight attendants fictional (although two women had promoted the memoir under these assumed names), the true author was in fact a successful mystery writer, Donald Bain, who had once worked for the public relations department of a major airline. If these revelations were not enough, the book (along with its three sequels) had all been dedicated in print to the true author.[33] Especially noteworthy was that this hoax had been perpetuated during the final decades of the 20th century, a period unprecedented in the mass media's ability to provide instant information for the general public.

If a masquerade on this scale could be successfully staged during the modern era, then how much easier it would have been to accomplish 400 years ago. Elizabethan and Jacobean societies were defined by a rigid class system in which hereditary rights of entitlement were outwardly symbolized by statutory dress codes. Literacy rates among the general population were dismally low, printing was a new technology, books were rare and expensive, public libraries did not exist, and there was no free press as we know it today. Minor infractions to the rules were routinely punished with death, disfigurement and incarceration.[34] This unstable society would erupt into civil war by 1642, leaving public institutions battered and confused for years to come. One by-product was the total abolishment of public theater. Given these conditions, the perpetration of an authorship ruse for a popular but politically charged writer such as William Shakespeare would have been no surprising accomplishment.

Perhaps the best modern-day analogy to Elizabethan playwriting is the Hollywood screenwriting industry. Most moviegoers do not know or care who writes the screenplay. Furthermore, just because someone is credited as screenwriter does not mean that he or she is the actual author.[35] In some cases, front men have been hired to take credit, the most notorious example perhaps being the blacklisted Hollywood screenwriters of the 1950s. This deception became the subject for Woody Allen's 1976 film *The Front*. To the extent that blacklisted writer Dalton Trumbo's concealment of his identity was a "conspiracy," then so was the facade of William Shakespeare, if in fact it was a facade. The word "conspiracy" is not typically used in this sense, but is always seemingly used in connection with the Shakespeare authorship question, more often than not to cast doubt on the mental stability of anyone trying to be curious.

Why It Matters

Any serious examination of the authorship question should be prefaced with an explanation of why it matters. For those who do not enjoy Shakespeare (or only pretend to), the question is certainly a non-issue; but for those who do, or at least think Shakespeare important, it should matter very much who he was. To know more about a writer's life is to have a better understanding and appreciation for the writer's work—plain common sense, one would think. The Bard's true identity may be a very small question in today's troubled world; and yet it goes right to the very heart of western culture.

Some argue that all literary biography is irrelevant. After all, many great writers were not great human beings, but this should not detract from our appreciation of their accomplishments. Therefore, we should focus solely on the text. On the other hand, it has become clear, especially in more recent years, that literary biography is essential to our understanding of historical literature.[36] Even if we could bypass the sordid details of a particular writer's life, to leave aside the world surrounding a book's creation too often renders it incomprehensible to later generations. To ignore this risks completely missing the writer's meaning and intent. Moreover, the "it doesn't matter" approach is most often interjected to mediate or avoid the authorship question altogether, a topic having the unique ability (at least among literary topics) of inflaming passions and bringing out the worst in its partisans. It has even been suggested that the non-biographical approach to literary criticism owes its origins to insecurity surrounding what we know about the English language's greatest craftsman. Given that Shakespeare seems to arouse strong personal feelings usually reserved for religion and politics, we should not be surprised that disdain for literary biography is so often invoked—a Missouri Compromise in the field of Shakespearean studies, if you will.

Method of Analysis

Traditionalists typically grimace at any mention of the authorship question and especially any reference to the person they identify as the author other than "William Shakespeare." Accordingly, use of the name *Shakspere* (pronounced with a short "a") generally provokes (and implies) derision, even though this in fact was the way the name was often spelled and pronounced before, during, and after Shakespeare's lifetime.[37] An impartial reader, however, can appreciate the need to temporarily distinguish between Shakespeare, the true author of the canon (whoever he may have been), and Shakespeare, the man who became known as the author; otherwise, attempts at genuine, rational analysis become muddled, if not completely stifled.[38] A traditionalist truly secure in the knowledge that "Shakespeare was Shakespeare" should have no difficulty in equating one with the other after a momentary separation. Accordingly, we shall identify the man born and buried in Stratford-upon-Avon as "Will Shakspere," and the true author of the works (whoever he may have been) as "William Shakespeare."

The most frequent analytical mistake made in connection with the authorship question is to reflexively equate all period references to "William Shakespeare" the writer with the man baptized as "Gulielmus, filius Johannes Shakspere" on April 26, 1564, in

Stratford-upon-Avon.[39] Jumping to this conclusion ignores the possibility that "William Shakespeare" may have been a pen name, with the actor Will Shakspere hired as a front man. Of course, any reference made to Shakespeare as a poet-playwright *and* in direct connection with Stratford-upon-Avon or with the actor *probably* means they were perceived as the same individual. We say "probably" because, as will be seen through the course of these pages, even connections with "Stratford" and play acting can be viewed ambiguously. Far more troubling is that such connections are surprisingly scarce and opaque to begin with. This scarcity holds true even after factoring into account Will Shakspere's humble origins, and is vividly underscored by comparison of his documented life with those of other common-born Elizabethan playwrights.[40]

If the Oxfordian theory is correct and "William Shakespeare" was in reality a pen name, then what was its origin? Most Oxfordians believe it harks back to the ancient "spear-shaker" goddess of wisdom and warfare: Minerva to the Romans, Athena to the Greeks. The name may have been originally derived from this popular Renaissance goddess. In addition, "Shake-speare" would tie in with de Vere's prowess as a three-time jousting champion. Lastly, the nearly identical name of Will Shakspere naturally leads to speculation that the pseudonym (if indeed it was one) may have been created from the necessity or preference of using a certain individual as a front man.

Anyone who glances at the endnotes to this study will immediately notice a heavy reliance upon the work of Dr. Alan Nelson from the University of California–Berkeley, whose recent biography of de Vere is required reading for anyone interested in the authorship question. Professor Nelson, it should be emphasized from the outset, is firmly orthodox in his authorship beliefs. His book, however, contains an indispensable and magnificent wealth of factual detail, much of which cannot be found outside of the source materials. Our respectful disagreement with Professor Nelson stems not from the facts but rather from his interpretation; we therefore found it useful to compare, whenever possible, the original Oxfordian biographer, Bernard M. Ward. We are furthermore deeply indebted to material published by the Shakespeare Oxford and de Vere Societies: when it's good, it's really good. Quotations from Shakespeare's contemporaries such as Cervantes and Montaigne are thrown in to add humor and perspective. Finally, readers will also notice some repetition. This is due to the repetitive themes within the canon, which are important and therefore worth repeating.

Because the Oxfordian theory places emphasis on Shakespeare's Italian and French connections (which de Vere had in spades), our analysis will not be restricted to English history, geography and literature. Given the author's ancestral heritage (which is part Italian) there may be accusations of ethnocentricity. There is probably some validity to this, although somehow the author believes that the Bard's reputation (as well as his own) will be able to survive an occasional outburst of cultural pride and prejudice. After all, part of the reason Shakespeare is the greatest poet and English the greatest language is that both are all-encompassing in terms of source material.

Thus this study is intended for Bardolators approaching Edward de Vere for the first time, via individual works in the canon. No doubt there will be a need to update this approach further, given the rapidly evolving state of the debate. While we offer no final answers on the authorship question, the solution to this old problem may still be within our reach. Open minds and a bit of curiosity, though, are needed. Above all, the Oxfordian theory should be viewed as a potential extension, rather than rejection, of traditional scholarship. All of the great orthodox commentators still maintain their rightful places on our bookshelves. What changes is how we read them. Taking this further, one could say that the true biography of Will Shakspere has yet to be written.

PART ONE

෨෨

COMEDIES AND ROMANCES

ഔ 1 ର

The Tempest

Most scholars, after agreeing that inspiration for this play came from an English ship-wreck in the Bermuda Triangle, completely diverge in their opinions regarding source material. They generally agree, however, that the work is a dazzling synthesis of many influences. Many believe that Shakespeare seemed to be striking a valedictory note, that *The Tempest* was one of his last works (if not his very last), and that Prospero represents the voice of the author. Prospero's speech "Our revels are now ended" (IV.i.148) is usually interpreted to have literal meaning.

The first publication was in the First Folio of 1623; therefore neither Will Shakspere (d. 1616) nor Edward de Vere (d. 1604?) lived to see it in print. When the play finally went to press it would have been at the mercy of editors; accordingly, whatever we see in the Folio is not necessarily what Shakespeare wrote. Furthermore, it is generally agreed that Shakespeare had editors and perhaps collaborators, both during and after his lifetime. Some critics, such as Dover Wilson, have suggested *The Tempest* went through several stages of revision.[1] Many Bardolators have noted the special place of the work as the very first play in the Folio, perhaps as Shakespeare's last play. The first recorded performances were in 1611 and 1613, both by the King's Men at Whitehall Palace. The 1613 production cele-brated the wedding of Princess Elizabeth to Frederick, Elector of Palatine. This event would have been in keeping with the theme of marital union in the story between Miranda and Ferdinand.[2]

Connections between *The Tempest* and the traditional biography of Will Shakspere are tenuous at best. Production notes for a recent Chicago performance inform us that Shakespeare "spent a lifetime struggling through disappointments in business, in love, betrayals of friends and, worst of all, the death of a child, his only son." The phrase "dis-appointments in business" is somewhat puzzling, given that Will Shakspere retired to the second largest house in Stratford-upon-Avon.[3] Others have tried to envision an aging, Prospero-like Shakspere sitting in his mansion at New Place, contemplating provincial retirement while suing neighbors over small debts and clashing with local authorities over the enclosure of public lands. But there is something wrong with that picture as well. Bio-graphical resonance abounds, however, if we allow ourselves to consider the possibility that Shakespeare may have been Edward de Vere.

Before exploring de Vere's personal connections to the sources and themes of *The Tempest*, let us examine one of the most frequent but not very convincing arguments against de Vere as Shakespeare. Orthodox scholars tend to date the writing of *The Tempest* to 1610, several years after de Vere's death, because many details from the storm scene are found in a document known as the Strachey letter, containing a lengthy description of an English shipwreck in the Bermudas circa 1609. The Strachey letter was written in 1610 and published in 1625, two years after the First Folio. The bromidic view among critics is that Shakespeare read this letter in manuscript and was inspired to write the play.[4] Leaving aside that the story is not, strictly speaking, about a shipwreck (everyone sails away happily at the end), there are bigger problems with this analysis.

To begin with, English shipwrecks in the Bermudas had been reported long before 1609, such as one in 1593 involving an expedition that included the *Edward Bonaventure*, a ship Edward de Vere himself once aspired to own. An account of this voyage had been published in 1600: Richard Hakluyt's *The Principal Navigations, Voyages, Traffiques and Discoveries of the English Nation*.[5] Second, as pointed out by Joseph Hunter and other orthodox scholars, most if not all of the corresponding details from the Strachey letter can be traced to authors popular at that time, such as Ovid, Virgil, and Ariosto. Even *The Acts of the Apostles* contains a lengthy passage in which St. Paul is shipwrecked on Malta.[6] For all we know, the Strachey letter may be repeating details found in these alternative sources or from an earlier, unpublished version of *The Tempest*.

One can assume for argument's sake that *The Tempest* does in fact incorporate the Strachey letter. What would this prove? Most agree Shakespeare had editors. Shakspere had died in 1616 and the play was first published in 1623. Would the existence of a post–1616 allusion prove Shakspere was not the main author? In a similar manner, the possible (though questionable) existence of a reference to an event after de Vere's death should not rule him out, at least for anyone who is not desperate to prove otherwise.

Connections between de Vere and sources for *The Tempest* are impressive and not particularly hard to discern. Ovid's *Metamorphoses*, widely regarded as Shakespeare's favorite book, was first translated into English by de Vere's uncle, Arthur Golding.[7] One of the most terrifying shipwreck stories ever written is found in Book XI. With respect to Virgil's *Aeneid*, the first English translation was by yet another de Vere uncle, Henry Howard, Earl of Surrey.[8] *The Aeneid* begins with a storm and shipwreck as Aeneas travels from Carthage to Naples, just like the characters in Shakespeare's *Tempest*. In contrast, connections between these books and Will Shakspere appear to be nil. As for the Strachey letter, its alleged monopoly of shipwreck data becomes, like many events in the play, illusory—that is, if we remove our blinders long enough to take a cursory look at popular literature of the 16th century.

Opinions dating *The Tempest* before 1610 have not been restricted to Oxfordians. Before refuting the Oxfordian theory became a priority during the late 20th century, Karl Elze had observed that Ben Jonson may have alluded to *The Tempest* in several of his own works, dating at least six years before the first recorded performance in 1611.[9] In addition, a German play similar to *The Tempest* titled *Die Schöne Sidea* was on the boards no later than 1604, though its relationship (if any) to Shakespeare's work is far from clear.[10] At the very least, there is general agreement that the Jacobean court masques of Ben Jonson and architect–set designer Inigo Jones were influential on Shakespeare the writer. This would appear a much stronger argument than the Strachey letter for inclusion of post–1603 elements in the play, if not overall authorship. Dover Wilson may have been right to suspect several stages of revision.

Modern scholars, including Geoffrey Bullough, have acknowledged that Shakespeare was influenced in some form or fashion by the tradition of Spanish prose romance, so brilliantly satirized during the same period by Cervantes in *Don Quixote*.[11] One such romance, *The History of the Palladine of England*, published in 1588 as an English version of *Amadis de Gaul*, was translated by Anthony Munday, servant and presumably secretary to Edward de Vere. Munday also dedicated his translation of the Spanish romance *Palmerin d'Oliva* to Oxford at about this same time.[12] Scholars disagree on which specific romances influenced Shakespeare's play, because many are filled with enchanted islands, magicians, shipwrecks, and the like, but the leading English translator of these works was in fact Anthony Munday, providing another direct link between Shakespeare's sources and de Vere.[13]

Another influence on *The Tempest*, as identified by Edmund Chambers, was the improvised Italian art form of *commedia dell' arte*.[14] Where did Shakespeare get this? Perhaps on one of the extremely rare occasions when troupes came to England to perform exclusively in the great houses of the nobility? Anything is possible, we suppose. Shakspere could have been in the right place at the right time. De Vere, on the other hand, spent nearly a year in Italy when this type of entertainment was soaring in popularity, and he likely would have had firsthand exposure. Furthermore, *The Tempest* has many character names and situations taken directly from 15th-century Italian history, which the author may have picked up from an English chronicle.[15] Another possibility is that the multilingual de Vere went directly to an Italian source, more specifically, his own personal copy of Francesco Guicciardini's *La Historia d'Italia*,[16] a book also owned and revered by Montaigne.[17]

In similar fashion, Montaigne's *Essays*, another recognized source for *The Tempest*, had been around since 1580 but were not translated into English until 1603, by John Florio. It is typically assumed the author read this translation, or he may have read the original French, because we know de Vere was capable of this.[18] In particular, scholars tend to agree that Shakespeare read Montaigne's famous essay *On Cannibals*, while others have noticed "Caliban" may be an amalgamation of the word "cannibal" and the name "Calvin."[19] John Calvin, spiritual father of the Puritan movement, had died in 1564, the same year Will Shakspere was born, and the 1560s witnessed the beginnings of the Puritan movement in England. Moreover, it seems Shakespeare the writer was not a fan of the Puritans, given his satirical treatment of them in the plays. Others have noted Caliban's similarity to the "wild men" characters in works such as Edmund Spenser's *The Faerie Queene*, which included a dedication sonnet to Oxford.[20]

De Vere's close proximity to Shakespeare's source material should be enough to grab attention by itself; if not, there are numerous connections with his personal life which are perhaps even more startling. As Antonio declares in *The Tempest*, "what's past is prologue" (II.i.252), and the back story for this play may have involved the troubled past between De Vere and Philip Sidney, Elizabethan courtier poet and war hero. The two men were rivals politically, personally, and poetically. This rivalry came to a head on a London tennis court in 1579 when a dispute arose over whose turn it was, culminating with de Vere bellicosely belittling Sidney as a "puppy." Events appeared to be moving toward a duel when the queen intervened, telling Sidney that de Vere outranked him and was therefore entitled to the tennis court. Then Sidney was ordered to apologize, which he refused to do, instead choosing to exile himself from politics.[21] Seven years later, Sidney was dead, a national hero, while de Vere was insolvent and in disgrace.

Philip Sidney was survived by his sister Mary, one of the most important literary patrons of the age, and to whose sons, William and Philip Herbert, Shakespeare's First Folio was dedicated as "the Most Noble and Incomparable Paire of Brethren." Mary and her husband, the Earl of Pembroke, resided at Wilton House near Salisbury in Wiltshire. An anecdote tells of the newly enthroned King James being invited in 1603 by Mary Sidney to stay at Wilton, who added that "the man Shakespeare" was staying there as well. We know that the King's Men performed at Wilton for King James soon afterward;[22] but during that same time, Mary Sidney and de Vere could well have been negotiating the future marriage of their respective children, Philip and Susan. Earlier, Philip's brother William had negotiated marriage with de Vere's daughter Bridget, and Oxford, in one of his letters, praised William's character.[23] Oxford's daughters were the nieces of Robert Cecil and the grandchildren of Lord Burghley, Elizabeth's chief advisor; after Burghley's death in 1598, Robert assumed his father's role as royal counselor. Oxfordians such as Eva Turner Clark have seen in Gonzalo, the wise counselor in The Tempest, perhaps a more sympathetic view of Burghley, as opposed to a less flattering portrait of him as Polonius in Hamlet.[24]

Susan Vere was sketched in costume by Inigo Jones while performing in Ben Jonson's Masque of Queenes on Twelfth Night, 1605, during celebrations in the aftermath of her marriage to Philip Herbert.[25] According to biographers of King James, the morning after the wedding night at the palace, the king got out of bed and ran to the bedroom of the newlyweds, burst in, jumped into their bed, and began quizzing them about their first night together.[26]

By this time, de Vere had presumably been dead about six months.[27] He had spent the last seven years of his life in relative isolation at King's Place in Hackney, suburban London. Oxfordians believe this is where many of Shakespeare's works began to take the final shape and form we know today. Reportedly, the house had an extensive library and study,[28] calling to mind Prospero's reminiscence that "my library was dukedom large enough" (I.ii.109–110). De Vere certainly resembled Prospero in the sense that he was repeatedly criticized for being too bookish for a nobleman, most notably by Gabriel Harvey in 1577.[29] Sadly, King's Place was heavily damaged during the Blitz of 1940 and finally torn down in 1955—a great loss.

Did Will Shakspere have connections with the Herberts? None that we know of, but Ben Jonson certainly did: they were his patrons.[30] In any event, the unification of the Vere-Cecil and Sidney-Herbert families, personally promoted by the king, symbolized a major reconciliation after the feuding between Oxford and Sidney more than 20 years earlier. It also parallels The Tempest, since Prospero's daughter Miranda is betrothed to Ferdinand, son of Prospero's long-time enemy Alonso.

In the play, Ariel reminds Prospero he once fetched him "dew from the still-vex'd Bermoothes" (I.ii.229). Commentators, beginning with the redoubtable Edmund Malone, have really latched on to this one.[31] "Bermoothes," we are informed by legions of scholars, means "Bermudas," as in the islands. That is one meaning. From there, many get carried away and assume the entire setting of the play is the New World, that it was inspired by exploration, and that this is the central theme of the play. A vocal minority of orthodox scholars, including Joseph Hunter and George Lyman Kittredge, have complained about these misconceptions, correctly pointing out the setting is the southern

Mediterranean, not the Americas.[32] When Miranda exclaims: "O brave new world, that has such people in it" (V.i.184–185). she is not referring to Native Americans, but rather to a group of Italian noblemen, none of whom she has ever seen before.

"Bermoothes" likely has double meaning. During Shakespeare's time, the "Bermudas" also referred to a London neighborhood, a notorious vice district, located just north of the Strand near Charing Cross and known for drunken street behavior. In his published works, Ben Jonson makes no fewer than three references to the London Bermudas (his childhood stomping grounds), all in the pejorative sense.[33] In the play, the excessive drinking of Stephano, Trinculo, and Caliban provides comic relief, and de Vere himself was not known for abstinence. Thus when Ariel speaks of fetching "dew from the still-vex'd Bermoothes," Shakespeare may well have been punning in reference to both the Bermuda Islands and the London vice district.

Some still insist the play is set in the New World, arguing that if Ariel's magic can transport him to the Bermudas, then it can transport the ship anywhere. Perhaps the best American candidate for Prospero's enchanted island is Cuttyhunk, Massachusetts. Aside from many similar descriptive details, Cuttyhunk was first explored in 1602 by an expedition sponsored through Henry Wriothesley, Earl of Southampton, a man whom both traditionalists and Oxfordians agree was close to Shakespeare the writer.[34]

As for the true geography of *The Tempest*, Prospero is usurped by his brother Antonio as Duke of Milan, located in northern Italy. Alonso is King of Naples, located in the south. When the tempest strikes, Alonso and Antonio are sailing back to Naples from Carthage in Tunisia, where Alonso has just married off his daughter. Even among readers who recognize a Mediterranean setting, however, the exact location of Prospero's enchanted island has been the subject of debate. Some have suggested one of the Aeolian Islands north of Sicily, perhaps Vulcano.[35] Joseph Hunter's original suggestion was Lampedusa, located south of Sicily and known as Orlando's island—from the same *Orlando Furioso* by Ludovico Ariosto that was a 16th-century best-seller.[36] *Orlando*, either in its original Italian[37] or the first English translation by John Harrington in 1591, was another work leaving its mark on Shakespeare the writer.

We believe that if Shakespeare had wanted to specify an island, he would have done so. Prospero's enchanted island could easily be a literary amalgamation of several places known to the author. Furthermore, de Vere's documented presence in Palermo would have given him personal experience with Sicily and environs, a world frequently evoked by the Bard. Given that de Vere was of Norman ancestry, it is also likely he would have taken a personal interest in the legend of the Frankish warrior Orlando.

Thus the play's major themes of personal valediction, social isolation, worldly dispossession, bookish wisdom, spiritual release, and marital unity between the children of former enemies are all strongly reflected by the last years of de Vere's life. Shortly after Queen Elizabeth's death in 1603, de Vere wrote a letter to his former brother-in-law Robert Cecil in a poetic, one might even say Shakespearean vein. He pleads with Cecil for old times' sake to help make sure the new king takes care of him, writing:

> In this common shipwreck, mine is above all the rest, who least regarded though often comforted of all her followers, she hath left to try my fortune among the altercations of time and chance, either without sail whereby to take the advantage of any prosperous gale, or with anchor ride till the storm be overpast.[38]

De Vere's allusion to personal shipwreck was not exaggeration; he died more or less impoverished, isolated, and far removed from the power centers of the Jacobean court. Oxfordians believe he was writing *The Tempest* at about this same time. King James promptly renewed de Vere's whopping £1,000 annuity and granted him custody of the Forest of Essex but, according to the official record, the 17th Earl died soon afterward in June 1604. Six months later, James sponsored the first festival of Shakespeare's plays, having seven of them performed at court during the holiday season of 1604–1605, concurrent with wedding festivities for de Vere's daughter at Whitehall Palace.[39]

ℰᴑ 2 ℛ

The Two Gentlemen
of Verona

What kind of mind, unless it's completely coarse and barbarous, could possibly be satisfied, reading how a tall tower full of knights goes sailing off to sea, like a boat on a good wind, and tonight it will be in Lombardy and the next day in the land of Prester John of India— or somewhere else that Ptolemy never wrote about and Marco Polo never saw? And to anyone who answers by saying that people who write such books are creating fictions and therefore aren't obliged to worry about fine points or truth, I say to them that the best lies are those that most closely resemble truth, and what gives the most pleasure is what seems most probable or possible.

—Cervantes, *Don Quixote* [1605][1]

One of the beauties of the Oxfordian theory is that plays and poems typically viewed as secondary in importance (about two-thirds of the canon, and hence generally neglected) now take on new meaning and interest. A prime example of this is *The Two Gentlemen of Verona*, a work that the great critic Harold Bloom pronounced "the weakest of all Shakespeare's comedies" and then dismissed with a short critique.[2] Bloom's view, not unreasonable if literary biography and the authorship question are ignored, represents the majority among orthodox scholars, many of whom believe *Two Gentlemen* was the Bard's first, tentative foray into playwriting. Viewed from the Oxfordian perspective, however, this play becomes a fascinating character study (of Shakespeare himself), plus a surprisingly informative lesson on the history and geography of Renaissance Italy, leading to the very crux of the authorship debate.

The Two Gentlemen of Verona was cited among Shakespeare's works by Francis Meres in 1598 but not printed until the First Folio of 1623.[3] There are no documented period performances. Edmund Chambers sums up the scanty record by noting that "The date can hardly be fixed with precision."[4] This has not stopped scholars, though, from postulating the early 1590s, based on stylistic grounds, at least for the version that has come down to us. We see no reason to disagree.

For those willing to expand their horizons before 1590, however (as some orthodox scholars are in fact willing to do), *Two Gentlemen* becomes a case study in the Bard's frequent use of foreign sources as a starting point for his own work. Among those who take the trouble, commentators generally agree that the heart of Shakespeare's story was lifted from an old Spanish play titled *Diana Enamorada* by Jorge de Montemayor. A lost, anonymous English version of this tale was performed at court by the Queen's Men in 1585, titled *The History of Felix and Philiomena*.[5] During this same period, Edward de Vere was sponsoring his own acting companies (which had some personnel overlap with the Queen's Men)[6] and was earning a reputation as "best for comedy"[7] among English playwrights, although no works under his name have survived. The early 1580s was also a time that saw de Vere trying to put his life back together (including his married life) after the follies and foibles of the late 1570s.

Another anonymous play from the same period (and one that has survived), titled *Two Italian Gentlemen: Fedele and Fortunio*, was performed at court in 1584 and 1585. This work probably influenced Shakespeare's play as well,[8] although to a lesser degree than *Felix and Philiomena*.[9] Scholars tend to believe that the author of *Two Italian Gentlemen* was Anthony Munday,[10] servant and secretary to Edward de Vere, who dedicated a number of works to his patron. This play was an English adaptation of the Italian *commedia erudite* known as *Il Fedele*, published in 1576[11] and written by the nobleman playwright Luigi Pasqualigo.[12] Bullough believed that Shakespeare's *Two Gentlemen* may have been influenced as well by the *commedia dell' arte* of the Italian nobleman playwright Flaminio Scala,[13] specifically his *Flavio Tradito*, not published until 1611 (in Italian).[14] In addition to these, Anthony Munday's Robin Hood plays have been viewed as possible models for the Bard's forest scenes in Act V.[15] If one was not enough, a second Elizabethan playwright who was a servant and secretary to Edward de Vere *and* who is widely believed to have influenced the writing of *Two Gentlemen* was John Lyly. Traces of Lyly's *Endimion*, *Sappho and Phoa*, and *Euphues* have variously been identified in Shakespeare's play.[16]

Given this background, it seems undeniable that de Vere was involved with this embryonic period of English drama (1576–1588) that influenced plays such as *Two Gentlemen*, even assuming he did not in fact later become Shakespeare the writer. The bigger question, though, is whether Shakespeare (given that he was a genius) absorbed his source material strictly in a secondhand manner from old books and plays, or whether this book-learning was reinforced by personal experience in life. Perhaps the ultimate issue is whether book-learning (and imagination) or personal experience (and the wisdom that comes with it) were more important to Shakespeare's creative process.

In the play, Valentine explains to Proteus that "Home-keeping youth have ever homely wits" (I.i.2), and one wonders if the author simply meant leaving Stratford for London, or in a wider sense, departing from England for the European continent. In terms of travel, was Shakespeare likely to have been in Verona, Milan, and Mantua (the settings of the play)? Some confusion does occur when Speed greets Launce with "Launce, by mine honesty, welcome to [Milan]" (II.v.1–2). In the First Folio text, "Padua" is printed, rather than Milan, which is clearly incorrect.[17] Taken as a whole, however, Shakespeare's geographical precision is usually astounding and underappreciated. Edmund Chambers recognized that the Bard "seems to have been remarkably successful in giving local coloring and atmosphere" to his Italian plays and "that he shows familiarity with some minute points of topography."[18] Dr. Ernesto Grillo of Italy went further by stating that "the topography is so precise and accurate that it must convince even the most superficial reader that the poet visited the country."[19]

Orthodox teachers and scholars tend to give tremendously short shrift to this topic, but we hope to dispel one popular myth, namely, that Shakespeare (whoever he was) supposedly had a very imperfect knowledge of Italy and made a lot of mistakes due to his assumed provincial education. On the contrary, our main argument is that Shakespeare the writer had an astonishingly detailed and accurate knowledge of Italy. Reasonable people may disagree on who Shakespeare really was, but it is wildly incorrect to say that Shakespeare just made up everything as he wrote.

Much has been written about Shakespeare's fascination with the great Renaissance city-states of northern Italy—Venice, Padua, Verona, Mantua, Milan, Genoa, Pisa, Florence, and Siena.[20] It so happens that Edward de Vere traveled to most, if not all of these places. As for the traditional author, Will Shakspere, we have no definite knowledge of his whereabouts outside London or his native Warwickshire. For de Vere, on the other hand, one can only marvel at the close parallels between his personal Italian experiences and the Italian influence on Shakespeare's work. If this be mere coincidence, then it is certainly one of the great series of coincidences in the history of world literature.

Attempts to refute Shakespeare's Italian expertise typically begin by citing Act I of *Two Gentlemen* in which both Valentine (I.i.54) and Speed (I.i.72) refer to Valentine's boat travel between the inland cities of Verona and Milan, with Mantua in between. Many, many commentators have gotten bent out of shape over Shakespeare's repeated insistence on this possibility.[21] Let us begin by saying that Venice is not the only Italian city with canals. During Shakespeare's time, an extensive canal system stretched all the way across the Po Valley from Venice (via the famous Brenta Canal),[22] west of Milan and the Lombard Plain as far as Turin. Remnants of this vast waterway system (begun in Roman times) still exist, and during the 16th century canals were *the* preferred mode of travel, as well as the most expensive and luxurious.[23]

The territory covered by *Two Gentlemen* includes the cities of Verona to the east, Milan to the west, and Mantua in between, southwest of Verona and southeast of Milan. Traveling from Verona to Milan, one first had to go south toward Mantua to get around the foothills surrounding Lake Garda. Later in the play (Act V), the lovers Valentine and Silvia steal away from Milan back to Verona on foot, along the northern land route that would have been used by travelers who were on the lam and did not want to be recognized as aristocrats—who all would have been traveling by boat. There has been some confusion because Sir Eglamour[24] speaks of forests to Silvia (V.i.11) and the Duke refers to mountains (V.ii.46), both of which are scarce in the Po Valley but not so scarce along this northern land route near the lake district. Anyone who has been there knows the close proximity of these forests and mountains.

A bird's-eye depiction of Mantua circa 1575 (the same year de Vere arrived in Italy) clearly shows that it (like Milan and Verona) was an inland port city—similar to Chicago— with lakes, canals, harbors and people sailing around in boats.[25] Some still insist that Shakespeare was wrongly referring to a sea voyage because Proteus threatens Speed (in so many words) not to worry about drowning in a shipwreck because he is going to personally kill him on dry land (I.i.148–150). If one ponders the size and scale of these waterways in period illustrations, or looks at the remnants today, one can easily see how people would have drowned, just as people occasionally drown in shipwrecks on the Chicago River or Lake Michigan. In Verona, the rapids of the River Adige were so treacherous that a canal was built to get around them. To this day, if one gets off at the Verona train station, the first sight encountered is this particular waterway, the *Canale Milani* or canal to Milan.

It seems incredible that so-called experts, in a frenzied rush to prove Shakespeare was a country bumpkin with no knowledge of Italy, have not picked up on this very basic information. Tenaciously, critics then point to Shakespeare's repeated references to the tide in Verona (II.iii.33–54) as proof of his coastal intentions. Recent research by Dr. Noemi Magri has shown, however, that flood levels of Veronese canals were known to rapidly rise and fall due to rainwater.[26]

Regarding Milan, the Braun and Hogenberg map of 1572[27] illustrates the dramatic circular pattern of Milan's once extensive urban canal system—a system that was instrumental in its growth. That is how Milan built its Duomo—the marble had to be shipped in on the canals. A good part of Milan's canal system still exists, including the Naviglio Grande, which in its heyday could handle huge shipping coming to and from the Adriatic Sea via the Po Valley. Any decent guidebook will tell this,[28] but during Shakespeare's time, there was no Michelin or AAA, nor did one just go to the nearest bookstore or public library for information. Books were rare and expensive; however, it is *possible* that Shakespeare had access to a travel guide, two or three of which were even written in English. If Shakespeare had access to Braun and Hogenberg, one could make a plausible argument that this book facilitated the dazzling display of local color in *Two Gentlemen.* To be clear, Shakespeare's plays are about people rather than places and are not photographic representations of Italy—characters sometimes have English names and there are allusions to Elizabethan London. The works are dramatic fiction, not travelogue; but to say Shakespeare does not show an unusual knowledge of his settings is a gross distortion.

Shakespeare shows amazing familiarity with Milanese landmarks, tossing these at the audience left and right. Silvia alludes to the Abbey of Saint Ambrose, out of the way from the center city (V.i.9). Even more out of the way is the obscure Well of St. Gregory, located near St. Gregory's Church and the Lazzaretto, completely beyond the old city walls, where Proteus tells Thurio to meet him (IV.ii.83). Shakespeare not only mentions the Well but uses it appropriately since Proteus needs an out-of-the-way spot. Here geographic detail serves the plot, but Elizabethan audiences likely would not have known the difference or cared. Conversation between the Duke, Thurio, and Proteus in Act III, scene ii, demonstrates that Shakespeare understood that the Ducal Palace (the Castello Sforzesco) was outside the city gates, as indeed it was. Dim-witted Launce correctly understands that this part of Milan is near the north city gate when he informs Speed that his master Valentine is waiting there (III.i.372–373). These are just a few examples.

Assuming that Shakespeare gathered all his Italian expertise from books and/or discussions over ale at the Mermaid Tavern, he still manages to fill a background in ways that other playwrights did not. For a contrast, read Ben Jonson's *Volpone*, set in Venice and utilizing local references. Jonson never went to Italy, but he did read books and he really piles this book-learning into his plays—and that is exactly what it feels like—book-learning. Shakespeare, on the other hand, always makes the audience feel like everything is coming from experience with a casual and offhand manner, never hitting us over the head with information.[29] Professional writers know how hard it is to fake this sort of thing, especially in a repeated and consistent manner. Regarding Italy, Jonson pretty much gives the audience what one would expect from an English Elizabethan playwright. He makes fun of Italians in general and Venetians in particular, including Italian food and wine (of all things), currency, salesmen, serving girls, courtesans, and husbands, whom he views either as foolish cuckolds or vicious pimps. Jonson's attitude makes a sharp contrast to Shakespeare, who never makes fun of any of these things. Shakespeare does, however, consistently make fun of commoners and the lower classes from all nationalities.

Another central question is whether the author was more likely to have had personal experiences similar to those of the characters in the play. We know very little of Will Shakspere's love life except that he left his wife Anne Hathaway and their three children in Stratford during the 1580s in order to pursue a London theatrical career, then much later returned to Stratford. Whether Anne came to London looking for him (as Julia goes to Milan looking for Proteus in the play) is unknown, although this scenario has been occasionally fictionalized.[30] Modern critics and audiences are rightfully repulsed by the faithless and violent behavior of Proteus, and are downright disgusted by Valentine's callous treatment of Silvia as a chattel by offering her to Proteus in the name of friendship (V.iv.83). Part of the reason *Two Gentlemen* has never been a popular play is that the unsavory and fickle Proteus does not fit the image of the author that most people want to have. Most want to believe that Will Shakspere (unlike Proteus) was driven away from home by economic hardship and a stifling provincial environment.

In the case of Edward de Vere, however, Proteus fits very well as a representation of the author. De Vere left his wife Anne Cecil in 1576 after returning from Italy (under the pretext of a paternity dispute) and lived a bohemian high life for the next five years. When Julia laments, "Poor wounded name! my bosom, as a bed / shall lodge thee till thy wound be thoroughly heal'd" (I.ii.111–112), one can easily hear the voice of the deeply wronged Anne Cecil, but not so easily that of Anne Hathaway. Moreover, one can easily imagine de Vere, as a playwright named "best for comedy" and who probably skewered others on the stage, feeling obligated (as atonement?) to do the same with respect to his own person, perhaps in the form of characters such as Proteus in *Two Gentlemen* and Bertram in *All's Well*. To repeat, orthodox scholars who have taken the trouble to look at the roots of this play usually find these in the early 1580s, a time that saw de Vere reconcile and move back with his wife Anne. In a similar fashion, Proteus (by the end of the story) finally recognizes Julia as his true love, rather than the idealized and unreciprocating Silvia, when he rhetorically asks, "What is in Silvia's face, but I may spy / more fresh in Julia's with a constant eye?" (V.iv.114–115).

✒ 3 ❦

The Merry Wives
of Windsor

The Merry Wives of Windsor is the only Shakespeare comedy (and one of only two Shakespeare plays) set specifically and entirely in England.[1] For this reason, it is typically held up as one of the Bard's quintessentially English dramas. Unfortunately, as in so many other things, this romantic notion crumbles under any kind of critical scrutiny. Three centuries after Shakespeare, the Italian composer Giuseppe Verdi would choose this subject for his final opera, *Falstaff*. Anglophiles view this work as an Italianized version of the play, but in reality, Verdi came full circle by taking an originally Italian tale that Shakespeare had adapted for his own purposes.

The first quarto of the play was published in 1602, indicating that it had been performed by the Lord Chamberlain's Men.[2] A popular legend, dating from 1702, claims that Queen Elizabeth herself commissioned the work because she wanted to see Falstaff in love. Geoffrey Bullough, as usual, went to the heart of the matter by observing that "This tradition may be true, but it tells us little except that *The Merry Wives of Windsor* was not the first Falstaff play."[3] A growing number of orthodox scholars, beginning with the late Leslie Hotson, believe the work was written for performance at installation ceremonies for the Knights of the Garter on April 23, 1597,[4] at Westminster, one of whose incoming members was the new Lord Chamberlain, George Carey, Lord Hunsdon.[5] We see no reason to disagree—one of the play settings is the "Garter" Inn in Windsor—but would add that *Merry Wives* is difficult to date. Chambers thought 1600–1601 but has been challenged on this estimate probably more so than for any other play. The normally confident Bullough begins his analysis by disclaiming that "This play presents many problems of dating and provenance."[6]

Orthodox scholars point to a wide variety of sources that Shakespeare may have drawn upon, but almost all agree that the Bard began with Italian short stories from the mid–16th century. In particular, the main plot involving Falstaff's escapades was derived from two collections, *Il Pecorone* ("The Blockhead") by Giovanni Fiorentino (also used by Shakespeare in *The Merchant of Venice*), and *Le Piacevoli Notti* ("The Pleasant Nights") by Giovanni Francesco Straparola. Fiorentino's Sienese story had not been translated into English during Shakespeare's time. An English version of Straparola's tale had appeared in the 1590 anonymous publication *Tarltons Newes out of Purgatory*; even here, however, the original Pisan setting for the tale was retained.[7] De Vere, it should be remembered, had traveled throughout Italy after these books had been published, spoke Italian, and was known to have owned Italian books.

The origins of the subplot in *Merry Wives* involving Fenton's courtship of Anne Page have given scholars far more difficulty. Bullough thought it may have derived as well from Straparola and *Tarltons Newes*, but he tentatively cautioned that "This is a surmise."[8] Chambers did not even venture a surmise. *Merry Wives* is another example in which the Bard transformed a popular story by embellishing it with a new subplot and new characters that seem to come out of left field. These often add life that the originals lacked, and the technique was a hallmark of his genius.

Shakespeare in *Merry Wives* appears to have been once again influenced by two uncles of Edward de Vere. The Arthur Golding translation of Ovid's *Metamorphoses* leaves its mark in a number of references to the legend of Actaeon (from Book III), particularly when Pistol refers to the dog "Ringwood" (II.i.118), a name found only in the Golding version.[9] Earlier, Slender wishes that he had in hand his copy of "Songs and Sonnets" (I.i.199), an acknowledged reference to the volume of poetry that showcased de Vere's uncle, Henry Howard, Earl of Surrey, and pioneer of the Petrarchan sonnet form in English.[10] Will Shakspere (or any other well-read Elizabethan) could have been familiar with these works as well, although there is no evidence that he owned or read books, let alone was related to these famous authors.

In Act V, Falstaff blusters to Ford that "I fear not Goliath with a weaver's beam" (V.i.22). This is nearly a direct quote from the Geneva Bible, which all scholars agree was the version read by Shakespeare. Roger Stritmatter identified this very same passage underlined in the Geneva Bible that was owned by Edward de Vere, and today owned by the Folger Library.[11] While this type of verbal parallel proves nothing in and of itself, a startling number of these parallels in de Vere's Bible, letters, and poetry must give serious pause to anyone not hopelessly obsessed with the traditional Shakespeare as true author of the canon.

In the finale to the play (V.v), Falstaff is tormented for his lustful pursuits by a group of "fairies" organized specifically for this purpose. This device borrows heavily from an anonymous play titled *Endimion*, usually attributed to John Lyly and published in 1591 but probably dating from the 1580s.[12] Lyly, in addition to being a servant and secretary for de Vere, dedicated literary works to his employer, most notably *Euphues His England*,[13] widely considered influential on Shakespeare. Lyly was closely associated with de Vere during the 1580s, particularly in the lease and sublease transactions involving Blackfriars Theater. During this same time, de Vere (probably with Lyly's help) was known to have sponsored acting companies, including a children's troupe (Oxford's Boys) in association with one Henry Evans, who appears as a character in *Merry Wives* as the Welsh parson "Sir Hugh" Evans, and who seems to stage-manage both children and townsfolk as they administer pinching punishment on the wayward Sir John.[14]

At the beginning of his landmark *William Shakespeare: A Study of Facts and Problems*, Edmund Chambers remarks that "William Shakespeare was born of burgess folk, not unlike those whom he depicts in *The Merry Wives of Windsor*."[15] This play in fact probably has the strongest overall biographical parallels for Will Shakspere—a sad comment given the overall lack of these in the canon, combined with the admitted scantiness of Stratfordian references contained even within this particular play. On the other hand, *Merry Wives* opens with a number of allusions that call to mind one of the more fascinating episodes, or legends rather, in the traditional biography.

Beginning with an anecdote repeated by Nicholas Rowe in 1709,[16] most biographers of Will Shakspere relate that his departure from Stratford-upon-Avon during the mid–1580s may have been hastened by an incident of deer-stealing. Several contradictory variations of the story were recorded, but the gist was that a not-so-young Will Shakspere (21 years old in 1585 when his twins were baptized) was caught rustling deer from private property and hauled before the local magistrate, Sir Thomas Lucy. Whether the deer and/or property belonged to Sir Thomas himself is uncertain, but all sources agree that Shakspere was unhappy with Lucy's judgment and retaliated by posting the satirical doggerel "Lucie is lowsie."[17] Before Sir Thomas could recover from this impertinence, Shakspere fled provincial Warwickshire for London and immortality.[18]

In Act I of *The Merry Wives* the country magistrate Justice Shallow confronts and upbraids Falstaff with "Knight, you have beaten my men, killed my deer, and broke open my lodge" (I.i.111–112). Before the unruly entrance of Sir John and his rowdy crew, Shallow, Slender and Evans engage in obscure banter regarding Shallow's coat of arms, which, according to Slender, has a "dozen white luces [i.e., fish]" (I.i.16). Evans chimes in with a "dozen white louses" (I.i.18). This recalls Shakspere's derisive pun against Lucy, and the Lucy coat of arms predictably sported luces, but had three instead of 12.[19] Oxfordians like to point out that 12 luces were featured on the forfeited coat of arms for John Dudley, Duke of Northumberland and father to Robert Dudley, Earl of Leicester,[20] and in the play, Shallow reminds Slender that the 12 luces are "an old coat" (I.i.17). Furthermore, Schoenbaum cautioned us that "Luces and louses" was "a predictable Elizabethan pun" and "In truth Sir Thomas [Lucy] does not sound very much like the tyrant of the tradition ... nor is he aptly caricatured as the dim-witted Shallow of *The Merry Wives of Windsor*."[21] In any event, we do not necessarily see a contradiction between these interpretations (multiple meanings and equivocation were standard fare), and Oxfordian Robert Brazil in his probing article on *Merry Wives* pointed out that heraldic discussions would have been perfectly in keeping with a play produced for the Garter induction ceremonies.[22] Even if the opening scene of *Merry Wives* has nothing to do with Sir Thomas Lucy, it is difficult (if not impossible) to forget the vivid image of a deer-poaching Will Shakspere.

Edward de Vere had documented connections with both Windsor and Warwickshire, while Will Shakspere only had the latter. De Vere was recorded as staying at Windsor Castle several times, and in one case was illustrated as an escort for the queen while carrying the sword of state (as Lord Great Chamberlain) in 1572.[23] That same year (1572), de Vere helped to stage an enormous mock battle at Warwick Castle and later sponsored a bear-baiting event in Coventry. Last but not least, de Vere's acting company was among several that swept through Stratford-upon-Avon during the early 1580s, immediately prior to Shakspere's (hastened?) departure from there.[24]

The hard-to-trace subplot in *Merry Wives* involving Fenton's courtship of Anne Page is not so obscure when viewed through the Oxfordian lens. After beating out several competing suitors, de Vere married Anne Cecil, daughter of his guardian Lord Burghley, in 1571. In the play, both Page (III.ii.73–74) and Fenton (III.iv.4) make reference to Fenton's high birth in relation to Anne, as was the case in real life between de Vere and Anne

Cecil. The character name of Fenton is itself easily identified with the writer Geoffrey Fenton, who in 1575 dedicated his *Golden Epistles* to Anne Cecil, Countess of Oxford.[25] As for Will Shakspere, his wife was named Anne as well, but beyond this single item, no other parallel facts are known.

Among Mistress Anne Page's rival suitors is Justice Shallow's "cousin" Abraham Slender, but who calls Shallow "uncle" (III.iv.38–39), and who bears a startling resemblance to Robert Dudley's famous nephew, the courtier poet Philip Sidney. Sidney, who was slender both in the physical and financial sense, had been a rival suitor to Anne Cecil—the two were betrothed at one point—before being surpassed by de Vere's superior title, wealth, and (presumably) charm, although in the long run everyone probably wondered whether the right choice had been made. In 1571, however, Sidney depended on inherited wealth from his mother (Dudley's sister) to become a truly eligible suitor, just like Slender in the play (I.i.275).[26]

The focus of attention, though, is the main plot revolving around Falstaff's lechery and the punishments devised for him by Mistress Ford and Mistress Quickly. As discussed for the *Henry IV* plays (see Chapters 19 and 20) that probably preceded *Merry Wives*, Shakespeare's Falstaff during the 1590s was recognized as a thinly disguised caricature of the historical Sir John Oldcastle by his irate descendents, William and Henry Brooke (father and son), the Lords Cobham. The Puritanical (and no doubt anti-theatrical) elder Brooke had replaced the popular Henry Carey upon his death in 1596 as Lord Chamberlain. Brooke then died on April 5, 1597,[27] and was replaced as Lord Chamberlain by the son of his predecessor, George Carey (the new Lord Hunsdon). Carey was then promptly admitted to the Order of the Garter on April 23, 1597, the ceremonies of which many believe had the premier of *Merry Wives* as its entertainment. The appointment of the new Lord Hunsdon as Lord Chamberlain (and his honorary knighthood) was probably an occasion of celebration and relief for all friends of the London public theaters. Brooke's shadow, however, still hangs over this play because the jealous Ford originally disguised himself under the name Brooke (in the first quarto), which was later censored into "Broome" (II.i.216–219) for the First Folio, despite spoiling several water puns in the text.[28]

Falstaff, on the other hand, is not merely a send-up of a Puritan icon: like Fenton and Ford, he reflects the author as well. Fenton represents the young de Vere courting his wife, but the cuckold-obsessed Ford reminds us that de Vere afterward falsely accused Anne of infidelity. Falstaff suggests the later de Vere, decayed in both reputation and fortune. Although the Oxfordian theory maintains that de Vere provided the Garter entertainment of 1597, de Vere himself was conspicuously and repeatedly rejected for this honor.[29] This would have made it an occasion both of nostalgia and bitterness. Falstaff declares in *Henry IV, Part II* that "I am not only witty in myself, but the cause that wit is in other men" (I.ii.9–10). Orthodox critic W.J. Courthope had a similar opinion of de Vere, specifically, that he "was not only witty in himself, but the cause of wit in others."[30] This ability may have allowed de Vere (like Falstaff) to provide laughs without necessarily being a member of the club.

❧ 4 ☙

Measure for Measure

Now laws remain respected not because they are just but because they are laws. That is the mystical basis of their authority. They have no other. It serves them well, too. Laws are often made by fools, and even more often by men who fail in equity because they hate equality: but always by men, vain authorities who can resolve nothing.
—Montaigne, *On Experience* [1592][1]

Measure for Measure was not published until the First Folio of 1623.[2] The only recorded period performance was at Whitehall Palace on December 26, 1604.[3] This production was part of what could be described as the first "festival" of Shakespeare plays, concurrent with celebrations surrounding the year-end wedding between Edward de Vere's daughter Susan Vere to Philip Herbert,[4] nephew of Philip Sidney and son of Mary Sidney. The wedding took place the following day, on December 27, 1604.[5] *Measure for Measure*, like *Othello* (performed at court a few weeks before), was listed in the revels as having been written by the poet "Shaxberd,"[6] and both works drew upon the Italian writer Cinthio as a primary source. Anne Barton, writing the introduction for *Riverside*, summed up the majority view among critics of all authorship persuasions:

> *Measure for Measure* stands then as the end of a development, the last word spoken in a particular kind of dramatic investigation which seems to have begun in the early 1590s and which extended itself through some eleven comedies before reaching this terminus.[7]

Barton added that "The play itself has some of the qualities of a farewell: a sense of dissatisfaction with its own dramatic mode..."[8] In bidding farewell to comedy, the Bard succeeded in turning every dramatic convention on its head, surprising audiences with each new development, oftentimes unpleasantly. Figuratively speaking, this was not the same comic playwright who had written (or rewritten) plays like *The Taming of the Shrew* many years before. Never a popular work, *Measure for Measure* is for most Bardolators a difficult pill to swallow. In trying to fully appreciate it, one would do well to remember that it was probably written to premiere before King James and a highly sophisticated court audience having their own unique prejudices. If the Oxfordian theory is correct, it was also written by a legally trained peer of the realm.

The title of the play is taken from Duke Vincentio's stern line "Measure still for Measure" (V.i.412), itself a paraphrase from the Sermon on the Mount (Matthew 6, following the Lord's Prayer).[9] The context relates to the statutory capital punishment of Angelo for fornication, who earlier had supposedly punished Claudio in the same manner for the same crime. In other words, an eye for an eye, or "death for death" (V.i.409). Claudio, however, is revealed not have been executed (to the surprise of everyone), and Angelo himself is then pardoned. The triumph of mercy and forgiveness toward all offenders at the end of the story reflects the superior moral values of the Christian New Testament over the harsher and less equitable rules and regulations of the Old Testament, a theme earlier explored by Shakespeare in *The Merchant of Venice.* While the true religious beliefs of Shakespeare the writer and Edward de Vere are likely never to be resolved, the Folger Library today owns a Geneva Bible that appears to be the same one purchased by the 19-year-old de Vere. By almost universal consensus, this was the same edition of the Bible used by Shakespeare. The Geneva English translation (predating the King James version) was so named because it originated from Geneva, Switzerland, adopted home base of John Calvin (1509–1564), spiritual father of the Puritan movement that was rapidly achieving political dominance in England at the time of the play's premiere.

Isaac Asimov classified *Measure for Measure* as an "Italian play," and so it is, at least in terms of primary source material.[10] The tale of the terrible bargain in which a woman must sacrifice her honor to save her brother's life was taken from the *Hecatommithi* by Cinthio—a pen name for Giovanni Battista Giraldi—published in 1565. This collection had also been used by Shakespeare for *Othello,* and no English translation existed at that time, although there was a French rendition from the original Italian.[11] While an English variation on the tale would appear a few years later, the Bard apparently knew Cinthio's work, as evidenced by his familiarity with a number of details unique to the Italian text.[12] Cinthio later dramatized the same tale in his play titled *Epitia,* published in 1582 but written no later than 1573, the year of Cinthio's death.[13] Cinthio's works belonged to the library of Lord Burghley, de Vere's guardian and father-in-law,[14] and it is possible that Cinthio's play was performed in Italy during de Vere's tour through that country in 1575–1576. The 17th Earl was known to have spoken fluent Italian (as well as French), owned Italian books, and was satirized as an Italianate Englishman. As for Will Shakspere, his familiarity with Cinthio's non–English works can only be assumed by those with traditional authorship beliefs.

Published in 1578, the play titled *Promos and Cassandra* by George Whetstone (1544?–1587?) tells a very similar story.[15] Although a variety of other minor sources have been identified,[16] Bullough emphasized that Shakespeare's play was "stimulated largely by" Cinthio and Whetstone.[17] Whetstone was a reformed libertine, most of whose writings were directed toward the uplifting of English moral standards and the condemnation of urban vice. In his prologue to *Promos and Cassandra* he criticized the fledging English dramatic arts as being too romantic, fantastical and vulgar, adding that plays should not be performed on Sundays. This view was in keeping with the Puritan movement to abolish the playhouses entirely, although Whetstone (as an aspiring playwright) did not belong to the extremist camp. This was the same period that saw de Vere highly active at court in a variety of dramatic and literary activities. Although Sunday plays were soon afterward legally abolished, Whetstone was not successful as a playwright, mainly because of his turgid writing style, and according to the *Dictionary of National Biography,* his "unwieldy play was never acted."[18]

In 1582, Whetstone published a prose version of the same tale as part of his pompously titled *Heptameron of Civill Discourses*.[19] *Heptameron* was dedicated to Christopher Hatton, one of de Vere's rivals at court, and to whom other writers hostile to de Vere and/or ambivalent toward the theaters were attached, such as Barnabe Riche and William Rankins[20] (see Chapter 13 on *Twelfth Night*). It seems as though these writers joined together to take potshots at de Vere (without mentioning his name, of course) under the patronage of Hatton, who may have been the earlier victim of de Vere's satire in a "pleasant conceit" performed at court in 1580. Whetstone then returned to soldiering, joining Philip Sidney at Zutphen in 1586, and later wrote an elegy for Sidney. His last book in 1587 was dedicated to Lord Burghley, de Vere's father-in-law.[21] While not much of a writer, Whetstone's name will forever be attached to Shakespeare's via *Measure for Measure*, and his idea of a moral and uplifting dramatic art was later picked up by Philip Sidney's sister Mary with more success in her *Antonie* of 1590. *Measure for Measure* (we believe) consciously took this concept to an entirely new level in its uninhibited juxtaposition of complex religious, legal and ethical issues with big-city low-life bawdry and street humor.

Before exploring the extensive similarities between the plot of *Measure for Measure* and de Vere's personal life, it should be noted that his son-in-law, William Stanley—probably the second most plausible "alternative" Bard after de Vere—has interesting connections to the play as well. In 1918 (two years before the Oxfordian theory was proposed), Professor Abel Lefranc published his discovery that the names and situations in Shakespeare's play had astonishingly close parallels to those in Paris circa 1582–1584. Stanley, like de Vere before him, had traveled extensively and this specific period found him in Paris hobnobbing with the French nobility. Lefranc noted that King Henry III of France had around this same time made one of his customary monastic retreats, leaving legal administration in the hands of one Jerome Angenouste (= Angelo), who immediately condemned to death one Claude Tonart (= Claudio) for the crime of fornication under an archaic statute.[22] Angenouste had recently broken off his engagement to a woman deprived of her dowry, being dependent on a brother who went bankrupt. This is like Mariana in the play, who is jilted by Angelo when she is deprived of her inheritance from a brother lost at sea (III.i.216). This woman (whose name has not survived) resided at a "moated grange" (III.i.264) near Beaulieu that had been granted by the king to her brother-in-law François d'Espinay Saint-Luc ("Saint Luke's"). As for Saint-Luc himself (= Lucio), he was one of the king's more disreputable companions. Other landmarks match. Near Paris was a "consecrated font / A league below the city" (IV.iii.98–99), known as the Fountain of Saint Genevieve at Nanterre. The king's favorite monastic retreat was located near the royal chateau at Vincennes (hence, Duke "Vincentio"), and the king assumes the moniker of Friar Lodowick (the only German name in the play), whose French equivalent is none other than Saint Louis of France. This is just a sampling of Lefranc's discoveries.[23]

Although Lefranc did not identify a real-life model for Shakespeare's Isabella (the key character in the Cinthio and Whetstone plays but under different names), he did learn that there was a nearby convent operated by the Order of "St. Clare" (I.iv.5) founded by the sister of Saint Louis, Saint Isabelle. This convent had a scandalous reputation for relaxed discipline,[24] and in the play we meet the novice Isabella advocating to Sister Francisca that the convent needs "a more strict restraint" (I.iv.4). At this point we must pause to insist that this is too much to be mere coincidence—the Bard somehow knew about these people and places. There would have been two sources for such information: the secret service files of Francis Walsingham[25]—access by de Vere would not have been out of the question—or from someone like de Vere's son-in-law William Stanley, who had been there at the time. Thus Shakespeare's "Vienna"[26] in *Measure for Measure* appears to be a euphemism for "Paris"—a city known to both de Vere and Stanley—and documented events provide the extensive material that embellishes the basic plot originally supplied by Cinthio and Whetstone.

The most prominent connection between de Vere's biography and the plot of *Measure for Measure* is that de Vere, like Claudio, was imprisoned for having sex outside the bounds of holy matrimony. This involved his affair with Anne Vavasor, who bore him a son (Edward Vere) in 1581, after which the queen promptly incarcerated them both in the Tower of London. This followed a year of scandalous charges and countercharges between the 17th Earl and his former Catholic associates, who accused him of every imaginable crime. De Vere seemed to have weathered this storm until it was revealed that he had impregnated one of Elizabeth's ladies-in-waiting, an intolerable infraction in the eyes of the queen. After having his jets cooled, de Vere was later released and reconciled with his wife, but then had to fight the formidable Thomas Knyvet, kinsman to his former mistress—an altercation that left him injured and possibly lame.[27]

On a more improbable level, Isabella in the play escapes the humiliation of sleeping with Angelo by successfully arranging for his jilted fiancée Mariana to take her place, unbeknownst to him (!), in Act III, scene i. In the sources, Cassandra and her predecessors sleep with the magistrate and then marry him afterward[28]—but the Bard resorts to substitution both in this matter and in Claudio's staged execution (IV.iii). Thus Shakespeare utilized the unlikely "bed-trick" device in both *Measure for Measure* and *All's Well That Ends Well*. It is nearly impossible to discuss this aspect of the canon without recalling that de Vere, among all Elizabethan noblemen, had his own unique associations with the bed-trick. Two separate sources record that de Vere conceived his first child by unknowingly sleeping with his wife when he thought he was with a third party.[29] This direct and highly unusual parallel between de Vere's life and one of the Bard's favored plot devices—one that is used twice—makes it difficult to deny that Shakespeare did not at least have the 17th Earl in mind when writing.[30] That Will Shakspere, if he was indeed the playwright, would even dare to suggest a scandal involving an earl (Burghley's son-in-law, no less) is more astounding still.

Moving from the prurient to the esoteric, *Measure for Measure* has been long recognized as a highly legalistic play reflecting jurisprudential sophistication on the part of the author. For example, the travesty of a courtroom in Act II, scene i, could only have been created by someone who first understood the law before effectively making a mockery of it. Angelo confidently begins the proceedings by declaring that "We must not make a scarecrow of the law" (II.i.1), but wavers as litigation drags on: "This will last out a night in Russia, / When nights are longest there" (II.i.134–135). Finally, he gives up, telling his deputy Escalus, "find good cause to whip them all" (II.i.137). Shakespeare also shows familiarity with obscure legislation, such as Mariana's right to dower upon the death of her newlywed husband Angelo for treason (V.i.422–425). Even those stubbornly skeptical of Shakespeare's legal expertise have admitted that the Bard got points such as this correct, though by accident, of course.[31]

Mark Twain, like many other doubters of the traditional Shakespeare biography, believed that the true Bard probably had some kind of legal training, based on canon:

> Shakespeare couldn't have written Shakespeare's works, for the reason that the man who wrote them was limitlessly familiar with the laws, and the law-courts, and law-proceedings, and lawyer-talk, and lawyer-ways...

Furthermore, Twain forcefully emphasized, mere book-learning was not enough to explain this expertise because:

> ... a man can't handle glibly and easily and comfortably and successfully the argot of a trade at which he has not personally served.[32]

For de Vere, a casual command of legalese would be explained by his training at Gray's Inn, combined with a lifetime of litigation, both on a mundane and grandiose level.[33] Will Shakspere, it must be admitted, was also involved in a number of lawsuits, although in comparison to de Vere his exposure to the courts would have been minuscule.

Shakespeare segues from law into religion. Bullough observed that the Bard "conceived the theme in terms more religious than his predecessors." Unlike the sources, Isabella is made into a novice and the Duke poses as a friar.[34] All ethical conflicts are ultimately resolved by public exposure and forgiveness. Bullough again:

> *Measure for Measure* is transcended by the law of compassion. The play is one of justice, severity, mercy, revitalization, and pardon, conceived not as allegory but in terms of individual human beings.[35]

In a sense, this is Shakespeare's most Christian play; yet it is also a work that has proved to be unpopular, especially with religious zealots who prefer to view strictly in terms of black and white the complex moral issues that are explored.

Although critics routinely classify Shakespeare's Angelo and Isabella as Catholics, they are really Puritans, or more specifically, moral absolutists. In this work, the Bard seemed very concerned about respectable appearances cloaking mischief. It is no accident that *Measure for Measure* contains one of the earliest uses of the word "sanctimonious" (I.ii.8), a word that Shakespeare appears to have made up.[36] The "fantastic" Lucio, a kind of Puritan foil, condemns a respectable gentleman (who says "Amen" to his face) with "Thou conclud'st like the sanctimonious pirate that went to sea with the Ten Commandments, but scrap'd one out of the table" (I.ii.7–9). In fact, Shakespeare gives us a whole gallery of disrespectable characters—Mistress Overdone, Constable Elbow, Kate Keepdowne, Froth, Pompey the Clown—all of whom would have deeply offended George Whetstone, and maybe Philip Sidney as well. Later, the executioner Abhorson observes that "Every true man's apparel fits your thief" (IV.ii.46). All of this would have been red meat to King James, who from day one of his reign showed hostility toward the Puritans. Carrying this idea further, the Duke pronounces:

> If thou art rich, thou'rt poor;
> For, like an ass whose back with ingots bows,
> Thou bear'st thy heavy riches but a journey,
> And death unloads thee [III.i.25–28].

This is an extraordinary statement if coming from the pen of the self-made entrepreneur Will Shakspere, but not at all surprising if from the bankrupt Edward de Vere, especially if recent research is correct in that de Vere made a dramatic escape from his creditors by faking his own death in 1604.[37]

How King James reacted to the first performance of *Measure for Measure* is unknown. Edmund Chambers, however, soberly noted that "When Puritanism gathered head under James, it was the sting of caricature which directly led to the renewal of the old controversy." As an example he cited the satirical play titled *The Puritan* (or *Widow of Watling Street*), which appeared in 1607 "written by W.S." and "acted by the Children of Paules."[38] Scholars reject *The Puritan* as a work by Shakespeare, but it seems to have been written with a Shakespearean attitude toward its subject matter. Some think it was the work of Thomas Middleton, although at least one leading Middleton scholar (Margot Heinemann) disagreed.[39] Given James' well-documented odium toward the Puritans, it may be that Shakespeare's *Measure for Measure* was the drama that truly began this "sting of caricature" trend, eventually leading toward *The Puritan* and other plays.

Lastly, we have the omnipresent Duke, a character that Shakespeare invented. Anne Barton, like most critics, saw him as a kind of stagemanager: "He [the Duke] is in fact a kind of comic dramatist." Barton may have come closer to the truth than she realized by noting that this "dramatist duke ... suggests an obvious parallel with Shakespeare himself."[40] How about a dramatist earl? If the Oxfordian theory is correct, then it seems natural (if not predictable) that de Vere would have played the role of his own stage manager in front of King James the night before the wedding of his youngest daughter. Furthermore, the listed playwright "Shaxberd" may not have been a scribal error, as is typically supposed; rather, it may have been an in-joke among peers.[41] This one and only period performance of *Measure for Measure* may have been the Bard's personal farewell to the comic genre, himself masquerading (or rather encoring after his supposed death in June?) as "the old fantastical duke of dark corners" (IV.iii.156) before finally disappearing from the public eye.

ఎ 5 ce

The Comedy of Errors

*It has often occurred to me that those of our contemporaries who undertake to write come-
dies (such as the Italians, who are quite good at it) use three or four plots from Terence
or Plautus to make their own.*

—Montaigne, On Books [1580][1]

Shakespeare's shortest play (1,777 lines), and one of only two that observe the classical unities of time and place (besides *The Tempest*), was not published until the First Folio
of 1623.[2] *The Comedy of Errors* had been associated with Shakespeare's name, however, as
early as 1598 by Francis Meres.[3] Although often criticized for its preposterous absurdities
of plot, this early work represents a sort of master thesis in the Plautine genre—as well as
stretching it beyond the boundaries of those constricts—besides just being a delightful
romp in slapstick humor. These attractive qualities were recognized and realized by Broadway in the 1938 Rodgers and Hart musical treatment of the play titled *The Boys from Syracuse*.

There is general agreement that the "comedy of errors" recorded in Philip Henslowe's
diary for a performance at Gray's Inn in 1594 refers to Shakespeare's play.[4] Gray's Inn,
incidentally, had been attended by de Vere in 1567. On New Year's Day, 1577, a lost,
anonymous play titled *The Historie of Error* was performed at Hampton Court by the Children of Paul's. At this time, de Vere was 26 years old and had recently returned to court
from his tour of the continent. Scholars of all authorship persuasions tend to believe this
was an early, primitive version of the play that Shakespeare the writer later revised into
the form published in the 1623 First Folio.[5] In theory it is possible for an orthodox scholar
to admit that de Vere, who was a noted playwright, may have written this early work (with
Will Shakspere later adapting it), but such an admission has never been made to the best
of our knowledge. This reluctance is probably due to the formidable backlash against the
Oxfordian theory that took place during the late 20th century, despite the fact that *A Historie of Error* belongs to a large group of lost, anonymous plays that were performed at
court during the late 1570s and early 1580s, with titles sounding remarkably like Shakespeare's. We concede the *possibility*, of course, that in early 1577 the 12-year-old Will
Shakspere may have been forwarding dramatic juvenilia from Stratford to London for royal
command performance.

The *Menaechmi* by the Roman playwright Plautus is the uncontested primary source
for the main plot of the twin brothers (whom Shakespeare gives identical names), but was

not translated into English until 1595.[6] Contrary to popular myth, there is a broad consensus among orthodox scholars that Shakespeare was capable of reading the Latin original. Edmund Chambers was firm: "I see no reason to doubt that Shakespeare could have read Plautus in the original."[7] Anne Barton, writing the introduction for *Riverside*, concurred: "Although William Warner's translation of Plautus' *Menaechmi* did not appear until 1595, Shakespeare had almost certainly read the play in Latin before that date."[8] Before proceeding any further with this analysis, it should be noted that the *Menaechmi* was part of the library of Thomas Smith, de Vere's childhood tutor and one of the most distinguished educators of the age.[9] Shakespeare did not stop with a single comedy by Plautus, however; he drew upon a second play, the *Amphitruo*, for the subplot of the twin servants (whom he also gives the same name). This work was not translated into English during Shakespeare's time, strengthening a general belief in the Bard's ability to read Latin.[10] De Vere's fluency in Latin was attested to during his lifetime[11]; as for Will Shakspere, it can only be presumed by the orthodox position.

A secondary source for *The Comedy of Errors* was the *Confessio Amantis* by John Gower, contemporary of Geoffrey Chaucer and to whom the latter dedicated his *Troilus and Criseyde* (another story dramatized by Shakespeare). Gower's *Confessio*, also a primary source for *Pericles*, provided Shakespeare's subplot for the sojourning father Egeon, based upon Apollonius of Tyre, a popular subject of ancient origin.[12] De Vere's most famous association with the name of John Gower is that both were cited in *The Arte of English Poesie* (1589) as being among the greatest English poets by George Puttenham (?), who added that social stigma of the times prevented de Vere as a nobleman from taking credit for his writing.[13]

The names of the twin brothers Antipholus are believed to have been taken from Philip Sidney's *Arcadia* (published in 1593), while the names of their twin servants Dromio derived from the anonymous play titled *Mother Bombie*, usually attributed to John Lyly and published in 1594.[14] Lyly was servant and secretary to de Vere, dedicating several works to the 17th Earl; conversely, Sidney was de Vere's arch-rival in poetry and most other things as well. Years after Sidney's death, however, de Vere's youngest daughter would marry Sidney's nephew in 1605, cementing a political alliance between the two families. Since the first publication of *The Comedy of Errors* was in 1623, we have no idea what earlier versions of this work may have looked like, and it is impossible to say with any certainty at what point specific character names and situations in the play were inserted.

On a very basic level, *The Comedy of Errors*, like *Twelfth Night*, shows a concern with the Plautine device of twin-ness. It would be remiss not to note that Will Shakspere fathered twins in 1585,[15] although de Vere may have had a personal interest in this theme as well, since it is possible that he and his sister Mary Vere were twins. This has not been established for certain, however, because all we have is a letter from their uncle saying they were both the same age.[16] More esoterically, Shakespeare in this play (and others) shows familiarity with the ins and outs of royal wardship.[17] In Act V, scene i, the Duke of Ephesus and Adriana (wife to Antipholus of Ephesus) engage in dialogue indicating that the match had been arranged by the Duke for the presumed-orphan Antipholus in recognition of his military service. The Duke acknowledges this to Adriana by telling her "And I to thee engag'd a prince's word, / When thou didst make him master of thy bed, / To do him all the grace and good I could" (V.i.162–164). Antipholus of Ephesus, like Bertram in *All's Well That Ends Well*, had his wife selected for him. This is similar to de Vere, who was a royal ward under Lord Burghley and married his daughter Anne Cecil with noticeable ambivalence in 1571.

Shakespeare also tosses in a gratuitous reference to contemporary French affairs when Dromio of Ephesus informs his master during a bawdy dialogue that parts of his wife's body are analogous to countries on the world globe. Dromio says that France was "In her forehead; arm'd and reverted, making war against her heir" (III.ii.123–124). Aside from the clever pun on the words "heir" and "hair," this line was a fairly transparent allusion to Henry IV (of Navarre), who consolidated his rightful claim to the throne only after much fighting and political maneuvering in a deeply divided France during the Wars of Religion.[18] In addition to his travels in France, de Vere was known to have received personal correspondence from Henry IV.[19]

Marriage is another serious theme that regularly intrudes upon the slapstick humor. The character of Luciana, invented by Shakespeare,[20] eventually weds Antipholus of Syracuse, whose brother, Antipholus of Ephesus, is already married to Luciana's sister Adriana.[21] The names of Luciana and her shrewish sister Adriana are suggestive of Anne Cecil, de Vere's first wife, but also (admittedly) to Will Shakspere's wife, Anne Hathaway. In 1582 an anonymous translation of St. John Chrysostom's *An Exposition upon the Epistle to the Ephesians* was published and dedicated to Anne Cecil,[22] perhaps written by her husband, who had recently reconciled with her. The city of Ephesus in Asia Minor on the Aegean coast, Shakespeare's chosen setting for the play, was closely associated with the aforementioned epistle by St. Paul that expounds on the institution of marriage (see Ephesians 5:22–33).[23] In a similar manner, the character of the abbess Aemilia is introduced by Shakespeare to turn the Plautine formula on its head in Act V by revealing herself (almost in the fashion of a *deus ex machina*) as both the long-lost wife of Egeon and mother of the twins Antipholus.[24] Aemilia (another favorite name among the Bard's secondary characters) cannot help but suggest one of the leading candidates for Shakespeare's Dark Lady, the Jacobean poetess Aemilia Bassano Lanyer, first proposed by orthodox scholar Alfred Leslie Rowse.[25]

Shakespeare's choice of Ephesus as a setting is fascinating on several levels. In addition to the city's associations with the Pauline epistle and marriage theme, Ephesus was noted in the Bible (see Acts 19:13–29) and elsewhere as having a reputation for sorcery and witchcraft.[26] Antipholus and Dromio of Syracuse, upon arriving in Ephesus, are bewildered by repeated instances of mistaken identity with their twins, and assume that this is attributable to the city's notoriety for occult activities. This is a subject, incidentally, that was known to have interested de Vere.[27] Combined with the Christian associations with St. Paul and matrimony, these factors provide a reasonable explanation for Shakespeare's choice of Ephesus as a setting.[28]

In Plautus, the action instead takes place at Epidamnum on the eastern Adriatic coast,[29] south of the "seacoast of Bohemia" in *The Winter's Tale*, so unjustly derided by Shakespeare's critics.[30] The Bard shifts the action to the remote eastern sector of the Hellenic world, but still uses Epidamnum as the location where Egeon's family is separated due to a storm and shipwreck (similar to *The Tempest*), as we learn through Egeon's flashbacks with the Duke in Act I, scene i. This passage, upon close inspection, once again reveals Shakespeare's geographic sophistication, especially with respect to the Mediterranean world. Egeon tells the Duke that after being thrown adrift near Epidamnum, their parties were separately rescued (and separated from each other) by ships coming from opposite directions via Corinth and Epidaurum along the Adriatic coast. Perusal of a map showing the respective locations of Syracuse, Epidamnum, Corinth, Epidaurum, and Ephesus reveals all this to make perfect sense,[31] although any audience not familiar with this part of the world becomes understandably confused. Why did Shakespeare bother us with all of this geographic detail, unless he perhaps wanted to show off or just could not help himself?

Although never in Ephesus, the presence of de Vere in Sicily and Venice, among other places, is documented.[32] At that time, the best way to travel between the two places was to take a Venetian galley south along the Adriatic coast, around the boot of Italy and past the Ionian Sea. There is no firm evidence that de Vere did exactly this, but it is certainly the most plausible scenario. For certain is Shakespeare's preoccupation with the Adriatic and Ionian coasts in a number of plays, including *The Comedy of Errors*, *The Winter's Tale*, *Twelfth Night*, *Othello*, *Julius Caesar*, *Antony and Cleopatra*, and *The Merchant of Venice*. It obviously fired his imagination. If de Vere was the true author, we may safely assume that these locales triggered an enthusiastic nostalgia.

Regarding Syracuse, the Sicilian home of Egeon's family, both the Duke (I.i.3) and Egeon (I.i.36) in the very first scene of the play refer to the city as "Syracusa" rather than the Anglicized "Syracuse"—a surprising choice unless coming from someone who had traveled there and was accustomed to the local pronunciation. Furthermore, *Riverside* commentator Anne Barton, with typical perception noted that

> Unlike Plautus, Shakespeare seems to have been less interested in the problems of the native twin angered by the perversity of a familiar world than he was in the more extreme situation of the traveler, especially vulnerable because far from home, who finds himself losing his own sense of self in an alien city of reputed sorcery and spells.[33]

Very true indeed. Like Antipholus of Syracuse, de Vere was a traveler in an alien world (perhaps in Syracuse itself) and surely knew the same feelings. In addition, like Egeon, who is proscribed merely for being an indigent Syracusan discovered in Ephesus, de Vere was an English Protestant touring Catholic Italy at a time when this could have been very risky business, if not a fatal undertaking. Lastly, the casual juxtaposition of Christian and pagan references in the play, which many commentators see merely as a cavalier attitude by the author, could be explained by personal experience as well. In the midst of a pagan setting, Antipholus of Syracuse declares, "Now, as I am a Christian, answer me" (I.ii.77). Such an outburst may seem odd to the uninitiated, but not for any Mediterranean traveler who has seen ancient temples converted into Catholic and Orthodox churches.

ဆ 6 ର

Much Ado About Nothing

Much Ado About Nothing, a perennial favorite among the comedies, was first registered and published in quarto during the year 1600.[1] There has been some speculation that the work titled *Love's Labor's Won*, cited by Francis Meres in 1598, may have referred to the same play, but orthodox scholars such as Edmund Chambers believe it was written afterward.[2] A number of other Shakespeare comedies, including *All's Well That Ends Well*, have a similar theme of hard-earned romantic triumph, but Oxfordian Charlton Ogburn, Jr. (among others), pointed out that Benedick and Beatrice seem to have points in common with Berowne and Rosaline, the thwarted (and verbose) couple from *Love's Labor's Lost*; hence, *Much Ado* could have been an appropriate sequel to the earlier play, but with a happier ending.[3]

Structurally, the most remarkable feature of this play is that Shakespeare took a very old and ancient story, adding his own original "subplot" that for most audiences becomes the main plot. The primary sources for the tale of the bride-to-be mistakenly accused of infidelity include the popular 16th-century novel *Orlando Furioso* by Ludovico Ariosto, first translated into English by John Harrington in 1591. Eight years prior to this, however (in 1583), a lost and anonymous English stage version of the tale was performed at court under the title of *The Historie of Ariodante and Genevra*.[4] During this same period there appears to have been a long list of anonymous plays at court that sound like alternative Shakespeare titles. These court productions were concurrent with the dawn of the London public theaters in Shoreditch, as well as de Vere's prominence as an impresario at the Elizabethan court.[5]

Other sources with similar main plots included Matteo Bandello's *Novella* (1554) and one of its French translations, François Belleforest's *Histoires Tragiques* (1559), which (like Shakespeare's play) set the action in Messina, Sicily.[6] The French version belonged to the library of Lord Burghley, de Vere's guardian (and later father-in-law), and de Vere himself was known to have spoken French, as well as Italian. Another parallel work likely known to the Bard (according to Geoffrey Bullough) was the anonymous play *Two Italian Gentlemen: Fedele and Fortunio*, performed at court in 1584.[7] Anthony Munday, de Vere's servant who dedicated works to his patron, is the favored author of *Two Italian Gentlemen*, an English adaptation of the Italian *commedia erudite* titled *Il Fedele*, written by Luigi Pasqualigo and published in 1576.[8]

Even before Harrington's English translation of Ariosto appeared in 1591, another similar version of Shakespeare's main plot was published in 1590 as Book IV of Edmund Spenser's *The Faerie Queene*,[9] which included a dedicatory sonnet addressing de Vere as "most dear" to the Muses.[10] Among the English sources, however, perhaps the most striking involves a direct quote in *Much Ado* from Thomas Watson's 1582 masterpiece *Hekatompathia*, a work that was lavishly dedicated to de Vere.[11] When Don Pedro slyly remarks to Benedick that "In time the savage bull doth bear the yoke" (I.i.261),[12] this is routinely cited as Shakespeare's own line when in fact the Bard was quoting Watson, or perhaps Watson's patron de Vere. Maybe it was the Bard's own invention after all.

As for Shakespeare's technical subplot (which in reality is the main plot) involving a war of the sexes between Benedick and Beatrice, scholars appear to be at a loss in terms of identifying source material. The idea of two people claiming to despise each other then being tricked into falling in love (after they are told by friends that one really adores the other) is unquestionably an example of the Bard's own dramatic genius. Chambers and Bullough noted that the verbal sparring in which the couple engages seems to have been influenced by an episode from *Il Cortegiano* ("The Courtier") by Baldessare Castiglione,[13] the 16th-century Italian best-seller translated into English by Thomas Hoby in 1561, and into Latin by Bartholomew Clerke in 1572. This latter edition included a Latin preface written by the 22-year-old Edward de Vere.[14] It must be admitted, however, that the monumental battle of wits depicted by Shakespeare used Castiglione as a mere suggestive starting point.

In contrast to the Sicilian natives of the story, Shakespeare's two leading male characters hail from northern Italy—Claudio from Florence and Benedick from Padua. De Vere, it must be remembered, traveled throughout Italy for almost a year, including Sicily. Edward Webbe proudly wrote of having witnessed de Vere issue an open jousting challenge in Palermo to all comers in defense of Queen Elizabeth's honor, to which there was no response, except as Webbe noted, that de Vere was afterward "very highly commended" and acknowledged across Italy as "the only Chavalier and Nobleman of England."[15] Some defenders of the traditional Bard have taken this one better by claiming that Will Shakspere was in fact born in Messina and later immigrated to Stratford-upon-Avon. These claimants have been Italians, of course.[16] On the other hand, the motivation is understandable given the Bard's keen fascination with Sicily, as evidenced by the canon.

Shakespeare seems to have constantly had Sicily in mind, with well over half the plays containing some kind of Sicilian point of reference. In theory, these could have been absorbed by any voracious reader, since a good part of classical and Renaissance literature has Sicilian settings, but traveling there (as de Vere did) would have reinforced this with personal experience. For example, the Bard shows an awareness of Sicily's former multinational rule. Don Pedro is from Aragon in Spain, which controlled the Kingdom of the Two Sicilies (based in Naples) during Shakespeare's time, and Pedro was the name of the first Spanish Sicilian monarch. Previously, Sicily had been governed by the French Angevins during the late 13th century, of which the Bard repeatedly displays his awareness in the *Henry VI* trilogy. After the Sicilian Vespers uprising of 1282 (the backdrop of Bandello's story, one of Shakespeare's sources), the Angevins were expelled and the Sicilians invited the Spanish Aragonese to rule over them, with that eventually becoming a permanent arrangement.

Another character in the play—the villain—is Don John, illegitimate brother to Don Pedro, and presumably named after Don John of Austria, the illegitimate brother of then-Spanish king, Philip II.[17] The historical Don John was also the leader of the Messina-based coalition fleet that defeated the Turks at the Battle of Lepanto in 1571. Shakespeare demonstrated his familiarity with the Straits of Messina in *The Merchant of Venice* with allusions to Scylla and Charybdis, the two mythological creatures[18] who guarded the straits (III.v.15–17). Curiously, Miguel Cervantes, who participated in the Battle of Lepanto and would have known Messina firsthand, also alluded to Scylla and Charybdis in *Don Quixote*.[19] Of course, Shakespeare and Cervantes could have simply picked up these names from Homer, although their retention would have been easier given firsthand encounters with these "monsters." Shakespeare presumably chose Messina as a setting based on the Sicilian background used in the Bandello-Belleforest source material, combining that city's associations with the name of Don John. Why he chose to use the name of Don John (which is not in the sources) is less apparent. Perhaps a patriotic Englishman such as Will Shakspere simply wanted to denigrate a Catholic hero; on the other hand, Don John had been long dead (since 1578) and was venerated by many Englishmen as a great Christian soldier who defeated heathen infidels. During de Vere's tour of Italy and Sicily, Don John was still alive and physically present in these environs. Whether there was any connection between de Vere's Palermo "challenge" and the historical Don John is unclear, although fascinating hypotheses have been put forward.[20]

In addition to the Italians, Spanish and French, one of Don John's companions is named Conrade, probably after the last German ruler of Sicily (1252–1268). At one point, Don Pedro makes a disparaging remark about the Germans (III.ii.35) and in *Edward III*, Shakespeare alluded to the Hohenstaufen dynasty that ruled over Sicily before the Angevins (III.i.35). So Shakespeare knew that Sicily had been successively ruled by the Germans, the French and the Spanish. Once again we are impressed with the presumed knowledge of a self-educated son of Warwickshire who never left England. For the same information, this commentator had to access a public library, even though his own grandparents had been born in Sicily.

In terms of the storyline, *Much Ado* touches upon several of Shakespeare's favorite themes. None of these have any known parallels with the traditional biography of Will Shakspere, but in the case of Edward de Vere, there are strong and suggestive counterparts. For one, Claudio falsely accuses his fiancée Hero of infidelity after witnessing a liaison between Don John's retainer Borachio and Hero's lady-in-waiting Margaret, whom he mistakes for Hero, as described in Act III, scene ii. The innocent and wrongly condemned heroine is a familiar figure in the canon, closely resembling de Vere's first wife Anne Cecil, from whom he separated after his return from Italy on suspicions that their first child was not his. Another reoccurring theme is illegitimacy of birth—Don John is literally a bastard (as was his real-life counterpart). This is a topic that Shakespeare's audiences are routinely confronted with (*Much Ado About Nothing*, *King Lear*, *King John*, *Henry VIII*, etc.); one cannot help but feel it was a subject near and dear to the author's heart. For Will Shakspere, there is no indication that the issue ever entered his life. In the case of de Vere, it was a topic of great concern, beginning with himself (at age 13) and continuing with his children, including an eldest daughter, whom he finally acknowledged after reconciling with his wife Anne.

Another one of the Bard's more striking creations (and not found in his source material) is Constable Dogberry.[21] Like Bottom in *A Midsummer Night's Dream*, Dogberry is both a laughingstock and an object of our sympathy. Both are portrayed by Shakespeare as jackasses (Bottom literally metamorphoses into one), and a flustered Dogberry refers to himself as such three times in quick succession (IV.ii.75–78), after Conrad calls him an ass twice (IV.ii.73). Orthodox scholars tend to have little to say about Dogberry, other than acknowledging that Shakespeare made him up. This is frustrating because he is one of the more remarkable minor characters in the canon. A refreshing exception to this silence was Anne Barton, who in her introduction for *Riverside* wrote about Dogberry at length. Paraphrase would only diminish her insightfulness, so we quote her comments here verbatim:

> Dogberry too is a character who customarily frights words out of their proper meaning.... He does so, of course, not because he is witty but because he is ignorant. A man with an exaggerated idea of his own merits and importance—"I am a wise fellow, and which is more, an officer, and which is more, a householder, and which is more, a piece of flesh as any in Messina" [IV.ii.80–82]—he relies upon language to overawe and impress people with whom he deals. To some extent, his verbal habits seem to have rubbed off on his associates.... Only Dogberry, however, consistently misemploys the grandest words he can think of as a way of magnifying himself.

Thus Dogberry butchers the English language. Attentive audiences, though, pick up little bits and pieces of his back story that endear him to us, as Barton notes:

> There is, nevertheless, something almost touching about Dogberry's unrequited passion for words in a play in which other characters possess a mastery of language that is positively dazzling. The suggestion that he is a man who "hath had losses" [IV.ii.84] is made only once, and not elaborated on by Shakespeare, but it is enough to explain the compulsion behind his speech style. Dogberry is a man who has, at some time in the past, suffered heavy financial and social setbacks. He has struggled onto his feet again, owns his own house, and has two gowns "and everything handsome about him" [IV.ii.85–86], but the doubt and the insecurity remain and cannot be banished. This is why he deals so constantly in self-magnification, bullies Verges, and becomes positively obsessed with the fact that he has publicly been described as an ass. Words are his one defense against the possibility that he may be slighted or misprized by the world. He uses them to keep the reality of his self and his situation at bay.[22]

Other than linguistic ambitions that exceed his abilities, Dogberry has done okay in life for someone dealt a bad hand. The question naturally arises: who (if anyone) was he? Did Shakespeare just make him up or did he know someone like Dogberry in real life? A look at another near-contemporary play may provide a clue.

In 1599, one year before Shakespeare's *Much Ado* appeared in quarto, Ben Jonson's *Every Man Out of His Humour* premiered. In her superb book *Shakespeare's Unorthodox Biography*, Diana Price has given a comprehensive summary of the many similarities between Jonson's object of satire—named Sogliardo—and a certain Elizabethan playwright of note.[23] Sogliardo, a pretentious socialclimber with some amateur theatrical background plus bogus intellectual aspirations, has (among other foibles) a tendency to affect foreign languages, simultaneously mangling words and distorting meanings—like Dogberry in *Much Ado*. More provocatively, Sogliardo obtains (through bribery) a coat of arms with the motto "Not Without Mustard"—a none-too-subtle slam on Will Shakspere's motto "Not Without Right,"[24] which he unsuccessfully applied for (on behalf of his father) two years earlier in 1596. Shakspere succeeded, however, in obtaining his coat of arms in 1599 (sans motto), the same year as Jonson's play. Sogliardo's crest is a boar (also Oxford's crest) minus a head—in other words, a swine without a brain trying to imitate de Vere. By that time, Shakspere had succeeded in becoming a homeowner (like Dogberry), after pulling himself up from the bootstraps (again, like Dogberry) following family financial hardships and what appears to have been a bad marriage. In Jonson's play, Sogliardo has a brother (Sordido) who hoards grain (as Shakspere was accused of doing) and a nephew (Fungoso) who is a clotheshorse, like the "upstart crow" in *Greene's Groatsworth of Wit*, typically assumed to be Will Shakspere. Chambers reluctantly recognized the Sogliardo association, but the normally unflappable Samuel Schoenbaum flinched at acknowledging it. In sum, Jonson's Sogliardo and Shakespeare's Dogberry appear to be close dramatic relatives, although the latter is certainly portrayed in more likeable fashion.

In the final analysis, though, it is Benedick and Beatrice who are Shakespeare's most memorable creations. Benedick, one of the Bard's prototypical and witty young noblemen, has been viewed by some as an idealized portrait of one of his patrons (Southampton, perhaps), but more perceptive critics such as Chambers dismissed this illogical notion.[25] A more plausible interpretation would be that Benedick represents the author's own mock-heroic view of himself—whom Don Pedro predicts will become "Benedick the married man" (I.i.267) and Beatrice taunts with "I wonder that you will still be talking, Signior Benedick: nobody marks you" (I.i.116–117).

As for Beatrice, the "Lady Disdain" (I.i.118) who urges Benedick to kill Claudio after he slanders the innocent Hero (Act IV, scene i), there can only be speculation as to whom she may represent—perhaps even as a composite, a favorite technique among great dramatists. From the Oxfordian point of view, we venture to guess that she (like Rosaline from *Love's Labor's Lost*) contains a good bit of Anne Vavasor, lady-in-waiting to Queen Elizabeth with whom de Vere carried on a disastrous affair through 1580. This was roughly concurrent with the same period in which anonymous plays that appear to have influenced *Much Ado* were performed at court. After giving birth to de Vere's illegitimate son (Edward Vere) in early 1581, father and mother (and child?) were incarcerated in the Tower of London by the queen, who considered dalliances between her courtiers and ladies among the most heinous of crimes.[26] After years of tolerated loose-canon behavior, this affair became the final straw that permanently wrecked de Vere's public reputation and career.

Both *Much Ado About Nothing* and *Love's Labor's Lost* are believed by Oxfordians to have existed in primitive versions (under different titles) that were performed at court during the late 1570s and early 1580s. Accordingly, Shakespeare's two battling pairs of lovers may have evolved from earlier models into the more complex creations that first appeared in print circa 1598–1600. If nothing else, Shakespeare's song "Sigh no more, ladies, sigh no more" (II.iii.62–63) seems to be a more mature response to de Vere's sonnet "Love thy Choice," beginning "Who taught thee first to sigh, alas, my heart?"[27] This poem was published as part of the 1591 collection titled *Tears of Fancy* by Thomas Watson, author of the same *Hekatompathia* that was quoted verbatim by Shakespeare in *Much Ado*.[28] By the late 1590s, even the rakish and profligate de Vere, humbled by permanent and self-inflicted setbacks, had probably become more philosophical and circumspect.

℘ 7 ℭ

Love's Labor's Lost

"You've said even more than you know, Sancho," said Don Quixote, "because there are people who exhaust themselves, investigating matters that, after all their learning and all their investigations, don't add a speck to our understanding and aren't worth remembering."

—Cervantes, *Don Quixote* [1615][1]

Love's Labor's Lost owns the distinction of being the first play printed under the Bard's name in 1598, as "Newly corrected and augmented by W. Shakespere."[2] That same year Francis Meres praised Shakespeare as the greatest of all English playwrights (while lauding Edward de Vere in the same pages) and cited *Love's Labor's Lost* as an example of his work.[3] The first quarto refers to a recent Christmas performance before the queen, and beyond this, scholars are left to conjecture the date of writing based solely upon stylistic grounds and topical references. Not surprisingly, this has led to a divergence of opinion. Geoffrey Bullough summed up the situation by noting that "The date of composition is much disputed."[4] William C. Carroll chirped in helpfully with "the play has always been the darling of the Shakespearean lunatic fringe."[5]

Using essentially the same methods as orthodox scholars to date the play (without being restricted to the assumption that Will Shakspere was the true author), Oxfordians postulate that the origins of *Love's Labor's Lost* are to be found in the literary fad of Euphuism during the late 1570s. On January 11, 1579, an exclusive court audience that included Queen Elizabeth and the French ambassador[6] were entertained by a lost, anonymous work titled *A Maske of Amasones and A Maske of Knightes*.[7] This piece, according to witnesses, featured a mock tournament in which six gentlemen were defeated by six ladies, not unlike the four gentlemen suitors in Shakespeare's play who are eventually outwitted and turned away by the Princess and her three companions.[8] Oxfordian scholar Dr. Felicia Hardison Londré of the University of Missouri–Kansas City (possibly the world's leading authority on this play) believes that the 1579 masque was a primitive version of *Love's Labor's Lost* later revised in 1592 and 1598 before its quarto publication.[9]

Identification of direct source material for Shakespeare's play has proved to be difficult and elusive. The indefatigable Geoffrey Bullough concluded that "The source-hunter [Bullough himself] has little to offer ... no one story has been found to cover the plot." Then he adds, "Shakespeare may have created his own plot."[10] We agree with this. We also agree with the assessment of Edmund Chambers that "*Love's Labour's Lost* suggests a courtly rather than a popular audience."[11] Shakespeare's most sophisticated and verbally adventuresome

49

comedy was not designed for mass consumption—it was written for connoisseurs, regardless of who the true author was. If Will Shakspere was the true author, then we can only assume that he was given a unique and specific opportunity to entertain his betters, to which he responded miraculously, to say the least. If the Oxfordian theory is correct, then *Love's Labor's Lost* was a play designed to entertain the queen and her court, written by a courtier with miraculous brilliance as well.

Although the storyline for Shakespeare's play appears to be original, all scholars with a clue have noticed parallels between the setup and historical events in France during the late 1500s. In 1578—one year before the *Maske of Amasones* in England—the Navarre court of the future King Henry IV of France was visited by his estranged wife, Marguerite de Valois (from whom he had been separated due to the Wars of Religion) along with her famed retinue of beautiful ladies-in-waiting or *escadron volant* ("flying squadron").[12] Moreover, many of Shakespeare's character names match French nobles of the period (Berowne = Biron, Longaville = Longueville, Dumain = de Mayenne, etc.).[13] Finally, it would be remiss not to note that these curious similarities to *Love's Labor's Lost* were first noticed by Professor Abel Lefranc, a noted anti–Stratfordian and advocate for William Stanley, Earl of Derby, as the true Shakespeare.[14] This information would have also been easily available to Stanley's father-in-law, Edward de Vere, who had traveled to France in 1575–1576, was fluent in French, and was known to have received correspondence from Henry IV.[15] Bullough noted that among the English nobility, Peregrine Bertie, Lord Willoughby, had the chance to extensively interact with King Henry during concerted (but ultimately thwarted) military operations in 1589, without mentioning that Bertie was de Vere's brother-in-law.[16]

Continuing in the French vein, Shakespeare's "little academe" (I.i.13) of Navarre appears to have been borrowed from *Academie Française* by Pierre de la Primaudaye, published in 1577 (two years before the *Maske of Amasones*) and translated into English in 1586. The dedication was made to King Henry III of France, Marguerite's brother and Henry IV's predecessor, to whom de Vere had been presented during his stay in Paris. The dedication reminds readers that this Academe was in the ancient, Platonic tradition of philosophy.[17] Platonic is not a word that usually comes to mind when describing Shakespeare's plays; then again, the Bard sends the ideals of the Academe crashing into the dust before the end of Act I, scene i, as Constable Dull hauls Costard the Clown before the King for having "sorted and consorted" (I.ii.258) with the country wench Jacquenetta. We do not know if Edward de Vere shared Shakespeare's skeptical attitude toward the Platonic ideal, but we do know that de Vere purchased a copy of Plato's works when he was 19 years old.[18]

Although the setting and characters of *Love's Labor's Lost* are ostensibly French, Shakespeare's virtuosic command of English Euphuism is the real star of the play. Professor Londré, in her introduction to a comprehensive collection of essays on the work, provided the following description of Euphuism:

> Arising from a self-consciousness about linguistics and literature that characterized Renaissance Italy, France, Spain, and England, Euphuism was an effort to explore and expand the possibilities of the English language through rhyming, antithesis, alliteration, "taffeta phrases, silken terms precise, three-piled hyperboles, spruce affectation" [V.ii.406–407], and lexical borrowings from classical Greek, Latin, and contemporary foreign languages. This courtly fad peaked in 1578. With its numerous examples of the

movement's characteristic verbal conceits (including the most rhymed lines in any Shakespeare play), *Love's Labour's Lost* is a textbook example of Euphuism.[19]

Londré, in concert with many orthodox scholars, noted that the leading published exponents of Euphuism during the late 1570s were John Lyly and Anthony Munday, both of whom had been de Vere's servants and presumably secretaries.[20] Lyly, in his best-seller *Euphues the Anatomy of Wit* (1578), acknowledged that he had been inspired by an unnamed nobleman, presumably his then-employer.[21] Conspicuous among de Vere's literary dedications are the Euphuistic works of the late 1570s and early 1580s, universally viewed as influential on Shakespeare, particularly on *Love's Labor's Lost*. These include *Euphues His England* (1580), also by Lyly, as well as *The Mirror of Mutability* (1579) and *Zelauto* (1580) by Anthony Munday.[22] One begins to wonder who was influencing whom. De Vere appears to have been the "acknowledged ringleader"[23] of the Euphuistic movement at court, standing in opposition to his arch-rival of the Areopagos, Philip Sidney. De Vere's identification with the figure of Euphues at the Elizabethan court by Lyly and Munday indicates he was not only articulate, but open to expanding the English language by coining new terms and phrases. When Costard spits out the impossible word "honorificabilitudinitatibus" (V.i.41), we may be getting a taste of de Vere's Euphuistic facilities via Shakespeare the writer.

A more troubling question relates to why the conventional Shakespeare would try to revive an elitist literary craze that was some 15 years out of fashion. Did someone tip him off that the queen wanted to walk down memory lane? Once again, Dr. Londré effectively went to the heart of the matter:

> the orthodox dating of the play to the 1590s (to make it fit the dates of Shakspere of Stratford-upon-Avon) posits that the author based his in-jokes upon topics that had been fashionable at court twelve to fifteen years earlier. How would a young man fresh from a small rural town have dared to write one of his first plays for and about court society? In fact, how could one who spoke Warwickshire dialect have acquired the verbal facility and sophistication to lampoon a linguistic fad that had flared briefly among courtiers when he was only fourteen?[24]

Resurrecting Euphuism during the mid–1590s seems counterintuitive, but Bardolators tend to swallow it because we are so attached to the traditional biography. Remove that obstacle, however, and everything seems to fall into place.

Peripheral influences on *Love's Labor's Lost* are numerous and diverse, yet direct connections with de Vere are unavoidable in almost every instance. The Pageant of the Nine Worthies in Act V is thought to be descended from a device with the same title that was arranged by Thomas Churchyard and performed before the queen in 1578.[25] Churchyard had a long personal and literary association with de Vere lasting over 30 years.[26] The pervasive influence of the Italian *commedia dell' arte* on the play has long been acknowledged,[27] and during his Italian tour de Vere likely had many opportunities to witness the leading practitioners of this improvised art form.[28] In Act IV, an enraptured Holofernes exclaims, "Ah, good old Mantuan! I may speak of thee as the traveller doth of Venice" (IV.ii.94–96). This is a reference to the Italian poet Mantuan—a pen name for Giovanni Baptista Spagnoli—whose works were translated into English, but more likely would have been appreciated by the multilingual de Vere who had traveled to Venice and surely Mantua as well.[29] Holofernes also praises (obligatory for Shakespeare) "Ovidius Naso" (IV.ii.123)—i.e., Ovid—whose works were first translated into English by de Vere's uncle Arthur Golding.

Beginning with John Thomas Looney, Oxfordians have tended to identify the prissy character of Boyet with de Vere's great poetic competitor Philip Sidney.[30] Scholars tend to agree that Shakespeare's simultaneous tribute to and send-up of Euphuism owes something to Sidney, whose Lady of May probably dates from the late 1570s. Apparently Euphuism influenced Sidney's clique as well, with experiments in rhyme being a feature of court drama advocated by the Pembroke circle and led by Philip's surviving sister, Mary Sidney.[31] This interaction between former rival factions would culminate in 1604 with the Vere and Sidney families intermarrying.[32]

Among the verbally sparring lovers in the play, it is Berowne and Rosaline who command most of our attention. To the orthodox view, they are generic; to Oxfordians, they represent the young wayward de Vere and most likely his mistress of the late 1570s, the lady-in-waiting Anne Vavasor.[33] Like Berowne in the mask of the "Muscovites" (V.ii.121), de Vere acted in at least one production, a 1579 court masque, and probably in others besides.[34] Berowne forswears the "Figures pendantical" and "maggot ostentation" (V.ii.408–410) of Euphuism, penning love sonnets to Rosaline instead (IV.iii.15). With respect to Shakespeare, critics have noted a kinship between Rosaline and the Dark Lady of the sonnets, but naysayer Edmund Chambers rightly objected that "Rosaline is throughout white-skinned; only her hair and brows are black...."[35] Indeed, when these untrained eyes look at a portrait of Anne Vavasor, they see brown hair and fair skin. Regardless of who the true Shakespeare was, we would humbly suggest that "Rosaline" may have been a real-life prototype that the Bard later allowed to morph into an even darker icon, utilizing similar poetic machinery he had earlier developed.

Our personal favorite character is the pendant Holofernes, whose historical identity (if there was one) has been debated by just about every commentator. Laying aside the authorship question for a moment, Shakespeare's contemporary Michel de Montaigne spoke for many of us when he wrote that:

> When I was a schoolboy I was often upset when I saw schoolmasters treated as buffoons in Italian comedies.... Placed as I was under their control and tutelage, the least I could do was to be jealous of their reputation. I tried to make excuses for them in terms of the natural conflict between the common man and men of rare judgment and outstanding learning—an inevitable one since their courses run flat opposite to each other. But the effort was wasted: it was the most civilized of men who held them in the greatest contempt.... This attitude goes back to the Ancients: for Plutarch says that scholar and Greek were terms of abuse among the Romans; they were insults.... As I grew older I found that they were absolutely right ... them most biggest clerks ain't the most wisest [quoting Rabelais from the vulgar Latin].[36]

Shakespeare gave us a number of memorable stage pendants (including one so-named from The Taming of the Shrew), but Holofernes represents the epitome. We feel bad for the guy even as we laugh at him.

Many, many Elizabethans have been suggested as models for Holofernes, several of whom had connections to de Vere, but among these the most enthralling is the Cambridge don Gabriel Harvey. The possibility of Harvey has been acknowledged by orthodox scholars such as Chambers,[37] but among Oxfordians, Looney once again led the charge, making a very persuasive case. In addition to the fact that Gabriel Harvey was a notorious pedant, Looney noted that Edmund Spenser nicknamed Harvey "Hobbinol" in his *Shepheardes Calender* of 1579[38]—there's that same year again. Of special interest was Harvey's relationship to his nobleman classmate de Vere, which apparently started out friendly but ended in mutual suspicion. In 1578[39] at Audley End, Harvey addressed the queen and her court in Latin, praising and exhorting a number of prominent individuals, including de Vere. Harvey windily lauded de Vere's literary reputation and accomplishments while associating him with the Roman spear-shaker goddess Minerva.[40] Shortly after this, however, Harvey became entwined with the Dudley-Sidney faction at court and his relationship with de Vere went downhill from there.

In 1580, Harvey's Latin *Speculum Tuscanismi* was published (without his knowledge) in which he satirized an unnamed Italianate Englishman, universally acknowledged as de Vere. Harvey's "Mirror of Tuscanism" is described in vivid detail as an eccentric and exhibitionist clotheshorse:

> Largebelied Kodspeasd Dublet, unkodpeased halfe hose,
> Straite to the dock like a shirte, and close to the britch, like a diveling.
> A little Apish Hatte, cowched fast to the pate, like an Oyster,
> French Camarick Ruffes, deepe with a witnesse, starched to the purpose.[41]

Harvey lambasts his subject as "a passing singular odd man," but hints de Vere also had a flair for espionage and was no novice when it came to putting on appearances. More specifically, Harvey refers to de Vere's "valorous" words and "womanish" works; yet seems to compliment him (perhaps ironically) as an "English Poet" who is "Delicate of speech" and "Not the like for discourser of Tongue."[42] Thus even de Vere's enemies, when attacking him, inadvertently drew attention to his eloquence and verbal abilities. In essence, Harvey portrayed de Vere as a man great in word only, not to mention outlandish dress.

Harvey's Italianate Englishman appears closely related to Shakespeare's "fantastical Spaniard" Don Armado. Holofernes gives us the rundown:

> His [Don Armado's] humor is lofty, his discourse peremptory, his tongue filed, his eye ambitious, his gait majestical, and his general behavior vain, ridiculous, and thrasonical. He is too picked, too spruce, too affected, too odd as it were, too peregrinate, as I may call it.... He draweth out the thread of his verbosity finer than the staple of his argument [V.i.9–17].

This also sounds a bit like Berowne. Like Berowne, Armado writes sonnets (I.ii.183), has the respect of the king (I.i.191), and is given surprisingly sympathetic treatment by Shakespeare, especially given that England fought for its very survival against the Spanish "Armada" in 1588.[43] Armado is both ridiculous and likable,[44] and it is he who has the last word in the play, preceded by his "Cuckoo" song (V.ii.900). Concerns over cuckoldry were on de Vere's mind in the late 1570s, being estranged from his wife Anne Cecil and questioning (rightly or wrongly) the paternity of his daughter. In Don Armado we may well be seeing the Bard's first tentative attempt at self-parody.

❧ 8 ❧

A Midsummer
Night's Dream

*My first taste for books arose from enjoying Ovid's Metamorphoses, when I was about
seven or eight I used to sneak away from all other joys to read it, especially since Latin
was my mother-tongue and the Metamorphoses was the easiest book I knew and the one
most suitable by its subject to my tender age.*
      —Montaigne, *On Educating Children* [1580][1]

Like *The Tempest*, *Love's Labor's Lost*, and *Titus Andronicus*, *A Midsummer Night's Dream*
seems to come directly from Shakespeare's imagination, with innumerable sources that
are still in the process of being identified some 400 years later. This "extraordinary synthesis of material" (Anne Barton)[2] ties together a story involving three distinct groups of
characters (four if one separates Theseus and Hippolyta from the other Athenians), transports the audience from an urban environment to the green world and back again, resolves
all conflicts in an unlikely fashion, and encores with a triple wedding and play-within-a
play. The dramatist had by this time become a complete virtuoso in stagecraft as well as
a walking encyclopedia of classical literary references. In 1595 (the usually favored date of
composition), Will Shakspere was 31 years old and had yet to receive any notice as a dramatist.[3] Edward de Vere was 45 and by 1589 had been acknowledged as best for "Comedy
and Enterlude" in *The Arte of English Poesie*.[4]

The first quarto of Shakespeare's most popular comedy was published in 1600. The
first definite reference to *Midsummer Night's Dream* was made in 1598 by Francis Meres; however, orthodox scholars are remarkably unanimous in their opinion that the play was written during the early to mid–1590s, based mainly on stylistic evidence. There is also
widespread belief, for sensible reasons, that *Midsummer Night's Dream* was written and premiered for the wedding of an Elizabethan nobleman.[5] Geoffrey Bullough's opinion was
typical: "The emphasis on weddings suggests that it was originally written for the marriage
of some noble."[6] One of the leading candidates for this occasion was the marriage on January 26, 1595, of William Stanley, Earl of Derby, to Elizabeth Vere, eldest daughter of
Edward de Vere. This gala event at Greenwich Palace was attended by the queen and an
unnamed play was performed afterward.[7] To this subject we shall return in a moment.

In writing of the sources, Edmund Chambers began with the qualification that "There
is no comprehensive source."[8] Bullough identified five major elements—all of which involve

multiple strands and debatable alternatives—and then did his formidable best to trace where each of these came from.[9] The action begins with the uneasy prenuptials between Theseus, the first legendary ruler of Athens, and his bride by-right-of-conquest, the Amazon queen Hippolyta. Most everyone agrees this was taken straight out of Chaucer's *The Knight's Tale*, based in turn on a suggestion from Plutarch's life of Theseus.[10] It is noteworthy that the young Edward de Vere was known to have personally owned copies of both Plutarch and Chaucer, which he purchased in 1569.[11] Furthermore, both Plutarch and Chaucer belonged to the library of his childhood tutor, Thomas Smith.[12] Thus de Vere had repeated exposure to these two authors his entire life. Aside from the considerable influence that Plutarch and Chaucer exerted on Shakespeare the writer, *The Knight's Tale* in particular seems to have been of interest to the Bard, since he used it as an imaginative springboard for both *Midsummer Night's Dream* and what is often viewed as his last direct involvement in a play, a back-seat collaboration with John Fletcher titled *The Two Noble Kinsmen*, usually dated around 1613. This topic calls for a brief digression.

The Two Noble Kinsmen was first published in a 1634 quarto as written by "John Fletcher and William Shakespeare" (note the billing order). Fletcher is also believed to have earlier collaborated with Shakespeare for *Henry VIII* and the now-lost play *Cardenio*.[13] *Two Noble Kinsmen* was not included in the First Folio of Shakespeare but did appear among Fletcher's complete works in 1679.[14] Regarding the orthodox Shakespeare's alleged retirement from the theater world at this point in time, Harold Bloom noted with honest candor that "Shakespeare's abandonment of his art is virtually unique in the annals of Western literature, nor can I think of a major composer or painter who made a similar retreat."[15] Professor Bloom then attempted, without much success, to explain why this happened. Oxfordians have their own explanation.

Although overlapping *Midsummer Night's Dream* with its interest in Theseus of Athens, *Two Noble Kinsmen* updated and highlighted another aspect of Chaucer's tale. This had been dramatized as early as 1566 in a lost play by Richard Edwards titled *Palamon and Arcite*, performed before Queen Elizabeth for graduation ceremonies at Oxford University.[16] The 16-year-old Edward de Vere participated in these same ceremonies, receiving his degree shortly afterward. Oxfordian researcher Katherine Chiljan made a plausible case that de Vere himself may have been involved in the production of *Palamon and Arcite*.[17] The close proximity of de Vere to this acknowledged precursor for *Two Noble Kinsmen* suggests that John Fletcher may have revised and updated an old piece of Shakespearean juvenilia, or perhaps a surviving torso of an update that de Vere attempted late in life. This scenario seems more intuitive than the Bard mysteriously retiring from his art years before his death.

Back to *Midsummer Night's Dream*. After establishing an Athenian backdrop for his play, Shakespeare transports the audience to the green fantasy world of Oberon, Titania, and Puck. As in other works in the canon, it is Shakespeare's green world where all conflicts must be resolved, in this case between the fugitive lovers and their persecutors. Bardolators are routinely lectured on how the Bard's love of nature was a reflection of his personal experience in the woods near Stratford-upon-Avon. However, there is not a shred of evidence that Will Shakspere lived or worked outside of an urban environment during his entire life. De Vere, on the other hand, was born in Castle Hedingham apart from the village itself, and showed a consistent pattern of escaping from the city whenever he

could, especially later in life. In 1573 (at age 23) we find him signing off from his "countrye Muses" in Wivenhoe, Essex.[18] By 1592, de Vere and his second wife had removed to
the London suburb of Stoke Newington, and then in 1596, even farther out to King's
Place in Hackney. Going to the limit, recent research by Oxfordian Christopher Paul
strongly suggests that de Vere did not die in 1604 as previously thought, but rather staged
his own death so as to escape from creditors and retire in peace and seclusion to the Forest of Essex.[19] Whether de Vere in fact died in 1604 or a few years later, there can be little doubt that he was a man who loved his rural escapes.

    Although Shakespeare's storyline was original, Ovid seems to have been presiding
over the creative process. This applies not only to the play-within-a-play, but to the inter-
nal (as well as external, in the case of Bottom) transformation of all mortal characters,
which in turn is facilitated by Oberon, Puck, and other members of the fairy kingdom.
Shakespeare, like many of his late Renaissance contemporaries, was clearly enthralled by
Ovid's fantastical tales of eroticism and trasfiguration. Ovid's *Metamorphoses* entered the
English language in 1565–1567 via Arthur Golding, the maternal uncle of Edward de
Vere.[20] At the time, de Vere was a teenage university student. Oxfordians are fond of spec-
ulating that his Puritan uncle may have allowed him a hand in the translation, but there
is absolutely no proof for this.

    There is proof, however, that John Lyly, the early Elizabethan dramatist and pre-
sumed author of the play titled *Endimion*, was a servant and secretary to de Vere, dedicating several works to the 17th Earl. Furthermore, *Endimion* is recognized as a likely source
for this aspect of *Midsummer Night's Dream*,[21] as well as for the staged, mock-fairy world of
The Merry Wives of Windsor. Particularly of note is Lyly's authorship of the work (not stated
on the anonymous 1591 quarto), but inferred from his involvement with the Children of
Paul's, who acted the play. The possibility that de Vere may have, if nothing else, heavily
influenced Lyly's writing (the two were closely associated during the 1580s) appears to be
another one of the great unmentionables for orthodox scholarship. This is despite de Vere
being repeatedly praised as a playwright by his contemporaries but leaving behind no
examples of his work.

    The fairy king Oberon, taken by Shakespeare from French literature,[22] tells Puck that
he once heard the song of "a mermaid on a dolphin's back" (II.i.150), and many orthodox scholars, even sensible ones such as Samuel Schoenbaum, have used this isolated line
in a frantic attempt to draw parallels with the life of Will Shakspere.[23] In 1575, when de
Vere was in Italy and the 11-year-old Will Shakspere was who knows where, Queen Elizabeth was entertained by Robert Dudley at Kenilworth in Warwickshire. One portion of
the entertainment, according to eyewitnesses, featured "Arion" singing on the back of a
mechanical dolphin. The remote similarity between this description and a single line in
Midsummer Night's Dream has produced reams of critical commentary, euphoric at the
opportunity to make a single connection between the canon and a mythologized, traditional biography. Laying aside all this excitement for a moment, reflection leads to doubt.
Spoilsport Edmund Chambers, for one, noted that "there is a generic quality about such
pageants, and the special feature of 'a mermaid on a dolphin's back' does not belong to
[this] occasion."[24] Indeed, Arion is not a mermaid, although in charity we could say that
Shakespeare merely improved upon a boyhood memory, assuming he traveled to Kenilworth. More importantly, the image of Arion singing on a dolphin's back was far from

being the exclusive property of those who attended the Kenilworth festivities. One could describe it as public domain, and the classically trained de Vere would have been familiar with the legend, along with most audiences; otherwise, why invoke it?

Not to belabor oft-made comparisons between the fairy queen Titania and Queen Elizabeth, almost unavoidable is the speculative relationship between Glorianna, Shakespeare's play, and Edmund Spenser's influential poem *The Faerie Queene*. In the final act of *Midsummer Night's Dream*, Theseus rejects a proposed nuptial entertainment touching upon "'The thrice three Muses mourning for the death / Of learning, late deceas'd in beggary'" (V.i.52–53). Chambers thought this may have referred to the 1595 death of the poet Torquato Tasso, who was active in Italy during de Vere's stay there.[25] A more likely candidate, however (since the line is vague on exactly who or what has died), would be Spenser's 1591 poem titled *The Tears of the Muses on the Neglect and Contempt of Learning*.[26] This same poem contains a lament by Spenser that "Our pleasant Willy, ah! Is dead of late...."[27] Will Shakspere at that time was 27 years old and not yet on anyone's radar as an artist, but Oxfordians believe Spenser may have been referring to a lull in de Vere's poetic and dramatic activities. The previous year (in 1590), Spenser had included a dedication sonnet to de Vere in *The Faerie Queene*, describing him as "most dear" to the Muses.[28] Eleven years earlier (in 1579, when Will Shakspere was 15), Spenser's *The Shepeardes Calender* included a rhyming match between "Willie" and "Perigot," probably references to de Vere and Philip Sidney, respectively, as court poetic rivals and the latter of whom was the dedicatee of Spenser's work.[29] While the identification of Spenser's "Willie" with de Vere is far from conclusive, it appears to be as plausible as any, given the surrounding circumstances. In any event, a degree of commonality between tributes by Shakespeare and Spenser to the queen are recognized by critics of all authorship persuasions.

And then there is Puck. Although "Robin Goodfellow" belonged to well-established English lore, Shakespeare's emphasis of this particular character name in lieu of the queen's earlier dalliance with Robert Dudley and later dotage on his stepson Robert Devereux (two Robin "Badfellows"?) comes across as somewhat bold. One would think only a peer of long acquaintance would have attempted it,[30] as opposed to an upstart, commoner dramatist on the make. Rather than dwell too long on this issue, suffice it to say that many scholars (such as Bullough) have believed that the Bard's immediate source for Puck may have been Reginald Scot's *Discovery of Witchcraft*, published in 1584.[31] Scot had attended Oxford University prior to de Vere,[32] and a few years later the young Earl would see military service in Scot's homeland. Moreover, de Vere was a man of his times with a noted fascination with the supernatural, and any book that offended King James (as Scot's was known to have done) would likely have caught the attention of the 17th Earl. For Will Shakspere, all of this must once again be assumed as there is no evidence, even of the anecdotal sort.

The metamorphosis of a man into an ass leads into the topic of Bottom and the "rude mechanicals," as characterized by Puck (III.ii.9). The 1566 William Adlington translation of *The Golden Ass* by Apuleius is often viewed as a leading candidate for Shakespeare's source.[33] Remarkably, this work was dedicated to Thomas Radcliffe, Earl of Sussex, who was de Vere's mentor at this time. If this were not enough, the dedication is dated September 1566, almost concurrent with de Vere's graduation from Oxford, Adlington's own university affiliation.[34] Thus we once again return to the Oxford graduation ceremonies of 1566.

Shakespeare, it should be remembered, takes Bottom to levels of prominence and poignancy that no author had previously suggested. This was clearly a character that fired his imagination, as well as a distant cousin of Dogberry from *Much Ado About Nothing*. Both, for example, while in the process of mangling the English language, confuse the words "odious" and "odorous," as Bottom (to the chagrin of Quince) botches his line by reciting "the flowers of odious savors sweet" (III.i.82).[35] Quince has a similar problem, though, and cannot annunciate the word "transformed" after Bottom emerges with a new look: "Bless thee, Bottom! Bless thee! Thou are *translated*" (III.i.117; emphasis added). After returning to "normal," Bottom then takes the cake with his soliloquy on "The eye of man hath not heard, the ear of man hath not seen, man's hand is not able to taste, his tongue to conceive, nor his heart report..." (IV.i.211–214), a neat misquotation of St. Paul (I Corinthians 2:9–10).[36] In the case of de Vere, we are fortunate enough to have his own personal copy of the Geneva Bible at the Folger Library, the version that orthodoxy tends to agree was Shakespeare's source.

On a more serious level, Bottom can generally be viewed by an audience in one of two ways. One is to interpret him as Will Shakspere's affectionate look back at his own tradesman roots. Another is to see him as Shakspere himself, through the eyes of de Vere. This latter (and obviously more controversial) interpretation, unfortunately for orthodoxy, tends to make more sense the harder we look at it. The Pyramus and Thisbe play-within-a-play (also taken from Ovid),[37] aside from being a parody of *Romeo and Juliet*,[38] also represents Bottom's figurative 15 minutes of fame before his noble overlords. Although Theseus condescendingly remarks that "For never any thing can be amiss, / When simpleness and duty tender it" (V.i.83–84), the labeling of the rude mechanicals by Philostrate is more indicative: "Hard-handed men that work in Athens here, / Which never labor'd in their minds till now" (V.i.72–73). The cold use of the word "which" (instead of "who") tells us all we need to know about the aristocratic attitude toward Bottom and his associates. Although the ineptitude of their performance is truly funny, the fact remains that the court of Theseus is deriving amusement and entertainment from this unintentional comedy. On the other hand, if Will Shakspere is represented by Bottom, then Shakspere certainly enjoyed more than 15 minutes of fame in the long run.

The last major plot element of *Midsummer Night's Dream* involves the fugitive lovers, Lysander and Hermia, along with their two pursuers, Demetrius and Helena. The normally intrepid Bullough had almost nothing to say on this topic, but then again, neither does anyone else. The comedies of John Lyly (under the influence of his patron de Vere?) have been suggested in a vague sort of manner, but with little to offer in the way of specifics.[39] This is surprising because the subplot of the four lovers inspired some of the Bard's most memorable quotes, such as Puck exclaiming, "Lord, what fools these mortals be!" (III.ii.115). Given this relative silence, we are bold enough to offer some conjectures, since orthodox scholarship does this on a routine basis, and in the sincere hope that further research may be encouraged, if nothing else to prove us wrong.

As stated previously, William Stanley married Elizabeth Vere in January 1595, and this wedding has been a leading contender for the event at which the play premiered. Stanley himself has been proposed as the true Shakespeare, and among the alternative candidates, his credentials are admittedly second only to his father-in-law's. In the play, Lysander notes that "The course of true love never did run smooth" (I.i.134), and this was apparently the case with William Stanley and Elizabeth Vere. Not long before the Stanley-Vere engagement, Elizabeth's guardian and grandfather, Lord Burghley, had negotiated her hand to Henry Percy, Earl of Northumberland, but she reportedly could not take a fancy to him.[40] Dare we compare Burghley with Shakespeare's Egeus, who attempts to marry off his daughter Hermia to Demetrius against her will? After overcoming various obstacles, not the least of which was Stanley receiving his inheritance, the wedding took place; later that same year (1595), the jilted Percy married Dorothy Devereux, the widowed sister of Essex. Neither marriage was noted for bliss, but the Percy-Devereux union was of note because although the couple lived apart (due to a lack of congeniality), Dorothy stood by Percy even after he had been falsely accused of treason and endured a lengthy imprisonment in the Tower of London.[41] A marriage of convenience perhaps; then again, maybe Dorothy tenaciously chased Percy in a manner similar to Helena's pursuit of Demetrius. Could the two weddings of 1595 be somewhat reflected by the adventures of the four lovers in the play? As Theseus oberves: "The lunatic, the lover, and the poet, / Are of imagination all compact" (V.i.7–8); in other words, reason and logic have little to do with matters of the heart.

ᔆ 9 ᙅ

The Merchant of Venice

The first quarto publication of *The Merchant of Venice* appeared in 1600; however, most orthodox critics agree the work dates from 1596 at the latest, with earlier versions perhaps going back even further.[1] In 1579 (this was three years after de Vere had returned from Italy and was beginning to get into serious financial straits), a lost anonymous play titled *The Jew* was performed at the English court. One witness (Stephen Gosson) wrote that the drama demonstrated "the greediness of worldly chusers, and bloody minds of usurers."[2] The following year (in 1580), another lost anonymous play titled *The History of Portio and Demorantes* (Portia and the Merchant?) was performed at Whitehall Palace by the Lord Chamberlain's Men, sponsored by de Vere's mentor Thomas Radcliffe.[3] In fact, during this same period there are numerous such works with designations sounding suspiciously like alternative titles for Shakespeare's plays. Whenever orthodox scholars condescend to notice this, it is usually remarked that Shakespeare may have been familiar with these.[4] De Vere, who was acknowledged by several contemporaries[5] as "best for comedy" (yet leaving no surviving examples of his work), seems as likely an author as any for these obscure early plays, although orthodoxy seems unwilling to contemplate this possibility.

Act IV, scene i, of *The Merchant of Venice* contains perhaps the most famous trial scene in all of drama. The merchant Antonio is brought before the Venetian high court by the Jewish moneylender Shylock for non-payment of debt. Shylock loaned 3,000 ducats for which Antonio gave surety with a written bond, that in the event of default, Shylock would be entitled (literally) to one pound of Antonio's flesh. Antonio does this for the sake of his young, gold-digging friend Bassanio,[6] who uses the money to successfully court Shakespeare's heroine, the rich heiress Portia. Antonio, however, loses all his assets when his trading galleys are lost at sea. Unable to repay, Antonio finds himself standing in judgment with an audience, both onstage and off, outraged at the thought of a Christian having to pay with his life for breach of contract with a Jew.

Orthodox scholars have been caught up in a desperate attempt to link events in the play to the 1594 trial and public execution of Roderigo Lopez, personal physician to Queen Elizabeth. Lopez, who was of Jewish ancestry, was convicted of attempting to poison the queen in return for bribe money from Spanish Catholics. This is called making a mountain out of a molehill. Far more impressive is the fact that Shakespeare drew upon details from a popular Italian book titled *Il Percorone* by Giovanni Fiorentino.[7] Remarkably, this story had not yet been fully translated into English. Not only does Shakespeare use all of the untranslated details, he adds a few of his own.[8]

As Antonio stands before the acting judge (the Duke of Venice), Shylock effectively argues his case by pointing out that Venetian law allows for human slavery (IV.i.90), which is comparable to owning a pound of flesh. No one disputes the facts and there is no cross-examination, no Perry Mason stuff—which is surprising for a courtroom drama. The issue is strictly whether the letter of the law should be observed, or if fairness needs to be achieved through some other equitable remedy. Antonio's now wealthy friend Bassanio offers Shylock 6,000 ducats (IV.i.84), twice the original loan amount. Shylock refuses and here shows his true colors. He's not interested in money; he's interested in killing Antonio. Shylock's entire suit is really about the pursuit of revenge by someone who has been an outsider in society his entire life, someone who in the past has literally been spat upon by Antonio and his cronies. In fact, everyone in the courtroom is revealed by Shakespeare to be bigoted to some degree. Shylock is seething with resentment and looking for the big payback. On top of this, his ungrateful daughter Jessica has just eloped with a Christian playboy, Lorenzo, one of Bassanio's friends.

At this point in the trial, the court brings in an *amicus curiae* played by Portia in disguise. First she delivers the greatest poetic speech in the English language on the virtue of mercy (IV.i.184–205), but that does not soften Shylock, who replies, "I crave the law" (IV.i.206). Portia then reminds everyone that Venetian commercial law is sacrosanct, since making exceptions would undermine foreign confidence in Venetian markets (IV.i.218–222). Shylock rejoices and gets his knife ready; but then Portia says that since the letter of the law must be observed, it must be observed absolutely. This means Shylock can draw no blood from his victim, since blood is not part of the contract (IV.i.306), and the portion of flesh must exactly equal one pound, no more and no less (IV.i.325). In the words of Supreme Court Justice John Paul Stevens, Portia "served justice by using one literal reading of the bond to trump another...."[9]

Shylock is unable to comply with this strict interpretation and backs off, saying he will now accept Bassanio's offer of 6,000 ducats (IV.i.317). Portia, however, says no, the terms of the contract must be honored to the letter (IV.i.322). Shylock offers to settle for the principal amount of 3,000 ducats, but Portia still insists on the letter of the law (IV.i.336–339). Defeated, Shylock is ordered by the court to give half his estate to Antonio, and the other half is forfeited to the Republic. The Duke announces that he will spare Shylock's life, and if he is contrite, may reduce half the forfeiture to a fine (IV.i.372). Thus Shakespeare shows a startling familiarity with the notorious Alien Statute of Venice, which provided the exact same penalty: forfeiture of half an estate to the Republic and half to the wronged party, plus a discretionary death sentence, to any foreigner (including Jews) who attempted to take the life of a Venetian citizen. Where would Will Shakspere have picked this up? Hanging out at the Mermaid Tavern, perhaps? That is one idea of the miracle of genius: Shakespeare as the greatest human sponge for knowledge that ever lived, reducing the Bard to some kind of idiot savant.

Concluding the trial, Antonio makes his own proposal, which is accepted by the court. Antonio gets half of Shylock's estate, but to be held in trust for Shylock's daughter; the other half Shylock gets to keep with the stipulation it goes to his new Christian son-in-law upon Shylock's death. Finally, Shylock is ordered to immediately convert to Christianity (IV.i.387–391). This last item is not in Shakespeare's source material. Shylock's next-to-last words are "I am content" (IV.i.393), surely the most ironic line in the history of drama.

In the incisive words of Harold Bloom, "One would have to be blind, deaf, and dumb not to recognize that Shakespeare's grand, equivocal comedy *The Merchant of Venice* is nevertheless a profoundly anti–Semitic work." Thus Bloom made it clear where he stands on the old (and very real) issue of anti–Semitism in the play.[10]

In spite of all this, Shakespeare was very daring for his time, taking a stock villain ("The Jew") and giving him a human, even sympathetic dimension—"Hath not a Jew eyes?" (III.i.59), etc. In the final analysis, however, Shylock is still a "Jew" and a villain. The trial scene and the entire play are loaded with innuendo, reinforced by repeated biblical quotations. Shylock's preference for the letter of the law seems a throwback to the Jewish Old Testament, while Portia's emphasis on mercy and search for equitable settlement reflect the superior moral values of the Christian New Testament. As Antonio says in the play, "The Devil can cite scripture for his purpose" (I.iii.99), and Shakespeare was apparently not above doing this himself.

As for the infamous "pound of flesh" penalty clause, some have remarked that the contract was illegal to begin with and that was the argument Portia should have used during the trial. Yes, today a contractual penalty clause authorizing death or disfigurement would be illegal; during Shakespeare's time, however, not necessarily. Such provisions were expressly allowed by Roman law, and these were in turn transmitted by the Code of Justinian to the city-states of northern Italy.[11] It was only thanks to the development of modern English civil law that such harshness was eventually mitigated. In fact, Shakespeare alludes to this penalty in another play, *Timon of Athens* (see Chapter 31).

Writing in England much later during the Enlightenment, Edward Gibbon looked back and observed that the "pound of flesh" penalty clause fell out favor because, as people became more civilized, they stopped enforcing it:

> The advocates for this savage law have insisted that it must strongly operate in deterring idleness and fraud from contracting debts which they were unable to discharge; but experience would dissipate this salutary terror, by proving that no creditor could be found to exact this unprofitable penalty of life or limb.[12]

On the other hand, just because enforcement stopped did not mean these laws were not on the books. If anyone in Shakespeare's play is on shaky legal ground, it is Portia. When she argues Shylock must take exactly one pound of flesh, this is contrary to Roman law, which expressly said one pound, *more or less*. In other words, the law allowed the creditor to kill or disfigure with impunity.[13] Perhaps Portia's eloquence is a forerunner to changes in civil law that would eventually renounce the validity of such harsh penalties.

Aside from showing a prodigious and astonishing knowledge of Venetian society, Shakespeare takes us right into the heartland of legal philosophy with *The Merchant of Venice*. The Bard consistently throws around legal terms in a casual and offhand manner, frequently converting this terminology into poetic expression. Not only does he know what these terms mean, but he does not have to think about it too hard, either. Legal terminology appears to have been second nature for him. As for the traditional author, we know that Will Shakspere was a litigious guy. He was involved in a number of lawsuits, like his father before him. On the other hand, litigiousness does not always equate into legal expertise.

Beginning in the late 18th century with Edmund Malone, volumes have been written on whether Shakespeare knew the law,[14] and Oxfordian scholar Mark Alexander has provided us with a thorough overview for the history of this debate. Throughout much of the 19th century, before the authorship question became a hot button issue, it was generally agreed that the Bard knew his law quite well, and later advocates such as the eminent English barrister George Greenwood come across in their writings as lucid, well-informed, and highly persuasive. As the authorship debate heated up, however, opposing points of view appeared. These maintained that Shakespeare's legal knowledge was faulty and/or that this knowledge could have easily been obtained by any intelligent person. The advocates for this more recent point of view always and without exception have been defenders of the traditional attribution of Shakespeare's authorship.

For example, the oft-cited Clarkson and Warren report of 1942 concludes that Shakespeare's legal knowledge was nothing special in comparison to his playwriting contemporaries. Anyone who reads this report with a grain of impartiality, however, will be surprised at the shallow statistical analysis upon which sweeping conclusions are made. Statistically, other playwrights are shown to have used similar numbers of legal references as Shakespeare, at least with respect to property law. Upon investigation, however, we learn that those other playwrights were members of the Inns of Court, or like John Fletcher, always collaborated with members of the Inns of Court. These are the playwrights who, like Shakespeare, used a lot of legal terms. This is the study that is routinely held up to show that Shakespeare's legal knowledge was not unusual. Compare Shakespeare, however, with playwrights who were not legally trained, such as Ben Jonson, and he completely stands apart.[15]

To reiterate, the point is not that Shakespeare frequently used legal terms (which he did), nor that he used them accurately (which he did), but rather that Shakespeare could consistently transform this legal terminology into dramatic poetry, far more so than his contemporaries. If that were not enough, Shakespeare takes the conflict between law and equity and makes it the centerpiece of a play. Then for good measure he throws in the Venetian Alien Statute. Not bad for a glovemaker's son from Warwickshire.

Most of these points were eloquently made long ago by Mark Twain, a.k.a. Samuel Clemens, in his classic essay *Is Shakespeare Dead?* Some have responded to Twain by pointing to Twain's own work *Pudd'nhead Wilson*, which accurately employs legal terminology despite Twain's lack of legal training.[16] Twain, by his own admission, had brought in outside professional help to make sure he got it right. Why could Shakespeare not have done the same? One response is that *Pudd'nhead Wilson* is a single book in a vast body of Twain's work, whereas legal expertise permeates the entire Shakespearean canon. That's why we notice it. If Shakespeare did not have vast legal knowledge, then he would have needed a full-time collaborator who did—like John Fletcher's acknowledged co-authors, who were lawyers. Even John Fletcher, however, could not infuse his works with poetic legalese, nor did Fletcher delve into the legal philosophy that became the centerpiece for *Merchant of Venice*. Not only was Shakespeare thoroughly engrained with legal knowledge, he used it in a way no other playwright has before or since. Another example often used as a non-lawyer writer who wrote convincingly about the law is Charles Dickens. Dickens' biography, however, reveals that, as a young man, he had worked in a solicitor's office.[17] Other old clichés are frequently rolled out as well. Shakespeare could have picked up his legal knowledge reading books or hanging out in the law courts just for fun (these are the same speculations that Twain satirized so mercilessly). Traditionalists insist that any uneducated genius would have a tremendous capacity for absorbing and retaining legalese (i.e., the human sponge theory). Most absurd of all, we occasionally hear that Shakespeare's legal knowledge was nothing special because that era was a litigious age in which law was a national preoccupation and legal allusions would have dominated the vernacular speech of the period. In other words, all Elizabethans had well developed legal minds! More than one person has found this line of reasoning not very persuasive.

More persuasive is that Edward de Vere studied law at Gray's Inn[18] and was involved in legal scrapes his entire life, typically brought on by his own impetuosity, profligacy, or both. By the late 1570s, de Vere was rapidly plunging toward insolvency, accelerated by a bad investment of £3,000 (as opposed to Shylock's 3,000 ducats). This investment had been used to back Martin Frobisher's exploration and unsuccessful search for a Northwest Passage. De Vere's money had been raised in the form of a bond raised by financier Michael Lok (sometimes spelled "Lock"), who may or may not have been a Christianized Anglo Jew. Add to this the prefix "Shy" (one meaning of which is "disreputable"), and it would be an understatement to say that the (otherwise mysterious) origin of Shylock's name is strongly suggested.[19]

Especially interesting was de Vere's litigation with his creditors, which often wound up in the English Courts of Chancery, or courts of equity, as opposed to the common law courts.[20] De Vere, like Antonio, could find no comfort in the letter of the law, so he turned to the spirit of the law for protection and/or redress. If that did not work, he sought favor from the queen herself, who provided it on more than one occasion.[21] De Vere was usually able to dodge the strict letter of the law, either simply because he was an Earl, or perhaps because he was contributing something else of value that has remained hidden from posterity. As we have seen, *The Merchant of Venice* is the quintessential poetic and theatrical argument in favor of the legal equity concept. In fact, it is the only one that we are aware of. Other playwrights used the word "equity," but how many used it as the crux of a play? In law school, students are taught, when engaged in a tough fight, to look beyond the letter of the law toward policy and intent, in order to make effective arguments. That is one of the few things in legal training that has not changed much since Shakespeare's time.

De Vere's biographical parallels with the storyline of *Merchant of Venice* are extensive,[22] but a few highlights are worth repeating. For starters, de Vere spent about a year in Italy when he was a young man, made Venice his base of operations, and would have had firsthand experience with the topographical settings and social trappings that the play so accurately presents. Like Shakespeare the writer, de Vere would have likely been familiar with the Rialto market (I.ii.19), as opposed to the Rialto bridge; he would have seen the Gobbo di Rialto statue situated within that market (in the play, Launcelot Gobbo is the Clown); and he would have used the *traghetto* ferry boats mentioned in the play (III.iv.53) that connect the city with the mainland.

Shakespeare knew about the great country estates approximately 20 miles west of Venice—a distance Portia specifies (II.iv.84)—and located along the Brenta Canal, such as Palladio's spectacular Villa Foscari. Dr. Noemi Magri of Mantua has made a very convincing case that the Villa Foscari was probably the Bard's inspiration for Portia's home, in the play called "Belmont."[23] At Belmont, Lorenzo's famous speech to Jessica, beginning "How sweet the moonlight sleeps upon this bank!" (IV.ii.54–65), is widely considered the greatest poetic description of an Italian moonlit evening in any language, supposedly written by someone who was never there.[24] Though not specific to Venice, Lorenzo's ecstatic praise of music (V.i.70–88) is often cited as the supreme example of its genre. While nothing is known of Will Shakspere's interest in music, de Vere, in spite of all his personal faults, was an acknowledged connoisseur. Foremost among all these details is the Venetian Ghetto itself, which is striking because in England there was no such thing. Un-Christianized Jews were outlaws. In Venice, de Vere, like Shylock, would have been legally classified as a foreigner and therefore subject to the Draconian provisions of the Venetian Alien Statute— legislation not found in England.

So who are the good guys and bad guys in *The Merchant of Venice?* Obviously, Shylock is a villain; but then again, not so obviously. He is human, at times even sympathetic, while his protagonists—Antonio, Portia, and the rest of Venetian society—can come across as dissolute, faithless, flippant, shallow, wasteful, rapacious—primarily concerned with gratifying their own appetites. The moral is perhaps best summed up by Portia, who remarks, "He that is well paid is well satisfied" (IV.i.415), a double entendre if there ever was one. Shakespeare has given us a dark comedy in which good and bad are not black and white, but rather various shades of grey, just like the real world. It is a lesson that both lawyers and laymen would do well to always remember.

❧ 10 ❧

As You Like It

As You Like It, along with *Twelfth Night*, represents the pinnacle of Shakespeare's comedic achievement. The play was recorded in 1600 with the Stationers' Register, presumably to preempt any contemplated piracy,[1] but was not published until the First Folio of 1623. Chambers and Bullough believed that it was written right before the turn of the 16th century, since the work was not mentioned by Francis Meres in 1598 and included a direct quote from Marlowe's poem *Hero and Leander*, also published in 1598.[2] On the other hand, since we have no idea exactly what text was registered in 1600, the First Folio may include revisions made after the original registration.

According to local legend, *As You Like It* was written at Billesley Manor, ancestral estate of the Trussell family and located approximately five miles west of Stratford-upon-Avon.[3] The tradition is of interest because it is possible (or at least not yet disproved) that Will Shakspere and Edward de Vere both had grandmothers named Trussell from this part of England. In the case of Shakspere, the maiden name of his maternal grandmother (Mary Arden's mother) is not known for certain, but some researchers (such as Charlotte Stopes) believed that she belonged to the local Trussell clan.[4] This possibility is routinely ignored by orthodox biographers, we suspect because they tend to downplay the more well-to-do, aristocratic (and Catholic) profile of Shakspere's Arden family branch. The Bard, as we all must believe, was of good yeoman, Protestant stock, untainted by any hint of snobbery or elitism. Furthermore, the mere thought of him as a poor country cousin to Edward de Vere is too horrible to even contemplate. In any event, Shakspere's physical presence in Warwickshire during this period seems to be confirmed by his purchase of New Place in 1597 and other third-party records from Stratford mentioning his name.[5] As for de Vere, his father's mother was Elizabeth Trussell, whose family hailed from nearby Staffordshire.[6]

According to tradition, the first performance of *As You Like It* was given before King James (by the King's Men) on December 2, 1603, at Wilton House, home of Mary Sidney Herbert, sister of Philip Sidney and mother to the "Incomparable Brethren" to whom Shakespeare's First Folio would be dedicated in 1623.[7] One of these two brothers was Philip Herbert, who the following year would marry the youngest daughter of Edward de Vere. Lore has it that Mary lured the new king to Wilton with the promise that she had "the man Shakespeare" with them.[8] Whether this was a reference to Will Shakspere (a member of the King's Men) or to de Vere, who may have been negotiating the marriage of his daughter, is unclear. Yet another legend holds that the role of old Adam in *As You Like*

It was taken by Shakespeare himself.[9] This is one of only two specific parts that the Bard is reputed to have played on stage (along with the Ghost in *Hamlet*). Again, whether these anecdotes refer to Shakspere or to de Vere (who was known to have acted at court) remains indeterminate.

That Will Shakspere was an actor connected with the London theater world is a reasonable conclusion under any scenario. Aside from numerous personal ties to theatrical entrepreneurs, other references, though often unflattering, appear to clinch his association with the acting profession. These include the infamous 1592 allusion to a "tiger's heart wrapped in a player's hide" from *Greene's Groatsworth of Wit*, as well as the 1602 objection to Shakspere's coat of arms application (on behalf of his father) with the contemptuous notation "Shakespeare ye Player by Garter."[10] His ultimately successful application for a coat of arms, by itself an amazing feat given his humble station in life, was indicative of his rising fortunes. Imposing at first glance is King James' royal warrant of 1603 naming William Shakespeare as a member of the newly christened King's Men acting company.[11] This was presumably a reference to Will Shakspere, although there is no mention of playwriting. The only real question with respect to Shakspere's profession is how he and a man of the theater such as de Vere managed to miss running into each other, which one could easily infer from the omission of this scenario in otherwise fanciful orthodox biographies.

Other actors are associated with the play as well. By 1600, the famous Shakespearean stage comedian Robert Armin had assumed principal duties as comedian for the Lord Chamberlain's Men (later to become the King's Men in 1603). It is thought that the great comedic roles of Feste in *Twelfth Night* and Touchstone in *As You Like It* were created for him.[12] The same year that the latter play was registered (1600), Armin recorded in his *Quips upon Questions* that he served a great lord in Hackney—de Vere being the only person to fit such a description at that time.[13]

One thing that most scholars do agree upon is that Shakespeare's primary source for *As You Like It* was the novel *Rosalynde, or Euphues Golden Legacy*, written by Thomas Lodge and published in 1590. Geoffrey Bullough noted that "His [Shakespeare's] play is more than an adaptation of Lodge's romance, but it must already be obvious that he drew much from it, both in detail and for his general conception."[14] Curiously, in his dedication to Lord Chamberlain Henry Carey (Lord Hunsdon), Lodge describes his patron as "wearing with *Pallas* both the launce and the bay...."[15] In other words, like Pallas Athena, the Greek spear-shaker goddess, Carey excelled both in the arts of warfare ("the launce") and wisdom ("the bay" or laurel wreath). This was considered the highest compliment one could pay to a true Renaissance man.[16] As Lodge's subtitle indicates, *Rosalynde* was written in the Euphuistic style, which had seen its heyday some 10 years before with authors such as John Lyly and Anthony Munday. Both Lyly and Munday had been servants to de Vere and dedicated several Euphuistic works to their employer, himself identified as the ringleader of this fashion at the English court.[17] As for Lodge, there have been no direct connections discovered to date between him and de Vere (other than both being graduates of Oxford); however, Lodge did later dedicate books to de Vere's daughter Elizabeth (*Prosopopœia* in 1596) and his son-in-law William Stanley (*A Fig for Momus* in 1595).[18]

One of the biggest misconceptions surrounding *As You Like It* is that the unequivocal setting is the Forest of Arden near Stratford-upon-Avon. Beyond using the name

"Arden," Shakespeare is non-specific, and a closer look at the Arden forest (as noted by orthodox scholars such as Asimov)[19] reveals a certain ambiguity. Lodge set his original version of the story in the French Forest of Ardenne between Bordeaux and Lyon.[20] Furthermore, Shakespeare retains many of the original French names plus adds new French names of his own. Another possibility is that Shakespeare the writer, like de Vere, was a Francophile of Norman ancestry. In the case of Will Shakspere, nothing is known or suggested in this regard. As previously mentioned, Arden was the maiden name of Will Shakspere's mother. With respect to de Vere—in addition to his other Warwickshire connections—he is believed to have inherited property in the Avon Valley (Bilton Manor in nearby Rugby) from his Trussell ancestors, later selling it off when forced to liquidate his estates.[21]

The creator of *As You Like It* also drew upon a wide a variety of secondary source material. These included Book IV of Edmund Spenser's *The Faerie Queene* (1590),[22] which contained a dedicatory sonnet addressed to de Vere, and the *Apology for Poetry* (1580),[23] written by Philip Sidney, de Vere's great poetic rival. Shakespeare's romantic lead is renamed after the hero of Ludovico Ariosto's *Orlando Furioso* (another tribute to de Vere's Norman ancestry?), translated by John Harrington in 1591; and no work by the Bard would be complete without a nod (by Touchstone) to Ovid (III.iii.8), translated by de Vere's uncle Arthur Golding in 1567. More idiosyncratic is the exotic allusion by Jacques to a "pantaloon" (II.vii.158). This stock character type from Italian *commedia dell' arte* would have been a highly rare spectacle in England during Shakespeare's time, but hard to miss in Italy when de Vere traveled there in 1575–1576. For Will Shakspere, we can only speculate as to how he may have come into contact with this foreign theatrical terminology.

Of the pastoral form itself, orthodox scholar Marjorie Garber of Harvard has written that

> From its earliest appearance pastoral had been used as mode of social critique: under the guise of merely talking about shepherds, poets could write critical and satirical accounts of government, politics, and religion (a priest was a "pastor"; his congregation was a "flock").[24]

Professor Garber quotes Shakespeare's contemporary George Puttenham, the presumed author of *The Arte of English Poesie* (1589), to this effect.[25] It should be noted as well that Puttenham, in the very same book, praises Edward de Vere as among England's best poets and playwrights, adding that social stigma of the times had prevented him from taking credit as such. De Vere himself seems to have enjoyed living away from the city, as evidenced by his spending the last years of his life in Stoke Newington and Hackney. As early as 1573, however, de Vere had indicated in his dedicatory letter for Thomas Bedingfield's translation of *Cardanus Comforte* that it had been written "From my newe countrye Muses at Wiuenghole," a reference to his rural estate at Wivenhoe in Essex.[26]

A rare example of Shakespeare quoting a contemporary writer occurs when Phebe the shepherdess, smitten with Rosalind in disguise as Ganymede, repeats the line from Christopher Marlowe's *Hero and Leander*: "Who ever lov'd that lov'd not at first sight?" (III.v.82). Another allusion to Marlowe seems to occur when Touchstone remarks to Audrey, "When a man's verse cannot be understood, nor a man's good wit seconded with the forward child, it strikes a man more dead than a great reckoning in a little room"

(III.iii.12–15).[27] History records that Marlowe was murdered in 1593 following an argument over a bill in a small tavern room. Partisans who argue that Marlowe was the true Shakespeare claim he was in fact spirited away to France where he continued to write plays. Two of the biggest obstacles to the Marlovian theory are that no definite proof of Marlowe's presence in France has come to light, and his serious writing style, while influential on the Bard, was incompatible with Shakespeare's humorous vein, often found even in the tragedies.[28] Like de Vere, he was a Cambridge graduate, but no definite connections between the two have been identified. Marlowe was certainly the most brilliant (and unstable) of the university wits involved in the great propaganda push of the English stage during the 1580s, and many of these writers (such as Lyly and Munday) did have documented associations with de Vere.

Probably the best-known lines in *As You Like It* (and some of the most famous in the canon) occur in Act II when the melancholic Jacques describes the "seven ages" of man, beginning with "All the world's a stage..." (II.vii.139–166). Wannabe Bardolators often take Jacques' pessimistic speech seriously, yet Jacques himself is an object of derision among the other characters, especially Touchstone, who later does a send-up of the "seven ages" philosophy with his own "seven causes for a quarrel" exposition (V.iv.4–103). Oxfordian researcher Christopher Paul demonstrated that the "seven ages" soliloquy appears to draw upon a number of sources having fairly unique ties to de Vere. These include mosaic artwork in Duomo of Siena (a city visited by de Vere); a 1575 book titled *Golden Epistles* by Geoffrey Fenton and dedicated to Oxford's wife Anne; and another work titled *Axiochus* from 1592, written by one "Edw. Spenser." Oxfordians believe that de Vere himself may have had an extensive hand in this pseudonymous collaboration, including a speech directly attributed to Oxford and given upon his victory at the Whitehall tournament of 1581.[29]

As noted by Bullough and others, *As You Like It* transcends its source material, with Shakespeare inventing numerous characters and situations whose meanings are still debated. The gloomy Jacques and his antithesis, the clown Touchstone, are foremost among these inventions. An astonished Jacques, who attends upon the banished Duke, tells us repeatedly that Touchstone is a former courtier (II.v.36 and V.iv.43) just as de Vere had been. As for Will Shakspere, it gives us pause to think of him daring to turn a courtier into a clown for the amusement of his royal audience. Even more enigmatic is the exchange between Touchstone and the country bumpkin William (one of the few characters named William in the entire canon), in which Touchstone asks him, "Art thou learned?" and William replies, "No, sir" (V.i.38–39). Traditionalists tend to be baffled by this scene while Oxfordians knowingly smile at it, especially when Touchstone sends William packing (V.i.40–59). So much for the Bard's sympathy for the common man. Perhaps Will Shakspere (the true author?) was trying to reassure his aristocratic patrons that Touchstone was not such a fool after all.

Another Shakespeare original, the country vicar Sir Oliver Martext, is brought in to marry everyone, but his role is bigger than necessary and he appears to represent yet another one of the Bard's gratuitous swipes at the Puritans. The name easily suggests an amalgamation of the well-known Puritan preacher Oliver Pigge with the controversial Elizabethan pen name of Martin Marprelate, instigator of a no-holds-barred pamphlet war that raged during the period immediately preceding William Shakespeare's appearance as a published writer.[30] Shakespeare later repeatedly showed his political sympathies in this conflict, Sir Oliver Martext providing only one example.

If Will Shakspere was in reality a front man for royally subsidized noblemen writing politically incorrect drama, then his Stratford background would have been especially useful. Warwickshire ministers were repeatedly noted for their defiance of ecclesiastical authority,[31] and East Warwickshire in particular was a Puritan stronghold, being one location that produced the first pamphlets under the name Martin Marprelate. Job Throckmorton, a leading candidate for Martin himself, hailed from Warwickshire.[32] Robert Dudley, Earl of Leicester, despite his shady reputation, was an early symbolic patron for the Puritans, and had a seat in the town of Warwick, not far from Stratford. It was in Warwick in 1585 that Leicester gave a permanent post and a pension to the influential Presbyterian advocate Thomas Cartwright at a time when he was viewed by the establishment church as a maverick.[33] In fairness, it should be added that Will Shakspere is likely to have been hostile toward the Puritans as well, given his rumored Catholic sympathies and (presumably) estranged wife, Anne Hathaway, herself thought to have come from a Puritan background.

This brings us to a central plank in the political platform of the Puritans: their intractable hatred for the public theaters. Sidney's *Apology* in 1580 was a response to loudly vented and widely circulated Puritan allegations that all poetry and drama are, in effect, lies and illusion encouraging others to engage in similar activities. Touchstone in the play adopts Sidney's Aristotelian defense of the arts when he pronounces that "The truest poetry is the most feigning" (III.iii.19–20).[34] Martext, for his part, defiantly views Touchstone as a "fantastical knave" (III.iii.106). Part of Shakespeare's effectiveness in presenting this conflict is that he used very light strokes rather than hitting us over the head. Everything has an innocent surface combined with a politically charged undertow—that is, if we dare to notice it.

Some audiences for this play have been surprised by the manner in which action suddenly winds down and conflicts are abruptly resolved in the forest, but this is how things generally transpire in Shakespeare's pastoral "green world."[35] Anne Barton, in the *Riverside* introduction, reminded us that "Arden is a place set apart from the ordinary world."[36] Bullough noted that earlier writers (such as de Vere's servant John Lyly) had utilized the "greenwood" device,[37] but it was Shakespeare who, artistically at least, took it to the bank. The forest is where characters must go in order to resolve their differences and heighten their personal awareness, sometimes not before they have gone slightly out of their minds.

Among the new discoveries regarding Edward de Vere in recent years, perhaps the most discombobulating is that de Vere appears not (as previously thought) to have died in the year 1604. Part of the basis for this surmise (once again, made by Christopher Paul) is that no fewer than three letters have surfaced, written after de Vere's supposed death in June 1604 and referring to him in the present tense as if he were still alive. Moreover, these letters were written by people who should have known whether he was in fact alive or dead.[38] Taken at face value, these documents seem to indicate that de Vere lived approximately three years longer than was originally thought, possibly dying sometime in 1607, rather than 1604. One theory put forth is that de Vere, who was hopelessly in debt and hounded by litigation, persuaded King James to grant him custody of the Forest of Essex (the Waltham Forest and Havering Park), where he retired to a hunting lodge in order to escape from creditors and live out the rest of his life in peace. Mr. Paul modestly notes that his research raises more questions than answers.[39] We hope for our part that these questions will be addressed in a serious manner by future scholarship.

In the play, Rosalind sees through Jacques by noting that "I fear you have sold your own lands to see other men's; then to have seen much, and to have nothing, is to have rich eyes and poor hands" (IV.i.22–25). One could not better describe de Vere's personal situation at the turn of the 16th century, although—to repeat—what was written for the Stationers' Register in 1600 and later for the 1623 First Folio is anyone's guess. Whether de Vere vanished into the Forest of Essex to live out his own Jacques-Touchstone fantasy is another unsolved mystery. If true, it would be hard to find a more fitting end for the Bard, metamorphosing like one of Ovid's tragic myths.

Also difficult to resist is the notion that in Shakespeare's two great cross-dressing heroines, Rosalind and Viola (from *Twelfth Night*), we may be catching a glimpse of de Vere's spirited, independent and literate second wife, Elizabeth Trentham (1559?–1612). De Vere had married this rich Staffordshire[40] heiress (and former Maid of Honour)[41] in late 1592 and she promptly provided him with a male heir in early 1593.[42] De Vere's biographer Professor Alan Nelson wrote that in Mistress Trentham, "Oxford had met his match" and described her as his "spokesperson and agent."[43] What little we know about the Countess Elizabeth indicates that she, like Rosalind and Viola in the plays, was an astute and strong-willed individual. Of course, another possibility is that Shakespeare's heroines represent the feminine alter-ego of the author himself.

ℬ 11 ℛ

The Taming of the Shrew

"And did you write it yourself?" the duchess asked. "I couldn't if I wanted to," replied
Sancho, "because I don't know how to read or write, just how to sign my name."
—Cervantes, *Don Quixote*, [1605][1]

One cannot underestimate the advantages that privileged social status would have
provided with respect to the world of Renaissance performing arts. For example, those
familiar with Cervantes' *Don Quixote* will recall that the second half of the novel dwells
on situations in which the Don and Sancho are both hoodwinked and mock-feted as
celebrities by the local nobility. These farces are orchestrated not by actors, but personally by the Duke and Duchess. During that period in history, the true impresarios were
not the fledgling professional actors (who also make appearances in Cervantes' tale) but
rather the nobility who patronized them and from whom the actors literally took their
cues. Whether involving dramatic scenarios, staging, costumes, music, dance, or the cho-
reography of any public spectacle, it was the upper classes who were the real masters of
what one could term the Elizabethan *Gesamtkunstwerk*.[2]

The comparison between *The Taming of the Shrew* and *Don Quixote* is appropriate
because just as Sancho Panza becomes governor of an island (or so he thinks), Shakespeare's
Christophero Sly is duped into believing he is a nobleman. This transpires during the
rarely staged Induction to the drama, in which the drunken and good-for-nothing Sly
awakens to find himself entertained by his noble-born deceivers. Thus begins Shakespeare's
famous play within its not-so-famous context. Before we are transported to Padua, however, the audience learns that Sly is "by education a card-maker" (Ind.i.19)—that is, cards
for combing wool—who recites a litany of information about Will Shakspere's native Warwickshire, including reference to one Stephen Sly (Ind.i.93), assumed kindred to Christophero.[3] Like the historical Will Shakspere, Sly has a tradesman background. He ineptly
brags of being descended from "Richard the Conqueror"[4] (Ind.i.4) before passing out,
thus enabling the aristocratic Huntsman and his entourage to have some fun at Sly's
expense. Oxfordians believe Sly to be a send-up of Shakspere himself,[5] while traditionalists are naturally horrified by this suggestion and refuse to even consider it. As for Sly's
boast of Norman descent, this would be a nice perk for Will Shakspere as the true author,
except that the very portrayal of him as the loutish tinker would easily offset any such
small gain.

Shakespeare's sexist comedy with subtle feminist overtones[6] was not printed until the First Folio of 1623.[7] The unanimous verdict among scholars is that the primary source was an earlier, anonymous play published in 1594, titled *The Taming of A Shrew*. Edmund Chambers noted that "*A Shrew* furnished the main structure of both plots, with their characters and entanglement, and of the induction," concluding that "Shakespeare himself probably used no other literary source than *A Shrew*...."[8] Geoffrey Bullough observed that "Until 1607 all bibliographical references were apparently to the latter [*A Shrew*]...." This echoed Chambers, who remarked that "The bibliographical data up to 1607 relate to *The Taming of A Shrew*, but it is clear that *A Shrew* and *The Shrew* were regarded commercially as the same...." Both pointed to 1607 because the third quarto of *A Shrew* was published that year; thus, Bullough and Chambers really meant that *until 1623* there was no distinction made between the two plays.[9] Orthodox critics are in somewhat of a bind because *The Shrew* is universally considered one of the Bard's earlier comedies; yet until 1623 its predecessor (*A Shrew*) had already seen three separate publications. Bullough sensibly tried to get around this by opining that *A Shrew* was "maybe Shakespeare's first shot at the theme...."[10] Chambers, however, resisted: "I adhere to the older view that it was used as a source-play...."[11] Bullough logically concluded that "The date of this play is in doubt."[12]

One of the noticeable differences between the two works is that in *A Shrew* Sly watches almost the entire play, interrupts the performance, is ejected from the audience, and returns at the end. In *The Shrew*, the opening Induction is expanded but that is the last we hear and see of Sly, whose continuing presence is assumed.[13] The first known performance of *A Shrew* (by the Earl of Pembroke's Men) is advertised in the 1594 quarto, which would have occurred sometime between 1592 and 1593.[14] Fourteen years earlier, however, on New Year's Day, 1579, at Richmond Palace, the Children of Paul's performed a play titled *A Morrall of the Marryage of Mynde and Measure*. Oxfordian Eva Turner Clark made a clever case for this being a primitive version of *A Shrew*, since Petruchio's "measures" win over the "mind" of Katherina.[15] This was the same period when de Vere was active as an impresario at court following his return from Italy in 1576.[16] Probably the most famous modern production of Shakespeare's play was the classic 1967 Franco Zeffirelli movie with Richard Burton and Elizabeth Taylor, also starring a young Michael York in the role of Lucentio. York, during his distinguished career both on stage and on the big screen, has become an outspoken Oxfordian in his authorship beliefs.[17]

Shakespeare did not invent the idea of a commoner being tricked into believing that he was a nobleman—the device is traceable back to *The Arabian Nights*.[18] Among English sources, a work on this theme by the early Elizabethan playwright and Poet Laureate Richard Edwards (d. 1566) was reportedly published around 1570, but was subsequently lost.[19] Edwards, praised as a dramatist (along with de Vere) by Puttenham and Meres,[20] had entertained the queen with his plays at Oxford University in August 1566.[21] This was during graduation ceremonies that included de Vere, who received his degree in September,[22] while Edwards himself died shortly afterward in October.[23]

Another minor Elizabethan playwright who seems to have influenced *The Shrew*, at least in terms of the romance between Lucentio and Bianca, was George Gascoigne (d. 1577), whose play titled *Supposes* was performed at Gray's Inn on December 26, 1566, two months after the death of Richard Edwards, and one month before de Vere was admitted to this institution on February 1, 1567.[24] Gascoigne's play was itself an English adaptation of *I Suppositi* by Ludovico Ariosto,[25] and was first published in 1573 as part of the collection titled *A Hundreth Sundrie Flowres*.[26] This beautiful but controversial book was eventually credited solely to Gascoigne in its second edition of 1575 (while de Vere was in Italy), retitled *The Poesies of George Gascoigne*. Oxfordians tend to view the work as authored by a number of courtier poets, including Gascoigne, de Vere, and Christopher Hatton.[27] Thus de Vere's shadow hangs over the English source material for *The Shrew* at almost every turn, including the obscure Richard Edwards and George Gascoigne, neither of whom became household names, but surely would have been known to the young earl. Will Shakspere during this same period was a child in Stratford-upon-Avon.

The storyline that most of us associate with *The Shrew*, however, is the "mastery in marriage" theme between Petruchio and Katherina, going back to ancient Plautine sources but which the Bard (via the author of *A Shrew*) notched up to degrees of previously unheard-of comic intensity.[28] Katherina sums up the so-called "Morall" of the story when she scolds the other wives with "Thy husband is thy lord" (V.ii.146). As for the "half-lunatic" (II.i.287) Petruchio of Verona, he introduces himself to Katherina by heaping verbal abuse upon her, repeating the name "Kate" 10 times in quick succession with almost scatological glee (II.i.185–190).[29] Bullough made a valiant attempt to identify this level of harassment in previous source material but finally admitted that "the fun begins" in *A Shrew*.[30] This is the aspect of the drama that truly sticks in the popular mind, as exemplified by the 1948 Cole Porter musical *Kiss Me, Kate*, the title of which quotes Petruchio's refrain in Shakespeare's play (II.i.318 and V.ii.179). Oxfordians are able to concisely resolve all of these problems by simply postulating that both *Morrall of the Marryage* and *A Shrew* were earlier versions of *The Shrew*, all written and subsequently revised by de Vere.

Apart from de Vere's suggestive proximity to the source material, Shakespeare's play seems to provide a soundtrack for de Vere's documented personal life. For starters, de Vere, like Lucentio, had traveled across northern Italy and wrote a letter from Padua in 1575, from which (along with earlier correspondence) we learn that he had borrowed money from two Italian financiers named Baptista Nigrone and Pasquino Spinola.[31] These have a jolting resemblance to the name of Baptista Minola, Katherina and Bianca's father.[32] More remarkable still is Shakespeare's often ignored command of the Italian language as Lucentio and Tranio trade expressions such as "Basta" [enough!] (I.i.198) and "Mi perdonato" [pardon me] (I.i.25). Then Petruchio greets Hortensio in Italian with "Con tutto il core, ben trovato" [with all my heart, well met] (I.ii.24), who in turn responds with "Alla nostra casa ben venuto, molto honorato signor mio Petrucio" [Welcome to our house, my most honored Signior Petruchio] (I.ii.25–26). Orthodox scholar Professor Ernesto Grillo described this as "pure Italian."[33] Perhaps Will Shakspere picked it up hanging out at the Mermaid Tavern. De Vere, on the other hand, was known to have been fluent in Italian, confirmed by testimony given to the Inquisition by Orazio Cuoco upon his return to Italy from England.[34]

As in *Much Ado About Nothing*, *The Taming of the Shrew* gives us (in the person of Gremio) a nod towards the pantaloon stock-character of *commedia dell' arte*, and specifically refers to him as such (II.i.37). Familiarity with this type of entertainment in England during Shakespeare's time would have required witnessing one of the rare documented performances at court or in a great house of the nobility (most likely performed in Italian), or—in the case of de Vere—traveling through Italy when this improvised art form was enjoying its greatest vogue of popularity. Both scenarios are possible but the latter is certainly more probable.

Perhaps the most amazing (and humorous) line in the play occurs in Act IV when Vincentio exclaims with incredulous contempt to the servant Tranio (posing as Vincentio's son, Lucentio), "Thy father! O villain, he is a sail maker in Bergamo" (IV.v.77–78). How the Bard accurately knew that the provincial inland town of Bergamo was a center for the sail-making industry[35] is anyone's guess, unless the Oxfordian theory is taken seriously, since de Vere traveled through this part of Italy. Shakespeare also knew about a country dance named after the town (the Bergomask), repeatedly invoked in *A Midsummer Night's Dream* (V.i.360, 368). Yet again—contrary to the popular image of Shakespeare as a writer who made many mistakes—we are awed by his repeated ability to toss out accurate, offhand minutiae on Renaissance Italy.

Upon his arrival, Petruchio calmly announces that "I come to wive it wealthily in Padua" (I.ii.75). Like Bassanio in *The Merchant of Venice*, Petruchio has this very specific objective in mind. De Vere himself was no stranger to gold-digging, having twice married women of means, and in both cases succeeded in dissipating their fortunes. In fact, de Vere (to the best of our knowledge) is the only Elizabethan courtier with the distinction of having twice married ladies-in-waiting to the queen *with her permission*.[36] Elizabeth obviously understood that de Vere was a spendthrift, and was notoriously vindictive toward courtiers who became involved with her ladies.[37] In spite of this, she gave him the green light not once but twice, suggesting that de Vere had some value to the state that has remained hidden from posterity. The suggestion that the queen did all this (including the grant of de Vere's prodigious annuity in 1586) just for the sake of keeping up appearances is at best an innocent one. For one thing, who else among her courtiers, many of whom seemed more deserving, received this kind of treatment?

While Petruchio's drunken and shameless pursuit of Katherina is somewhat reminiscent of de Vere, Katherina herself invites a search for real-life prototypes. We begin by noting that de Vere's half-sister was named Katherine, and this appears to have been less than an ideal sibling relationship. At age 13 and shortly after his father's death, de Vere had his title (and legitimacy of birth) legally challenged by his older half-sister's husband, the Baron Windsor.[38] Although Oxford managed (with the help of his guardian, Lord Burghley) to retain his earldom, this experience surely did less than endear the two to each other.

While de Vere's relations with his half-sister Katherine may have been no walk in the park, those with his other sister (and possibly his twin), Mary Vere, appear to have been only slightly better. Mary Vere, like Katherina in *The Shrew* (and like Maria from *Twelfth Night*), was noted for being adept at dishing out verbal abuse.[39] It has been correctly observed that Katherina seems to be a near relation to Maria, just as Petruchio resembles Maria's beau, Sir Toby Belch. Oxfordians such as Eva Turner Clark and Charlton Ogburn, Jr., were quick to pick up on these similarities.[40]

Approximately one year before *Morall of the Marryage* was performed at Richmond Palace, Mary Vere was married to Peregrine Bertie, Lord Willoughby, after a stormy courtship that received opposition from both families.[41] De Vere apparently objected to the stridently Protestant views of Bertie's clan, and Bertie's family, particularly his mother, objected to de Vere himself. Bertie, who later proved to be one of Elizabeth's better generals, seems to have taken the whole thing in stride, placidly noting in a letter to Mary that her brother "sweareth my death."[42] Some Oxfordians see him along with Sir Toby Belch as a model for Petruchio,[43] especially given his flamboyant portrait at Grimsthorpe Castle, providing us with a demeanor not unlike that of Richard Burton as Petruchio in the Zeffirelli film version. After Peregrine's wedding to the shrewish Mary Vere, however, there were reported problems, with Thomas Cecil predicting in a letter to his father Lord Burghley that Mary "will be beaten with that rod which heretofore she prepared for others."[44] Then, instead of killing Bertie as he had previously threatened, de Vere socialized with him. This followed in the wake of de Vere's messy affair with Anne Vavasor in 1581 and his precipitous fall from royal favor, as many of his other former friends deserted him.[45]

The Taming of the Shrew, aside from being a classic example of Elizabethan slapstick and farce, also provides a good seminar in Shakespeare's early comedic style, perhaps even his first plateau in that genre. The Bard began with an existing story and then added his own original subplot, which takes over as the new main plot and brings the whole thing to life in a way that his sources never could. One typically has no idea where this extra material came from, that is, if we adhere to the traditional biography of Will Shakspere. If the Oxfordian theory is given a fair hearing, then we can see how the original subplot-turned-main-plot of Petruchio and Katherina ties directly into the author's (that is to say, de Vere's) personal life. If this were not enough, Shakespeare grafts on a third plot—the Christophero Sly Induction—that makes little or no sense if we adhere to orthodox authorship beliefs. The best that can be said is that Shakespeare the writer was fond of the play-within-a-play device presumed to be fashionable at that time.[46] Other than the Bard having a bit of technical fun (282 lines' worth), one may wonder why he bothered, especially when so many subsequent productions have not. If Christophero Sly represents Will Shakspere, however, then we may be witnessing the upstart thespian from Warwickshire receiving a reminder from his noble benefactors who the real masters of illusion were.

ഇറ 12 ൽ

All's Well
That Ends Well

The first printed appearance of *All's Well That Ends Well*—in fact the first definite, recorded mention of the play—is in the First Folio of 1623.[1] It has been hypothesized that the mysterious play titled *Love's Labor's Won*, cited by Francis Meres in 1598 as an example of Shakespeare's work, may be an early version of *All's Well* under a different title.[2] Edmund Chambers, with marvelous understatement, added that "There is little external evidence on the date of the play."[3] *All's Well* has never been one of Shakespeare's more popular dramas, and commentators have tried to explain, among other things, why the Bard was attracted to such an odd story. Another reason *All's Well* has been widely discussed is that it contains enormous amounts of esoteric knowledge regarding the history and geography of France and Italy, as well as Renaissance literature and courtly social customs. To acquire this knowledge, the genius who was the author had to have been a prodigious reader, if not a prodigious liver of life.

Orthodox scholars, using very speculative and stylistic justification, tend to date the writing of *All's Well* to the turn of the 16th century.[4] Oxfordians, however, do a little speculating themselves. On Twelfth Night, January 6, 1579 (Will Shakspere was 13 years old), an anonymous, lost play was performed by the Lord Chamberlain's Men for an exclusive court audience at Richmond Palace, titled *The Historie of the Rape of the Second Helene*.[5] Oxfordians postulate this was an earlier version of *All's Well*,[6] because the name of Shakespeare's heroine is Helena and because she contrives to sleep with her husband Bertram against his knowledge—he thinks that he has slept with someone else. This unusual plot device,[7] the so-called bed-trick, is used by Shakespeare in not one but two of his plays, the other being *Measure for Measure*. Although Helena's bed-tricking of Bertram is not a "rape" in the modern sense of the word, during Shakespeare's time there were multiple shades of meaning, one of which was ravishment in which the degree of force used was debatable.[8]

During this period, plays such as *The Rape of the Second Helene* were often performed privately for the queen and her court. Moreover, up until the early 1580s, many anonymous, lost plays with names sounding suspiciously like alternative titles for Shakespeare's works were performed exclusively for the Elizabethan court.[9] This is not widely discussed because Will Shakspere was only a teenager, and no one claims he was such a genius that he was a prolific adolescent playwright. Perhaps by coincidence, 1579 was also the year the popular saying "all's well that ends well" first appeared in print in modern English. This was from *Ars Adulandi* by the poet Ulpian Fulwell,[10] a book dedicated to none other than de Vere's own mother-in-law, Mildred Cooke Cecil, Lady Burghley.[11]

The uncontested primary source for *All's Well* is the tale of "Giletta of Narbona" from *The Decameron* by the great Florentine writer Giovanni Boccaccio.[12] This was a variation of the "Patient Griselda" legend[13] that Shakespeare also employed for *The Winter's Tale*. The library of de Vere's guardian (and later father-in-law), Lord Burghley, contained a copy of Boccaccio in the original Italian,[14] a language in which we know that de Vere was conversant. Boccaccio's tale, however, had been translated into English by William Painter in his *Palace of Pleasure*, dating from 1566.[15] For some reason, Shakespeare was drawn to this peculiar story; then he goes on to embellish his own version with many characters and situations not found in Boccaccio.

An acknowledged secondary source for *All's Well* was the anonymous play titled *The Weakest Goeth to the Wall*,[16] first published in 1600 and, as advertised on the frontispiece, performed by the Earl of Oxford's Men. Both Chambers and Bullough agree that the Bard drew upon this work by using the highly unusual and Frenchified word "lustique" or "lustick" (meaning "lusty"), when Lafew quips "*Lustick*, as the Dutchman says" (II.iii.41).[17] As for Oxford's Men, de Vere, like his father and grandfather before him, sponsored acting companies throughout his life. For example, in 1580 de Vere took over the Earl of Warwick's company, which became known as Oxford's Men. This group was one of several that, after performing in London, toured the provinces during the early 1580s, including Stratford-upon-Avon.[18] A possible link to *All's Well* is suggested by this point—a small point perhaps, but interesting and not otherwise noticed unless one looks through the Oxfordian lens, as we call it.

All's Well is set in France and Italy, and Shakespeare's geography tends to be more sophisticated than he is usually given credit for. In Act V, Helena's entourage travels from Marseilles to Roussillon, a distance described as "four or five removes" (V.iii.31); that is, four or five relay stations along a coach or horseback route. This has troubled scholars because "Roussillon" is usually associated with the French Pyrenees province, and this is where Boccaccio partially sets his original version of the story. The stretch between the Pyrenees and Marseilles is pretty rough terrain—certainly more than four or five relays. There is, however, more than one Roussillon in France. On his way back from Italy, de Vere returned through France up the Rhone Valley from Marseilles to Lyon, like Helena in the play. Just a few kilometers south of Lyon is the small town of Roussillon, in the province of Dauphine. A 16th-century chateau (still standing) was once owned by the Count of Roussillon, which is Bertram's title in *All's Well*.[19] There is no proof that de Vere stayed here, but he would have at least passed by.

The previous year (in 1575), de Vere had arrived in Paris. This was three years after the infamous St. Bartholomew's Day Massacre, in which French Catholics committed mass murder against their Huguenot countrymen. Oxford was treated very well, being received by King Henry III himself. Although de Vere was technically an English Protestant, he was rumored to have Catholic sympathies and later secretly converted, although he then turned around and renounced Catholicism.[20] This flip-flopping reminds one of the French witticism, "Paris is well worth a mass."[21]

Shakespeare's French king is reminiscent of Francis I, who ruled until 1547. Although the Bard does not specify which French king he had in mind, nor make any pretense at precise history, he was no doubt influenced by the reputations of recent French monarchs. Like Shakespeare's French king, Francis lived to an old age and was constantly vacillating between good and bad health; however, he was a great lover of the ladies and was widely admired both by subjects and foreigners for his religious toleration and generous patronage of the arts. His great mistake was to wage war against the Holy Roman Emperor, Charles V, and he never recovered politically from this military defeat.

The grandson of Francis I, King Henry III, was the French monarch when de Vere passed through France in 1575 and 1576. As history vividly records, Henry was no boy scout. In addition to his involvement in the St. Bartholomew's Day Massacre and persecution of religious dissenters, Henry was known to have been quite a sexual adventurer and somewhat of a jokester. When told by the English ambassador that Oxford had an attractive wife, he reportedly said (in French), "Then you make a beautiful couple."[22] How do we know de Vere could understand French? Among other things, we have a letter written in French by de Vere when he was 13 years old,[23] and another letter written in French to Oxford in 1595 by Henry the Great himself.[24]

The action shifts from France to Italy when Bertram escapes from his forced marriage to Helena by running off to fight for the Florentines in one of their periodic wars against the Sienese. Shakespeare's French King says, "The Florentines and the Senoys are by th' ears" (I.ii.1); that is, they have each other by the ears. This is a translation of a very real Italian colloquialism.[25] Florence and Siena are geographically very close to each other, being separated by the Chianti wine region. Much of the play is centered around famous wine country (Chianti, the Rhone Valley), and blind inebriation is one explanation making the bed-trick device dramatically plausible. De Vere also traveled to these places and was certainly criticized for his lack of sobriety.[26] Then again, if de Vere was Shakespeare it would not be the first time in history a great writer had a drinking problem.

De Vere's presence in Siena, Florence, and France during his travels is well documented. Like Boccaccio, he traveled far and wide. In fact, an earlier dramatic version of Boccaccio's tale was popular in Siena during the 16th century, titled *Virginia* and written by the Sienese playwright Bernardo Accolti.[27] It is interesting that such a titled work was apparently well-known in a city that was visited by de Vere during the time of the English Virgin Queen, and based on the same story as *All's Well That Ends Well*. Along these lines, viewing Shakespeare through the Oxfordian lens may eventually reveal new insights. In any event, the Bard appears to have been fascinated by the city of Siena, which is mentioned or alluded to in many of his plays. There might also be a connection between Accolti's title and the bawdy banter between Parolles and Helena on the subject of virginity at the end of Act I, scene i.

Italy provides the settings for key events in the play, both in love and war. Helena follows Bertram to Florence and conspires with the locals to win her husband back. Several scenes are set both in and around the Palazzo Vecchio or Ducal Palace, a place surely known to de Vere or any tourist who passes through Florence to this day. A long-standing feud between Florence and Siena culminated in 1555 when the Florentines under Duke Cosimo de' Medici brutally defeated the Sienese once and for all. Cosimo was a younger contemporary of Francis I and the last Duke of Florence to wage war against Siena. He was admired both for his military prowess and enlightened government, which included patronage of famous artists. Cosimo died, however, in 1574, so when de Vere arrived in Italy in 1575, the Grand Duke of Florence was Cosimo's eldest son, Francesco.[28] De Vere's enemies claimed that Oxford, while drunk, bragged of having been temporarily placed in command of a cavalry unit during a conflict between Florence and Genoa.[29] Recall that in *All's Well*, Bertram is appointed General of the Horse by the Duke of Florence. This detail is not found in Boccaccio, where Bertram serves the Florentines in a much lesser capacity. Bullough, among others, found this odd.[30] Why would Shakespeare turn Bertram into such a high-ranking commander? Once again, applying the Oxfordian theory makes things a little more interesting.

Bertram, second only to Hamlet among Shakespeare's characters, bears a keen resemblance to the young Edward de Vere. Exactly like Bertram in the play, de Vere became a royal ward after his father died and left home to live away from his mother at court. This was under the supervision of William Cecil, the future Lord Burghley, who was raised to the nobility by Queen Elizabeth in 1571, concurrent with his daughter Anne's marriage to de Vere. Burghley had originally come from the merchant class and was therefore socially beneath Oxford, as was his daughter, at least until Elizabeth changed all that with her royal prerogative,[31] similar to what Shakespeare's French King offers to do for Helena (II.iii.117–118). This is only the beginning of similarities between Shakespeare's Bertram and de Vere.[32]

The Bard invents numerous characters not found in Boccaccio's original story. These include Bertram's mother, the Countess, the wise counselor Lafew, the Clown Lavatch, the Duke of Florence, and a whole gaggle of minor French and Florentine characters[33]— many of whom, it has been persuasively argued, resemble real Frenchmen and Florentines of the time.[34] Lafew may represent a more favorable view of Lord Burghley,[35] in contrast to the spymaster Polonius in *Hamlet*, since he embodies the sober and prudent advisor— the same role Burghley often played at the Elizabethan court. Geoffrey Bullough exclaimed, "How far this is away from Boccaccio!"[36]

Another character not found in Boccaccio (perhaps the most memorable one in the play) is Parolles, the verbose and cowardly companion of Bertram, whom he leads astray. Many see Parolles as a forerunner of Falstaff, albeit a leaner and meaner version without any of Falstaff's likable qualities.[37] Parolles in French means "words"[38]—in other words, all talk,[39] and that pretty much sums up the character, whose true colors are finally revealed to Bertram by the end of the story. Shakespeare gives us a vivid portrait of Parolles—swaggering, boastful, deceitful, and prurient. Among the many controversial figures known to have associated with de Vere, one in particular appears to fit this description, at least according to period accounts. This was the ineffable Henry Howard, de Vere's first cousin and arguably the most disliked man at court during Shakespeare's time. Howard's older brother Thomas, the Duke of Norfolk, had been executed for high treason in 1572, but Henry managed to survive by laying low and convincing everyone that he was harmless. Like de Vere, he was extremely well educated and traveled, but unlike de Vere, he never allied himself with Burghley and the Protestant majority at court. De Vere broke with his cousin in 1580 after denouncing him as a traitor in front of the queen, and he later referred to Howard as "the most arrant villain that lived"[40]—quite a statement if coming from Shakespeare. It does not seem too far-fetched to say that we may be catching a glimpse of Howard's personality in the character of Parolles.

In the climactic finale to the play, Diana Capilet (the object of Bertram's infatuation) accusatorily challenges the young Count with "Look so strange upon your wife?" (V.iii.168). De Vere's biography is highly suggested by this. After marrying Anne Cecil with noticeable ambivalence (similar to the way Bertram marries Helena), de Vere separated from his wife and lived apart from her for five years. This break occurred over a paternity dispute involving their daughter Elizabeth. Initially, de Vere said the child was not his, because he had supposedly left for his Grand Tour before Anne conceived. Later, however, de Vere reversed himself, acknowledged the child as his own, reconciled with Anne and moved back with her. After the fact, there was a story circulated, recorded in two separate sources, that de Vere had conceived his first child by unknowingly sleeping with his wife when he thought he was sleeping with someone else, i.e., the bed-trick.[41] Thus we have another very direct and unusual (to say the least) parallel between the biography of Edward de Vere and one of Shakespeare's more bizarre storylines, one the Bard used twice, in fact. For Will Shakspere, we simply do not have any information that would suggest any of these numerous connections to the play's sources or storyline.

One of our favorite lines from *All's Well* occurs when the Clown is hauled before the Countess to answer for sleeping around and the Countess says to him: "The complaints I have heard of you I do not all believe. 'Tis my slowness that I do not, for I know you lack not folly to commit them, and have ability enough to make such knaveries yours" (I.iii.9–12). In other words, she does not know if he is innocent or guilty, but that he is capable of anything, and that's bad enough. Lavatch, like many of Shakespeare's clowns, personifies the author's festive alter-ego in contrast to Bertram, who is portrayed not too glamorously. Both Bertram and Lavatch are, in turn, foils to the virtuous character of Helena. If *The Rape of the Second Helene* was in fact an early draft for *All's Well That Ends Well*, then perhaps the play reflects de Vere coming to grips with his own bad behavior toward his wife, in which case Bertram would represent Shakespeare's own unvarnished and unflattering self-portrait of the artist as a young man.

∽ 13 ∾

Twelfth Night

This subliminal comedy belongs to a sizeable group of plays that did not appear in print until the First Folio of 1623.[1] The first definite reference to a performance (circa 1602) at the Middle Temple in London was recorded in the diary of barrister John Manningham.[2] Traditionally, *Twelfth Night* is dated around 1600 because, prior to the Middle Temple performance, the work probably took one to two years to write and produce. Occasionally, someone has the effrontery to question this guesstimate. For example, anyone may ponder the famous sketch of the Swan Theater from 1596 by Dutch scholar Johannes de Witt, the only detailed period drawing showing the interior of an Elizabethan playhouse.[3] The scene being depicted on stage shows a man with a staff bowing before a surprised-looking woman seated next to her lady-in-waiting. Many believe this to be the scene from *Twelfth Night* where Malvolio approaches Olivia and Maria wearing yellow stockings, cross-gartered (Act III, scene iv). If so, this would indicate that *Twelfth Night* was on the boards by at least 1596.

Oxfordians such as Frank Davis take it further by pointing to an 18th-century work titled *Desiderata Curiosa* (1732) by Francis Peck, who proposed publishing "a pleasant conceit of Vere, Earl of Oxford, discontented at the rising of a mean gentleman in the English court circa 1580."[4] They postulate that this mysterious manuscript (now lost) was an early version of *Twelfth Night*. If correct, then the "mean gentleman" obviously refers to the character of Malvolio, and the play was in fact often known by this alternative title.[5]

The basic plot of *Twelfth Night* goes back to Plautus and the ancients; however, many scholars agree that the primary source was a 16th-century *commedia erudite* known as *Gl'Ingannati* (The Deceived) and its prologue companion piece, *Il Sacrificio* (The Sacrifice)—usually printed and performed together. These were written and produced by the Acadamia degl' Intronati (Academy of the Astounded), a group of anonymous Sienese noblemen, and were first performed and published during the 1530s.[6] *Gl'Ingannati* was very popular—perhaps the best-known play to come out of Siena. Variations subsequently proliferated across Europe, although a true and complete English translation did not appear until the 20th century.[7]

Like *Twelfth Night*, *Gl'Ingannati* deals with a brother and sister who are accidentally separated and later reunited. The sister must disguise herself as a boy and pay court to a lady in the name of her master whom she loves herself. Later, the brother and sister are mistaken for each other, and eventually, the brother and the lady get together, as do his sister and her master.[8] As Fabian in *Twelfth Night* would say, "an improbable fiction"

(III.iv.128). By contrast, *Il Sacrificio* is a short, allegorical farce in which the characters renounce love and pay mock sacrificial homage to Minerva, the Roman spear-shaker goddess of wisdom and warfare.[9] During this time in Italy, the first serious excavations for ancient statuary were yielding remarkable discoveries. Members of the Intronati were likely familiar with these and were possibly inspired to create the ceremonial devotion to the image of Minerva. *Il Sacrificio* also has a character named "Malevolti," a possible forerunner to Shakespeare's Malvolio.[10]

The title of *Twelfth Night* refers to the evening of January 5/6—the night before the Christian Feast of the Epiphany, or secular Feast of Fools, as it was also known during Elizabethan times. The holiday was a carryover from pagan times, associated with carnival mood and licentious behavior.[11] *Gl'Ingannati–Il Sacrificio* was affiliated with this same festival. Shakespeare's work makes no reference to the Epiphany, although its connection to the Sienese plays surely explains the title. The frontispiece for a 1569 edition, today in the Chicago Newberry Library, specifically advertises itself within this context. The subtitle, prologue and text all refer to carnival entertainment for the eve of the Feast of the Epiphany, or Twelfth Night.[12]

There is a decent possibility that de Vere saw these two plays being performed in Siena, from where he wrote a letter to his father-in-law Lord Burghley on "Tenth Night," January 3, 1576.[13] While no proof has surfaced to support the claim, it does not seem too far of a stretch to say that de Vere may have been in town on January 4 and January 5 (the climactic nights of the festival) to witness performances of Siena's most popular dramas. *Il Sacrificio*, the prologue piece, was typically performed on "Eleventh Night" (January 4/5), and *Gl'Ingannati* on the following evening of Twelfth Night (January 5/6). If de Vere was in attendance, he would have seen the mock sacrificial homage to the spear-shaker goddess Minerva that was an integral part of this entertainment. He may have also been exposed to the anonymous, group-work ethic of the Intronati, possibly even meeting their leader, the nobleman playwright Alessandro Piccolomini.[14]

A short English prose spin on the plot of *Gl'Ingannati* was later published in 1581 and is often suggested as an alternative source. This was the tale of *Apolonius and Silla* by Barnabe Riche, taken from his *Farewell to Militarie Profession*. Scholars uncomfortable with Shakespeare's ability to draw directly upon yet-to-be-translated Italian material tend to cite Riche as a source for *Twelfth Night*, rather than *Gl'Ingannati*. Bullough, while favoring Riche as a primary source, admitted that the Bard probably drew upon the original Italian play for at least some of the material.[15] Edmund Chambers went further by stating that *Gl'Ingannati* "comes nearer to Shakespeare's handling," while to Riche, "his debt was not very great."[16] Regarding the character of Malvolio, Bullough added that "no one has yet to find Shakespeare a debtor."[17]

Shakespeare's play also contains a number of secondary sources with connections to de Vere. Orsino alludes to the legend of the Egyptian thief (V.i.118–119), which is probably taken from a 1569 book dedicated to the 19-year-old Oxford, Thomas Underdowne's English translation of *An Aethiopian History* by Heliodorus.[18] In addition, the original ancient source for the story, the *Menechmi* by Plautus, was found in the library of Thomas Smith, de Vere's childhood tutor and one of the outstanding intellectual personalities of the Elizabethan era.[19]

This brings us back to de Vere's "discontent" in 1580 over the ascendancy of a "mean gentleman" at court. In 1580, Will Shakspere was 16 years old and still living in Warwick-shire, but in London, there was a man of humble origins whose meteoric rise to promi-nence would have been hard for anyone to miss. This was Christopher Hatton, captain of Queen Elizabeth's bodyguards. Hatton, because of his common background, was the sort of person to incur the enmity of the old nobility, and Sir Christopher's letters indi-cate that he and de Vere disliked each other.[20] To aggravate the situation, Hatton had recently made a fortune beyond his wildest dreams by investing in the global piracy expe-dition of Francis Drake, while de Vere had bankrupted himself by investing in Martin Frobisher's unsuccessful search for a Northwest Passage.[21] Hatton, in the words of Malvo-lio, had "greatness thrust upon" him (II.v.146).

Soon afterward (in 1581), Hatton was the dedicatee of the aforementioned *Farewell to Militarie Profession*. In this same book, Riche gives a bizarre account of an unnamed English nobleman, whose description fits de Vere in every detail, engaged in what could be interpreted as a public cross-dressing incident. According to Riche, this nobleman appeared on horseback in the streets of London wearing very effeminate French attire, possibly to lampoon the queen's latest French suitor, François de Valois, along with his retinue, who were in England at that time.[22] This remarkable anecdote comes from a fol-lower of the same man (Hatton) who may have been satirized (as Malvolio?) in de Vere's "pleasant conceit" from the previous year, and from an author (Riche) often cited as an English source for *Twelfth Night*. It would appear that the old de Vere-Hatton rivalry con-tinues to this very day as a debate over Shakespeare's original source material.

Apart from the question of whether Malvolio is in fact a caricature of Hatton,[23] Shakespeare's motives in creating the character deserve a closer look. Based on the canon, few would claim Shakespeare had Puritan sympathies. The best single example of the Bard's attitude is his portrayal of Malvolio, who is derided by Maria and Sir Toby as a Puritan (II.iii.140–147). Sir Andrew also expresses a loathing for Brownists (III.ii.31), who were the first Puritan-like separatists in England. The relationship between the Puritans and Shakespeare is typically ignored or glossed over by modern commentators. Two obser-vations, however, can be made with certitude. First, the political ascendancy of the Puri-tans in England during this period in history was absolute and omnipresent. Second, the Puritans were dedicated, mortal enemies of the public theaters. This attitude (and polit-ical trend) would culminate one generation later in 1642–1648 with a decisive Puritan vic-tory in the English Civil War, resulting in the demolition of the playhouses and temporary consignment of Shakespeare to oblivion.

The genesis of organized, Calvinist opposition to the theaters coincided with the opening of the first playhouse in 1576. The London Council had already clamped down hard on play activity within its jurisdiction, and the Burbages built their first theaters just outside the city limits in Shoreditch. Immediate commercial success brought down fury from the pulpit, with preachers blaming all personal and social ills on the new form of entertainment, including outbreaks of plague and the London earthquake of 1580.[24] In *Twelfth Night*, Feste the clown scandalously hints to Orsino that Sunday church bells sum-mon everyone to the playhouse (V.i.36–40). This stampede may well have occurred directly from church, where furious preachers watched helplessly as parishioners bolted during the sermon. By 1583, the city had persuaded the Privy Council to adopt similar measures outside the city, with no performances allowed on Sundays or Holy Days, while plays, playhouses, and players all were vigorously licensed and regulated.[25] The crackdown of 1583 also led traveling companies such as Oxford's Men to tour the provinces, including Stratford-upon-Avon.[26]

Among the other writers sponsored by Hatton (besides Riche) was one William Rankins, who in 1587 issued an all-out attack on the acting profession titled *A Mirror of Monsters,* amazing in its vicious and inflammatory rhetoric.[27] Then in 1588 (the Armada year), Rankins dedicated to Hatton a work titled *The English Ape, the Italian Imitation, the Footesteppes of France*—or, the Englishman who apes Italians and dances like a Frenchman. This pamphlet condemned all foreign affectations in the English nobility, and was surely aimed at de Vere. After Hatton's death in 1591, however, Rankins did an about-face and earned his living as a playwright—he was on the payroll for Henslowe's company.[28] If you can't beat 'em, join 'em.

While Oxfordians believe that Hatton was the main object of satire (as Malvolio) in *Twelfth Night,* there appear to have been other targets as well. Sir Philip Sidney, courtier poet and English war hero, seems to have inspired Sir Andrew Aguecheek. De Vere and Sidney had a troubled relationship before the latter died fighting in the Low Countries in 1586. Both were rival suitors for de Vere's first wife, Anne Cecil, and each belonged to competing political factions at court. Above all, both were rival poets. This rivalry came to a head in 1579 on a London tennis court where the two men engaged in their infamous quarrel. According to eyewitnesses, there was disagreement over whose turn it was, culminating with de Vere's belittlement of Sidney as "a puppy." Sidney reportedly challenged de Vere to a duel but, in arbitrating the case, the queen told Sidney that Oxford was in the right as his social superior. Sidney was then ordered to apologize, which he refused to do, choosing instead to exile himself from court. Along these lines, *Twelfth Night* has not one but two mock duel scenes, both involving Aguecheek, one against Viola, disguised as Cesario (Act III, scene iv) and another against her twin brother Sebastian (Act IV, scene i). Oxfordians tend to think all of this was inspired by de Vere's squabbles with Sidney.[29]

Like Sebastian in *Twelfth Night,* de Vere possibly had a twin sister. We say "possibly" because the only evidence is a 1563 letter from their uncle stating that Mary Vere and her brother were the same age.[30] In fairness it should be remembered that Will Shakspere had a twin daughter and son (the latter died as a child), although making the imaginative leap to Viola and Sebastian is like jumping over the Grand Canyon. While Viola (one of the Bard's most likeable heroines) does not seem to have much in common with Mary Vere's known personality, there is another character in *Twelfth Night* that bears more resemblance to de Vere's sister. This is Maria, Olivia's lady-in-waiting, who is (like Mary Vere was reported to have been)[31] sharp-tongued—Sir Andrew at one point calls her a shrew (I.iii.47)—and it is she who comes up with the ruthless scheme to trick Malvolio. It has been rightly observed that Maria seems to be a close relative of Kate from *Taming of the Shrew,* and that Sir Toby Belch is similar to Petruchio.[32]

Mary Vere's husband was Peregrine Bertie, Lord Willoughby, whom some Oxfordians see as an inspiration for both Petruchio and Sir Toby Belch.[33] One may easily gather from his portrait at Grimsthorpe Castle that Bertie was, to borrow Kate's description of Petruchio, a "mad-capped ruffian and a swearing Jack"[34]; nor does he appear to have been a teetotaler. Peregrine Bertie—Petruchio Belch? Sounds like a derogatory nickname for a brother-in-law. This is the man who married de Vere's sister, apparently against the wishes of both families. According to Bertie, de Vere at one point threatened to kill him.[35] True love prevailed, however, and while the marriage was reportedly an unhappy one,[36] there is an interesting footnote. After the couple was said to be having difficulties, we find Bertie and de Vere socializing together.[37] This is reminiscent of the Bard's rough but affectionate portrayal of Sir Toby. Shakespeare, as we know, usually started with existing stories and then added his own original subplots, and these often bring the story to life. Assuming Will Shakspere was the author, we have no idea where this extra material came from, but if we consider de Vere as the possible author, then we can see how these tie directly into the author's personal life.

On another level, in *Twelfth Night* Shakespeare offers a curious wealth of geographic information. Although the play has Italian roots, the Bard moves the setting to Illyria along the eastern Adriatic coast, which during the 16th century was being hotly disputed between the Venetians, the Hapsburgs, and the Ottomans.[38] Viola and Sebastian hail from "Messaline," which may refer to northern Syria near the great trading city of Aleppo,[39] and located along the western perimeter of the famed Silk Road to India and China. Shakespeare seems preoccupied with world trade, and when Viola exclaims "Then westward-ho!" (II.i.134), she is repeating a popular slogan of the day. Sir Toby offhandedly labels Olivia a "Cathaian" (II.iii.75), that is, an investor in East Indian trade, and praises Maria as his "metal of India" (II.iv.14). Then Maria compares the lines in Malvolio's face to a "new map with the augmentation of the Indies" (III.ii.78–80), alluding to the first global maps in England. Two ships are also mentioned by name—the *Tiger* and the *Phoenix*, both well-known English vessels of the period. The *Tiger* is believed to have voyaged in the direction of Aleppo during the early 1580s,[40] and the very name of the ship suggests the Far East. The *Tiger* was also associated with the previously mentioned Martin Frobisher,[41] in whose unsuccessful searches for a Northwest Passage de Vere had been a heavy investor.

Another hallmark of this transcendent work is the stripping away of gender. Viola, who during Shakespeare's time would have been played by a boy, at one point finds herself disguised as "Cesario" while lamenting an alter-ego sister who had died for love (II.iv.107–121). Viola is then confused with her twin brother Sebastian (and vice-versa), and Antonio's bond with Sebastian seems to go beyond that of conventional male friendship. Olivia becomes infatuated with Viola/Cesario, who in turn must conceal her love for Orsino but speaks of it hypothetically to him (II.iv.107–108). Even Orsino's affection for the "boy" Viola/Cesario has raised a few eyebrows. All of this confusion aside, Shakespeare's remarkable ability to look beyond gender makes his characters all the more profoundly human, and his female characters uniquely so among Elizabethan playwrights. Like other Shakespearean works, *Twelfth Night* hints at bisexual relationships, and de Vere, whatever the truth may have been, had a reputation for living an alternative lifestyle.[42]

Orsino's opening line "If music be the food of love, play on" seems to challenge any Puritanical assumptions the audience may have, and *Twelfth Night* is arguably Shakespeare's most musical play. The heroine's name is Viola, and Sir Toby refers to the violas da gamba when boasting of Sir Andrew's accomplishments (I.iii.26). Dances are catalogued as well—the galliard (I.iii.128, 133), the coranto (I.iii.129), and the jig (I.iii.129). The play also contains some of the Bard's most memorable songs, including "O Mistress Mine" (II.iii.34–52), the melody for which was published in 1599 as part of Thomas Morley's *First Book of*

Consort Lessons.[43] That same year, Morley published John Farmer's *First Set of English Madrigals*, which was lavishly dedicated to Oxford. Farmer flatters de Vere by stating that his musical talent exceeded that of many professionals, though for him music was just a hobby.[44] De Vere patronized other musicians as well, such as the madrigalist Henry Litchfild,[45] and at one point was the landlord of Elizabethan composer William Byrd. One of the most popular pieces attributed to Byrd is *My Lord of Oxenforde's Maske*—a title containing yet another reference to de Vere's involvement in the theater world.[46] De Vere also once had the audacity (in private company) to express loathing for the queen's singing voice.[47]

In his younger days, de Vere was no less acclaimed as a dancer. His schoolboy curriculum included dancing among his exercises, and it was remarked that the queen admired his skills, high praise given her own reputation as an accomplished dancer.[48] In one of de Vere's famous displays of temper in 1578, he refused to exhibit these skills before French ambassadors, despite repeated commands from the queen.[49] De Vere also kept as house servants a Venetian choir boy, Orazio Cuoco, and a boy acrobat or "tumbling-boy" from the John Symons company.[50] Looking beyond these foibles, even de Vere's critics admit that he was a dedicated and sophisticated connoisseur of music and dance. It can be safely said that whoever Shakespeare was, he was probably very musical, given the expertise displayed in the canon. With respect to Will Shakspere, there are no indications to what extent (if any) he was interested in music.

ഇ 14 ര

The Winter's Tale

The Winter's Tale, like The Tempest, saw its initial publication in the First Folio of 1623,[1] and the earliest known performance was noted in the diary of the astrologer Simon Forman, who saw it produced at the Globe Theater in 1611. Based on this sole reference, orthodox scholars tend to date the writing around 1610.[2] In 1594, however, 17 years prior to Forman's account, an unpublished play titled A Winter's Night's Pastime was entered with the Stationer's Register.[3] The year 1594 also saw publication of Shakespeare's two narrative poems, which, like The Winter's Tale, have classical roots in Ovid, along with less than subtle references to Italian Renaissance art. As for the colorful Simon Forman, it is through his diaries that we know something about the poetess Aemilia Bassano Lanyer, one of the leading candidates for Shakespeare's Dark Lady.[4] Perhaps by coincidence, there is a character in The Winter's Tale named Emilia, who is a lady-in-waiting for Queen Hermione.

The best-known character in the play, however, is probably the bear that devours Antigonus in Act III. Indeed, Exit, pursued by a bear (III.iii) may be the most famous stage direction in theatrical history. Another bear reference is made as the Clown disparagingly tells the rogue Autolycus that "He haunts wakes, fairs, and bear-baitings." (IV.iii.101–102). As most students of Elizabethan drama know, a bear-baiting arena was located down the street from the original Globe, and there has been some interesting scholarly debate on whether a real bear (a small, trainable one) was originally used in The Winter's Tale.[5] More interestingly, Edward de Vere was known to have sponsored a bear-baiting event on at least one occasion in Warwickshire.[6]

The play is also notorious for containing the best-known of Shakespeare's alleged geographical bloopers, occurring in Act III, scene iii, where the action is assigned to the "sea-coast of Bohemia." As everyone knows, Bohemia and the modern-day Czech Republic are a long way from the Adriatic coast. Commentators beginning with Ben Jonson have jumped all over this one to prove how clever they are and what a bumpkin Shakespeare was.[7] The point deserves scrutiny because Shakespeare's geography lessons, contrary to popular myth, are usually right on target.

The Winter's Tale is set in Sicily and Bohemia. During Shakespeare's time, the best route between the two places was across the Adriatic Sea. Ownership of the eastern Adriatic sea coast has been hotly disputed over the ages by many nations, including the Venetians, the Hapsburgs, the Ottoman Turks, and the Kingdom of Bohemia. This area centers around the Istrian Peninsula, south of the Julian Alps. To the northwest is the Italian seaport of Trieste, and to the southeast is the Croatian seaport of Rijeka. During the late

16th century, this territory was being aggressively disputed by the Venetians and the Hapsburgs, because whoever controlled it had a piece of the eastern trade routes.[8]

As early as the 9th century, before Bohemia had been Christianized by Saints Cyril and Methodius, the Kingdom of Bohemia (based in Prague) was a military and commercial power to be reckoned with, especially after the death of Charlemagne when the Holy Roman Empire was in a state of chaos. This power culminated in the late 13th century when Bohemia, under King Ottakar II, extended its control all the way from the Baltic to the Adriatic. So at one point Bohemia had not one but two sea coasts. After Ottakar was killed in battle, this power waned and Bohemia was absorbed back into the Holy Roman Empire, yet even then retained its separate identity. This information can be found, not in some obscure publication, but rather in the *Encyclopedia Britannica*, which includes a detailed map.[9] Even after Bohemia was re-incorporated into the Holy Roman Empire, it was still a world power. In 1355 the Bohemian-born Charles IV became Holy Roman Emperor, and made Prague his capital. Toward the end of the 14th century, Prague became the third largest city in Europe, behind only Rome and Constantinople. Historical atlases for this period show how Prague at this point still had direct, legal access to Adriatic ports.[10]

By Shakespeare's time, the Hapsburgs controlled the Kingdom of Bohemia and dominated the eastern sector of the Holy Roman Empire, eventually extending their control as far east as Transylvania. This expansion process had begun in 1526, when the king of Bohemia and Hungary and his army were annihilated by the Ottoman Turks at the Battle of Mohacs. The result of this disaster was that everyone in southeastern Europe handed the baton to the Hapsburgs and begged for protection. That marked the real beginning of the Hapsburgs as a world power. When the Hapsburgs were not busy defeating the Turks, they were fighting the Venetians for control of Trieste, eventually winning that contest as well. Even then, Bohemia retained access rights to the Adriatic, but as a satellite of the Hapsburgs.[11] At this same time, the map of Europe was shifting pretty much along religious lines, Protestant versus Catholic. Even though Bohemia was technically a Hapsburg satellite and part of the Holy Roman Empire, greater Bohemia, extending to the Adriatic Sea, was often viewed as a separate identity with its own religious classification— basically Catholic but showing signs of wavering. Seven years after Simon Forman witnessed a performance of *The Winter's Tale* at the Globe, Prague became the flash point of the Thirty Years' War.[12] By now perhaps the point has been beaten to death, but Shakespeare's alleged blooper is in reality a reflection of our own modern ignorance of history and geography.

Those who get their geography wrong usually get other things wrong as well. In *The Winter's Tale*, Shakespeare praises Giulio Romano, the most famous and talented artist to emerge from the tutelage of Raphael, as "that rare Italian master" (V.ii.98). This is in reference to the supposed statue of Hermione. Critics have been bothered by this because Romano is known primarily as a painter[13]; yet, the original inscription on Romano's tomb noted that he was also a sculptor and architect, like many other Renaissance artists.[14] A Titian portrait of Romano depicts him holding architectural plans, so we assume this is how he wanted to be remembered—as a multifaceted artist.

Moving beyond superficial opinions, the undisputed primary source for *The Winter's Tale* is Robert Greene's novel *Pandosto*, first published in 1588[15] and which, incidentally, gives Bohemia a sea coast as well.[16] Greene was a graduate of Cambridge and Oxford, which were also Edward de Vere's alma maters.[17] During the 1580s Greene was closely associated with a circle of writers surrounding de Vere, most of whom are considered highly "influential" on Shakespeare. We know Greene was part of de Vere's circle because, for one thing, in 1584 Greene's *Gwydonius* or *The Card of Fancy* was published with a lengthy and elaborate dedication to Oxford, in which Greene discreetly hinted that de Vere was both a generous patron of writers and an eminent writer himself.[18] Thus Edward de Vere was a major patron for the author universally credited as Shakespeare's source for *The Winter's Tale*—or perhaps Greene got the story from Shakespeare (that is, de Vere) to begin with. In addition, Greene is usually credited with writing the infamous *Greene's Groatsworth of Wit*, originally published in 1592. *Groatsworth* contains what many consider to be the first reference to Shakespeare as the "upstart crow." This is not the place to go into the myriad complexities of this document, supposedly written by Greene on his deathbed, but suffice it to say that the issues of who actually wrote the obscure and awkward text of *Groatsworth* and what was actually meant within are far from settled.[19]

Another Elizabethan work with commonalities to *The Winter's Tale* is the 1598 play titled *Parismus, the Renowned Prince of Bohemia*.[20] The author is credited as "E. Forde" (a curious resemblance to "Edward Oxenford," as de Vere often signed his name) and usually equated with the shadowy playwright Emmanuel Forde. Both *Parismus* and *The Winter's Tale* feature a Bohemian bear, a Bohemian prince, and (of course) a Bohemian setting.[21] The word "Bohemian," both then and now, connotes the geographical place *and* a certain style of living; that is, a somewhat morally carefree lifestyle associated with artists, writers, and poets—a lifestyle epitomized by Edward de Vere. De Vere could have easily been viewed as the proverbial Prince of Bohemia in London, just as Polixenes was the literal King of Bohemia in Shakespeare's play.

The original source for the main plot in *The Winter's Tale* (as well as Greene's *Pandosto*) involving the vindication of a long-suffering wife was derived from the legend of the patient Griselda, as retold by Boccaccio and Chaucer, among others.[22] We know that de Vere's guardian, Lord Burghley, kept a copy of Boccaccio (in the original Italian) in his library.[23] We also know, as documented in Burghley's account books, that de Vere purchased a volume of Chaucer's works when he was 19 years old.[24]

Many of the character names in the play are from Plutarch,[25] a French translation of which de Vere purchased at the same time he acquired the Chaucer.[26] The celebrated English translation of Plutarch by Thomas North was in fact based upon the earlier French translation by Bishop Jacques Amyot, the same edition that de Vere bought as a teenager. De Vere was known to have been versed in both French and Italian, and his adolescent purchase of French and Italian books represents only one of many examples that demonstrate this ability.

By general consensus, Shakespeare's favorite writer was Ovid.[27] The whole idea of a statue coming to life (or seeming to come to life, as Hermione does in the play) is a variation on the Pygmalion legend from Book X of the *Metamorphoses*.[28] This famous work was first translated into English by de Vere's uncle Arthur Golding and published in 1567. Oxfordians are fond of speculating that the teenage de Vere assisted his uncle in the process, although there is no proof to this effect. Coincidentally, Shakespearean actor Leslie Howard, who had Oxfordian sympathies in his authorship beliefs, won an Oscar for his role as Professor Henry Higgins in the original 1938 film version of *Pygmalion*, George Bernard Shaw's updated stage rendering of the story that later became the hit musical *My Fair Lady*.

Likely sources for *The Winter's Tale*'s subplot involving a long-lost infant were two Greek romance novels: Thomas Underdowne's 1569 translation of *An Aethiopian Historie* by Heliodorus, and Angel Day's 1587 translation of *Daphnis and Chloe*, by Longus.[29] Underdowne's work contains an extravagant dedication to the young Edward de Vere,[30] while Angel Day had been de Vere's personal secretary. In the previous year (1586) Day had dedicated *The English Secretary* to his patron, describing Oxford as "ever sacred to the Muses," a phrase later echoed in a dedication sonnet to Oxford by Edmund Spenser in *The Faerie Queene*.[31] Spenser's poem, incidentally, is yet another work seen as having affinities with Shakespeare's play.[32]

As with *The Tempest*, de Vere's personal connections with the themes and subject matter of *The Winter's Tale* are even more striking than his close proximity to the source material. William Cecil, Lord Burghley, was Queen Elizabeth's chief advisor for 40 years, as well as Edward de Vere's guardian and later his father-in-law. De Vere's marriage to Burghley's daughter Anne Cecil, however, was not a happy one. To make a long story short, he treated her very badly, including what was probably a false accusation of infidelity.[33] Thus the documented facts of de Vere's life tie directly into the plot of *The Winter's Tale*, since Leontes falsely accuses his wife Hermione of adultery. This is a recurring theme in Shakespeare, as well as in all *commedia dell' arte*: the guileless heroine accused of infidelity by a raging, jealous lover.[34] Most Oxfordians agree that these Shakespearean heroines are memorials to de Vere's first wife, Anne Cecil. Like Leontes in the play, de Vere lost an infant son (in 1583), perhaps seen as divine punishment for the mistreatment of his wife.[35] In fact, the title of the play paraphrases a line in which Mamillus, the doomed son of Leontes, tells his mother Hermione that "A sad tale's best for winter" (II.i.25).

De Vere's mother-in-law was the formidable Mildred Cooke Cecil, Lady Burghley, one of the best educated women of her times. Lady Burghley was known to have been highly critical of her son-in-law, especially for his neglect of her daughter.[36] The fiery character of Paulina in *The Winter's Tale*, who steadfastly berates Leontes for his irrational indictment of Hermione, may well have been modeled at least in part on Lady Burghley. Paulina eventually marries Camillo, the royal advisor banished by Leontes for his loyalty to Hermione, and a figure who may represent a more favorable view of Burghley than the negative characterization of Polonius in *Hamlet* (similar to Gonzalo in *The Tempest*). In one of the more famous lines from the play, Paulina proclaims, "It is a heretic that makes the fire, not she which burns in't" (II.iii.115–116). That pretty much sums up the moral of the story, if there is one.

De Vere's first wife, Anne, and his mother-in-law, Lady Burghley, both predeceased him in rapid succession between 1588 and 1589, about the same time Robert Greene's *Pandosto* appeared in print. Their shared tomb and effigies in Westminster Abbey include lengthy obituaries that omit any mention of de Vere; presumably, he would have been familiar with this monument.[37] Remarkably, Anne Cecil was publicly eulogized by Wilfred Samonde as "another Grissel for her patience"—a direct reference to the legend of the patient Griselda, the original plot source for both *The Winter's Tale* and *Pandosto*.[38] Shakespeare again refers to the Griselda legend in *Taming of the Shrew*, almost quoting

Samonde verbatim.[39] It was obviously a theme that resonated. Unlike the Pygmalion story, Hermione only appears to be a statue in the eyes of Leontes, and her transformation or metamorphosis takes place in his own mind's eye. This would not be a surprising attitude coming from de Vere, who was likely feeling remorse over his own past conduct. As Paulina somberly reflects in the play, "What's gone and what's past help should be past grief" (III.ii.222–223).

Oxford's eldest daughter by Anne Cecil was Elizabeth Vere, whose paternity in 1575 was the cause of the ruckus that led to a five-year break between de Vere and his wife. The issue was whether he had left for Italy by the time Anne had conceived. Initially, de Vere said no, the child was not his, and separated from Anne for five years, living a Bohemian-style high life in the interim. Later, de Vere moved back with his wife and came to accept the child as his own—just as Leontes eventually accepts Perdita as his daughter in the play, realizing his insane accusations against Hermione were unfounded.[40] Shakespeare was certainly obsessed with the idea of an innocent and wrongly accused heroine. If de Vere was in fact the author, it seems to suggest how he viewed his own situation in retrospect.

During the early 1590s, Elizabeth Vere was betrothed to Henry Wriothesley, Earl of Southampton, dedicatee of Shakespeare's two narrative poems and viewed by many as the Fair Youth of the sonnets. To repeat, there are kinships between these narrative poems and *The Winter's Tale*. Perhaps de Vere wrote *A Winter's Night's Pastime* (circa 1594) with his eldest daughter in mind, just as he may have written the poems that were dedicated to her then-fiancée. In the play, Perdita eventually weds the Bohemian Prince Florizel, and in real life, Elizabeth Vere, after the engagement to Wriothesley was broken off, married William Stanley, Earl of Derby, in 1595. In any event, all of Shakespeare's comedy-romances reflect a father's concern for a daughter's marital options. In the case of *The Winter's Tale*, this is combined with acknowledgment of the daughter's paternity and regret over false accusations against the daughter's mother. Shakespeare the writer seems to have had a certain Elizabethan nobleman in mind.

ꙮ 15 ꙮ

Cymbeline

Shakespeare's three late romances, *The Tempest*, *The Winter's Tale*, and *Cymbeline*, share a concern over the marital fates of their respective young heroines (Miranda, Perdita, and Imogen). Given that Edward de Vere had three surviving daughters by his first marriage, all of whom wed during the last years of his life, one is tempted to draw parallels with Shakespeare's final romantic trilogy. In *The Tempest*, Miranda's union with the son of her father's enemy suggests the betrothal of Susan Vere and Philip Herbert, nephew of de Vere's late, great rival Philip Sidney. The belated reunion between Perdita and Leontes in *The Winter's Tale*, followed by her wedding to a Bohemian prince, is reminiscent of Elizabeth Vere's delayed acknowledgment by her father and subsequent marriage to the wealthy William Stanley. Last but not least, Imogen in *Cymbeline* rejects an unwelcome suitor who is forced upon her, in favor of the lover that she prefers. This more than hints at the plight of Bridget Vere, who married Francis Norris after rejecting another admirer who was found to be quite unacceptable.

Like the other two works in the trilogy, *Cymbeline* was not printed until the First Folio of 1623, long after the death of whoever the author may have been. The play was witnessed by the astrologer Simon Forman in 1611, about the same time he saw *The Winter's Tale* produced at the Globe,[1] and the same year *The Tempest* was performed at court. This tells us little about the dates of composition, however, as evidenced by works such as *As You Like It*, which was entered with the Stationers' Register many years before publication or any definite, recorded performances. Furthermore, new plays were sometimes revised from old ones, such as *The Taming of the Shrew*. Independent-minded commentators such as Samuel Taylor Coleridge believed that *Cymbeline* was "a play written by the Master in his youth and re-written in his last theatrical years."[2] Geoffrey Bullough simply concluded that "The date of *Cymbeline* is uncertain."[3]

Over 30 years before Foreman's diary entry on December 28, 1578, the Lord Chamberlain's Men performed an anonymous, lost play at Richmond Palace titled *The History of the Crueltie of a Stepmother*. In Shakespeare's drama, the heroine Imogen is subjected to the cruelty of her stepmother, who is described as such by Cornelius (V.v.30–31); Oxfordian Eva Turner Clark postulated that the work performed at Richmond was a primitive version of *Cymbeline*.[4] In fact, *Crueltie of a Stepmother* belongs to a rather large group of lost, anonymous court dramas from that period having titles with strong Shakespearean overtones. Furthermore, in 1578 the Lord Chamberlain was Thomas Radcliffe, Earl of Sussex and mentor to Edward de Vere. De Vere concurrently was engaged in a wide variety of literary and dramatic activities following his return from Italy in 1576.[5]

Like Shakespeare's other late romances, *Cymbeline* draws upon a dizzying array of source material. The primary source for the main plot comes from Boccaccio's *Decameron*,[6] also a main source for *All's Well That Ends Well*, but this portion not translated into English until long after Shakespeare's time. Sensible Bardolators of all authorship persuasions agree that Shakespeare the writer was capable to some degree of reading Italian, and it is documented that de Vere spoke Italian, owned Italian books, and was satirized as an Italianate Englishman. Furthermore, Boccaccio belonged to the library of Lord Burghley, de Vere's guardian and later father-in-law.[7] Another Italian book recognized as a minor source for the play is *Jerusalem Delivered* by Torquato Tasso, translated into English in 1600.[8] Although there are no documented direct connections between Tasso and de Vere, the latter was in Italy while Tasso was active, and he moved in the same Venetian environs. This included the church of Santa Maria Formosa, which faced the famed literary salon of Domenico Venier, frequented by Tasso and others.[9]

One of the play's many interesting facets is that *Cymbeline* takes an Italian Renaissance story (set in France, Italy, and the Middle East) and transports it to Roman Great Britain at the dawn of the Christian era. A few basic facts are taken from Holinshed's *Chronicles*, but Boccaccio's plot remains, and this in turn had very ancient origins.[10] Regarding the story of a husband who wagers on his wife's fidelity and is tricked into believing that he has lost, Edmund Chambers noted, "The wager theme is widespread in romantic literature."[11] Shakespeare cleverly appropriates this old Mediterranean tale for a British setting and allows the English armies to defeat the Roman legions in magnanimous fashion, but he still could not resist setting several of the scenes in Italy. Raphael Holinshed's multiple connections with de Vere are discussed in the history plays, but it is suggestive that the first edition of the *Chronicles* was published in 1577, one year before *Crueltie of a Stepmother* was performed at court.[12]

As to Shakespeare's subplot of a cruel stepmother, the waters appear far murkier. Geoffery Bullough remarked that this theme was commonplace as well but gave no specific examples save for *Snow White*, which he admitted had not been translated and was probably unknown in England at the time.[13] In addition, the device of a wicked stepmother's son (Cloten in the play) seeking the hand of an unwilling heroine appears to be the Bard's own invention. It is of course possible that the mysterious play *Crueltie of a Stepmother* may have provided material. Shakespeare went to the trouble of eliminating the villain Jachimo's desire to possess Imogen[14]—which is inherent in the sources—and transfers this desire to the repugnant Cloten, just as he did the same with the characters of Iago and Rodrigo in *Othello*. Jachimo and Iago are close relatives, dramatically speaking, both using appearances to deceive their victims.

Space does not permit a comprehensive source listing for *Cymbeline*, but a few are especially noteworthy. *Certaine Tragicall Discourses of Bandello*,[15] translated into English in 1567 by Geoffrey Fenton, has been recognized for its similarities with Shakespeare's escape-to-the-wilderness theme.[16] Fenton (also a character name in *The Merry Wives of Windsor*) was a writer connected with the de Vere household, dedicating his 1575 *Golden Epistles* to Oxford's wife, Anne Cecil.[17] Furthermore, Belarius—the name of the banished lord living in the Welsh mountains—is thought to have derived from the 1588 novel titled *Pandosto* by Robert Greene.[18] Greene was another author associated with de Vere, elaborately dedicating his *Gwydonius* or *The Card of Fancy* to the 17th Earl in 1584.[19] Other minor details, such as the sleeping potion used by Imogen, are viewed as being adapted from William Adlington's English translation of *The Golden Ass* by Apuleius,[20] a work dedicated in 1566 to the same Thomas Radcliffe who was de Vere's mentor and Lord Chamberlain of the acting company that later produced *Crueltie of a Stepmother* at court.[21] While it cannot be proven that de Vere had documented connections to every single book that may have influenced the creation of *Cymbeline*, we continue to search in vain for any such affiliations with Will Shakspere.

Another minor influence on *Cymbeline* that underscores this entire problem is the Thomas Underdowne translation of *An Aethiopian Historie* by Heliodorus, first published in 1569 and verbosely dedicated to the 19-year-old Edward de Vere, who not for the first or last time in his career was repeatedly praised for being accomplished in the humanities.[22] J.M. Nosworthy, editor of the *Arden Shakespeare* edition, was among critics who recognized the influence of this book on Shakespeare's play, particularly the vision sequence of Posthumous in Act V, scene iv.[23] Others have tried to deflect these similarities by announcing that Shakespeare did not write his plays entirely (a remarkable admission!), and that the vision sequence in *Cymbeline* is one such example. On this point, we tend to side with Bullough, who wrote that "Shakespeare's prophets and ghosts often speak mediocre verse, and although the ghosts here are more banal than usual I see no reason to bring in another playwright."[24] This does not prove de Vere was Shakespeare; on the other hand, how many books did Thomas Underdowne dedicate to Will Shakspere? For that matter, how many commendatory verses did Will Shakspere receive at all?[25]

Last but not least, there is Ovid's *Metamorphoses*, which Jachimo observes Imogen reading in the crucial bedchamber scene (II.ii.45–46).[26] In addition to the first English translation of Ovid being completed by de Vere's uncle Arthur Golding in 1567,[27] the previous year at Oxford University the young earl had himself received a poetic tribute from George Coryate as one who attracted "the love of the muses in such great measure...."[28] Perhaps by coincidence, Book V of the *Metamorphoses* tells of the dramatic meeting between Minerva and the Muses on Mount Helicon; thus within the space of a few months we have the Roman spear-shaker goddess and de Vere both associated with the Muses in print. This was also about the same time that Raphael Holinshed, author of the *Chronicles* that provide the setting for *Cymbeline*, was sitting on a jury that would absolve de Vere of a murder charge.[29]

Parallels between the multiple plots of *Cymbeline* and de Vere's biography are too numerous to list; however, a short sampling followed by a few close-ups may give an inkling of their extensiveness. Like Cymbeline, de Vere had two sons, one legitimate, Henry de Vere, by his second wife, Elizabeth Trentham, and one illegitimate, Sir Edward Vere, by his mistress Anne Vavasor.[30] Although Henry de Vere was still a teenager at the time of his father's death, Edward Vere had already begun to establish a military reputation in the family tradition, similar to Guiderius and Arviragus in the play. The historical Cymbeline (Cunobelinus) had his capital at Colchester in Essex, not far from Castle Hedingham where de Vere was born[31] and closer still to his "countrye Muses" house at Wivenhoe.[32] Like Posthumous, de Vere traveled far afield to France and Italy, and Shakespeare refers to Jachimo as "Sienna's brother" (IV.ii.341), that is, the brother of the Duke of Siena.

This was a city from which de Vere wrote one of his well-known letters. Posthumous is tricked into believing his wife has been unfaithful, just as de Vere notoriously appears to have been—a theme so near and dear to the Bard—and has a vision (V.iv) of his dead parents and brothers. De Vere showed a strong interest in the occult and is reported to have had nightmare visions of his dead mother, who prophesied the future to him.[33]

The dastardly Jachimo, to repeat, appears to be another incarnation of Iago, who in turn greatly resembles a composite of de Vere's disreputable, Machiavellian retainer Rowland Yorke and de Vere's dissembling first cousin, the Catholic sympathizer Henry Howard. Yorke was at de Vere's side when he broke with his wife Anne Cecil in 1576 and probably contributed to this separation, with Howard acting as a destructive go-between.[34] The moral to the story in Shakespeare's source Boccaccio is that deceivers often wind up at the mercy of those whom they deceive, and such was the case with Henry Howard. After a sensational and scandalous series of countercharges involving treason and immorality in 1580–1581 between de Vere and his adversaries, Howard was let off easy in that he was merely imprisoned and later released.[35] Later he was restored to royal favor (particularly during the Jacobean era), just as Jachimo is forgiven by Posthumous in the play (V.v.418–419), a detail not found in Boccaccio.

By far the most striking parallels, however, are found with respect to de Vere's daughter Bridget, her suitors, and her marriage. We begin by noting that Bridget Vere, like her sisters and most Elizabethan noblewomen, had marriage negotiated for her by elders when she was a young teenager. At age 13, under the guardianship of her grandfather Lord Burghley and uncle Robert Cecil, she was betrothed to Henry Brooke, the new Lord Cobham and very wealthy Warden of Cinque Ports, whose Puritan ancestor Sir John Oldcastle had been so mercilessly satirized by Shakespeare as Sir John Falstaff. Robert Cecil had earlier married Brooke's sister, and events appeared to be moving toward an even closer alliance between these families (whose common enemy was the Earl of Essex) when the engagement was suddenly called off.[36] Brooke later married that same year but was abandoned by his wife in 1603 when he was caught up in a plot against the new King James, spending the remainder of his life in prison. Brooke's contemporaries went on record to describe him as a fool[37]; it seems that Bridget Vere dodged a bullet by not marrying him.

In Cymbeline, the unwelcome suitor of Imogen, Cloten, is repeated described by his peers as a fool (I.ii.21, 24 and IV.ii.112, 116). After Cloten is beheaded, Imogen's brother Guiderius coolly remarks that "Not Hercules / Could have knock'd out his brains, for he had none" (IV.ii.113–114). Even Cloten's love song, "Hark, hark, the lark at heaven's gate sings, and Phoebus gins arise" (II.iii.20–21) is possibly the most ridiculous warbling ever set for male voice (more fit for a soprano) and comes off more as a parody. Then again, Puritans such as Brooke were not known for their appreciation of music. By way of contrast, the dirge-duet of Guiderius and Aviragus, "Fear no more the heat o' the sun" (IV.ii.258) is one of the Bard's most profound song lyrics. Although there is no proof, we would wager good money that the sons of Edward de Vere had more musical appreciation than did Lord Cobham. As for Brooke's mother, Frances Newton Brooke,[38] Lady Cobham, little is known of her; however, this would make an intriguing topic for further study.

Following unsuccessful marriage negotiations with the Herbert family,[39] Bridget Vere, at age 15, married Francis Norris, later to become Earl of Berkeley, in 1599. In Cymbeline,

Imogen tries to placate her angry father by telling him that "I chose an eagle, / And did avoid a puttock [kite]" (I.i.139–140). Cymbeline is not impressed: "Thou took'st a beggar" (I.i.141). *The Dictionary of National Biography* informs us that Francis Norris was "impetuous and quarrelsome," at one point fighting a duel with his wife's first cousin, Peregrine Bertie,[40] and himself committing suicide in January 1623, shortly before the publication of the First Folio. This came after engaging in fisticuffs at Parliament and falling into disgrace as a result. Shakespeare's Posthumous is also impetuous, quick to believe his wife's infidelity and ordering her death, joining the Romans to fight against the Britons, and then striking Imogen in disguise as Fidele (V.v.228), before realizing that he himself needs forgiveness almost as much as Jachimo.

With respect to money, Norris did not inherit a title until the year after his wedding, upon the death of his grandfather in 1600. Before then, it is likely he lived on a slim budget since his father, William Norris, had died the year Francis was born, in 1579. Along these lines, Shakespeare chose the name Posthumous because the character's father Sicilius was "deceas'd as he [Posthumous] was born" (I.i.39–40). "Posthumous" normally suggests one born after a father's death, but the Latin word literally means "last"[41] and in Shakespeare's play it is unclear whether Sicilius literally predeceased the birth of his son. In the case of Francis Norris, his birthdate is recorded as July 6, 1579, while his father's death is reported to have occurred on Christmas Day of that same year. Thus William Norris outlived his son's birthday by approximately six and one-half months. Anecdote has it that William Norris accurately foretold his own death (more supernatural interest), which appears to have been sudden and unexpected, not unlike the death of the 17th Earl's own father when he was a child.[42] An alarmed de Vere may have seen a bit of himself in his short-fused, prospective son-in-law. Then again, perhaps he would have agreed with Imogen that an eagle is better than a kite.

✂ 16 ✄

Pericles

Pericles was entered with the Stationers' Register in 1608 and printed (by a different publisher)[1] in 1609, as having been written by William Shakespeare, but was not included in the First Folio of 1623. It found only gradual acceptance into the canon later in the 17th century, and was included in the Third Folio of 1664 (along with a number of believed spurious works). The first quarto of *Pericles* was also published the same year that two other controversial Shakespeare works were printed, *Troilus and Cressida* and the sonnets. The 1609 frontispiece advertised that the play had been produced by the King's Men at the Globe Theater,[2] but the date of the first performance is unknown. Although the first quarto claims that the play had been "much admired" and "sundry times acted,"[3] years later Ben Jonson would sneer at *Pericles* (without mentioning Shakespeare's name) as a "stale" and "mouldy tale," adding that audiences at public playhouses ("the common tub") applauded just about anything: "There, sweepings doe as well / As the best order'd meale."[4] This harshness (coming from the son of a bricklayer), while not totally undeserved, does disservice to an interesting work that becomes particularly fascinating when viewed through an Oxfordian lens.

Edmund Chambers began his analysis by stating the obvious: "In some form the play must have existed before Blount's registration entry of 20 May 1608."[5] He noted that two of the primary sources were John Gower's *Confessio Amantis* (possibly the 1554 edition)[6] and Laurence Twine's short novel titled *The Patterne of Paynfull Adventures* (1576), with the latter being adapted into yet another novel by George Wilkins, *The Painfull Adventures of Pericles Prince of Tyre*, published in 1608. The previous year (1607) also saw a new edition of Twine's work printed, and this flurry of activity led Chambers to the sensible surmise that "The reprinting of Twine's story in 1607 possibly dates the revival."[7] He then concluded:

> I incline to find a solution in the view that there was an earlier play, that a new version was written by Shakespeare and another, and that the novel [by Wilkins] was not the source of the play, but was put together by Wilkins, not directly from any dramatic text, but from reminiscences of both versions, with the help of a liberal resort to Twine.[8]

Thus not only was Gower viewed as the main source, Shakespeare was approaching the story secondhand from another unknown playwright who had adapted Gower.

Geoffrey Bullough more or less agreed that Gower and Twine were primary sources,[9] and that Shakespeare had probably undertaken to revise someone else's play:

> *Pericles* is probably a piece conceived, planned and perhaps written by someone else, which Shakespeare undertook to improve and did so perfunctorily (maybe in haste) except for the second half where the themes aroused his interest and so led him largely to rewrite and ... replace the original material.[10]

Bullough concluded that *Pericles* represented Shakespeare's "preliminary shot in a new romantic campaign" that would later come to full fruition in *The Winter's Tale* and *Cymbeline*, which deal with similar themes.[11] Given the play's reputation for uncertain dating and authorship, there is a surprising consensus that the Bard's role was that of a reviser,[12] including a large school of thought that Shakespeare mainly rewrote the last three acts of the play.[13] In general, *Pericles* is typically viewed as a Shakespearean fragment that was originally discarded but later readmitted back into the canon.

In the climactic finale to the play (V.iii), after being reunited with his long-lost (and presumed dead) daughter Marina, Pericles is then restored to his wife Thaisa, whom he also believed to be dead. This is similar to the reunion of Egeon and Aemilia in *The Comedy of Errors*, and for this aspect of the story Shakespeare drew upon the ancient tale relating to Apollonius of Tyre, as retold by Gower, Twine and others.[14] Although John Gower and Edward de Vere were together praised as great writers in *The Arte of English Poesie* (1589), there have been no definite connections made between de Vere and the works of Gower, who appears as the Chorus in *Pericles*. This is a rather unique situation in the canon, since almost every other major source either was dedicated to de Vere or his family, was written by one his relatives or servants, was accessible through the private libraries of his guardian or tutor, or was personally owned by him. We note that documented connections between any of these books and Will Shakspere is nil. As for de Vere's limited connections with Gower, scholars appear to agree that *Pericles* was not originally Shakespeare's play; therefore this is not necessarily surprising.

A connection between de Vere and Laurence Twine, on the other hand, is strongly suggested by the record. Laurence Twine and his brother Thomas graduated from Oxford University in 1564, two years before de Vere received his degree from the same institution. Moreover, both of the Twine brothers contributed to the 1573 translation of *The Breviary of Britain*, a book dedicated to de Vere and praising his interest in history, geography, and all learning in general. Thomas Twine also went on to study medicine at Cambridge, another de Vere alma mater.[15] This is the brother of the author whom Shakespeare saw fit to draw upon in his revision of the play, or at the very least, saw fit to allow intermingling with Gower's tale in the original draft.

In changing the name of the title character from Apollonius to Pericles, orthodox scholars agree that Shakespeare drew upon the tale of Pyrocles from Philip Sidney's *Arcadia*, first published in 1590.[16] Before his death in 1586, Sidney's career had intersected with that of de Vere's as an opponent in almost everything—not the least of which was poetic style and philosophy. Much later (in 1605) the Vere-Cecil and Sidney-Herbert families decided to bury the hatchet and intermarry, with Sidney's nephew Philip Herbert[17] marrying de Vere's youngest daughter Susan. This alliance between former rival clans may have been partially influenced by the gradually rising tide of Puritan political opposition to the monarchy and peerage. In any event, the match was certainly encouraged by King James, and there can be no doubt that, at the very least, de Vere would have kept tabs on the posthumous literary productions of his famous and former literary competitor. One thing that Bardolators of all authorship persuasions can agree upon is that Sidney influenced Shakespeare, and in the case of de Vere, there are a number of direct connections, whereas with Will Shakspere there are none.

The first two acts of *Pericles* can easily be seen as a sentimentalized portrait of the young Edward de Vere. For starters, de Vere—like Pericles in the play—was a jousting champion, winning tournaments in 1571 and 1581 (twice), plus delivering an unanswered challenge in Palermo, Sicily,[18] and according to a 17th-century Neapolitan *tirata*, making a cameo appearance on stage as a jouster.[19] The first of these victories, in 1571, was immediately proceded by de Vere's wedding to Anne Cecil, just as Pericles marries Thaisa shortly after winning the tournament prize in the play. Like the title character, de Vere was known for his wanderlust and traveled far and wide (though not to the eastern Hellenic world where the play is set). Like Pericles' daughter Marina (IV.i)—and like Hamlet—de Vere had at least one encounter with pirates during his travels.[20]

Pericles, while revealing his identity in Act II, states that his education has been "in arts and arms" (II.iv.82)—note the order—and gains attention for his skills in the performing arts, as well as jousting. Thaisa's father King Simonides declares Pericles a "music master" (II.v.36) and "the best" (II.iv.108) for dancing. Nor is Pericles' passion for music superficial; later, when reunited with Marina, he ecstatically praises "The music of the spheres!" (V.ii.229), as alarmed bystanders (who hear nothing) try to humor him. Like Castiglione's model courtier, Pericles is highly accomplished in both soldiering and the humanities.

De Vere not only helped to sponsor a Latin translation of Castiglione's book in 1572, but took its lessons seriously as well, for he was noted both as a musician and dancer at court. In 1599, composer John Farmer's *First Set of English Madrigals* was dedicated to de Vere with unsparing praise for his musical talent.[21] De Vere patronized other musicians as well, and was once a landlord to the composer William Byrd, whose popularly attributed piece titled *My Lord of Oxenforde's Maske* makes another reference to the 17th Earl's theatrical involvement.[22] De Vere was also praised as a dancer; it was remarked that Queen Elizabeth, widely admired for her own skills, delighted in him as a partner.[23] One may argue whether de Vere was the true Bard, but there can be no argument that he was committed to the performing arts (like Shakespeare's Pericles) and may have even provided some inspiration for Shakespeare's title character. For Will Shakspere, there is nothing to indicate that he had the slightest interest in music or dancing—or jousting, for that matter.

In *Pericles*, the antitheses to the evil King Antiochus and his daughter (from whom Pericles flees) are King Simonides and Thaisa, both presented as virtuous and innocent victims of fate. Once again, parallels with de Vere's life are evident. In the play, Pericles marries Thaisa, they have a daughter, and then he is quickly separated from both. In real life, de Vere married Anne Cecil, she bore him a daughter (Elizabeth Vere), and then they were separated—but at his own instigation, with de Vere alleging (by implication) that the infant was not in fact his daughter. Five years later there was a reconciliation with de Vere acknowledging paternity, but then Anne Cecil died in 1588, leaving de Vere with three daughters and (most likely) a degree of acrimony among his Cecil in-laws. Upon his reunion with Thaisa, Pericles expresses both joy and a kind of remorse: "O, come, be buried a second time within these arms" (V.iii.93). De Vere, whatever his faults may have been, could easily have known such feelings based on personal experience. Once again, we must query whether the author or authors of this play had de Vere's biography in mind.

In 1595, Elizabeth Vere married the wealthy William Stanley, Earl of Derby. Stanley, like his father-in-law de Vere, has been proposed as the true Bard, first tentatively during the 19th century and then more forcibly in Professor Abel Lefranc's 1918 book, *Sous le Masque de Shakespeare* ("Behind the Mask of Shakespeare") and Georges Lambin's 1962 work, *Voyages de Shakespeare en France et en Italie* ("The Voyages of Shakespeare in France and Italy").[24] Among other connections, Stanley was known to have traveled far and wide, including the eastern Mediterranean world that is the setting for *Pericles*. Like de Vere, Stanley was noted by contemporaries as a playwright but left no examples of his work under his own name. In 1599, four years after his marriage to Elizabeth, correspondence by the Jesuit agent George Fenner indicated that Stanley—who was a potential rallying point for English Catholics—was only busy writing plays for "the common players."[25] An interesting tidbit concerns a portable writing desk that de Vere apparently owned and left at the Stanley residence on Canon Row during a 1596 visit.[26] There are many Bardolators today who wish they could see that piece of furniture.

It is tempting to identify Shakespeare's Marina in *Pericles* with Elizabeth Vere, and Marina's future husband Lysimachus with William Stanley. During the second of the infamous brothel scenes in Act IV, Lysimachus "rescues" Marina (who is fending off would-be customers) by giving her money to buy her way out. She promptly recruits the help of Boult for this purpose, after admonishing his lack of moral values: "For what thou professest, a baboon, could he speak, would own a name too dear" (IV.vi.178–179). If one adopts a Vere-Stanley interpretation, all of this resonates since Stanley was known more for achieving his ends through wealth and brains rather than use of force—in contrast to, say, his hot-headed, jousting champion of a father-in-law.

By now it should be obvious that we are suggesting a scenario in which Shakespeare's *Pericles* may have been originally drafted into a performing version by William Stanley, attracted to Gower's characters by similarities to members of his own family. At some point, de Vere was then invited to revise, and did so up to a point, before disregarding the work and turning his attention to the superior merits of *The Winter's Tale*. Earlier, in 1594, an unpublished, anonymous play titled *A Winter's Night's Pastime* had been entered with the Stationers' Register,[27] and this may have been an earlier attempt by de Vere to address the same themes. If in fact this was the original version of *The Winter's Tale*, then these particular themes were better suited to de Vere's own personal story, incorporating the follies and guilt of King Leontes, as well as the suffering caused by his separation from wife and daughter. The material of *Pericles* may have thus been abandoned because it failed to fully satisfy the artistic needs of Shakespeare the writer.

PART TWO

ഈരു

HISTORIES

ഇ 17 ശ

King John

Shakespeare's *King John* did not appear in print until the First Folio. Francis Meres listed the play among Shakespeare's works in 1598,[1] but this is the only definite reference before 1623. Edmund Chambers wrote that "There is practically no external evidence to fix the date of the play before its mention by Meres in 1598."[2] Geoffrey Bullough concurred: "The date of composition is hard to decide."[3] Herschel Baker, in his *Riverside* introduction, concluded, "The date of *King John* ... is difficult to fix."[4] We agree with these traditional viewpoints.

Another point of agreement is that Shakespeare's primary source was an earlier anonymous play titled *The Troublesome Raigne of King John*, published in 1591, reprinted in 1611 (as written by "W. Sh."), and then again in 1622 (one year before the First Folio) under the name "W. Shakespeare."[5] Herschel Baker firmly concluded, "That *The Troublesome Reign* and *King John* are somehow intimately related is not open to dispute." Dover Wilson went even further by stating that the earlier play was Shakespeare's *only* source.[6] Edmund Chambers, representing the majority view, opined that "Shakespeare must have kept the old book before him."[7] We see no reason to disagree with any of this, but would add that the playwright probably had his *own* book in front of him. Curiously, among the traditionalists, one is hard-pressed to find anyone who believes that the young Will Shakspere was the author of *Troublesome Raigne*, even though it was expressly attributed to him in two later quarto publications.[8] The idea of Shakespeare revising his own works goes against the popular image of the Bard as a purely spontaneous genius, although multiple quartos universally credited to him clearly demonstrate that these plays had several different performing versions.

It is also generally agreed that both *King John* and *Troublesome Raigne* have their roots in a 1538 drama by John Bale titled *King Johan*, one of the very earliest English history plays.[9] This "violently anti–Catholic"[10] work was revised in 1561, probably for a special command performance before the queen. During that same year, Elizabeth visited Castle Hedingham in Essex,[11] home of the 11-year-old Edward de Vere and his father John, the 16th Earl of Oxford. While there is no evidence as to what entertainment was given at Hedingham for that occasion, it is known that John de Vere was a major patron for John Bale throughout his career.[12] The 17th Earl would continue the Vere family tradition of patronage toward dramatists, in addition to being himself a noted playwright. It would be some 30 years after these events that Shakespeare's anonymous source was published. Bullough noted that

> In *The Raigne* the author's purpose was to modernize Bale's presentation of John as a
> pre–Reformation opponent of Church abuses and papal power and to use him as a mir-
> ror in which all would see the dangers of domestic dissension and foreign
> interference....[13]

Shakespeare's later version would be along these same lines.

The frontispiece for *Troublesome Raigne* noted that it had been performed by the Queen's Men acting company,[14] formed in 1583 and then later disbanded in 1588.[15] This was the crucial historical period preceding the Spanish Armada that also saw a major Puritan offensive against the public playhouses. Concurrently, de Vere sponsored his own acting companies and there was in fact some overlap in personnel between Oxford's Men and the Queen's Men.[16] At approximately the same time, Will Shakspere is believed to have migrated to London from Stratford-upon-Avon, following visits to Stratford by these groups of players.

The composition of *Troublesome Raigne* (presumably during the late 1580s) probably owed something to the second edition of Holinshed's *Chronicles*, published in 1587.[17] This is generally considered a direct or indirect source for all of the history plays. The previous year (in 1586), de Vere had been awarded his prodigious lifetime annuity of £1,000 by the crown.[18] Oxfordians believe this was an attempt by Elizabeth to channel and transform de Vere's theatrical activities into public propaganda that would help unify the English people in the face of the Spanish onslaught. Even assuming de Vere was not Shakespeare, this would seem to be a reasonable explanation (as opposed to a mere maintenance allowance for his earldom), especially given the queen's notorious disinclination toward handouts.

Shakespeare's play deals primarily with the latter reign of King John, who ascended the English throne upon the death of his brother Richard I (surnamed the "Lion-Hearted") in 1199, and who died in 1216. In terms of the chronological events portrayed, *King John* is therefore the earliest of Shakespeare's English history plays. This was a period in which England was being racked by internal disputes while simultaneously being threatened from papal-sanctioned foreign (French) invasion. These were timely themes for the English in the 1580s.[19] King John cuts to the chase when he proclaims "No Italian priest shall tithe or toll in our dominions" (III.i.153–154). Faulconbridge, in the closing speech of the play, sums it all up by declaring, "This England never did, nor never shall, lie at the proud foot of a conqueror" (V.vii.112–113)—an interesting statement coming from the playwright. Aside from earlier Roman and Saxon conquests, anyone with a passing interest in history knows that England was ruthlessly and permanently conquered by William of Normandy in 1066, during the century prior to events depicted in the play. Of course, if Shakespeare the writer was of Norman descent, then the sweeping boast of Faulconbridge would have some merit.[20] We know little or nothing of Will Shakspere's ancestry before the early 16th century, although there is a wonderful anecdote that he once referred to himself as William the Conqueror after stealing an assignation from fellow actor Richard Burbage.[21] Edward de Vere, on the other hand, was descended from one of the oldest and most illustrious Norman families in England, and the family seat at Castle Hedingham was (and still is today) a famous Norman fortress in East Anglia.

Some commentators, desperate to find links between Shakespeare's storylines and the traditional biography, have suggested that the death of the young Arthur in Act IV and the grief of his mother Constance may have found inspiration from the tragic demise of the 11-year-old Hamnet Shakspere in 1596. Constance, in anticipation of Arthur's death, despairs that "Grief fills the room up of my absent child" (III.iv.93). Later, Arthur's dying words "Heaven take my soul, and England keep my bones!" (IV.iii.10) could well express the sentiments of any patriotic Englishman. Other orthodox commentators, such as Herschel Baker, have been less impressed: "attempts to fix a date from alleged topical allusions ... to the death of Shakespeare's son Hamnet (1596) in Constance's laments for Arthur do not impart conviction."[22] In either event, de Vere could have laid claim to the same kind of grief, losing an only son in 1583.[23] This same period (the early 1580s) was pivotal in the history of English drama, with both de Vere and Will Shakspere moving toward some kind of collision course as touring actors swept through Stratford-upon-Avon. This was about the same time de Vere tried to piece his life back together after the personal upheavals of 1580–1581.

Much of Tudor society had embraced the new public playhouses with gusto, thereby providing impetus for conversion of English drama from private courtly entertainment for the privileged few to public propaganda for the masses. This effort was naturally spearheaded by the nobility, but in partnership with ambitious commoners such as the Burbages. Suffice it to say, if not for the patronage and protection of the nobility and crown, Elizabethan theater would never have been born, let alone survived. De Vere's prominent role in this process may have been formalized with his enormous and otherwise inexplicable annuity grant. Shakespeare's plays, especially the histories, would have certainly been viewed by Elizabeth (and later James) as propaganda. Indeed, to forget this aspect of the canon is to lose much of its meaning. Even the comedies and tragedies, when not diverting the rabble's attention away from their hard and uncertain lives, reinforced the superiority of the nobility and justified hereditary rights of authority. Shakespeare's works, in the political sense, were the Tudor and Stuart version of (to borrow Walter Lippmann's phrase) "manufacturing consent" among the English people. To facilitate this, the voice of "Shakespeare" could have been easily assigned to a member of the target audience.

This is P.R. 101, and a good analogy is the modern-day newspaper, such as the *Chicago Tribune*, which derives its name from the tribunes of ancient Rome who protected the plebian rights against the land-holding aristocracy (or "patricians"); hence "tribune" connotes "voice of the people." Never mind the *Chicago Tribune* is a huge corporation whose shareholders are mostly wealthy individuals; yet the paper is not called the "Chicago Patrician" but rather the "Chicago *Tribune*," suggesting that it represents the common interest above all. In a similar fashion, by attributing Shakespeare's works to Will Shakspere, the sponsors of the First Folio may have side-stepped the political stigma that most Jacobean readers would have attached to high-ranking authorship.

The ambitious and energetic Will Shakspere would have been a good candidate for this assignment: a provincial, possibly semi-literate actor with a middle-class background, and a name that approximated the designated pseudonym. He was also not a Puritan—perhaps even a Catholic sympathizer fleeing an unhappy Puritan marriage, eager to do almost anything as an agent-employee of the nobility to achieve financial security and respectability. Shakspere's death in 1616 made him an even better candidate; by 1623 he was a deceased Warwickshire "gentleman" with connections to the London theater world, unable to say or do anything to contradict the intentions of his former benefactors. Ben Jonson was also an excellent choice to write and edit the First Folio introduction: son of a bricklayer, Anglican convert from Catholicism, and associate of everyone involved.

Returning to de Vere's personal connections with the events dramatized in *King John*, his direct ancestor Robert de Vere, the Third Earl of Oxford, was a contemporary of John (as was Robert's brother Aubrey, the Second Earl). In fact, Robert de Vere was one of the 25 noblemen who in 1215 forced the king to sign the Magna Carta, thereby restricting his royal prerogatives. Soon afterward, in retaliation, John declared war against the barons, who in turn appealed to France for help. The French invasion and John's struggle against it during the last year of his life essentially form the backdrop of Shakespeare's play; yet there is no mention whatsoever of the Magna Carta,[24] nor of Robert de Vere. These glaring omissions could be interpreted simply as the author trying to avoid trouble with his noble patrons, who (in the 16th century) were probably less enamored of the Magna Carta than modern-day Americans. On the other hand, portraying the deposition of an anointed monarch in *Richard II* or taking a swipe at King James' Scottish ancestors in *Macbeth* were no problem for the Bard.[25]

It may be significant that Castle Hedingham (de Vere's ancestral home) was among the fortresses reclaimed by John as he fought back against his rebellious barons and their French allies.[26] Add to this the 16th Earl's patronage of John Bale, author of *King Johan* (rewritten and performed for Elizabeth in 1561 as she toured the region), and there seems little room for doubt that de Vere would have been intimately familiar with this dramatic tradition and the historical events behind it. As for the absence of Robert de Vere in the play, either the author was uncharacteristically worried about offending the 17th Earl, or alternatively, he wanted to erase the memory of someone (an ancestor?) who opposed the English monarchy at a time of crisis—a man perhaps viewed as a divider rather than a uniter.

By contrast, Philip (a.k.a. Richard) Faulconbridge, the dashing bastard son of John's predecessor Richard I, is a rallying point for everyone. His soliloquy at the end of Act II, beginning "Mad world, mad kings, mad composition!" (II.i.561) is probably the best-known speech in *King John* and expresses one of the great epiphanies in Shakespeare's history plays. After John and the French conclude an ignoble treaty, Faulconbridge cynically observes, "That smooth-fac'd gentleman, tickling Commodity, Commodity the bias of the world" (II.i.573–574). This "Commodity" or self-interest is viewed as a threat to England's national unity so urgently needed to fend off foreign invaders. Taking his cue from corrupt leaders, Faulconbridge promises that "Since kings break faith upon commodity, Gain be my lord, for I will worship thee" (II.i.597–598). By the end of the play, though, it is Faulconbridge who is the true patriot and man of action who saves the day, rather than the unscrupulous king.

Like the bastard Edmund in *King Lear*, Faulconbridge is one of the Bard's more notable creations.[27] Aside from Shakespeare's disconcertingly prolific use of the word "bastard" in the canon, both Faulconbridge and Edmund reflect the author's preoccupation (or obsession?) with legitimacy of birth.[28] Edward de Vere, aside from having at least one illegitimate son (Sir Edward Vere), and harboring doubts as to whether his eldest daughter (Elizabeth Vere) really belonged to him, was himself accused of illegitimacy when he was 13 years old.[29] Eventually, de Vere's birthright was confirmed, but scars must have remained. When the queen, herself having firsthand experience in these matters, report-edly called him a bastard (in jest?), he privately swore never to forgive her.[30] It is not hard to imagine de Vere having a defiant attitude toward his own alleged bastardy and being more concerned with the inherent nobility of his own genes—like Faulconbridge in the play, who explicitly wants to be known as the son of Richard the Lion-Hearted, legitimate or not. As for Will Shakspere, nothing is known whether he ever had to struggle with issues of this kind. One might argue that in Elizabethan England everyone had to be con-cerned with birth, title, and class (especially an ambitious social climber like Will Shakspere); on the other hand, Shakespeare the writer seemed unconcerned with per-sonal, economic upward mobility, but was apparently mesmerized by an assumed and intrinsic superiority of breeding. Faulconbridge and Edmund, whether doing good or evil for personal gain, are not exactly underprivileged to begin with.

On a more subconscious level, the entire play seems to be heavily concerned with issues of personal identity.[31] Faulconbridge, despite his ignoble birth, has a glorious pedi-gree and emerges as the true hero of the story. John holds power as king, but has a weak claim to the throne and even weaker ethics to justify it. His nephew Arthur has a good, legitimate claim, but is in reality a powerless boy whose insufferable mother Constance cannot save him from a pointless death. Concerns about personal identity are not what one would expect from the traditional Shakespeare during the 1590s (by then London's most popular and successful poet-playwright) unless success bred doubts. If "William Shakespeare," however, was a pseudonym for an identity-insecure Edward de Vere, then these issues begin to take on profound and subtle overtones that go beyond the rah-rah nationalism on the surface of the play. Thus, if we elect to take the Oxfordian theory seri-ously, *King John* holds great interest despite its flawed reputation among Bardolators in general.

❧ 18 ❧

Richard II

The Tragedie of King Richard the Second was first published in a 1597 quarto with the subheading: "As it hath been publikely acted by the right Honorable the Lorde Chamber-laine his Servants." This anonymous work made no mention of the author. The follow-ing year (1598), the second quarto appeared, adding that the play was "By William Shake-speare."[1] Incidentally, 1598 is the first year that Shakespeare's name was printed as a playwright,[2] although anonymous quartos had been published since 1594. Both the first and second quartos of Richard II sport a frontispiece logo depicting a man or boy with his left arm weighed down by a ball and chain, and his right arm (with wings) reaching toward heaven. In the background, God is seen beckoning from a cloud. This image is appropriate for the drama, because Richard's last words (as he is murdered by assassins) are "Mount, mount, my soul! Thy seat is up on high, whilst my gross flesh sinks down-ward, here to die" (V.v.111–112).

At age 23, Edward de Vere had written similar words: "virtue yet will ever abide with us, and when our bodies fall into the bowels of the earth, yet that shall mount with our minds into the highest Heavens."[3] Thus both de Vere and Shakespeare (24 years later) use the poetic image of mounting a steed to describe the ascent to heaven from death. The de Vere quote is taken from his introduction to the Thomas Bedingfield English translation of De Consolatione by Girolamo Cardano, better known as Cardanus Comforte. This earlier work has been cited by orthodox scholars as the book Hamlet carries as he feigns madness to Polonius, since it contains ideas similar to those expressed in the "To be, or not to be..." speech. It has been further noted that Hamlet and King Richard have many verbal similarities as characters.[4] Would that we had anything even rumored to have been written by Will Shakspere when he was 23 years old, let alone something that was similar to the canon.

Although both quartos refer to public performances by the Lord Chamberlain's Men, the first known production of Richard II was a private one, reportedly occurring on Decem-ber 9, 1595, at the Canon Row house of Edward Hoby. Robert Cecil, son of Lord Burgh-ley and a personage of growing importance in his own right, was invited for the occasion.[5] Down the street on Canon Row lived Cecil's niece Elizabeth Vere Stanley (de Vere's eld-est daughter), who earlier that same year had married William Stanley, Earl of Derby. Within months of this union, however, rumors of Elizabeth Vere's marital unfaithfulness began to surface, particularly in connection with another prominent figure at court, Robert Devereux, Earl of Essex. At the same time, de Vere (who had been spending time at Canon

Row with his daughter and new son-in-law) revealed in a letter to Burghley that he had received "diverse injuries and wrongs" from Devereux.[6] Such were the events leading up to the first conjectured performance of *Richard II*. The year 1595 is also when most scholars believe the play was written.[7]

The de Vere–Devereux feud is fascinating because Shakespeare's play will forever be associated with the Essex Rebellion of 1601, an abortive attempt by Devereux to take over the government. Devereux, after many years of favoritism from the queen, resorted to this rash act of desperation after a series of military and financial disasters that were mostly his own fault. Concurrent with the uprising, Essex and his followers arranged to have *Richard II* repeatedly performed at the Globe Theater and elsewhere in London, depicting as it does the overthrow of an anointed English monarch.[8] After the rebellion was suppressed and Devereux executed, the queen, when later reminded of these performances, angrily remarked, "I am Richard II, know ye not that?"[9] De Vere led the jury of peers who found Devereux guilty of treason.[10]

Among Devereux's followers was the 28-year-old Henry Wriothesley, Earl of Southampton, who in 1593–1594 had been the conspicuous dedicatee of Shakespeare's first two published works (as well as, many believe, the "Fair Youth" of the sonnets), and whom almost all commentators agree was close to Shakespeare the writer. Wriothesley had, a few years earlier, been engaged (by his guardian, Lord Burghley) to Elizabeth Vere, and later during the Jacobean era, became a close political ally of de Vere's son, the 18th Earl of Oxford.[11] Wriothesley, unlike his mentor Devereux, was spared execution and sentenced to life in the Tower of London. More than one commentator has been surprised by Shakespeare not being called to account or even mentioned in these legal proceedings, despite his presumed personal connections to Wriothesley, and his play's high profile during the rebellion. Although Augustine Phillips was summoned to explain the circumstances under which these performances had taken place—they had been well-paid to produce an "old play," he said[12]—there seems to have been a distinct presumption that Shakespeare the writer was innocent of any sinister intent. This is in stark contrast to the case of John Hayward, who was imprisoned at about the same time for dedicating a work to Devereux on nearly identical subject matter, *The First Part of the Life and Reign of King Henry IV*.[13] Shakespeare, it seems, was not merely untouchable, but aloof as well. Was he given special license because he was universally loved? The Puritans certainly did not love him, and they controlled Parliament. In any event, one would here (as in other places) expect the Bard to have at least shown his face, but once again we are disappointed.

Shakespeare's primary source for the play appears to have been the second (1587) edition of Holinshed's *Chronicles*, since Act II, scene iv, uses a line (8) not found in the original 1577 publication.[14] The second edition of Holinshed was dedicated to William Brooke, Lord Cobham, whom we shall meet again in two sequel works, *Henry IV, Parts I and II* (see Chapters 19 and 20). As for numerous other historical documents that Shakespeare seems to have drawn upon, Dover Wilson made the prescient observation that the Bard more likely drew upon an earlier, lost play, written by someone who was "soaked" in English history.[15] Even assuming that de Vere was not Shakespeare the writer, could he have been this "someone"?

Both of Shakespeare's great historical tetralogies require a bit of genealogical background for non–English history buffs. Richard II was the younger son of the powerful

Edward III, who ruled England from 1327 to 1377. Edward's elder son and namesake was the "Black Prince" of Wales who inflicted such havoc on the French during the Hundred Years' War. The Black Prince, however, predeceased his father in 1376, leaving his younger brother Richard as heir to the throne. Richard was then eventually overthrown by his first cousin, Henry "Bullingbrook,"[16] son of King Edward's brother John of Gaunt, Duke of Lancaster.[17] *Richard II* begins with the characters pointing fingers at each other over who was to blame for the recent murder of King Richard's virtuous but outspoken uncle, Thomas of Woodstock.

As a side note, the turn of the 14th century was the age of Geoffrey Chaucer. A lavish cover illustration to an early 15th-century Cambridge manuscript of *Troilus and Cresyde* by Chaucer depicts the author in a lectern, surrounded by the royal court of Richard II.[18] Chaucer, who was patronized by three successive English monarchs,[19] was in many ways a model example of an artist who came from the merchant class and rose to prominence through his own genius, hard work, and the patronage of the nobility. The surprisingly numerous details known about his life include this exquisite contemporary representation, beautifully executed in color (this was before the invention of printing), dating immediately after the author's own epoch, in one of his own books, and advertising Chaucer as he performed in front of his noble patrons. Two centuries later, we find nothing remotely similar for William Shakespeare.

We do find in 1596,[20] however, the anonymous play titled *The Raigne of King Edward the Third* (now generally attributed to Shakespeare), being published in quarto. This engaging work covers the period before Richard came to the throne, and deals with the heroism of the Black Prince at the Battles of Crécy (1346) and Poitiers (1356), set against King Edward's personal struggle for self-mastery over his own sexual passions. In one of the more memorable scenes, the married King Edward dictates a love poem to his secretary Lodwick, addressed to the married Countess of Salisbury, with whom the king is smitten (Act II, scene i). Oxfordians, like many traditionalists, believe that secretarial dictation played a significant role in the creation of Shakespeare's works, and this scene may provide us with a glimpse into that process as King "Edward" (de Vere?) struggles to both find the right words and make sure his transcriber gets things correct.

Another anonymous play, attributed by some to Shakespeare, that touches upon historical events prior to King Richard's fall from power was *Thomas of Woodstock*. This mysterious work is a genuine prequel to *Richard II*, although it has been debated whether *Woodstock* is an authentic Elizabethan manuscript or a later forgery.[21] The story deals with events at the outset of Richard's reign leading up to the murder of his uncle. Taken as a group, *Edward III*, *Thomas of Woodstock*, and *Richard II* portray England's political descent from the golden age of the warrior-king Edward and his warrior-son, the Black Prince, to the decadence and corruption of Richard's government, thus setting the stage for the king's deposition by the more able and worthy Bolingbroke in 1399.

Shakespeare's license with historical facts has been well documented, and *Richard II* is no exception. Perhaps most noteworthy among these departures is Shakespeare's complete erasure of Edward de Vere's direct ancestor, Robert de Vere, Ninth Earl of Oxford. According to all accounts, Earl Robert was King Richard's best friend and worst influence, with some chroniclers accusing the two men of having (in the words of one) "obscene familiarity" with each another. Whatever the truth was, it is uncontested that Robert de

Vere's odious sway over the king was viewed censoriously by his peers and hastened Richard's political downfall. In spite of this, Shakespeare makes absolutely no mention of Robert de Vere in *Richard II*. One obvious explanation for this conspicuous absence is that Shakespeare did not want to offend the 17th Earl of Oxford. Depicting the overthrow of an anointed English monarch on the public stage was of course no problem. Oxfordians, on the other hand, believe that Edward de Vere, as the true author of the play, wanted to blot out the memory of his most infamous ancestor.

In place of Robert de Vere, Shakespeare substitutes as the king's favorites the effete and sycophantic trio of Bagot, Bushy, and Green. These three "caterpillars of the commonwealth" (II.iii.166) lead Richard astray in all things.[22] Alluding to this problem, the Duke of York complains to his brother Gaunt about the numerous, corrupting influences on the king, particularly Italian fashions of dress among the younger men, which is singled out as an example of frivolity and "apish" behavior (II.i.21–23). Earlier in 1580, precisely such criticism had been leveled against Edward de Vere. Gabriel Harvey's memorable caricature of an Italianate Englishman, universally acknowledged as de Vere, described him in vivid detail ("apish" is one word used) as an affected imitator of foreign fashions in dress. Harvey lampooned his subject as "a passing singular odde man" who spoke "valorous" words but performed "womanish" works.[23]

Richard II begins with Bolingbroke, the future Henry IV, eloquently challenging Thomas Mowbray, Duke of Norfolk, to trial by combat. By Shakespeare's time, however, jousting had become strictly a spectator sport, more entertainment than military exercise. De Vere's successful career as an athlete would have provided him invaluable experience in the arts of Elizabethan pageantry and showmanship. His three tournament victories in 1571 and 1581 (twice), along with his unanswered Palermo challenge in Sicily, established his reputation as a master of the tilt.[24] To accomplish this, de Vere would had to have been a crowd pleaser, comfortable with the rituals of heraldry and providing lavish costuming, along with dramatic visual spectacle. This included the writing of speeches for these events, one of which (from 1581) still survives.[25] In addition, a surviving Neapolitan *tirata* suggests that de Vere once did a cameo in a staged mock tournament.[26]

Much of the action in the play takes place at Windsor Castle. There are several engravings of de Vere in his hereditary role as Lord Great Chamberlain, including one depicting him as an escort for Queen Elizabeth at Windsor Castle in 1572.[27] This is about the same period he wrote the prefatory material for *Cardanus Comforte*. Obviously, de Vere's various ceremonial roles at court would have placed great emphasis on pomp and display—valuable skills for the accomplished stage dramatist that he was noted to have been.[28] Although it is not unreasonable to suppose Will Shakspere was familiar with Windsor Castle, or that he had witnessed jousting and other royal spectacles, there are no anecdotes (let alone evidence) suggesting this is the case.

De Vere's fall from the royal favor that he enjoyed earlier in his career was precipitous. By the 1590s he had gone from being the "glass of fashion and the mould of form"[29] to "disgrac'd, impeach'd, and baffled" (I.i.170) like Mowbray in *Richard II*. Mowbray's complaint "Take honor from me, and my life is done" (I.i.183) could well have applied to de Vere. Moreover, this dominant theme in the Shakespearean canon could have easily used de Vere's life as a cautionary tale. Few Elizabethans lost as much in public reputation and esteem as did Oxford and still managed to stay alive. De Vere's knack for survival, combined with his staggering £1,000 annuity,[30] suggest that his talents were considered valuable in ways that have yet to be sufficiently recognized by conventional history.

In another well-known passage, the imprisoned King Richard, shortly before he is murdered, reflects on his fate: "I'll give ... my large kingdom for a little grave, a little little grave, an obscure grave" (III.iii.147–154). The theme of obscure burial also appears in Shakespeare's sonnets and other works, as if the Bard worried that his identity would be unknown to future generations. This does not fit with the traditional biography, because the name William Shakespeare was well known in London by 1593, and his grave marker has surely become the world's most famous shrine of literary pilgrimage.[31] Shakespeare's concerns, however, tie in perfectly with the life of Edward de Vere, who was buried in the remote cemetery of St. Augustine's Church in Hackney, a suburb of London (Borough of Stratford),[32] and whose name has barely resurfaced over the last century. His physical monument, such as it was, has long since vanished and de Vere (as he probably foresaw) received an obscure burial similar to that of King Richard II. Oxford expressed similar concerns for literary endeavors in his prefatory epistle to *Cardanus Comforte*, writing that it would be wrong to "bury and insevill [i.e., entomb] your works in the grave of oblivion" and accordingly, he would "erect you such a monument [i.e., a book]."[33] Like the author of Shakespeare's sonnets, de Vere seems to have valued literary monuments more highly than other types of memorials.

❦ 19 ❧

Henry IV, Part I

In an era dominated by the Wars of Religion, it is somewhat surprising to the modern reader how infrequently (if ever) Shakespeare makes direct reference to these events. One may hypothesize that the Bard's popularity was partly due to this avoidance, since the overlap between religion and politics was (and still is) an inflammatory issue. Moreover, in an age of government censorship—there was no such thing as a free press—it would have been obviously dangerous to broach this topic. On the other hand, dramatic satire of both Papists and Puritans (performed for the personal amusement of Queen Elizabeth and King James, no less) is well documented. Thus it seems reasonable to suppose that Shakespeare did in fact address these concerns, but perhaps in a more subtle and indirect (if not oblique) manner.

One thing that most commentators can agree upon is that Shakespeare the writer achieved a high-water mark in his second great historical tetralogy with *Henry IV, Part I*. Both Edmund Chambers and Geoffrey Bullough believed the play to have been written around 1596. The first quarto appeared anonymously in 1598; however, that same year Francis Meres praises Shakespeare as the greatest English playwright and lists *Henry IV* as an example of his work. The following year (in 1599), a second quarto added that the play had been "Newly corrected by W. Shake-speare."[1] Also in 1599, the Globe Theater in London was constructed, despite fierce Puritan opposition to the public playhouses.

Before the Globe, London's original theater district was located north of the city limits in the neighborhood known as Shoreditch. It was here that the Burbage family built their first two outdoor playhouses during the late 1570s, the Theater and the Curtain.[2] It is likely that the *Henry IV* plays saw early public performances by the Lord Chamberlain's Men at these venues. Further to the south was the neighborhood of Eastcheap, legendary home to the Boar's Head Tavern that is the scene of so much nonsense and shenanigans in *Henry IV*.[3] De Vere's own company of players (Oxford's Men), toward the end of his life, in 1602, were among those granted special permission by the queen to perform at one of the several taverns in London then known as the Boar's Head.[4] The image of the boar also figures prominently in the Vere family coat of arms,[5] and the 17th Earl himself was compared unfavorably to a boar by his rival Christopher Hatton in a letter to the queen.[6] For most of his adult life, de Vere lived near or within these precincts, including the mid–1580s when he owned Fisher's Folly, a large house down Bishopsgate Street from the Burbage playhouses.[7] Immediately north of the Shoreditch neighborhood were suburban Stoke Newington and Hackney (Borough of Stratford), where de Vere spent the last years of his life in seclusion and retirement.[8]

Orthodox scholars generally agree that the second edition of Holinshed's *Chronicles* (1587) was the main source for Shakespeare.[9] This book is often viewed as a spark plug for the wave of English history plays that came afterward. For example, E.M.W. Tillyard wrote that "the publication of a second edition of Holinshed's Chronicle in 1587 did more to forward the growth of the English Chronicle Play than the defeat of the Spanish Armada in 1588."[10] On the other hand, one cannot rule out the possibility that the Bard drew upon the same sources as Holinshed.[11] The second edition was dedicated to William Brooke, Lord Cobham, who succeeded Henry Carey as Lord Chamberlain in 1596[12] and who figures prominently in the story of Shakespeare's Falstaff, as we shall see in *Henry IV, Part II*. As for Raphael Holinshed, he (like de Vere) had been attached to the household of Lord Burghley, to whom the first edition of the *Chronicles* had been dedicated in 1577.

Orthodox scholars also pretty much agree that another major source for Shakespeare was an anonymous history play titled *The Famous Victories of Henry the Fifth*. The first quarto of *Famous Victories* appeared in 1598 (the same year as the first quarto of *Henry IV, Part I*), but this play existed at least as early as 1594, because it is mentioned in Henslowe's diary. Geoffrey Bullough, among others, has suggested that *Famous Victories* may have been produced even earlier (before 1588), based on a reference made by the comedian Richard Tarlton, who died that same year.[13] Oxfordians tend to believe that *Famous Victories* was written by de Vere as an early draft for the same historical events covered by the *Henry IV* and *Henry V* plays.[14]

In reviewing the hundreds of parallels between Shakespeare's storylines and the biography of Edward de Vere, one must be cautious, if for no other reason than the universality of Shakespeare's themes can have some biographical resonance with almost anyone. In the case of *Henry IV, Part I*, however, there is an example so unique to de Vere's life that one must, at the very least, assume that Shakespeare the writer had the 17th Earl of Oxford in mind. In Act II, scene ii, Falstaff and his motley crew commit highway robbery at Gads Hill (between Gravesend and Rochester) before they are quickly in turn robbed by Prince Hal. This is the same location where in May of 1573, two of Lord Burghley's servants, William Faunt and John Wotton, were attacked by three of Oxford's men.[15] In a letter to Burghley, Faunt and Wotton complained that the instigator of the incident was none other than Burghley's own son-in-law, de Vere.[16] Some believe that the two victims had been caught spying on de Vere for their employer, an activity that Burghley was known to have initiated on more than one occasion, and in one instance with respect to his own son.[17] Burghley also complained at one point of his son-in-law's association with "lewd servants" who were socially beneath him (reminiscent of Prince Hal), and who presumably included the many actors and writers whom de Vere was known to have patronized.[18] In an interesting coincidence, Burghley died in 1598, the same year that *Henry IV, Part I* first appeared in print.

On a more general level, Shakespeare's Lancastrian bias in the history plays has been widely discussed by commentators of all authorship persuasions. This slant is not surprising given that the Tudor dynasty had been more or less aligned with the Lancastrians against the Yorkists during the civil strife and contentions in 15th-century England. In fact, any Elizabethan playwright would have been foolish to take an opposing viewpoint. It should be added, however, that Edward de Vere's ancestors had fought hard for the Lancastrians,[19] and in his case, such sympathies would have been predictable. If de Vere was Shakespeare the writer, then the partisan stance of the history plays would have been a natural outgrowth of the author's family heritage, in addition to being the politically correct choice.

In the plays, this Lancastrian bias is illustrated by Shakespeare's very sympathetic view of King Henry IV. Highly conjectural but fun to contemplate is the remarkable likeness between the Gheeraedts portrait of de Vere and an alleged portrait of Shakespeare's King Henry IV, now classified by art experts as a paint-over or an Elizabethan actor in costume.[20] Some believe the Gheeraedts, despite the clear labeling, is not de Vere but rather his father, the 16th Earl, based on the style of clothing and facial hair. If this is really his father, then it stands to reason there would be some physical resemblance anyway, and as for the older style of clothing, retro fashions are not a recent invention. Moreover, retro would not be inconceivable for a guy like de Vere, who was known as an eccentric dresser and someone chronically short of money. One must keep in mind that the Elizabethan nobility was obsessed with projection of personal image, and portraiture was an important aspect of this. For example, various portraits of Queen Elizabeth often look like different people. Whether the Gheeraedts is the 16th or 17th Earl of Oxford seems irrelevant; what really matters are the Lancastrian heritage and theatrical traditions among the Vere family.

In contrast to the serious-minded and guilt-ridden king, Shakespeare presents the young Prince Hal (before his metamorphosis into Henry V) as a riotous, carousing prankster who is still under the bad influence of Falstaff and his disreputable band at the Boar's Head Tavern. The myriad youthful (and not so youthful) indiscretions of Edward de Vere—of which drunkenness was probably the least infraction—need hardly be catalogued at this point. Suffice it to say that Prince Hal is one of the Bard's arch-typical nobleman heroes (in fact, almost all of his heroes and heroines are nobility), but one who hangs around the rabble too much. Shakespeare's overtly class-conscious and elitist worldview has troubled more than one commentator, and we can only assume that if the true author was Will Shakspere, then he must have been kissing up to his aristocratic patrons by necessity. Others have less convincingly suggested that the groundlings at Shakespeare's theaters knew deep down that they were inferior beings and thus aspired to something higher, and could do this vicariously through the noble characters in the plays. On the other hand, if we stipulate that the Bard himself was a haughty nobleman, then these interpretative problems vanish.

Another foil to Prince Hal is Henry Percy, surnamed Hotspur and son of the Earl of Northumberland. Frontispieces to both the first and second quartos give second billing (ahead of Prince Hal and Falstaff) to Hotspur,[21] who has always been a very popular character, in spite of the fact that he was a rebel who is killed at the end of *Part I* by Prince Hal in single combat at the Battle of Shrewsbury. It should be noted that Hotspur's direct descendent, Henry Percy, Ninth Earl of Northumberland, was a prominent nobleman during Shakespeare's time. There is no evidence as to whether Percy approved of his ancestor being portrayed on the public stage as a likeable but rebellious hothead. It is safe to assume, however, that had he objected, changes would have been made if the true author was Will Shakspere. The Ninth Earl was in fact known as an accomplished soldier who fought with distinction in the Low Countries and against the Armada. Later he was nicknamed the "Wizard Earl" because of his scientific interests and patronage.[22] In Shakespeare's play, Percy's ancestor is almost glorified into a symbol of bygone chivalry and champion of feudalistic values. This is another major subtext of Shakespeare's history plays—that feudalism is a good thing, along with all of the privileges and prerogatives that it afforded the nobility. During the Elizabethan era, these old-fashioned values were being eroded by the rising merchant middle class, represented by people like Burghley, Cobham, and the Puritans, with their more modern and egalitarian values. In this sense, Hotspur is anachronistic—a throwback and very admirable in many ways, apart from his rebelliousness and impetuosity. This multidimensional quality is what often makes the Bard's characters so interesting.

Later during the Jacobean era, Percy was falsely implicated in the Gunpowder Plot of 1605 and spent 15 years in the Tower of London before being released. While allowed special privileges during his imprisonment that enabled him to pursue non-political interests, a cloud of disloyalty always hung over Percy's career and reputation due to his family's Catholic associations. Percy's father (the Eighth Earl) had died in the Tower under suspicious circumstances during Elizabeth's reign because of these connections.[23] This is parallel to Hotspur and his father Northumberland (who turns traitor as well) in the *Henry IV* plays. Like Percy and much of the older English nobility, de Vere had often been suspected of harboring Catholic sympathies and his loyalty to the crown was frequently under scrutiny. Like Percy, de Vere more than once served in a personal military capacity against foreign Catholic threats to England, received occasional favor from the queen, and married into a Protestant family. Of particular interest is that Percy was considered as a marriage candidate for de Vere's eldest daughter Elizabeth around 1592.[24] This is about the same period that Henry Wriothesley, Earl of Southampton,[25] was also being considered as a husband for Elizabeth Vere, although neither proposed match ever materialized. Percy's subsequent marriage in 1595 to the sister of de Vere's enemy Robert Devereux may have been viewed by Oxford as an example of a good man going bad (like Hotspur). This event took place, incidentally, shortly before most scholars believe *Henry IV, Part I* was written. Percy, however, would prove more astute and resilient than Wriothesley in terms of remaining unscathed by the Essex Rebellion six years later. In any event, Percy's entire career can be viewed as a case study on how a man of visible sense and ability had to watch his step very carefully during the Wars of Religion, and how his own potential for doing public good was severely handicapped by these external forces.

In a memorable opening speech from the play (Act I, scene i), King Henry expresses admiration for the rebel Hotspur's valor, implies that he wishes his own son Prince Hal was more like him, and that Englishmen in general should be uniting and going off to crusade in the Holy Land, rather than killing each other in civil wars. Of course, "Britons unite" would have been a very timely political message in Elizabethan England. Coming full circle in *Henry IV, Part II*, King Henry on his deathbed advises his son Prince Hal to encourage foreign military adventures, which often make good distractions away from domestic troubles, adding that it is good "to busy giddy minds with foreign quarrels" (IV.v.213–214)—some things never change. Shakespeare's great contemporary Montaigne had a few years earlier expressed a similar sentiment, having witnessed France being ripped apart by religious dissension:

> There are many today who use similar arguments, wishing that the heat of civil commotions among us could be diverted into some war against our neighbors, fearing that

those aberrant humours which now dominate the body politic would, if not discanted elsewhere, continue to maintain our troubles at fever-pitch, finally entailing our complete collapse.[26]

Montaigne, like Shakespeare, recognized that foreign policy can sometimes be used to divert public attention away from domestic strife and civil conflict. The Percy Rebellion of 1403 predated the Reformation, but for the groundlings at Elizabethan public theaters, King Henry's double-edged remark could have been heard as code for a green light to beat up on Catholic insurgents before English Protestants tore each other to pieces, which was exactly what the Protestants of the next generation did.

Shakespeare recognized the same problem developing in England that Montaigne had experienced firsthand in France. The relatively new establishment church strove in vain to hold a middle-of-the-road posture (the *via media*) between the rising power of Puritan extremists and opposing Englishmen whose families had recently been Catholic, or who still were, but remained loyal to the crown. These political events in Shakespeare's England formed the backdrop for the English Civil War of 1642–1648, which ended in the overthrow of the monarchy. The triumphant Puritans immediately proceeded to outlaw and demolish the playhouses, thus consigning William Shakespeare and his works to over a century of oblivion.

Like Shakespeare's other great plays, *Henry IV, Part I* offers many facets of meaning and interpretation. One example appears to be a subtle allegory for the religious and political strife of that epoch, as represented by Hotspur, Prince Hal, and Falstaff. That the play speaks so loudly to audiences over 400 years later demonstrates our affinity with the Elizabethan and Jacobean political dilemma, at least with respect to this particular theme. While the very idea of a mandatory, state-sponsored religious denomination is alien to the modern American Bardolator, this is precisely the atmosphere in which Shakespeare was active. During that time, Catholics, Puritans, and Anglicans glared at each other with increasing hostility and loathing, while the monarchy struggled to hold together the national fabric. This effort was conducted in the face of simultaneous foreign threats and internal implosion, the latter eventually becoming a reality, and at the expense of the humanist values that Shakespeare the writer so obviously held dear. Hotspur, despite his admirable qualities, must eventually be suppressed by Prince Hal in the name of his father the king, for the sake of maintaining the social order. At least, this is the first step in the overall process, as dramatized in *Henry IV, Part I*. The second step is to turn our attention to Falstaff, who devolves from being the humorous miscreant of *Part I* to an albatross around the neck of the English state in *Henry IV, Part II*. Falstaff's ultimate banishment by the new king, Henry V, will be a sad but necessary act of good statesmanship.

℘ 20 ℂℛ

Henry IV, Part II

Not widely discussed among historians is the disturbing fact that construction of the Globe Theater in 1599 was completed despite formidable opposition from Puritan influence within the government. The aftermath of the London Plague (1592–1593) had strengthened a coalition of religious conservatives, who opposed the playhouses on moral grounds, and local businessmen who only wanted peace and quiet in order to control the spread of disease. Thus, when Blackfriars Theater was shut down by the Privy Council in 1596, even people like George Carey, Lord Hunsdon, the patron of Shakespeare's acting company, and Richard Field, printer of Shakespeare's narrative poems, both signed the petition in favor of closure.[1] Carey's father had died earlier that year and was replaced as Lord Chamberlain by William Brooke, Lord Cobham, a man with Puritan sympathies and hostile to the public playhouses.[2] Brooke's appointment as Lord Chamberlain gave the London mayor and aldermen courage to write a long letter to the Privy Council in 1597, condemning the English stage *en totem*. In response, the Council promptly banned all theatrical activity and ordered the immediate dismantlement of all playhouses.[3] Fortunately, this decree was never enforced, thanks to pressure from more sensible quarters, which presumably included the queen herself. Brooke died later that same year and was replaced as Lord Chamberlain by the son of his predecessor. This provided encouragement for the Burbages to transfer their theater operations to Southwark during the winter of 1598–1599, after thumbing their noses at a difficult landlord in Shoreditch.[4]

These events form an important backdrop to Shakespeare's *Henry IV* plays, with *Part I* first appearing in the quartos of 1598–1599. In 1600 the first quarto of *Part II* was published, unambiguously advertising that the work was written by William Shakespeare and performed by the Lord Chamberlain's Men. The 1600 frontispiece changed the billing order of the characters to King Henry IV, King Henry V, and Sir John Falstaff,[5] the latter being one of the Bard's most inspired creations. Most scholars believe that *Part II* was written soon after *Part I*, and that both parts were possibly written as one long play.[6] *Part II*, however, is a much darker work than *Part I*, with less tavern humor and no great battle scenes. Military success is achieved through treachery and subterfuge rather than valor and heroism. In the final act, Prince Hal is transformed into King Henry V and banishes the morally degenerate Falstaff from his presence. Henry's chilling denial of Falstaff, "I know thee not, old man" (V.v.147), is one of the most piercing lines in the canon.

Where did Shakespeare come up with Sir John? He is not in any of the history books; yet, regarding Falstaff's origins, one is struck by the unanimous verdict of scholarship.

Everyone more or less agrees where he came from: Sir John Falstaff was originally derived from the historical figure of Sir John Oldcastle, Lord Cobham, who was famous during the times of Henry IV and Henry V. There is also general agreement that Shakespeare initially named the character Sir John Oldcastle, and vestiges of this remain in the version known today. For example, at one point in *Part I*, Hal jokingly refers to Falstaff as "my old lad of the castle" (I.ii.41–42). Even more remarkable is that Oldcastle's direct descendent, William Brooke, Lord Cobham, was a powerful Elizabethan nobleman. It is rightfully assumed that Brooke forced the name of the character to be changed from Oldcastle to Falstaff. Edmund Chambers was firm: "As to the fact of this substitution there can be no doubt."[7]

The historical Sir John Oldcastle had been lionized in print a generation earlier by John Bale,[8] who is credited with writing the first English history play (*King John*) and had been patronized by de Vere's father, the 16th Earl of Oxford. In Bale's 1544 work titled *Brief Chronicle*, Oldcastle is portrayed (and illustrated) as a patriotic warrior-hero; however, not everyone saw him that way. In addition to being a soldier, Oldcastle was a follower of the Lollard religious dissident and Purtian forerunner John Wycliffe, and this got him into a lot of trouble. Then Oldcastle made the huge mistake of falling out with the new king, Henry V (formerly Prince Hal), and became an outlaw before he was eventually captured, condemned, and burned at the stake in 1417.

Oldcastle was controversial right up through Shakespeare's time. Many saw him as an early Protestant martyr and, as such, he was informally canonized by the Puritans. This is how he was portrayed by Bale and later by John Foxe in his 1563 *Book of Martyrs*,[9] which horrifically illustrated Oldcastle's execution. An opposing view of Oldcastle, typically held by the nobility, was that religion was just used as an excuse for his feuding with Henry V and as a pretext for being an outlaw.

The second edition of Holinshed's *Chronicles* was published in 1587 and continued the tradition of presenting Oldcastle as a heroic martyr—"a valiant capteine and hardie gentleman."[10] The conspicuous dedicatee of this historic volume was none other than Oldcastle's lineal descendent, William Brooke, Lord Cobham.[11] Just a coincidence, orthodox scholars would probably say. We would say that a disgruntled Edward de Vere took one look at the 1587 dedication and decided to have some fun with this guy. Eventually, Oldcastle would be renamed Falstaff; however, that was not the end of it. In the epilogue to *Henry IV, Part II*, a speaker comes on stage to emphatically remind the audience, in so many words, that Falstaff is *not* Sir John Oldcastle (who was, of course, a hero), and that no one should think otherwise. That, in our opinion, may have been a good example of the biting humor that earned de Vere his reputation as "best for comedy" among observers like Francis Meres and George Puttenham. The presumed influence of the *Chronicles* on Shakespeare[12] and de Vere's personal connections with Raphael Holinshed (d. 1580) are discussed in reference to *Henry IV, Part I*.

The previous year (in 1586) Queen Elizabeth had granted de Vere what would become a lifetime annuity of £1,000, at that time an extraordinary amount of money.[13] The reasons for this prodigious award from a famously tight-fisted monarch have never been satisfactorily explained by conventional history. The suggestion that it was necessary to maintain de Vere's status in the face of insolvency reflects a degree of naïveté with respect to money matters, not to mention a lack of appreciation for Elizabeth's parsimony

in the face of pending war with Spain. A more plausible explanation is that the monarchy viewed de Vere's acknowledged theatrical expertise as a propaganda weapon, and did
everything it could to encourage, say, history plays, so as to help unite Britons against foreign threats. Among the peerage (that is, among those having the most at stake), few
would have been better qualified than de Vere for the task of creating patriotic drama
such as the *Henry IV* plays. Later, upon the accession of King James in 1603, this annuity was promptly renewed, even though de Vere was about the last person in the world
whose political support was needed by the new theater-loving monarch. Other high-ranking nobility, such as Henry Percy or William Brooke's son Henry Brooke, were expected
to simply tow the line or were cashiered.

Although de Vere was a noted playwright and man of the theater, no works under
his own name have come down to us. The very idea of a nobleman secretly writing plays
with a front man to take credit went back to the ancients and Terence—himself an
influence on the Bard. One may argue whether Terence was indeed a front man, but there
can be no argument that many of Shakespeare's contemporaries, such as Montaigne,
believed it to be true. Amusingly, Montaigne's English translator M.A. Screech felt a need
to take issue with his source on this point in a footnote:

> Terence *may* have been a Carthaginian slave freed by Terentius Lucanus. In the *Prologue*
> to the *Adelphi* (15–21), he says he is flattered by the imputation that great men helped
> him write his comedies, which may or may not mean what Montaigne thinks it means.[14]

Elizabeth's tutor Roger Ascham also believed it, which strongly suggests that the queen
herself held this view.[15] In any event, authorship questions (especially commoners versus
noblemen in the eyes of British professors) have always been a surefire way to raise hack-
les in academia. The point is that during the Elizabethan period there was at least a perceived precedent for this sort of thing.

During Shakespeare's time, the nobility both sponsored theatrical groups and often
provided them with artistic material. This should not surprise, given that theatrical activities were considered an appropriate, desirable, and even necessary part of a nobleman's
education. Montaigne commented on this phenomenon as well:

> Acting is an activity which is not unpraiseworthy in the children of good families; I have
> subsequently seen our Princes actively involved in it (following the example of the
> ancients) and winning honor and praise.[16]

Along these lines, both de Vere and his children are recorded as having performed in
court masques. De Vere's upbringing in a house that sponsored acting companies and
playwrights (John Bale among them), his recorded associations with playwrights, actors,
and theaters, plus praise of de Vere himself as a playwright, all suggest that he was a master in the arts of entertainment and illusion, and was recognized as such by his own contemporary peers. Shakespeare's noblemen tend to be the same way. For example, in *Henry
IV, Part II*, Prince John of Lancaster gives a bravura performance as he tricks the traitors
Hastings, Mowbray, and Scroop into disbanding their army before promptly arresting
them (IV.ii).

In addition to his noted skills in poetry, music, dance, and jousting, de Vere held the hereditary office of Lord Great Chamberlain (to be distinguished from the post of Lord Chamberlain that was held by the Careys and William Brooke, among others). In this office he was entitled and obligated to play various ceremonial roles at court, with emphasis on pomp and display. For example, he participated in the coronation of King James in 1603, just as his father had assisted in Queen Elizabeth's coronation in 1558.[17] At the very least, de Vere played a very public and symbolic role in major events of the era. In a sense, courtiers such as de Vere were the true impresarios of that time, being constantly "on stage" in the public eye. During his participation in the Royal Progress of 1580, de Vere, according to an eyewitness, incited laugher from the crowds by gesturing with his white staff of office.[18] One can only imagine. Moreover, the very name of Falstaff suggests letting fall a staff representing a symbolic dignity.[19]

Getting back to Falstaff, the contrarian view of Sir John Oldcastle eventually manifested itself in the anonymous history play titled *The Famous Victories of Henry Fifth*, another widely acknowledged source for Shakespeare's *Henry IV* and *Henry V*.[20] Although not published until 1598—by this time Lord Burghley and William Brooke were dead—*Famous Victories* is believed to have hit the boards sometime during the late 1580s. This was roughly concurrent with de Vere's annuity grant (1586) and the dedication to Brooke in the second edition (1587) of Holinshed.[21] In *Famous Victories*, Sir John Oldcastle is portrayed not as a warrior-hero or religious martyr, but as a ridiculous scoundrel.[22] Is it so outrageous to suggest that de Vere may have written this work? The notion seems plausible even if de Vere was not in fact Shakespeare the writer.

Why Shakespeare chose to make Oldcastle an object of ridicule has long perplexed scholars, especially given that his descendent William Brooke was a big man at court and most certainly proud of his lineage from Oldcastle. To repeat, in 1596 Brooke was named the new Lord Chamberlain, despite his censorious attitude toward the public theaters. Concurrently, Shakespeare wrote (or rewrote?) two plays in which Brooke's most famous ancestor is portrayed as a cowardly and garrulous rogue. If this were not enough, Brooke's Puritan sensibilities would have been surely offended by the bawdiness of Shakespeare's tavern scenes, startling even by today's standards with character names such as Mistress Quickly and Doll Tearsheet.

Conventional wisdom would have us believe that Brooke, sometime before his death in 1597, protested that his illustrious ancestor was being ridiculed on the public stage. Shakespeare then had to change the name to Falstaff, which he had already used in *Henry VI, Part I*, drawing upon the historical Sir John Fastolfe, and making a slight change in spelling.[23] Among orthodox scholars, Geoffrey Bullough really puzzled over this episode. How could Shakespeare have made such a blunder? This was an era when playwrights were routinely arrested, imprisoned, and tortured for giving even the slightest offense. Nevertheless, we are to understand Brooke merely "complained" that Shakespeare was making fun of his ancestor and demanded that the name be changed. If Will Shakspere was the true author, it would seem that he was lucky not to have his head put on a stake. Bullough reluctantly concluded that Shakespeare must have unwittingly copied the name from *Famous Victories* and not been aware of the implications.[24] The unmentionable alternative is that the true Shakespeare knew exactly what he was doing.

William Brooke's son Henry Brooke became the new Lord Cobham upon his father's death in 1597. The only point resembling any kind of disagreement among scholars is specifically whether Henry or his father had taken exception to their ancestor being turned into Falstaff.[25] In all likelihood, neither father nor son took to it very kindly. That same year (1597), it is interesting to learn that Henry Brooke appears to have been considered as a marriage candidate for de Vere's daughter Bridget (see Chapter 15).[26] This would seem to argue against hard feelings between the two families, unless the proposal represented a sort of olive branch. More importantly, Henry Brooke during this same period was a sworn adversary to Robert Devereux, who was unquestionably loathed by de Vere. Furthermore, Robert Cecil (de Vere's former brother-in-law and Bridget Vere's uncle) was already married to Henry Brooke's sister Elizabeth.[27] It may well have been that at this point in time, at least for Devereux's opponents, closing ranks overruled all other considerations. Another marriage candidate for Bridget Vere in 1597 was William Herbert, future co-dedicatee of Shakespeare's First Folio, but this match did not materialize, either.[28] Instead, Bridget would eventually marry Francis Norris in 1599.[29] As for Henry Brooke, his subsequent career was a fiasco. Following the bad example of his ancestor Oldcastle, Brooke conspired against the new king, James I, and was imprisoned for life in 1603 after being reprieved from a death sentence on the scaffold.[30] Before this occurred, however, the story of Shakespeare's Falstaff had one more strange but amusing chapter.

Immediately after the *Henry IV* quartos appeared, an anonymous play was published in 1600, bombastically titled *The First Part of the True and Honorable Histories of the Life of Sir John Old-castle, the Good Lord Cobham*. In this work, Oldcastle is portrayed as a Puritan hero the same way he had originally been presented before *Famous Victories* and the *Henry IV* plays. Furthermore, *Sir John Old-castle* alludes disparagingly to Shakespeare's Falstaff and reminds us yet again that Oldcastle is not to be confused with Falstaff. So not only was Shakespeare compelled to change the name, but another drama was brought out to present Oldcastle in a favorable light. A short time later—this is still 1600[31]—yet another, second quarto of *Sir John Old-castle* was published, with "William Shakespeare" credited as the author.[32] This is called backpedaling. Shakespeare's apology to the Lords Cobham perhaps? No, because for this work Henslowe recorded in his diary that he had paid a team of authors: Anthony Munday, Michael Drayton, Robert Wilson, and Richard Hathaway.[33] Henslowe also paid for a sequel ("part two") which is either lost or was never written because William Brooke died and Henry Brooke went to the Tower. So Shakespeare may have changed the name to Falstaff but did not write a subsequent play to glorify Oldcastle. He let his colleagues do that, or perhaps his employees, since Munday had been de Vere's servant and (presumably) secretary as well. Above all, Shakespeare the writer had the last laugh, because Sir John Oldcastle is today forgotten, but Sir John Falstaff will live as long as there are stages to be performed upon.

❧ 21 ❧

Henry V

"A knight errant knows everything, Sancho, as he must," said Don Quixote, "for in days gone by a knight errant might have to deliver a sermon, or a lecture, right in the middle of the king's camp, as if he were a graduate of the University of Paris, from which we may conclude that the lance has never blunted the pen, nor the pen the lance."
—Cervantes, *Don Quixote* [1605][1]

Shakespeare's quintessential warrior-king has suffered at the hands of modern critics and audiences, many of whom, and not without some justification, view him as a grasping, war-mongering, and overgrown juvenile delinquent. If this were not enough, he comes across as a clumsy lover after the fighting is done. On the other hand, King Henry is an effective speech giver, besides being a man of action, and to underrate him for his shortcomings is to give the play a very shallow reading. Taken as a whole, *Henry V* is a magnificent pageant representing the Elizabethan national triumph over internal dissensions and foreign threats, and will remain popular as long as nation-states and the English language exist.

Opposing views of Henry are conveniently available for everyone to see in two classic films: the 1944 production by Laurence Olivier and Kenneth Branagh's 1989 updated version. During World War II as the Allies invaded France, Olivier presented the conquering English king as a great liberator, with the help of skillful editing and subtle interpretation.[2] Forty-five years later, Branagh gave the world a more unvarnished take on these accomplishments, veering disconcertingly close to portraying the "star of England"[3] (V.Epilogue.6) as an invading oppressor and empty-headed butcher of innocent life.[4]

Historically, the play deals with events surrounding the last decisive English victory of the Hundred Years' War. The Battle of Agincourt was fought on October 25, 1415, the feast day of "Crispin Crispian" (IV.iii.57).[5] As usual in the history plays, Shakespeare in *Henry V* took great liberties with documented facts and succeeded brilliantly in terms of dramatic effect. For example, in the play Henry's wedding to the French Princess Katherine immediately follows triumph in the field, whereas in real life it took five more years of fighting to consolidate English gains.[6] More remarkable (and less remarked upon) is Shakespeare's stagecraft, with the Bard able to effectively reinvent English history while remaining surprisingly faithful to the record. Shakespeare's history plays were created by someone who lived and breathed the national epic (thus enabling him to pick and choose where best to mythologize), rather than one who had merely taken a crash course in the source materials.

A truncated quarto version of the play was first published in 1600, while the definitive text was not printed until the First Folio of 1623.[7] Although the Spanish Armada was defeated in 1588, England remained at war with Spain throughout the reign of Elizabeth. Moreover, during this period England was racked with internal dissensions, from Catholic insurgents and even more so from Puritan fanatics who rejected outright the supremacy of the crown as head of the Anglican Church. England's survival—indeed, its prosperity and subsequent colonial expansion—were surprising to those observers who could not see beyond these overt problems. In one sense, Henry V was a contemporary allegory of this phenomenon. England, despite all of its apparent handicaps, was the little engine that could. As a propaganda vehicle, the play was superlative, drawing upon "true events" from the country's past to dramatize how a ragtag, disparate group of people with little in common except one dread sovereign could still achieve a difficult objective, and do so against tremendously long odds.

While Elizabethan audiences imagined an English army invading France, the contemporary reality was that England was invading nothing, except perhaps North America. This was the result of prudent foreign policy by Queen Elizabeth and King James, both of whom hated war (especially the financial expense of it), and did everything in their power to divert English militarism into constructive channels such as home defense and volunteer expeditionary forces. In the play, by invading France Henry is following the deathbed advice of his father in Henry IV, Part II (IV.v.213–214), who advocated that Englishmen should take out their aggression on foreign adversaries before they took it out on each other. Shakespeare's great source Plutarch, in his life of Camillus, says the Romans had a similar policy, assuming that unless a permanent wartime footing was maintained, civil war would automatically result. The Chorus in Henry V informs us that "Now all the youth of England are on fire" (II.Chorus.1), and Henry successfully exports this youthful enthusiasm to France, much to the grief of the French. It should be added that the defensive-postured reigns of Elizabeth and James—both stingy with blood—were followed immediately by the English Civil War.

Admittedly, a propaganda masterwork of national unification such as Henry V could have been written by anyone with the proper abilities and background, which (in theory, at least) could have included Will Shakspere. It must also be conceded, however, that as a propaganda piece, any play would have been more effective if credited to a commoner rather than to a royally subsidized nobleman. This was particularly true since the politically ascendant Puritan opposition to the playhouses was reaching a fever pitch.

Orthodox scholars agree that Shakespeare's main source was Holinshed's Chronicles,[8] first published in 1577 and dedicated to Lord Burghley. A second expanded edition was then published after Holinshed's death and dedicated to Lord Cobham in 1587, the year before the Armada invasion.[9] Few people would have been as well placed as de Vere to have access to Holinshed's work, with Lord Burghley as his guardian and later father-in-law. In addition to belonging to the same household to which Holinshed was attached, de Vere found himself being judged innocent by Holinshed as a juror after his killing of Thomas Bricknell in 1567.[10] This cozy arrangement between Holinshed, Burghley, and de Vere reflected a more flexible interpretation regarding conflict of interest for those times. In the play, King Henry has the opportunity to pardon his old friend, the hapless Bardolph, for the crime of looting but instead opts to have him hanged (Act III, scene vi).

Holinshed certainly showed more mercy toward de Vere in real life than did King Henry toward Bardolph; then again, both probably did what was politically expedient.

In addition to the *Chronicles*, a variety of other sources for the play have been discussed, many of which Holinshed probably used; furthermore, Shakespeare the writer may have bypassed Holinshed to do the same. Two of these (noted by Bullough)[11] include the writings of Tacitus (in French) and the Englishman John Smithe, both found in the library of Lord Burghley.[12] De Vere presumably had easy access to these while Will Shakspere had difficult access at best.

Another independent source was the anonymous play titled *The Famous Victories of Henry the Fifth*, published in 1598, registered in 1594, and written no later than 1588.[13] This fascinating, uneven work also provided material for Shakespeare's two *Henry IV* plays and introduced an early version of the buffoonish Falstaff (as Sir John Oldcastle). *Famous Victories* was exhaustively analyzed by Oxfordian scholar Ramón Jiménez, who determined (among other things) that it was probably written by de Vere as a direct response to the dramatic rules advocated by his poetic rival, Philip Sidney. Sidney, in his *Apologie for Poetrie* (published in 1595 but written circa 1582), stressed the inappropriateness of mixing serious historical drama with low comedy. *Famous Victories* (like Shakespeare's plays) does precisely this.[14] In the larger context, Sidney wrote his treatise to defend the poetic and dramatic arts from the severe drubbing these had been recently receiving from Puritan critics. Part of Sidney's defense was to admit that there had been some excesses and abuses in the playhouses, and that these should be toned down. We believe that de Vere responded by turning the Puritan sympathizer and *Chronicles* dedicatee Lord Cobham into Sir John Falstaff, who provides comic relief during the serious-minded *Henry IV* plays.

The connections between *Henry V*, Sidney, and de Vere multiply upon closer examination. In Sidney's *Apologie*, writers such as John Lyly, author of *Euphues*, is singled out for criticism. Lyly was, not surprisingly, associated with de Vere as his secretary and among those who dedicated Euphuistic works to his employer. De Vere himself personified the figure of Euphues at the Elizabethan court, in opposition to Sidney.[15] *Henry V* contains a direct paraphrase of Lyly's *Euphues* when the Archbishop of Canterbury delivers a formal disquisition to the king on how his subjects should be obedient because "For so work the honey-bees" (I.ii.187).[16] A more dramatic association occurs a few moments later when Henry is mockingly presented with tennis balls as a gift from the Dauphin. The king chillingly responds that "When we have match'd our rackets to these balls," the result will be that "thousands weep more than did laugh at it" (I.ii.261–295). Scholars have noted that this passage shows an intimate knowledge of tennis (at that time an exclusive sport for noblemen) with technical terms converted into poetic images.[17] Apparently the Bard either played tennis or was a keen observer. As for de Vere and Sidney, their most infamous encounter occurred in 1579 on a London tennis court when de Vere belittled his rival as "a puppy" after a petty dispute over whose turn it was to use the facility.[18]

In terms of dating the play, *Henry V* provides a good example reflecting the shallow flimsiness often found in orthodox reasoning. In Act V, the Chorus interjects:

> Were now the general of our gracious Empress,
> As in good time he may, from Ireland coming,
> Bringing rebellion broached on his sword. [V.Chorus.30–32]

Parroting each other, critics often declare this to be a definite reference to the Earl of Essex's punitive Irish expedition of 1599. Aside from the fact that the Irish have been rebelling against the English since time immemorial, the lines in question were not printed until the 1623 First Folio. Thus the implied Irish rebellion could have occurred either before[19] or after 1599, often with happier results for the English than the abortive Essex campaign that ended with his disgrace and downfall.

The same critics should spend more time addressing Shakespeare's amazing use of the French language in *Henry V*. To give only one example, the banter between the Princess Katherine and Alice in Act III, scene iv, shows enough sophistication to make bawdy French puns while the two women try to learn the dialect of their English conquerors. Proponents of Will Shakspere have occasionally cited his recorded lodgings at the London residence of the Huguenot refugee Mountjoy as a possible source of his French expertise; furthermore, "Montjoy" is the name of the French herald in the play. This speculation, however, falls apart under critical analysis. For one thing, the name of Montjoy is found in the chronicles;[20] secondly, as Samuel Schoenbaum has noted, the play was certainly written before Shakspere was Mountjoy's tenant.[21] A more plausible speculation is that de Vere, repeatedly noted for his fluency in French, used the play as a vehicle to show off his multilingual skills.

Returning to the dubious character of King Henry, it is not difficult to see in Shakespeare's portrayal an image of the man that de Vere wanted to be but never was. Along with his heroic deeds, Henry is a talker. He is capable of both persuading his men to charge fortifications ("Once more unto the breach, dear friends, once more") (III.i.1) and, using reverse psychology, to hold their ground when attacked ("he which hath no stomach for this fight, / Let him depart") (IV.iii.35). More impressively, he is able to force the garrison of Harfleur to surrender merely by threatening rape and pillage (III.iii.1–43). Like Don Quixote's ideal Knight-Errant, Henry excels at oration. The limitations of this skill, though, are acknowledged in the play, including when a boy in the trenches reflects that "Men of fewest words are the best men" (III.ii.36). De Vere was not a man of few words. He is reported to have said that in Italy he was praised "for his eloquence another Cicero and for his conduct a Caesar" while delivering orations in various cities.[22] Back in England, this tendency was even more pronounced, with Gabriel Harvey's devastating reference to de Vere as a man of "valorous" words and "womanish" works.[23] This sounds more like the playwright that de Vere was noted by his contemporaries to have been.

Shortly before English history plays such as *Famous Victories* began making their appearance on the public stage, the disgraced and bankrupt de Vere was awarded a prodigious annuity of £1,000 by Queen Elizabeth in 1586 for unspecified reasons. Opponents of the Oxfordian theory strenuously maintain that this was merely a face-saving device for Burghley's son-in-law, but such an explanation fails to satisfy any half-open mind. For one thing, a far easier face-saving device would have been to do away with the wayward 17th Earl, and Elizabethan power brokers were not above using such tactics. It seems as though de Vere had something to offer that has remained concealed from conventional history. A far more plausible interpretation is that de Vere was recruited for the great Tudor propaganda push of the late 1580s. Most Oxfordians have postulated de Vere's authorship of *Famous Victories*, a reasonable hypothesis regardless of whether he was the true Shakespeare.

An interesting side note for both *Henry V* and *Famous Victories* involves the respective use and non-use of de Vere's ancestor Richard de Vere, 11th Earl of Oxford, as a character. According to history, the 11th Earl was present at Agincourt but played a limited role. Curiously, Oxford is inflated to almost absurd heroic proportions in *Famous Victories*; if de Vere was the author one can imagine why.[24] By contrast, Shakespeare's *Henry V* goes to the opposite extreme: the Earl of Oxford is completed omitted as a character. Since the 11th Earl played a minor role in events, de Vere may have later judged it better to expunge him from the record rather than to faithfully dramatize his mediocrity.[25]

In weaving his tapestry of national unity, the Bard supplies a galaxy of colorful secondary characters, beginning with the Welshman Fluellen. Both orthodox scholars and Oxfordians have recognized close similarities between Shakespeare's curmudgeonly captain and the Elizabethan Welsh soldier (and author) Roger Williams, who was associated with de Vere and his family at various times throughout his career.[26] In fairness, it should be added that Will Shakspere may have known this person as well, although there is no record of it (as in the case of de Vere).

Another example of the comic interludes so objected to by Philip Sidney occurs whenever Fluellen tries to interact with his Irish and Scotch allies. Along with the dim-witted Irishman "Macmorris," Shakespeare's portrayal of the Scottish captain "Jamy" is especially offensive, if for no other reason that no one, not even after 400 years, can understand what he is saying. These men simply cannot communicate with each other, and yet are willing and able to fight together under Henry's banner: a good lesson for contemporary Elizabethans. De Vere's literary rival Sidney may have been horrified but Shakespeare's audiences were no doubt delighted, as they still are today.

Dissensions among the lower ranks of Englishmen are more sinister in nature. Falstaff dies offstage (II.iii),[27] while his disreputable companions Bardolph and Nym are later hanged for various infractions. Only Pistol survives, vowing bitterly to become a thief upon his return to England (V.i.87). These men represent the worst elements of English society; they are engaged in constructive activity only when obeying orders. A realistic attitude perhaps, but much easier one would think if coming from a privileged nobleman such as de Vere, than from the self-made Will Shakspere.

Regarding Shakespeare's view of royal authority in *Henry V*, there are no uncertainties. King Henry is the unambiguous, supreme head of church and state. Anglican archbishops answer to their monarch personally and all theological issues are resolved by the king on the eve of battle. Distinguished Oxfordian scholar Dr. Daniel Wright, apart from the authorship question, made the general observation that

> Henry, like the England he represents, signifies in his person the achievements of Anglicism. He is the patient deliverer of the national Church ... from its bondage to a tyrannical Roman authority—a tyranny personified by the affected and un-English Richard [II]; and he is the repudiator of the fanaticism and hypocrisy of Puritanism—as parodied by the unregenerate Falstaff.[28]

Wright further noted that King Henry "personifies the character of the new Church of England,"[29] while continually invoking the name of God in all his endeavors (over 30 times to be exact),[30] and directing that the *Te Deum* be sung after victory. Thus Henry is presented as both military hero and high priest of the state-sponsored religion.

None of this was taken for granted at the time. Presbyterians, Puritans, and separatists of all shades, while recognizing the English monarchy as their lawful sovereign, either
shied away from or firmly rejected the king or queen as supreme head of the church. The
overbearing message of *Henry V* flies directly in the face of this reluctance, most notably
on the eve before Agincourt as Henry engages incognito in theological debate with his
troops, particularly the defiant Michael Williams. It has been pointed out by orthodox
scholars such as Lily Campbell that this lengthy dialogue is dramatically unnecessary,[31]
but absolutely essential for English propaganda purposes. The stubborn Williams finally
agrees with the king that "every man that dies ill, the ill be on his own head, the King is
not to answer it" (IV.i.186–187) but nevertheless accuses Henry of gullibility for his alleged
faith in the king and challenges him to a duel after the battle (IV.i.196–202). William's
comrade John Bates then admonishes them both: "Be friends, you English fools, be
friends, we have French quarrels enow, if you could tell how to reckon" (IV.i.222–224).[32]
When later confronted with the true identity of his royal adversary, Williams successfully
gains pardon by pleading an egalitarian defense (IV.viii.50–56), as surely would any good
Puritan under similar circumstances.

Henry V ends with a wedding, symbolic of English national unity. Typically, Shakespeare's "happy" ending also leaves the audience with a bitter pill, predicting the War of
the Roses following Henry's death, and more subtly, allowing us insight into the limitations of Henry's own character, as he warns Katherine: "For these fellows of infinite
tongue, that can rhyme themselves into ladies' favours, they do always reason themselves
out again" (V.ii.155–157). Henry claims to be a "plain soldier" (V.ii.149) (like the Caesar
who so exasperated Cicero by describing himself in similar terms while addressing the
Senate), but the audience knows better. As for de Vere, perhaps he, like Shakespeare's
King Henry, moved incognito among his audience (his "subjects"?) under an assumed identity, both for his own protection and to better gauge their temper.

&o 22 c&

Henry VI, Part I

Writing the introduction for *Riverside*, Herschel Baker rightfully observed that Shakespeare's *Henry VI* trilogy has inspired "more scholarship than admiration,"[1] but that may be beginning to change. Recent creative productions have demonstrated that there is much in these oft-maligned works to be esteemed and enjoyed. It is unnecessary to waste much ink pointing out the obvious; namely, that the Bard rewrote English history and these plays represent a vision of the past that never happened. In striking contrast to Shakespeare's use of Plutarch, which is highly faithful to recorded ancient events, his adaptations of Holinshed and Hall often reflect a dramatic imagination completely unrestrained by the agreed-upon facts. We can only assume that Shakespeare was well aware of the liberties he was taking, not out of ignorance, but rather for the sake of dramatic and propagandistic effect. This was a writer who knew his English history so thoroughly inside and out that he was able to convincingly rearrange it in a manner that, for many of us, Shakespeare's version of historical events have replaced those that actually occurred. In particular, the *Henry VI* trilogy appears to have been a hothouse for the flowering of Shakespeare's genius in the chronicle play genre.

The trilogy deals with the meltdown in English civil and military affairs transpiring toward the end of the Hundred Years' War, followed immediately by the internecine chaos and outrages that marked the War of the Roses. *Henry VI, Part I* specifically covers the time period (very roughly speaking) from the funeral of Henry V in 1422 to the heroic death of Lord Talbot in France at the Battle of Castillon in 1453—a red-letter year in European history as the Hundred Years' War ended simultaneously with the Ottoman conquest of Constantinople. The play's coda portrays the fateful marriage pact between Henry VI and Margaret of Anjou, which had actually occurred earlier in time but was moved ahead by the Bard in order to provide a transition into *Henry VI, Part II*. The turbulent mid–15th century, in addition to witnessing the collapse of English pretensions in France, saw Englishmen turn on themselves in a horrific manner that the Elizabethan government wished to avoid repeating during the late 16th century, to say the least. That it succeeded in this objective was no small feat, given that one generation later (in 1642), England would explode into yet another bitterly contested civil war.

How much of the play, if any, was actually written by Shakespeare the writer has been highly debated; but this holds true for much of the canon as well. *Henry VI, Part I*, like 17 other works, made its printed debut in the First Folio of 1623,[2] years after the death of whoever the author was. Although Thomas Nashe in his *Pierce Penniless* of 1592 made an allusion to Lord Talbot on stage,[3] we have no idea to what extent this early version resembled the play printed 33 years later, nor do we know for certain in what order the trilogy was written. No less eminent authorities than Geoffrey Bullough and Edmund Chambers went head to head on these issues. Chambers acknowledged that "there are certainly several styles in the play" and believed that *Part I* was written after Parts II and III as a prequel.[4] Bullough, on the other hand, took the view that Shakespeare was "the only writer in the early nineties who possessed the skill to bring such order out of the straggling narrative" and "we cannot be sure that Shakespeare did not write all of *I Henry VI*." Moreover, Bullough felt that *Part I* was written first.[5] We are inclined to side with Chambers on these issues, with all due respect to numerous dissenters.[6] For one, Shakespeare later followed up (by popular and/or royal demand) his two masterful *Henry IV* plays with the less brilliant *Merry Wives of Windsor*, which seems to have been written in haste, so he was not above doing this sort of thing. Second, the encore-prequel (*Part I*)—if it was such—could have been farmed out to other writers after the Bard had himself written essential parts and provided direction for the balance. Third and most important, the first three acts of *Part II* seem to form their own independent set-up for events that follow, and we would conjecture that *Part I* was written later to provide more background information on the political and military setbacks leading up to the War of the Roses.

To the limited extent that the play is historically faithful, Shakespeare's two main sources were Holinshed's *Chronicles* (published in 1577 and 1587) and Edward Hall's *The Union of the Two Noble and Illustre Famelies of Lancastre and Yorke*, definitively published in 1550.[7] Hall's classic work belonged to the library of de Vere's childhood tutor Thomas Smith,[8] and Raphael Holinshed dedicated the first edition of his landmark opus to Lord Burghley, de Vere's father-in-law. In addition, Holinshed was attached to the Burghley household at the same time de Vere was a young ward there, and sat in judgment (as a juror) over the 17-year-old earl after his killing of Thomas Bricknell in 1567.[9] Holinshed later retired to Warwickshire and died around 1580, but no known connections have been discovered between the chronicler or his famous book and Will Shakspere, who was a teenager at the time.

The traditional biography of Shakespeare would have us believe that the young entrepreneurial genius initially established his reputation among colleagues and insinuated himself with his betters by churning out jingoistic, patriotic potboilers such as *Henry VI, Part I*. There is nothing inherently wrong with this view. Anyone not recognizing the latent Tudor propaganda in these works—covertly supported by Elizabeth and her peers—has less than a superficial understanding of the canon. This theatrical propaganda campaign was used not only to unite England against Catholic foreign threats, but after the 1588 defeat of the Spanish Armada, to unite Englishmen among themselves as well. More specifically, it was used to remind English Anglicans, Catholics and Puritans that a house divided against itself would not stand. That public stagecraft was often aimed against this domestic threat is documented.[10] Any patriotic Englishman, including Will Shakspere, would have supported the effort, especially if there was money to be made. As for Edward de Vere (an acknowledged playwright), there were a number of additional reasons why he would have likely been involved. One was the strong Lancastrian bias of his family.[11] Another was that in 1586, the normally austere Queen Elizabeth, in the face of imminent war, granted de Vere an astonishing £1,000 annuity for unspecified purposes.[12] Some say this was so the bankrupt and wayward son-in-law of Lord Burghley could keep up appearances, which makes about as much sense as pouring a canteen of water over a cactus plant in the desert.

It was no coincidence that the Martin Marprelate controversy commenced with England's November 1588 victory celebration over the Spanish Armada. With the removal of immediate foreign threat, English religious radicals focused their hostility on the Church of England, the decadent old aristocracy, and the fledgling public theater. Writing under a pseudonym, Martin himself employed a devastating, theatrical style while exposing the many shortcomings of the Anglican Church to a delighted and wide public audience. Incredibly, though, Martin fell under criticism from those whose views he advocated so effectively, not for the content of his pamphlets, but for method he used. He himself acknowledged the problem: "Those whom foolishly men call puritans like of the matter I have handled, but the form they cannot brook." Historian Patrick Collinson explained that "He [Martin] made fun of a solemn matter and defiled the cause with unprecedented scurrility." Martin is then compared to popular satirists and playwrights such as Thomas Nashe and John Lyly, who aimed their writings directly at "the people," bypassing more proper and official channels.[13]

Also engaged in the printed counterattack on Martin were playwrights such as John Lyly, Thomas Nashe and Robert Greene—all of whom had associations with de Vere.[14] Another response to Martin, perhaps the wittiest of all, came from one self-styled "Pasquill Cavaliero of England," whom Oxfordians believe was de Vere himself.[15] It is possible that de Vere's state subsidies were temporarily channeled in this direction and that Oxford's Boys were connected with Paul's Boys, the children's acting troupe disbanded for performing outrageous anti–Martinist plays.[16] In any event, Shakespeare's *Henry VI* plays with their "Englishmen unite" message hit the boards during the early 1590s concurrent with the cantankerous height of the Marprelate disputation.

An outstanding example of the highly slanted, agitprop nature of the history plays is Shakespeare's vicious portrayal of Joan of Arc in *Henry VI, Part I*. The Maid of Orleans, before she was christened Saint Joan during the 20th century, was fodder for English polemicists. Her dramatic entrance into history, inspiring the French to raise the English siege of Orleans in 1429, was the strategical turning point of the Hundred Years' War. Shakespeare, for his part, portrays Joan as a witch and a strumpet. When she is finally captured and brought to trial, first she denies her common-born father—"I am descended of a gentler blood. Thou art no father of mine" (V.iv.7–9)—then argues that she is a virgin, then that she is pregnant, and then tries to name three different fathers, before being dragged off to execution kicking and screaming—presumably with the groundlings cheering all the way. Bullough observed that "Admirers of Joan of Arc have found it hard to believe that Shakespeare would write an attack on her which goes far beyond anything found in Hall or Holinshed...."[17] Admirers of Shakespeare have found it hard to believe as well, to the extent they often deny that Shakespeare even wrote the play or at least these portions of it. We note, however, that Shakespeare's Joan never does as much harm to the English on the battlefield as the amazingly vilified Queen Margaret later does behind the scenes in Parts II and III of the trilogy, and few deny the Bard credit for her portrayal.

One of the rare points of agreement among scholars regarding *Henry VI, Part I*, is that Act II, scene iv—the so-called Temple Garden scene in which York and Somerset quietly declare war on each other—was written mostly if not entirely by Shakespeare. One good reason for this belief, aside from the mastery of the writing, is that there is absolutely no basis for it in the chronicles.[18] When York "stands upon the honor of his birth" and plucks "a white rose," followed by Somerset's oath to "maintain the party of truth" and picking of "a red rose" (II.iv.27–37), nervous bystanders realize this is a far more serious breach than the previous blustering and chest-thumping from other antagonists. De Vere's own connection with this scene is that he studied law at nearby Gray's Inn which, along with the Middle Temple, was one of the four London Inns of Court.[19] The scene opens with the characters quibbling over "nice sharp quillets of law" (II.iv.17), an activity that the legally trained and lifelong litigant de Vere would have been well acquainted with, probably far more so than Will Shakspere, whose documented courtroom exposure was sporadic at best.

Lastly, *Henry VI, Part I* holds the distinction of introducing the name (if not the fully developed character) of Sir John Falstaff to the English stage. This was actually a corruption of the historical Sir John Fastolfe (a name used in some modern editions of the play), who like Joan of Arc did not deserve the ridiculous treatment he receives from the Bard. Shakespeare the dramatist, however, needed an English scapegoat who was a "coward" (I.i.131) and perhaps decided to change the name slightly, playing upon his own name ("shake-speare" versus "fall-staff"). Oxfordians maintain that this was a play on a pseudonym[20] whose origins went back at least to the 1570s. For example, on January 1, 1576, George Gascoigne helped to win for himself the title of English Poet Laureate by presenting the queen with his *Tale of Hemetes the Heremyte*, in which Gascoigne described himself as "A poett with a Speare." In 1575, while de Vere was out of the country, Gascoigne also appears to have hijacked some of de Vere's poetry with the second edition of *A Hundreth Sundrie Flowres*, retitled *The Poesies of George Gascoigne*.[21] De Vere, upon his return from Italy in 1576, may have decided to engage in some one-upmanship by selecting a similar monicker for future use.

৯১ 23 ৫৯

Henry VI, Part II

Those critics of Shakespeare's *Henry VI* trilogy who find fault with the historical distortions and imperfections of structure, character development, etc., could probably not produce anything half as good if confronted with the same source material. Forty-nine years of complex international relations and English domestic upheavals are compressed by the Bard into a few hours of remarkable stagecraft, interspersed with many poignant moments of poetry and personal reflection. All indications are that these three works were written quickly and produced soon afterward to great popular and critical claim. The magnitude of Shakespeare's achievement can never be discounted—and, oh yes, the feuding Anglican, Puritan, and Catholic factions in England during this same period managed to keep a relatively united front. Thus the propagandist function of the English history plays was achieved as well, at least temporarily.

Henry VI, Part II may well have been the first play in the trilogy, followed by *Part III* and then *Part I* as a prequel.[1] *Part II* covers the 10-year period of events from Henry VI's marriage to Margaret of Anjou at Tours in 1445 to the first Battle of St. Albans, fought in 1455.[2] Acts I through III deal with the complex machinations leading up to Duke Humphrey's murder, followed by insurrection and civil war in Acts IV–V. At St. Albans in Act V, Yorkist forces achieve a stunning victory (in history, thanks to a flanking maneuver by the aggressive Earl of Warwick) and kill the two Lancastrian leaders, Somerset and Clifford. This pitched battle opened the War of the Roses and was roughly equivalent to the Battle of Bull Run during the American Civil War, in that rebel forces dealt a surprisingly effective (and almost terminal) blow against armies loyal to the existing government. The first four acts of *Part II*, however, literally set the stage for this epic conflict that was to last on and off for the next 30 years.

The first reliable text for *Part II* was published in the First Folio of 1623; in 1594, however, a "bad" quarto—usually assumed to be a corrupt, memorial reconstruction— was published as *The First Part of the Contention betwixt the Two Famous Houses of Yorke and Lancaster.* This was an anonymous publication with no mention of the author, although a later entry with the Stationers Register in 1600 named "William Shakespeare" as playwright. Impresario Philip Henslowe mentioned in his diary a 1591 performance at the Rose Theater by Lord Strange's Men of "harey the vj" as a "ne[w]" piece (again with no mention of the author), although which play of the *Henry VI* trilogy this entry referred to is unclear.[3] Whether the various bad quarto and First Folio publications of this play reflect an organic creative process or merely the faulty memories and greedy dispositions of those involved is irrelevant; either way, there were bound to be revisions for an authoritative text that appeared so long after the death of the author. As for Lord Strange's Men, these actors were sponsored by Ferdinando Stanley, Earl of Derby, whose brother William would succeed to the earldom and four years later (in 1595) marry de Vere's eldest daughter, Elizabeth (see Chapter 8).

Once again, Holinshed and Hall (particularly the latter) are considered the main sources.[4] Once again, de Vere had easy access to these works through the library of his childhood tutor Thomas Smith (for Hall) or through his father-in-law, Lord Burghley, to whom the first edition of Holinshed's *Chronicles* was dedicated in 1577. When speaking of Shakespeare's access to the specific books that enlightened commentators agree the Bard had on hand, the issue of access becomes critical. It is known for a fact that de Vere purchased and owned books, had books dedicated to him, and had a direct pipeline to the best libraries in England at a time when there were no public libraries and buying a book was similar in expense and difficulty to purchasing the most advanced and up-to-date computer technology today. For Will Shakspere, before he became rich and famous, we can only assume that he was granted access by someone who had this privilege, such as Henry Wriothesley or Richard Field.[5] There is no record of this, of course, and even after the name Shakespeare became a commodity there are no records or anecdotes that the man from Stratford-upon-Avon owned printed material or made an effort to do so.

Returning to *Henry VI, Part II*, the first three acts delineate the devious manner in which most of the characters shamelessly gang up to destroy the virtuous Duke Humphrey, the king's uncle and only good counselor near his person. So subtly and realistically is this process portrayed that one can only marvel at the author's seemingly instinctive and familiar grasp of the swirling political intrigues attaching to an inner royal court. The Duke of York, a man that everyone should be worried about, lays low and waits in the wings until the powerful Humphrey is disposed of by his petty, jealous rivals, and only then makes his move. The beginning of Humphrey's end occurs when his wife, Duchess Eleanor, is convicted of witchcraft (thanks to her hated rival, Queen Margaret), almost immediately after her husband's exposure and condemnation of the fake Simpcox miracle in Act II, scene i. These scenes of character obsession with the supernatural are drawn out by the Bard in lurid detail, and we should remember that Edward de Vere himself had a noted fascination, if not obsession with the occult.[6]

Long before Duke Humphrey is entrapped by his enemies, however (beginning in *Part I*), he makes the mistake of locking into a death struggle for power with his kinsman, Cardinal Beaufort. Humphrey tries to bring Beaufort to justice for his notorious greed and avarice, to which Beaufort more or less confesses on his deathbed (III.iii.2). The Humphrey-Beaufort feud, seemingly so pointless to non-students of English history and so ultimately destructive because it draws everyone's attention away from the more dangerous York and Somerset, is given curious prominence by the Bard as well. In this conflict we may well be seeing an analogue for the dormant but rumbling breach between the English church and state during the late 1580s and early 1590s. While English Catholics had been effectively reigned in, Anglicans and Puritans were engaging in a bruising war of words à la the Martin Marprelate controversy which 50 years later would become more than verbal. We suspect that Shakespeare's Duke Humphrey and Cardinal Beaufort, respectively, personify the Elizabethan elite peerage and mercantile middle class, along with their differing religious allegiances and personal priorities. The weak and powerless king seems to speak as chorus when after Beaufort's guilt-stricken death he instructs witnesses: "Forbear to judge, for we are sinners all" (III.iii.31). With the double demise of Humphrey and Beaufort at the end of Act III, the English state immediately plunges headlong into chaos.

In Act IV, the forces of evil are unleashed, beginning with Jack Cade, whose rebellion (orchestrated by York—at least according to Shakespeare) provides some of the most notable and troubling scenes in the canon. As Cade's army of thugs and ragamuffins enters London unopposed, Dick the butcher exclaims: "The first thing we do, let's kill all the lawyers" (IV.ii.76), possibly quoted out of context more often than any line in the canon. Shakespeare portrays Dick and his companions as louts and ruffians, and the Bard wanted to kill all the lawyers like he wanted a hole in the head. Recall that de Vere was a legally trained aristocrat who surely had an aristocratic bias for law and order. Soon after Dick puts in his two cents, Cade, under the pseudonym of Mortimer, announces that "Now is Mortimer lord of this city. And here sitting upon London Stone, I charge and command" (IV.vi.1–2). The London Stone that Cade strikes with his staff was a famous landmark in the city center, and was adjacent to Oxford House, one of de Vere's early town residences.[7]

The barbarity of Act IV, scene vii, almost defies description. As Cade condemns Lord Say to death, he catalogues Say's "crimes": "Thou hast most traitorously corrupted the youth of the realm in erecting a grammar school ... thou hast caus'd printing to be us'd" (IV.vii.33, 36). But the final straw comes when Say insults Cade's Kentish homeland in Latin,[8] to which he responds, "Away with him, away with him! He speaks Latin" (IV.vii.57). Not only did de Vere speak Latin and cause printing to be used, he had been involved with the establishment of a grammar school at Earls Colne in his native Essex.[9] Had de Vere been in London during Cade's insurrection, the 17th Earl probably would have found himself strung up before anyone else. In fact, it is rather easy to imagine de Vere as Shakespeare the writer imagining himself as poor Lord Say.

Where Shakespeare came up with his furious harpy and engine of destruction, Queen Margaret, is truly anyone's guess, unless de Vere was thinking of the harpy on his own coat of arms.[10] After Jack Cade is ingloriously dispatched by an honest yeoman from Kent (IV.x), Margaret moves to stage front and center and pretty much stays there for the rest of the trilogy. As she emerges as one of Shakespeare's greatest villainesses in *Parts II* and *III*, Margaret reveals herself to be the mistress-master of manipulation. Her puppets include her husband (the king), her son (the Prince of Wales), Suffolk (her lover), Beaufort and then Buckingham as political intriguers, and finally Somerset and Clifford as soldiers. Even Warwick eventually falls under her spell in *Part III* and pays for it with his life. Most of those who defend her cause die, usually at the hands of the Yorkists; then again, many of those who oppose her die as well. After she succeeds in disposing of Duke Humphrey and his wife, her chief target becomes York, although he (and his sons especially) prove to be more formidable opponents.

Although many of de Vere's apologists would probably resist the comparison, there are a number of parallels between de Vere's dalliances with lady-in-waiting Anne Vavasor and Queen Margaret's scandalous attachment to Suffolk in the trilogy. Earlier in *Part I*, the smug and self-satisfied Suffolk treats Margaret as a prize of war, chauvinistically remarking that "She's beautiful and therefore to be woo'd: / She is a woman: therefore to be won" (V.iii.78–79). By the time she becomes queen, however, Margaret completely turns the tables and becomes Suffolk's boss. Like the illicit lovers in the play, de Vere and his mistress brazenly carried on their affair at court to great approbation, although the queen did not pick up on it until a son was born, just like Queen Margaret appears to have Suffolk's son, who is passed off as the king's instead. Suffolk, like de Vere, was condemned and punished (though in capital fashion for the murder of Duke Humphrey), and his last words before execution are "Suffolk dies by pirates" (IV.i.138), just like de Vere is reported to have almost been killed by his pirate captors on the English Channel in 1576.[11] The wooing scene in *Part I* is not in any of Shakespeare's sources, and the relationship between Margaret and Suffolk in *Part II* appears to be entirely the Bard's own invention.[12]

Another one of Margaret's traits that makes audiences love to hate her is the queen's abusive way with words. During the parlay before the climatic battle of St. Albans in Act V, Margaret inaugurates the deterioration of peace talks by referring to York's four sons as "the bastard boys of York," suggesting that they serve as hostages "for their traitor father" (V.i.115–116). Shakespeare's prolific and effective use of the word "bastard" in this and many other plays cannot help but to remind us that de Vere personally struggled with issues of illegitimacy his entire life. After having his own legitimacy of birth challenged at age 13, and then later as an adult taunted as a "bastard" by the queen,[13] de Vere questioned for many years whether his own eldest daughter belonged to him. Whenever the ultimate insult is required, this is the exact word that the Bard usually resorts to.

York responds to Margaret's aspersions with Shakespeare's favored affront regarding the French-born queen—not her Frenchness (surprisingly) but rather her royal connection to the Kingdom of the Two Sicilies, seated in Naples. York declares her a "Blood-bespotted Neapolitan" and "Outcast of Naples" (V.i.117–118); throughout the trilogy we are repeatedly reminded that she is technically a Sicilian princess. For example, the wedding between Henry VI and Margaret in Act I is presided over by the "Kings of France and Sicil" (I.i.6), implying that these countries now lord it over England. This is really outrageous stuff that typically flies over the heads of audiences. Margaret's father, a penniless and exiled French nobleman, had been ousted from his Sicilian claims by the Spanish Aragonese, who were England's real threat (and pretty much dictated policy to France as well) when the *Henry VI* plays hit the boards. De Vere, it should be remembered, had spent time in both Sicily and France during his Grand Tour in 1575–1576, and probably passed through Naples as well. The predictable thing for Shakespeare to do would have been to bash Margaret's French roots, but instead (as was often the case), he had Sicily and Naples on his mind, and drags those images (however inappropriately) before us.

Last but certainly not least, Act V of *Henry VI, Part II* introduces the world and posterity to Shakespeare's version of York's son Richard, later to become King Richard III. Everyone, including Clifford, scoffs at Richard as a "heap of wrath, foul indigested lump, / As crooked in thy manners as thy shape!" (V.i.157–158), and the belligerent young Clifford chimes in by calling him a "Foul stigmatic" (V.i.215). The young Plantagenet, however, will prove to be his father's frightening right hand in battle. Before hostilities are commenced, Clifford, Warwick, and Richard exchange a vivid series of bear-baiting images that foreshadow the upcoming horrors of combat. Warwick's own badge depicts a "rampant bear chain'd to a ragged staff" (V.i.203), a bear that he is about to unleash against the Lancastrians. This is another one of Shakespeare's favorite images in the canon. De Vere, aside from his other Warwickshire connections, is known to have once sponsored a bear-baiting event in Coventry.[14] Will Shakspere, as a Warwickshire native, would probably have known much of this as well. He certainly would have been familiar with bear-baiting, although it is surprising that there is no record of his entrepreneurial instincts trying to make a profit from it, with an arena located just down the street from the Globe Theater. Defenders of the traditional biography assume, of course, that he would have been too high-minded to engage in such activities.

ℬ 24 ℛ

Henry VI, Part III

Herschel Baker, in his introduction for *Riverside*, aptly described *Henry VI, Part III* as "a play of battles."[1] The action begins in the aftermath of the Yorkist victory at St. Albans in 1455 and concludes with the temporary end of Lancastrian resistance following the murder of Henry VI in 1471. This crime had been immediately preceded by the devastating 1–2 knockout punch delivered by the Yorkists at Barnett and Tewkesbury, both fought in 1471. Fourteen years later (in 1485), the two houses would unite with the marriage between Henry Tudor, Earl of Richmond, and the Princess Elizabeth Plantagenet. Within the 16-year period covered by *Part III*, however, Shakespeare condensed the horrific seesaw nature of the lengthy conflict into five acts that dramatize in stunning fashion the "universe of battle" (to borrow Geoffrey Ward's phrase).[2] The eventual reconciliation of Yorkists and Lancastrians signaled the end of the seemingly endless hostilities that many Englishmen viewed as divine punishment and/or expiation for the unlawful deposition of King Richard II in 1399.

Like its predecessor work, *Henry VI, Part III* was not published in a "respectable form" (Geoffrey Bullough) until the First Folio of 1623. A "bad" anonymous quarto, however, appeared in 1595 as *The True Tragedie of Richard Duke of Yorke*.[3] A subsequent edition of *True Tragedie* in 1600 indicated that the play had been performed by the Lord Pembroke's Men, referring to the acting company sponsored by William Herbert, Earl of Pembroke, later to be Lord Chamberlain and co-dedicatee of Shakespeare's First Folio. Herbert had once negotiated to marry de Vere's daughter Bridget and his brother would eventually marry Bridget's sister Susan. Thus early performances of both *Parts II* and *III* are associated with acting companies sponsored by families whose sons married de Vere's daughters.[4] Most scholars agree that *Part III* was written immediately after *Part II*, although Bullough cautioned that "The early history and authorship for the play [*True Tragedie*] are still much debated."[5] At the end of the day, it can be safely concluded that no one can definitively say exactly how and when these plays originated, although a documented flourish of activity during the early 1590s is readily apparent.

Holinshed, Hall, and Fabyan were Shakespeare's acknowledged starting point for his massive dramatic compression of historical events.[6] Bullough, who meticulously read through the originals, came away amazed: "To a reader of the sources ... it [*Henry VI, Part III*] seems ... astonishing ... in its handling of sprawling, recalcitrant material."[7] Even more astonishing is how Will Shakspere supposedly and conveniently managed to get his hands on these valuable chronicles without leaving a trace of ever having owned, borrowed, or read a book. De Vere, on the other hand, was unavoidably tied to Holinshed via Lord Burghley, plus had access to Hall and Fabyan through the library of his tutor Thomas Smith.[8] Above all, his documented trail of literary and dramatic activity cut a wide swath through the annals of Elizabethan England. For Will Shakspere, we must (yet again) assume, presume, conjecture, speculate, and guess as to how he acquired rare and expensive reading material, the chronicles being only isolated examples in the canon. The concept of public libraries did not exist and would not exist until the 18th century when the self-educated American genius Benjamin Franklin decided that such a thing would be a good idea. Moreover, it is certainly no coincidence that the mythos of William Shakespeare as the ultimate self-taught, poor-boy-made-good took shape at about this same point in history. The widespread belief that everyone had a certain right to information was a product of the Enlightenment and not before. The Bard thus became a convenient exemplar of pulling oneself up by the bootstraps, and he remains one to date, although the icon is being gradually eroded.

Act I, scene iv, of *Henry VI, Part III* is one of the most stirring scenes in the entire canon. York is captured following his disastrous engagement with the Lancastrians at Wakefield in 1460. After the murder of his son Edmund in cold blood (I.iii), York himself faces mocking (on a mole hill with a paper crown) and senseless, summary execution at the hands of Queen Margaret, but not before he dishes out one of the most stinging invectives in the history of drama. Addressing her as "She-wolf of France, but worse than wolves of France / Whose tongue more poisons than the adder's tooth!" (I.iv.111–112), York labels his deadly antagonist an "Amazonian trull [i.e., prostitute]" (I.iv.114) and once more reminds everyone that her father is "King of Naples / Of both the Sicils" (I.iv.121–122). Then comes the real zinger as York pronounces the final judgment of history on Queen Margaret: "O tiger's heart wrapp'd in a woman's hide!" (I.iv.137). Even Margaret's allies on stage are impressed.

York's eloquent condemnation had repercussions outside of Elizabethan theaters. The first arguable allusion to Shakespeare the writer occurred in the infamous *Greene's Groatsworth of Wit* of 1592, where an actor called "Shake-scene" is derided as an "upstart crow" and who (paraphrasing York's line) had a "tiger's heart wrapped in a player's hide."[9] Whether the author of *Groatsworth* was referring to Will Shakspere as a playwright or as a front man is not made explicit; in fact, whether the author of *Groatsworth* was indeed the playwright Robert Greene (supposedly writing on his deathbed) has been challenged on more than one occasion.[10] Suffice it to say that these issues are far from being resolved. As with many Elizabethan works, a cursory read of the awkward and obscure text of *Groatsworth* defies any clear and singular interpretation. It is worth repeating that deliberate equivocation at that time and place in history was often necessary for the self-preservation of any writer, and the suspected real author of *Groatsworth*, Greene's associate Henry Chettle, was in fact compelled by the authorities to issue a subsequent apology.[11]

Oxfordian authors Richard Whalen and Joseph Sobran, along with authorship agnostic Diana Price, have analyzed the *Groatsworth* puzzle as well as anyone to date. On a very basic level, Whalen rightfully wondered that so many orthodox scholars vehemently insist a clear meaning is plainly evident from such an ambiguous and opaque document. Sobran, like others who take the trouble to reflect, noticed a disconnect between the upstart crow actor and Shakespeare the writer.[12] Price humorously characterized

Groatsworth as "Shakespeare's first clipping" in his "theatrical scrapbook" and underscored that Greene's authorship was challenged almost from day one.[13] Lastly, it should be recalled that the credited author of *Groatsworth*, Robert Greene, was associated with de Vere toward the end of his career and dedicated his *Guydonius* or *Card of Fancy* to the 17th Earl in 1584.[14] Whether Greene or Chettle in fact penned *Groatsworth*, perhaps it was Will Shakspere the front man that was being objected to, as opposed to William Shakespeare the writer.

York's cruel and sudden demise at Wakefield invigorated rather than discouraged the forces led by his sons, and it would be 25 years before the Lancastrians really recovered. In early 1461, York's eldest son Edward was declared king at Westminster and a few weeks later a massive gathering of opposing English armies faced off at Towton near the city of York. Towton represented the apex of carnage during the War of the Roses, as a terrified Europe stood back and watched, too frightened to intervene. In Act II, scenes ii through vi, without actually naming the terrible place that was dreadfully synonymous with civil mayhem, Shakespeare leads us through a battle in which Yorkists, Lancastrians, and the best archers in the world hammer away at each other for six hours in a blinding snowstorm. At one point (II.v), King Henry watches in horror as a son recognizes that he has killed his father, while another father realizes that he has killed his son. At the end of the day, the Lancastrians retreated to Scotland, leaving the field to the victorious Yorkists and 38,000 slain.[15] As the fire-eating young Clifford dies on stage with an arrow through his neck, Warwick and the three sons of York mock the corpse. The insatiable Richard Plantagenet only regrets that young Clifford cannot be killed again (II.vi.79–84). Thus ends Shakespeare's blood-chilling account of this horrendous fight.

There is no indication that Will Shakspere was ever a soldier, although this has been occasionally theorized by traditionalists given the apparent familiarity of the author with military life displayed in the canon. Either Shakespeare the writer had personally experienced the alternating feelings of boredom and terror that war inspires, or his imagination could accurately reconstruct these based on interaction with others who had experienced it. As for Edward de Vere, he was no one's idea of a hero but we do know a few things. We know for one that at age 20 he participated in the Earl of Sussex's savage punitive campaign in Scotland during the Northern Rebellion. For another we know that in 1574 and 1584 he briefly visited the Low Countries while the Dutch were fighting for freedom against the Spanish. We know that in 1575–1576 he traveled across the continent as the French, Germans, and Italians engaged in various civil hostilities amongst themselves. We know that he witnessed the Armada campaign in 1588, however much on the periphery. When not witnessing the real thing, de Vere apparently liked to pretend, being a three-time jousting champion and choreographing a huge mock-battle at Warwick Castle[16] in 1572 for the queen's entertainment, an event so large in scale that the locals were frightened out of their wits. Later in 1578, soldier-author Geoffrey Gates dedicated his book titled *The Defense of Militarie Profession* to de Vere,[17] while urging the permanent establishment of an English standing army.

Returning to Shakespeare's play, the Yorkists followed up their hard-earned victory at Towton by sending Warwick to France as an ambassador. His mission was to arrange a marriage of alliance between the French and the new English king, Edward IV. No sooner has the French king, Louis XI (Lewis), agreed to Warwick's proposal than word arrives that the impulsive and sensual Edward has made a common-born woman (Elizabeth Woodville, Lady Grey) his queen, to the great anger of the French and humiliation of Warwick. Also present at this summit in Act III, scene iii, are none other than Queen Margaret with her son, returned to her homeland and petitioning for help. Accompanying them is the young John de Vere, 13th Earl of Oxford, de Vere's great-great-grandfather. Before word arrives of Edward's double-dealing, Warwick and Oxford exchange blunt but respectful opinions as to who their rightful king should be, restating their respective Yorkist and Lancastrian sympathies (III.iii.107–108), serving as a reiteration of the Temple Garden scene from *Part I*, which in fact may have been written afterward. After Warwick is informed of Edward's marriage, he immediately switches sides, patches things up with Queen Margaret and is off with Oxford to make war against his former sovereign.

Act IV displays the Bard's miraculous abilities at historical compression as the events of 10 years are more or less coherently reduced to eight scenes. In short order, Warwick and Oxford are joined by the defectors Montagu and Clarence, and a surprised King Edward is taken prisoner while King Henry is released from prison and restored to the throne. Thus Warwick, the "Proud setter-up and puller-down of kings" (III.iii.156–157), enjoys his last moment of triumph. Thanks to the subtlety and single-handed determination of Richard Plantagenet (now Duke of Gloucester), however, Edward is quickly sprung from prison, a new Yorkist army is raised, and King Henry is once again taken into custody. The stage is now set for Henry's unhappy reign to end.

In a final act of betrayal, Clarence turns against his father-in-law Warwick to rejoin his brothers Edward and Richard (V.i). At the ferocious Battle of Barnett, fought on Easter Sunday in 1471, despite Oxford's victory on the left wing, Warwick was beaten on the right by Richard, now serving in the same battering-ram capacity for his brother Edward that he once filled for his father York. The crucial moment came when, thanks to lack of communication and heavy fog, Warwick's men did not recognize Oxford's contingent coming to their rescue and fired a volley of arrows at their would-be reinforcements.[18] At the end of the engagement, Oxford and his survivors fled, leaving King Henry's "Hector" (IV.viii.25) Warwick and his brother Montagu dead in the field. Curiously, although Barnett is located near London, Shakespeare opted to place much of the action in Acts IV and V in Warwickshire and Coventry, both for events which occurred there and those that did not. This is obviously a point in favor of Will Shakspere, although de Vere had strong Warwickshire connections as well (especially Coventry and Warwick Castle). Perhaps the most important point to remember is that the Earl of Warwick is the center of attention at this point in the play and Warwickshire was his home base of operations.

Far more striking is the prominence that Shakespeare gives to the Earl of Oxford, whose father and brother had died in the Lancastrian cause (III.iii.101–105). "Valiant Oxford" (V.i.1) emerges as a hope for the future toward the end of *Part III*, even more so than Henry Tudor, Earl of Richmond (Queen Elizabeth's grandfather), who makes his entrance in Act IV, scene vi. In addition to historical feats of valor performed by the 13th Earl, Shakespeare gives him credit for things he did not do, such as being present at the Battle of Tewkesbury where he is supposedly taken prisoner.[19] If Will Shakspere was the true author, we can only assume that he was flattering the 17th Earl of Oxford. On the other hand, if de Vere was the playwright, then he was obviously glorifying one of his more illustrious ancestors. Regardless of who the author or authors were, everyone can at least agree on Shakespeare's blatant Lancastrian bias throughout the history plays. For Will Shakspere, the origins of such bias are unknown, other than he may have been understandably buttering up the then-current English monarchy and peerage; after all, to do otherwise would have at bare minimum earned him a one-way ticket back to Stratford-upon-Avon and the none-too-tender jurisdiction of Sir Thomas Lucy. As for de Vere, his ancestral sympathies are well-documented and there for everyone to see.

Henry VI, Part III concludes, fittingly enough, with the Battle of Tewkesbury in 1471, fought three weeks after the Lancastrian disaster at Barnett. Queen Margaret's son, Prince Edward, is butchered before her eyes by Clarence, but she is spared (V.v), presumably because the audience enjoys her suffering so much. The hapless King Henry is then dispatched, fittingly enough, by the future King Richard III, thus setting the stage for Shakespeare's final play in his first historical tetralogy. In a startling last dig, we learn that Margaret's father has raised a ransom for her by pawning his alleged kingdom of Sicily (V.vii.38–40), a complete absurdity, although she was in fact eventually redeemed by the king of France.

From the Oxfordian point of view, it is uncertain whether the Henry VI trilogy was Shakespeare's first venture into the chronicle play genre; most likely it was not. It probably was, however, the Bard's first blockbuster within the public sphere, necessitating a concealment device for the author. Apart from the documented and still-pervasive social stigma regarding publication of nobleman writers, a more fundamental problem was the need to maximize the effectiveness of this not-too-subtle propaganda. The great American poet and champion of the common man (and outspoken anti-Stratfordian) Walt Whitman had this to say about Shakespeare's history plays:

> Conceived out of the fullest heat and pulse of European feudalism—personifying in unparalleled ways the medieval aristocracy, its towering spirit of ruthless and gigantic caste, with its own peculiar air and arrogance (no mere imitation)—only one of the "wolfish earls" so plenteous in the plays themselves, or some born descendent and knower, might seem to be the true author of those amazing works, works in some respects greater than anything else in recorded literature.[20]

Wolfish earls, indeed. The last thing that 16th-century groundlings wanted to hear was a haughty nobleman of the realm encouraging them to put aside their differences and die for their country. Revelation of the Bard as a decadent peer living off the royal largess, however, would have been music to the ears of both English Catholic and Puritan extremists who were unhappy with the status quo and wanted to do away with it.

ℰ❀ 25 ❀℞

Richard III

*"...it's one thing to write as a poet, and very different to write as a historian. The poet
can show us things not as they actually happened, but as they should have happened..."*
—Cervantes, *Don Quixote* [1615][1]

On both sides of the Atlantic there is an organization known as the Richard III Society, whose members devote themselves to making sure that history gives a balanced view of Shakespeare's most villainous king. We applaud their efforts. Most Bardolators are aware that Shakespeare engaged in some serious embellishment of the facts both for the sake of dramatic effect and Tudor propaganda.[2] While Richard was certainly no saint, the smear campaign conducted against him by five successive Tudor monarchs following his defeat and death at the Battle of Bosworth in 1485 appears unprecedented in the annals of English history. Not widely known is that Shakespeare was far from the first writer to denigrate him. Indeed, Shakespeare's *Richard III* can be aptly described as the greatest hits of Richard's alleged villainies—both real and imagined. Audiences of this play need to always bear in mind that the victor of Bosworth, Henry Tudor, Earl of Richmond, was the grandfather of Queen Elizabeth I. Accordingly, Shakespeare's accommodation of the Tudor dynasty's Lancastrian sympathies can make the work of D.W. Griffith look like child's play.[3]

The publication history of *Richard III* is confusing, even to the experts. The first quarto of the play was published anonymously in 1597, followed by a second quarto under the name "William Shake-speare" in 1598.[4] A total of six quarto editions appeared before the First Folio of 1623, all somewhat different, thus creating major difficulties for most editors. In addition to these, an earlier anonymous work, *The True Tragedy of Richard III*, had been published in 1594. Given this profusion, *Richard III* can rightfully be included among the Bard's most popular plays from its very inception.[5]

Unflattering portrayals of Richard began to appear from the winners of Bosworth very early on. One of these, *The History of King Richard the Third*, published in 1513 during the time of Henry VIII, was written by none other than Thomas More, and orthodox scholars agree it contains many elements later used by the Bard.[6] This particular work is also believed to have an eyewitness source—John Morton, Bishop of Ely, who appears as a character in Shakespeare's play.[7] Another acknowledged source was Edward Hall's *The Union of the Two Noble and Illustre Famelies of Lancastre and York*, published in 1550 during King Edward VI's reign.[8] More and Hall were relied on to a fair extent by Raphael Holinshed,[9] whose *Chronicles* were first published in 1577. All of these works were hostile to the memory of Richard, understandably so since to be otherwise during the Tudor era would constitute immediate grounds for censorship or worse. As for Edward de Vere, his ancestors, particularly John de Vere, the 13th Earl of Oxford, had fought hard to overthrow Richard and establish Henry VII as king. In addition, the 17th Earl himself was part of same Cecil household (as a royal ward) that patronized Holinshed, who dedicated the first edition of his *Chronicles* to Lord Burghley. Holinshed also was among the jurors who absolved de Vere of a murder charge in 1567.[10]

Among Shakespeare's recognized sources, however, the most intriguing is the anonymous play titled *The True Tragedy of Richard III*, first published in 1594 and believed to have been written earlier. The quarto informs us that the play had been performed by the Queen's Men, a group known to have personnel overlap with de Vere's own acting company.[11] Herschel Baker, in his introduction for *Riverside*, admitted that the *True Tragedy* is "a crude but not wholly unsuccessful attempt to combine the motif of Senecan revenge with the English history play."[12] Others such as Geoffrey Bullough firmly acknowledged the obvious, that Shakespeare was well acquainted with this work and probably had it close at hand when he produced the 1597 version.[13] Other orthodox scholars have averted their eyes to the implications of this earlier work, even after admitting that an evolving process of revision is reflected by nearly insurmountable textual problems existing between Shakespeare's quarto and First Folio texts.

Very little can be said about the close relationship between Shakespeare's play and the *True Tragedy* that has not already been said by Oxfordian scholar Ramón Jiménez. Myriad similarities in language and structure are found. One typical example occurs when Richard cries out, "A horse, a horse! My kingdom for a horse" (V.iv.7), echoed in the *True Tragedy* with "A horse! A horse! A fresh horse!"[14] Both plays repeat historical errors not found in the source material.[15] Shakespeare even quotes a line from the *True Tragedy* in *Hamlet*.[16] Taken as a whole, the evidence strongly points to Shakespeare's *Richard III* as belonging to the large group of plays drawing upon anonymous works with near-identical titles and printed only a few years earlier. Analysts can choose two different views: either Shakespeare was revising someone else's work and putting his name to it, or he was revising and improving his own earlier effort. Orthodoxy tends to shy away from this latter scenario because the idea of the Bard as anything other than a spontaneous creator of full-blown masterpieces is abhorrent to them.

Among the identified secondary sources for the play is the collection known as *A Mirror for Magistrates*, with the 1563 edition including a poem on Mistress Jane Shore written by the soldier-poet Thomas Churchyard.[17] Shore, who was mistress to Richard's brother King Edward IV and later to Lord Hastings, is a lightning rod in the play for criticism. Churchyard had a long association with de Vere, beginning in 1567 when de Vere sent him on a mission to the Low Countries, through at least 1590 when he rented London lodgings in de Vere's name. In between, he published a commendatory letter for *Cardanus Comforte*, dedicated to and prefaced by de Vere in 1573. His poems also appeared alongside of de Vere's in the collection titled *A Paradise of Dainty Devices* (1576), and he promised to dedicate future works to de Vere (though he never did so) in two 1580 pamphlets, *Churchyardes Charge* and *Churchyardes Chance*.[18]

One of the more striking secondary influences on *Richard III*, though infrequently commented upon, is the anonymous history play titled *Arden of Feversham*, published in 1592,[19] two years before the *True Tragedy*. In Shakespeare's play, Richard's first victim is his brother George, Duke of Clarence, who while imprisoned in the Tower of London relates a dream to his guard that foreshadows his own death (I.iv.9). This passage has a striking resemblance to the dream speech given by Arden in the anonymous play that anticipates his murder. Arden's wife conspires with their servant Michael in hiring two killers to commit the deed, just as Richard arranges with Tyrrel to hire two assassins for George in Shakespeare's play. Curiously, the names of two killers in *Arden of Feversham* are "Shakebag" and "Black Will,"[20] possibly intended as a practical joke against Will Shakspere.

The true story of Arden's murder (in 1551) was taken directly from Holinshed's 1577 edition of the *Chronicles*. Oxfordian Eva Turner Clark believed that this incident was dramatized two years later for a court performance by the Lord Chamberlain's Men at Whitehall on March 3, 1579, as the anonymous (now lost) play titled *The History of the Murderous Mychaell*. De Vere himself acted in a production at Whitehall during that same Shrovetide season, and Clark believed that he was also involved with *The Murderous Mychaell*.[21] A more dubious association with de Vere had occurred earlier in 1573 when his former servant George Brown murdered one George Saunders, apparently in collaboration with the victim's wife, similar to earlier events involving Arden. Two separate accounts of this latter-day crime were published in 1577 by Holinshed and de Vere's uncle, Arthur Golding, the English translator of Ovid. A third account was published by de Vere's servant Anthony Munday in 1580, then dramatized in yet another anonymous play, *A Warning for Fair Women*, in 1599.[22] Thus de Vere had connections with every single writer of the period who covered the Saunders murder, including Holinshed, who chronicled the original Arden case. These incidents of course reflect only one single episode from *Richard III*—one, however, that sets the tone for the entire play. *Arden of Feversham*'s relationship to *Richard III* is further strengthened by the numerous verbal parallels between the two plays noted by Clark.[23]

The arranged murder of George in *Richard III* comes off as dastardly in the extreme given that Richard and George had fought together at Barnett and Tewkesbury in 1471 to place their brother Edward on the throne. The play begins here as Richard delivers his soliloquy "Now is the winter of our discontent made glorious summer by this son of York" (I.i.1–2). Richard then informs the audience of his true objective, and the first obstacles he must remove are his own two brothers. De Vere was accused of plotting murders for hire, just like Richard, although in fairness it should be added that these accusations came from enemies that he had accused of treason.[24] After the body count has accumulated, Richard at first struggles with his conscience, frankly admitting, "I am a villain" (V.iii.191), but he quickly reverses himself with "yet I lie, I am not" (V.iii.191). Finally, he faces up to his crimes and delivers his own judgment, "Guilty! guilty!" (V.iii.199). This sounds suspiciously like remorse, a near universal emotion, but even more believable if being voiced by Edward de Vere during the 1590s.

Of all the alleged crimes committed by Richard, the most heinous (and the one that signals the beginning of his downfall) are the murders of his two young nephews, Edward, Prince of Wales (and briefly King Edward V), and his younger brother Richard, Duke of York, after they have been confined in the Tower. This is partially facilitated by King Richard's sudden claim that the boys are illegitimate and not his lawful nephews.[25] Thus we are once again led by the Bard into a prolonged dramatic conflict over the issue of bastardy, as in *King Lear, King John, Much Ado About Nothing,* and other plays. De Vere, as most Oxfordians know, had to deal with this issue his entire life, beginning with himself, and then later with his own children; plus this was known to have been (understandably) a hot button issue for him. Also like the two young princes, de Vere did a stint in the Tower of London in 1581. This came in the aftermath of his extramarital affair with Anne Vavasor, which along with other accumulated follies, effectively wrecked his political career and reputation. It seems as though the Bard, in rewriting English history, enjoyed latching on to any particular aspect of that history that also applied to the contemporary Earl of Oxford.

By an unhappy confluence, Richard's evil henchman in the play (also named in the chronicles) is James Tyrrel, while the name of de Vere's stepfather was Charles Tyrrell. Whether the two were related is uncertain,[26] but if de Vere had a hand in the creation, one can only imagine what distasteful associations he had with the man who married his mother not long after his father's death. Although there is no clear-cut evidence of Hamlet-like hostility between de Vere and Charles Tyrrell, there is no indication that they were close, either. Tyrrell left de Vere a horse in his will (the young earl had once given him a horse), but de Vere later dreamt of his stepfather's ghost holding a whip[27]—not a fond memory, to be sure. The historical James Tyrrel supposedly confessed to his crimes during the reign of Henry VII,[28] but the truth of the matter is a strong point of contention between Richard's apologists and his critics. One thing all Bardolators can agree upon is that Shakespeare had a hefty Lancastrian bias in the history plays; the portrayal of James Tyrrel is only one example of this. In the case of de Vere, there would have been additional reasons for wanting to vilify the family name of Tyrrell, if in fact de Vere was the true author.

In contrast to widespread fascination with the murder of the two young princes, the intriguing topic of Richard's refined skill at faking religious piety is inexplicably avoided by most commentators. In fact, when not committing murder or grasping at power, he takes a lot of trouble to appear benevolent.[29] The Bard clearly had great contempt for this personality type, and chose to make it a hallmark feature of his greatest political villain. For example, Richard does not sleep around and is never caught, as Buckingham puts it, "dallying with the brace of courtesans" (III.vii.74). His courtships of Lady Anne and the Princess Elizabeth are conducted with all due propriety. He works hard at being chummy with the Bishop of Ely (III.iv.31–34)—before lowering the boom on Hastings, that is. When Buckingham artfully manipulates "the citizens" into offering Richard the crown, the latter pretends to be cloistered in meditation, emerging only with appropriate reluctance and a book of prayer in hand, flanked by two clergymen (III.vii.94–99). One of the more devastating scenes (Act II, scene i) occurs when, after exchanging insincere reconciliation with his enemies, Richard announces that George is dead, hurrying his elder brother Edward to the grave while casting suspicions on the same individuals whom he has just embraced.

Even more striking is Richard's puritanical attitude toward sex. From the very beginning, he is quick to condemn, both openly and by insinuation, the illicit relations between Mistress Shore and his brother the king (I.i.98–100). Then, after Edward's death, he does the same thing to Hastings, using it as a prelude to accusations of witchcraft that result in Hastings' immediate execution (III.iv.71). Richard is highly adept at advocating conventional sexual mores in order to further his own political agenda. This is a surprising choice for an Elizabethan playwright to make during an era when Puritan influence in Parliament was rising and would continue to grow for the next half-century. Of course, any self-respecting dramatist at that time would probably have taken a highly jaundiced view of the Puritans, since the latter were determined to put the playhouses out of business—and would eventually succeed in doing so. De Vere himself was notorious for loose sexual behavior, although it would be unfair to assume that Will Shakspere was any different.

In addition to Richard's startling witchcraft allegations against Mistress Shore and the Dowager Queen, this play, like so many others in the canon, abounds in supernatural references. Like his murdered brother George, Richard has nightmare visions on the eve of Bosworth, and his defeat and death are foreshadowed by a solar eclipse (V.iii.276–283). Similarly, Lord Stanley dreams of a deadly boar when he realizes that Richard is about to do away with Hastings (III.ii.10–11). Nothing is known of Will Shakspere's interest in the occult, but there can be no doubting de Vere's enthusiasm, having patronized John Dee and other astrologers of the day.[30] As for dreams and visions, de Vere allegedly conversed with the dead, including his deceased mother (who appeared as a prophetess), and, as previously mentioned, he had a very threatening vision of his dead stepfather, among other things.[31]

The boar symbolism relating to Richard's badge[32] easily connects to de Vere as well. The Vere coat of arms prominently featured boars; plus there were a number of other associations that he and his family had with this particular beast. For example, de Vere himself was once unflatteringly alluded to as a boar by his rival Christopher Hatton.[33] As a noted playwright, especially for comedy, we assume that de Vere's talent included an ability to verbally skewer one's adversaries in a very boar-like manner. This would likely be true even if he was not in fact Shakespeare the writer.

Shakespeare's use of the Earl of Oxford as a character in *Richard III* and other history plays is indicative. John de Vere had played a conspicuous role in the War of the Roses, culminating with his Tudor alliance at Bosworth. Eminent Oxfordian scholar Dr. Daniel Wright observed that, in direct contrast to Richard's tormented conscience on the eve of battle, the 13th Earl proclaims, "Every man's conscience is a thousand men, / To fight against a guilty homicide" (V.ii.17–18).[34] This is one of many examples in the canon where a past Earl of Oxford is either unnecessarily glorified or whose misbehavior is expunged from the record. Perhaps Shakespeare was just trying to compliment the current Earl of Oxford; on the other hand, even complimenting Elizabethan nobility could be highly risky business.[35] A far safer course, especially for a playwright, would have been to say as little as possible regarding powerful personages and to not stray too far from the chronicle record.

De Vere was known to have been a skillful public speaker, and boasted of himself as such.[36] It is hard to imagine the Bard as anything else. In the play, the contrasting pep talks of Henry (V.iii.237–270) and Richard (V.iii.314–341) to their respective armies at Bosworth underscore their personal differences. Henry addresses his soldiers as "loving countrymen" and then proceeds to invoke the name of God six times, tossing in Saint George and the holy saints for good measure. Regarding their adversaries, he generously proclaims that "those whom we fight against / Had rather have us win than him they follow." Richard follows in the next scene by labeling Henry's army as a collection of "vagabonds, rascals, and runaways," "scum of Britains and base lackey peasants," "stragglers," "overweening rags of France," "famish'd beggars," "poor rats," and "bastard Britains" (there's that word again). No mistaking good guys and bad guys here.

Many other characters in *Richard III* seem to relate to people in de Vere's life: Thomas Stanley, Lord Derby, was an ancestor of de Vere's son-in-law William Stanley; the tragic Lady Anne at times resembles de Vere's first wife Anne Cecil; and even the doomed Prince Edward is reminiscent of a younger, precocious de Vere.[37] Among the secondary characters, however, the true standout is Richard's mother, the Duchess of York, who repeatedly scorns Richard, even after he becomes king. This animosity was invented by Shakespeare.[38] Before cursing her son and disowning him for good, the Duchess furiously upbraids Richard:

> Thou cam'st on earth to make the earth my hell.
> A grievous burthen was thy birth to me,
> Tetchy and wayward was thy infancy;
> Thy school-days frightful, desp'rate, wild, and furious,
> Thy prime of manhood daring, bold, and venturous;
> Thy age confirm'd, proud, subtle, sly, and bloody,
> More mild, but yet more harmful—kind in hatred.
> What comfortable hour canst thou name
> That ever grac'd me with thy company? [IV.iv.166–175].

This sounds like de Vere, who was no one's idea of a model son. Furthermore, happy mother-son relationships are virtually nonexistent in the canon. With Richard's final break from his mother, we may be catching a glimpse of the True Tragedy of Edward de Vere.

ℬ 26 ℛ

Henry VIII

The broad consensus among commentators is that Shakespeare's last history play was brought to completion by other hands. It did not appear in print until the First Folio of 1623,[1] and there are no recorded performances before 1613. Though never one of the Bard's more popular works, *Henry VIII* is the only history play—indeed the *only* Shakespeare drama—that touches directly upon *the* big issue of the day, namely, the turbulent overlap between religion and politics among our European ancestors. Thus it provides curious insight into the unspoken anxieties of Jacobean society. *Henry VIII* represents the chronological culmination of Shakespeare's great English history cycle, with events leading to the dawn of the Elizabethan era. The play dramatizes the concurrent births of the English Reformation and the Princess Elizabeth in 1533, as well as the intertwined conflicts surrounding these occurrences.[2]

The leading candidate for Shakespeare's collaborator on this underappreciated work is the Jacobean playwright John Fletcher (1579–1625), who may have completed ideas originally sketched out by the Bard himself.[3] Like the great Renaissance painters who often farmed out brushstrokes to assistants and colleagues, Shakespeare the writer probably had a degree of help from other writers, actors, and editors, both during and after his lifetime. Recall that 18 plays (one of which was *Henry VIII*) did not appear in print until 1623; thus what we see is not necessarily what the Bard himself wrote.[4] This helps to explain the staggering, nearly superhuman range of vocabulary and style in the canon, although this was a time when the English language was in flux, which also partially accounts for the seemingly endless verbal inventiveness. Although *Henry VIII* was certainly performed late during the life of Will Shakspere (d. 1616), one cannot categorically rule out the possibility that the final 1623 First Folio text contained some degree of posthumous collaboration.

Edmund Chambers was understandably uneasy with assigning firm dates to this work. He admitted that "The reversion to the epic chronicle at the very end of Shakespeare's career is odd. I have sometimes thought that an earlier plot may have been adapted."[5] Given that Shakespeare's other history plays were written during the 1590s, for him to have revisited an old genre does seem counterintuitive. Since it is unlikely that Queen Elizabeth would have sanctioned any play dealing with her origins and birth (no matter how flattering), it is reasonable to suppose that the work represents an early Jacobean commission that possibly had some delay before its first production. As for Chambers' conjectured "earlier plot," no such work has ever been identified,[6] although Shakespeare's original, unfinished (?) manuscript may have provided this.

As for the primary source material, one need not go much further than Holinshed. Although other secondary sources have been suggested, Geoffrey Bullough was definite: "The main source for *Henry VIII* was Holinshed's *Chronicles*...."[7] Raphael Holinshed belonged to the large circle of patronage extended by Lord Burghley (de Vere's guardian), and would have been surely acquainted with the young earl (and vice-versa). As for Will Shakspere, there are no known connections between him and the author whose *Chronicles* were not far from the Bard's fingertips as he reimagined English history.

Henry VIII has the distinction of receiving the most infamous single performance of a Shakespeare play, taking place at the Globe Theater in London on June 29, 1613.[8] According to eyewitnesses, the highly combustible thatched roof of the playhouse caught flames after a mock canon was fired in Act I, scene iv, and the entire edifice promptly burned to the ground, although miraculously, no one perished.[9] Immediate public reaction emphasized that the conflagration represented God's wrath against the wickedness epitomized by the playhouses. Just as the London earthquake of 1580 (which had rocked the theaters) was interpreted by Puritan preachers as a warning to their flocks, the burning of the Globe in 1613 was viewed as a divine rebuke to anyone who would support this kind of entertainment. Samuel Schoenbaum noted sardonically that these same preachers were infuriated when less than a year later a second Globe Theater was constructed on the very same site.[10] In 1642, however, the Globe and other playhouses would be closed and demolished following Puritan victory in the English Civil War.

In many ways, King James had laid the groundwork for these conflicts. With the accession of James in 1603 (and official peace with Spain), the Puritans began to truly focus their earnest and exclusive attention on domestic affairs. Although an enthusiastic patron of the theater, James did not have a Lord Burghley to deal with the religious conservatives, nor Elizabeth's spotless image for personal morality. While James had received a Calvinist education, he was no friend to the Puritans; in fact, his entire reign seems to have been a reaction against them. Upon taking the throne, James was confronted by a Puritan majority in Parliament making what he viewed as presumptuous, self-righteous demands. Having received an earful of Calvinism from his childhood tutors, James was allergic to all forms of proselytizing, and enjoyed private performances in which Puritan characters were portrayed with the long ears of an ass.[11] Rebuffing their requests for church reforms at the Hampton Court Conference of 1604 immediately got James off on the wrong foot with the Puritans, but he threw them a bone by agreeing to sponsor the first authorized English translation of the Bible. At first glance, it seems incredible that Shakespeare was not one of the 47 scholars chosen to work on the project[12]; however, playwrights were considered too disreputable for religious work. Given the climate of the times, a nobleman playwright would have been even more politically incorrect. Had de Vere lived to participate, it would have been done secretly, although he had once drunkenly boasted that he could write "a better and more orderly scripture in six days."[13] Regardless of whether de Vere was Shakespeare, he would have been viewed as the embodiment of the elite peerage, as well as everything considered wrong with the nobility.

Given that *Henry VIII* deals with the theme of state-sponsored religion more than any other Shakespeare play, this flourish of royally endorsed Bible activity between 1604 and 1611 seems a natural prelude. In 1611 the King James Bible was finally published but greeted with suspicion by those Puritans who were partial to the old Geneva translation.

More ominous for the monarchy in 1612 was the death of the popular Prince Henry, one of the few people viewed favorably by all sides and, before his untimely demise, seen as a small glimmer of hope for the future. These events, along with the growing, mutual defiance between the king and Parliament, formed the backdrop to the 1613 appearance of *Henry VIII*, a play that none too subtly reinforces the religious supremacy of the English crown over all competitors. Not surprisingly, the work concludes by praising the reign of James as an extension of Elizabeth's (V.v.39–55).

While modern takes on King Henry VIII tend to catalogue his six forays into the institution of holy matrimony, Shakespeare had other, more narrowly focused concerns: specifically, Queen Elizabeth's royal legitimacy as Henry's daughter.[14] Modern audiences who take for granted Elizabeth's iconographic legacy as the Virgin Queen tend to forget that during her own time she was viewed by enemies of the Anglican Church as no more than King Henry's bastard (and heretic) child by Anne Boleyn. The Catholic Church refused to recognize Henry's second marriage or divorce from his first wife, Catherine of Aragon ("Katherine" in the play), prompting an English Reformation that would not be consolidated until later during Elizabeth's reign. De Vere, as we know, had several brushes with these issues, having his own legitimacy challenged as a child and later with two of his children. The Queen reportedly taunted de Vere for being a bastard (literally and/or figuratively), which was taken unkindly by the 17th Earl.[15]

In addition to Elizabeth's disputed right to the throne, Glorianna had to live (like her father before her) in the shadow of Queen Isabella I of Spain, the mother of her father's first wife Catherine and grandmother of her half-sister Mary. It is difficult (if not impossible) for our modern Anglocentric sensibilities to fully appreciate the regard in which Isabella was held in Christendom during that time. Born a Castilian princess in 1451 (about the most insecure title one could hold), Isabella consecrated her life to the establishment of an earthly, Christian political dominance in the wake of the Ottoman conquest of Constantinople in 1453. Given the unique opportunity to choose her own suitor, the teenage princess opted for a man (Ferdinand of Aragon) who, from all accounts, was not the sharpest knife in the drawer, but had steadiness and other qualities that Isabella appreciated. In quick succession, northern Spain's warring kingdoms were unified, Muslims were driven from the Iberian Peninsula (after a seven-century hold), the Inquisition was established, Jews were expelled, the fanatical Christopher Columbus was hired as a pious gamble in exploration, and Conquistadors were unleashed against the New World. By the time Isabella died in 1504 at age 53, Spain had become the most powerful empire on earth. This was all accomplished by one generation and posterity can only marvel at the personal dedication (however misguided on occasion) that was required and surely inspired by the example of Isabella herself.

Elizabeth's mother, Anne Boleyn—"a spleeny Lutheran" (III.ii.99), as Wolsey calls her—had neither Catherine of Aragon's pedigree nor the support of world opinion, but she did have a temporary hold on Henry's affections, and the king desperately wanted a male heir, which Catherine could apparently no longer produce. Catherine had earlier given Henry a daughter who would go on to lead a violent Catholic backlash against the English Reformation, forever earning her the unflattering sobriquet of "Bloody Mary." Not surprisingly, Mary does not make an appearance in Shakespeare's play. Elizabeth's first great political victory would be staying alive during her half-sister's reign of terror.

Also conspicuously absent from the events depicted in Shakespeare's play is Thomas More, martyred into Catholic sainthood by the king for his opposition (on principle) to Henry's divorce from Catherine and hasty remarriage to Anne Boleyn.[16] The omission of More as a character is underscored by the reverent portrayal of Thomas Cramner, Archbishop of Canterbury, who supported the king's break with Rome,[17] and by the depiction of Cardinal Wolsey as a brilliant but ultimately tragic and misguided counselor.[18] Thomas More was, however, the subject of another Elizabethan play at least partially attributed to Shakespeare and appropriately titled *Sir Thomas More*. This work apparently never made it past the manuscript phase (presumably because it was censored),[19] but is nevertheless of great interest for being one of the few surviving Elizabethan play manuscripts. The work is even more famous because one of the collaborating, anonymous playwrights (known as "Hand D") is thought by many true believers to have been the Bard himself. Unfortunately, attempts to analytically connect "Hand D" with Will Shakspere's six accredited, scrawled signatures, though Herculean in effort, at the end of the day have slightly more scientific credibility than those made on behalf of the Shroud of Turin. Furthermore, both Chambers and Schoenbaum, though they earnestly wanted to believe, admitted that the original draft of *Sir Thomas More* was probably written by Anthony Munday,[20] servant and secretary to Edward de Vere.

Another character omitted from *Henry VIII*, but given a prominent role in *Sir Thomas More* (for no apparent reason), is the poet Henry Howard, Earl of Surrey, who was de Vere's uncle,[21] English translator of Virgil, and pioneer of the English sonnet form that Shakespeare later adopted. Surrey would be one of the last people executed by Henry before his death in 1547, on what was probably a trumped-up charge of treason. Oxfordian Joseph Sobran observed that the author of this play went to considerable trouble in changing historical facts so that Howard would be presented in a favorable light. Not the least of these changes included making him old enough to participate in events, when in fact he was only a teenager at the time.[22]

In recent years, the alleged Catholic sympathies of Will Shakspere have become a popular (and potentially explosive) topic of debate. To say that the strident patriotism of Shakespeare's history plays was written by someone in allegiance to the Church of Rome may be more controversial than saying Shakespeare was not Shakespeare. Putting the shoe on the other foot, Edward de Vere had his own experimentation with Catholicism during the 1570s, before dramatically renouncing his Catholic associates in the presence of the queen on December 16, 1580.[23] One difference, therefore, between de Vere and Will Shakspere (assuming the latter had covert Catholic sympathies) is that de Vere confessed and recanted in the very presence of his monarch. If the Oxfordian theory is correct, then it is not difficult to surmise that, in return for Elizabeth's royal forgiveness, the theatrical de Vere was instructed to become the unofficial propagandist for the English Reformation (via Shakespeare's history plays). The unsavory alternative (again, assuming that Will Shakspere was a secret Catholic) is that the creation of this towering pro-Anglican corpus was in reality an act of cynical masquerading committed for the sake of monetary profit.

Almost every Bardolator at one time or another indulges in speculation, and this one is no exception. We believe de Vere could never bring himself to finish *Henry VIII* because of hard feelings with Elizabeth that remained even after her death in 1603.

Whether this situation was partly or entirely his own fault is irrelevant. The fact remains that, after 1581, de Vere never fully recovered the goodwill of his prince, notwithstanding his staggering annuity grant in 1586. By 1593, de Vere was complaining to Lord Burghley, "that in place of receiving that ordinary favour which is of course granted to the meanest subject, I was browbeaten [by the queen] and had many bitter speeches given me."[24] If bruised feelings still remained by 1603 (as was likely the case), then the act of writing a history play in praise of the Virgin Queen's legitimacy and birth may have been just a little too much for the author. For Will Shakspere, there is absolutely no indication of any ambivalence that he may have had toward his monarch (even had he dared), whereas for de Vere there is plenty. Why did Shakespeare the writer not eulogize the queen upon her death? One subtle moral of the play is summed up by Norfolk, who prudently warns Buckingham in regard to Wolsey, "Heat not a furnace for your foe so hot that it do singe yourself" (I.i.140). If de Vere did in fact have a hand in the creation of Shakespeare's astounding history cycle, it may have been that he (like Buckingham in the play) got more than he bargained for in the end. For one, he may have found himself ultimately at the mercy of an icon that he himself had helped to create.

PART THREE

৯৯৩

TRAGEDIES AND POEMS

∾ 27 ∾

Troilus and Cressida

One thing that most Bardolators can agree upon is that Shakespeare the playwright delighted in blending genres and defying categories. *Romeo and Juliet* starts out as a comedy until Mercutio is killed and then makes an about-face into high tragedy. *Love's Labor's Lost* is a comedy in which the boy does not get the girl. Ancient history is retold as both tragedy (*Antony and Cleopatra*) and romance (*Cymbeline*). *The Merchant of Venice* is often classified as a "dark" comedy. *Hamlet* is suffused with the influence of *commedia dell' arte*. *Titus Andronicus* mixes horror with over-the-top humor. English history plays are in a category by themselves, a category that the Bard himself more or less invented. Regarding *Troilus and Cressida*, however, Samuel Taylor Coleridge wrote that "There is no one of Shakespeare's plays harder to characterize."[1] If this were not enough, *Troilus* possibly has the most bizarre publication history of any play ever written. "What is it?" and "Where did it come from?" become threshold questions among scholars for which there has been little consensus to date.

Troilus and Cressida was entered with the Stationers Register in 1603 as having been acted by the Lord Chamberlain's Men (later to become the King's Men), but was not printed until 1609,[2] having been reregistered and published by a different partnership than the original registrar. This is only the beginning of complications. The **Historie** (emphasis added) *of Troylus and Cresseida* by "William Shakespeare" was advertised as having been performed by the King's Men at the Globe Theater, but almost immediately this blurb was replaced in another 1609 publication that deleted these references.[3] Furthermore, this corrected edition added a lengthy, anonymous introduction, presumably written by the publisher, that defies any clear-cut interpretation.[4] Beginning with the enigmatic invocation "A never writer, to an ever reader,"[5] the introduction describes *Troilus and Cressida* as "a new play, never staled with the stage, never clapper-clawed with the palms of the vulgar ... [or] ... sullied with the smoky breath of the multitude,"[6] then proceeds to repeatedly and insistently label the work as a comedy.[7] The advertisement continues with the warning that "when he [Shakespeare] is gone and his comedies out of sale, you will scramble for them...."[8] Startlingly, the publisher brags of his piracy, having obtained the manuscript in spite of "the grand possessors' wills."[9] Fourteen years later, *Troilus and Cressida* was republished in the First Folio of 1623, again in a mystifying manner. Originally consigned among the tragedies, it was replaced by *Timon of Athens* at the last minute and then reinserted between the histories and tragedies, with no mention whatsoever in the table of contents. The header reads *The **Tragedie** (emphasis added) of Troylus and Cresida.*[10]

Some commentators have tried to explain this confusion as being the result of copyright disputes, but it may be that 17th-century editors were just as puzzled as their 21st-century counterparts. Some of these critics, after laying out a scenario in which half of Jacobean London was supposedly involved, will turn around a few pages later and remind us that play authorship was not that big a deal at the time. Oxfordians speculate that the spurt of unauthorized Shakespeare publications in 1609 was triggered by de Vere's widow, the Countess of Oxford (one of the "grand possessors"?), selling her house at King's Place in Hackney, with certain contents that probably included de Vere's papers. As to the classification of *Troilus*, Geoffrey Bullough, in a rare slip (for him), joined the proverbial smart set by calling the play a "savage comedy."[11] More egregiously, the second edition of *Riverside* listed *Troilus* among the comedies.[12] Who's kidding who here? Love is betrayed, Hector dies, and almost everyone lives unhappily ever after. The biggest casualty, however, is the cherished Homeric ideal of western civilization, which receives the rudest squashing ever endured at the hands of a poet. Would we call *Hamlet* a comedy just because there are funny moments?[13] Edmund Chambers, above the fray as usual, sensibly observed that "if the play is thought of as tragedy rather than comedy, it falls into place as a development of the critical attitude to life already apparent in *Hamlet*."[14]

Bullough summed up the state of affairs with "How long before the 1603 entry in Stationers Register *Troilus* was written has been much debated."[15] There were no definite recorded performances before the 19th century, although the publication history seems to indicate that private audiences may have seen the work during Shakespeare's time.[16] Oxfordians postulate that the origins of *Troilus* go back at least to December 27, 1584, when an anonymous, lost play titled *The History of Agamemnon and Ulisses* was performed by Oxford's Boys, the children's acting troupe sponsored by de Vere.[17] Everyone from Edmund Chambers to John Thomas Looney has recognized at least a possible connection between this early work and Shakespeare's play, given the large speaking roles of these two characters and that the tragedy of the two lovers is set against the much larger backdrop of the Trojan War.[18] In 1584, Will Shakspere was 20 years old and dreaming of escape from Stratford-upon-Avon, perhaps inspired by de Vere's other acting company (Oxford's Men), which had barnstormed through Warwickshire during the early 1580s.[19] As for the 34-year-old de Vere, during this same period he was heavily involved in a wide variety of theatrical and literary activities.

For source material, Shakespeare used Homer's *Iliad* as his starting point.[20] The first English translation was by George Chapman in 1598, usually assumed to have been utilized by the Bard.[21] We first note that the library of de Vere's guardian and father-in-law Lord Burghley contained an Italian translation of the *Iliad*,[22] and that de Vere (like the Queen) was known to have been fluent in Italian. Moreover, George Chapman and de Vere apparently knew each other quite well. We base this statement on Chapman's 1613 play, *The Revenge of Bussy d'Ambois*, in which Chapman portrays de Vere in an almost mythological, heroic light, similar to one of Homer's characters:

> Of England, the most goodly fashion'd man
> I ever saw: from head to foote in form
> Rare, and most absolute; hee had a face
> Like one of the most ancient honor'd Romanes,
> From whence his noblest Familie was deriv'd;

> He was beside of spirit passing great,
> Valiant, and learn'd, and liberall as the Sunne,
> Spoke and writ sweetly, or of learned subjects,
> Or of the discipline of public weales;
> And t'was the Earle of Oxford...

This from the man who first translated Homer into English. The encounter between the two men is portrayed as having taken place on the continent during the 1570s.[23] For Chapman, de Vere seemed to embody the aristocratic values endorsed by Ulysses (whether sincere or not) in Act I, scene iii, of *Troilus*.

Like other Renaissance humanists, the Bard appears to have been fascinated with the fall of Troy, based on the number of canonical allusions. For example, in *The Rape of Lucrece* (see Chapter 39), the action comes to a dead halt as the heroine recites a lengthy digression giving a pictorial representation of the Trojan War. Outside the world of classical scholarship, it is not generally known that the source for many of these legendary events is not Homer, but rather Virgil's *Aeneid*. The influence of this work on Shakespeare's *Troilus*, along with Ovid's *Metamorphoses*, has been recognized as well.[24] In the case of both ancient authors, the first English translations were by de Vere's uncles: Ovid by Arthur Golding, and Virgil by Henry Howard, Earl of Surrey. Given these various connections, we are at a loss to name another Elizabethan nobleman who would have been better placed than de Vere for second-natured familiarity with the Trojan legend, as told by Homer, Virgil, and Ovid.[25] In his own personal letters, de Vere would use the image of Aeneas (a character in Shakespeare's play) to describe French Huguenot refugees in England following the St. Bartholomew's Day Massacre of 1572.[26]

Combined with the Trojan War setting is the ill-fated love affair between the two lead characters. This main plot is not found in the ancient sources but was developed during the 14th century by Giovanni Boccaccio in his *Filostrato*, which in turn was further delineated by Geoffrey Chaucer in his own version of *Troilus and Criseyde*. Bullough identified the latter as the main source: "Obviously Shakespeare's Troilus in love is from Chaucer."[27] Also obvious from biographies of de Vere was his 1569–1570 purchase of a stack of books that included a volume of Chaucer. Whether this particular volume included *Troilus and Cresyde* is unknown, but no matter, de Vere could have also accessed it through the library of his tutor, Thomas Smith.[28]

Several inferior versions of the Troilus and Cressida story appeared in English after Chaucer but prior to Shakespeare, and it is generally agreed the Bard may have been familiar with some of these. For example, in *The Poesies of George Gascoigne* (1575), the tale is repeatedly alluded to, and cited by Bullough as a possible source.[29] Further investigation reveals that *Poesies* was a second edition of the 1573 anthology titled *A Hundreth Sundrie Flowres* in which Gascoigne's poetry was intermingled with that of other anonymous and pseudonymous noblemen, including one who signed his name *Meritum petere, grave*,[30] and which happened to include all of the aforementioned references to Troilus and Cressida. Although Gascoigne later claimed all of these poems under his own name, Oxfordians beginning with Bernard M. Ward have made a convincing case that these were in reality the work of de Vere, who was touring Italy in 1575 when the later edition was published. De Vere would not have challenged the authorship of these poems for the same reason he may have used a pseudonym in the first place; however, the 1575 edition of *Poesies* was recalled by censors for unknown reasons in 1576, shortly after de Vere had returned to England.[31]

Troilus and Cressida is about sex and war, in that order. Thersites, deformed in mind and body (like the author?), declares "Lechery, lechery; still, wars and lechery: nothing else holds fashion" (V.ii.194–195)—a modern sentiment, to be sure. The ill-fated lovers, or "pair of spectacles" (IV.iv.14), as Pandarus calls them, are the foremost victims of the twisted world they inhabit. Viewing these characters through the Oxfordian lens naturally leads to conjecture on real-life inspirations, fallible though these may be. Our first choice for the doomed romantic entanglement between the title characters is the ruinous extramarital affair that de Vere carried on during the late 1570s with Anne Vavasor, lady-in-waiting to the queen. His career never recovered from the scandal and he himself barely escaped with his life.[32] Our vote for the scheming Pandarus goes to de Vere's first cousin (and Anne Vavasor's kinsman) Henry Howard, son of the poet. During this period, de Vere was separated from his wife Anne Cecil (daughter of the arch–Protestant Lord Burghley) and consorting with Catholic sympathizers such as his cousin Howard and the infamous Charles Arundel, who later referred to de Vere as his "monstrous adversary." De Vere, for his part, afterward tagged Howard as "the most arrant villain that lived."[33] Before denouncing these two men before the queen on December 16, 1580 (after having confessed to his dalliance with Catholicism),[34] de Vere had no doubt been encouraged in his liaison with Anne Vavasor by Howard, Arundel and company, just as they surely discouraged him from reconciling with his Protestant wife.[35] This reconciliation did eventually take place in 1581, which probably saved de Vere's life, though not his reputation. All this occurred, however, not before he broke off with Anne Vavasor (who bore him a son), had been incarcerated, and incurred the odium of countless individuals, many of whom were quite powerful.

Cressida presciently observes that "Men prize the thing ungain'd more than it is" (I.ii.289), but she cannot follow her own advice. Professor Marjorie Garber, in her great essay on *Troilus and Cressida*, noted that Cressida is the one Shakespearean lover who is "genuinely unfaithful"[36] but who is also at the mercy of forces beyond her control. She is "merely a woman, first overidealized, then undervalued, finally dismissed...."[37] Garber rightfully concluded that Shakespeare hopelessly stacks the cards against his heroine:

> For Cressida herself, struggling not only against the political will of the Greeks and Trojans but also against her character's notorious literary history, there is, alas, no reservoir of personal agency, however much she tries to summon it.[38]

Troilus responds to Cressida's unfaithfulness and subsequent communiqué with "Words, words, mere words, no matter from the heart" (V.iii.108)—a very Hamlet-like response.[39] Professor Garber also observed that "In some ways we might say that *Troilus and Cressida* ... is a play that might almost have been written by Hamlet."[40] We would go one further and say that it *was* written by Hamlet, figuratively speaking. Perhaps in the Hamlet-Ophelia and Troilus-Cressida relationships we are seeing de Vere's retrospective feelings toward two of the more important women in his earlier life.

At this point it should be stated that we are not trying to ignore Will Shakspere; rather, nothing is known of his life that would suggest any similar parallels. For de Vere, on the other hand, biographical allusions extend to the subplots. Achilles has a less-than-respectable relationship with Patrocolus, who according to Ulysses, when not in bed with Achilles, amuses him by mercilessly mimicking the other Greek commanders (I.iii.150–151), and whose death finally provokes Achilles into the field. De Vere, it can never be forgotten, faced a hailstorm of sodomy allegations[41] which he inexplicably was able to weather,[42] but this cloud presumably hung over him for the rest of his life.

The background political message of *Troilus*, though laced with cynical irony, is summed up by Ulysses in his oft-quoted but frequently misunderstood speech advocating the observance of "degree, priority, and place" (I.iii.86). This same theme of unity was likely emphasized in the 1584 court production of *Agamemnon and Ulisses*. "English courtiers and noblemen unite" (read: be obedient) would have been a very timely message in 1584, with the court racked by internal dissension and the Spanish Armada invasion only four years off. England wanted to be like the Greeks, not the Trojans, and de Vere by this time may have been doing penance by helping to mount a campaign. By the early 17th century, however, this sort of thing may have also turned sour for the author, as reflected by his tone. As a side note, Ulysses also makes a comparison to "the glorious planet Sol / In noble eminence enthron'd and spher'd" (I.iii.89–90), which no less of an authority than Isaac Asimov took as indication of the Bard's geocentric sympathies in the then-current debate over the Copernican theory.[43] We take a far more ambiguous view of these lines. Equivocation, rather than sincerity, is the strong point of Shakespeare's Ulysses, and his astronomical similes can be taken either way.[44]

As for Shakespeare's true worldview in *Troilus*, pessimism is pervasive. Hector's death (V.ix), like that of Troilus and Cressida's relationship, is sordid and tawdry. Perhaps a more charitable view is expressed by Ulysses, who tells Achilles that:

> Time is like a fashionable host
> That slightly shakes his parting guest by the hand,
> And with his arms outstretch'd, as he would fly,
> Grasps in the comer: welcome ever smiles,
> And farewell goes out sighing. (III.iii.145–149)

Hector takes it one step further, telling Ulysses that "The end crowns all,[45] / And that old common arbiter, Time, / Will one day end it" (IV.v.224–226). Such an outlook would not have been surprising coming from Edward de Vere in 1603, toward the end of his own strange journey through life.

∾ 28 ≪

Coriolanus

Coriolanus was not printed until the First Folio of 1623 and there is no recorded performance prior to the Restoration era.[1] Edmund Chambers wrote that "There is practically no concrete evidence as to date...." Geoffrey Bullough had a similar opinion: "the date of composition is doubtful." Bullough then grapples with a more important question: "What led Shakespeare to write this play on a comparatively minor and early figure in Roman history?" Chambers notes, almost in a defensive tone, that "There is no reason to suppose that Volumnia was inspired by Shakespeare's mother, who was buried on 9 September 1608."[2] This statement assumes, of course, that Shakespeare the writer was Will Shakspere. We, on the other hand, would speculate that Shakespeare the writer tackled this subject because he had a personal response to it. *Coriolanus* is a good example of how a supposedly minor work that has befuddled critics and audiences can shine with clarity once viewed through the Oxfordian lens.

Shakespeare's primary source material was provided by Plutarch's *The Lives of Noble Grecians and Romans*. This great book had been first translated into French by Bishop Jacques Amyot in 1559, and then into English (using the Amyot translation) by Thomas North in 1579. The original Amyot translation of Plutarch was also among several books purchased by the 19-year-old Edward de Vere—the receipt for this purchase still exists in the account books of his guardian, Lord Burghley.[3] De Vere, who was conversant in French, also had access to the Roman historian Livy (usually considered a secondary source for the work) through Burghley's library.[4] As for Will Shakspere, we have absolutely no records, rumors, or anecdotes regarding the books that he may have owned or had access to.

Another supposed secondary source for *Coriolanus* is William Camden's *Remains of a Greater Work Concerning Britain*, published in 1605. In Act I, scene i, of the play, the patrician Menenius Agrippa tries to calm the plebeian mob by comparing the mutually dependent relationship between the two social classes with the dependency of various bodily members on the stomach. This same fable, containing similar details from the speech of Menenius, is found in Camden's work, leading to a widespread conclusion that *Coriolanus* was written sometime after 1605. This analysis, however, has several shortcomings. For one, Plutarch tells the fable as well, but with fewer details. Second, who is to say whether Shakespeare was copying Camden or vice-versa? Camden's *Remains* also praised Shakespeare as a playwright[5]; therefore, it is plausible (if not likely) that Camden had Shakespeare's play in mind at the same time he was praising him. Third, Camden himself had sources (besides Plutarch) for the fable,[6] and the possibility that he and Shakespeare drew upon the same material should not be ruled out. Moreover, all reasonable scholars agree that Shakespeare the writer had editors and collaborators, both during and after his lifetime; thus, even if certain references to a particular source do in fact exist, this does not conclusively establish that the work had not been written earlier. Overall, the conjectured use of Camden is a very flimsy reason to date a play for which there is no publication or performance record during the author's lifetime.

Plutarch begins his life of Caius Martius (surnamed Coriolanus) by noting that violent men who lose their fathers at an early age often use this as an excuse for their own bad behavior. According to Plutarch, this was in fact the case with Coriolanus.[7] In a similar manner, Edward de Vere's father died when he was 12 years of age.[8] Will Shakspere's father John, on the other hand, lived well into his son's adulthood. As for Volumnia, the mother of Coriolanus, she is representative of the troubled, dysfunctional relationships between mothers and sons in the canon (when these relationships are dramatized at all), and exemplified by other works such as *Hamlet*, *All's Well That Ends Well*, *Richard III*, and *Cymbeline*. When Coriolanus laments, "O mother, mother! What have you done?" (V.iii.182–183), we are perhaps hearing the emotional climax of the play. Little is known of de Vere's mother Margery Golding, except that she remarried shortly after his father's death, and then died in 1568, not long before her son purchased his copy of the Amyot Plutarch. We also know that de Vere's enemies claimed that he had spoken of having nightmare visions of his mother after her death.[9]

Husband-wife relationships in Shakespeare also tend to be less than idyllic, and *Coriolanus* is no exception. Whereas Volumnia is overbearing and domineering, Virgilia is painfully meek and subservient to her husband. This is reminiscent of de Vere's first wife Anne Cecil, who predeceased him in 1588, and who (from all accounts) was the innocent victim of de Vere's mental cruelty on more than one occasion.[10] Nothing specific is known of relations between Will Shakspere and his wife Anne Hathaway, except that he left her and their children behind in Stratford-upon-Avon to pursue his London theatrical career. Frank Kermode, in his introduction to the play for *Riverside*, noted that while Shakespeare took the characters of Volumnia and Virgilia from Plutarch, he then amplified their fierce and pacific qualities, respectively.[11]

Familial relations aside, the most striking feature of the Coriolanus' personality— indeed, his "tragic flaw"—is his inflexible and haughty, patrician attitude toward the plebeians. This pride and contempt for the rabble accelerates his undoing. Kermode (quoting Wyndham Lewis) describes Coriolanus as:

> "an astonishingly close picture of a particularly cheerless ... snob, such as must have pullulated in the court of Elizabeth"—a schoolboy crazed with notions of privilege, and possessed of a "demented ideal of authority." ... He is an ugly political innocent: "What his breast forges, that his tongue must vent." There is no gap between his crude mind and his violent tongue. And such men are dangerous.[12]

All this sounds like a portrait of Edward de Vere. Aside from our fascination with British academics who accuse anyone of snobbery, another question is naturally raised. How would Will Shakspere, if he were the true author, dare to write a play in which the tragic downfall of an aristocrat is caused by his snobbish attitude toward the common people?

This was an age in which dress code distinctions between the English social classes were sanctioned by law. Nevertheless, Shakespeare not only had the audacity to make class war-fare the backdrop of a story, he turned a nobleman's bad attitude into a cautionary tale as well. It is true that Shakespeare softens the edges somewhat by making the plebeians and their tribunes more unruly and self-serving than they are in Plutarch.[13] We are skep-tical, however, that such concessions (?) would have mollified the patricians of Elizabethan and Jacobean England. More likely, these fine tunings reflected the author's own aristo-cratic bias. Looking at the big picture, one must eventually ask: where are the populist heroes and heroines in Shakespeare? Certainly not in the Roman plays, and not in the English history plays, either.

Returning to Plutarch, his *Lives* are structured so that each Roman biography is paired with one Greek, followed by a short comparison of the two for purposes of moral edification. Plutarch was demonstrating to his Roman patrons that their Latin heroes of yore had close parallels with Hellenic predecessors. In the case of Coriolanus, Plutarch compares his biography with that of the Athenian general Alcibiades, who makes an appearance in Shakespeare's *Timon of Athens*. Shakespeare the writer obviously had read this section of Plutarch with great interest. Plutarch noted that while Coriolanus and Alcibiades had numerous similarities (both were treated ungratefully by their country, turned against it, relented, and then were killed), there were also striking differences between the two. For one, Alcibiades was known to have been notoriously loose in his personal morals, while Coriolanus was reputedly above reproach outside the sphere of politics. Conversely, Alcibiades was praised for his affability and slowness to take offense; Coriolanus was known for unsociability and a quick temper. Shakespeare was apparently interested in these opposing personalities, as well as the general common theme of divided political allegiance that is examined in both biographies.

In the case of Will Shakspere, assuming that he in fact had secret Catholic sympa-thies (as his father John probably did), such divided political allegiance during the Wars of Religion would make some sense. The divided loyalties of Coriolanus, however, have nothing to do with religious doctrine. His anger and resentment are kindled by personal affronts and fanned by elitist notions of privilege and power. In the end, his fury is blunted only by appeals from mother and wife. Beyond the hotly debated issue of Will Shakspere's alleged Catholic sympathies, connections between the play and his personal life (if any) remain concealed from the view of history.

For Edward de Vere, on the other hand, affinities with the personality of Coriolanus multiply beyond his presumed aristocratic sympathies. For starters, during and after his trip to Italy, de Vere was known to have flirted with Catholicism before renouncing it in the presence of Queen Elizabeth at Greenwich Palace on December 16, 1580.[14] Thus, like Will Shakspere, historians often see a cloud hanging over de Vere's loyalty to the Angli-can Church.[15] In addition to his nobleman's bias and secret experimentations with the Catholic faith, de Vere was above all noted for his hot-temperedness, again similar to the tragic hero of Shakespeare's play. Sometimes this anger was directed against common tradesmen with whom he had monetary disputes, including one instance late in life when de Vere threatened to have a joiner "laid by the heeles."[16] Furthermore, just as Coriolanus is rejected by the people for the office of Consulship, Oxford was repeatedly rebuffed for membership in the Order of the Garter by electors. Boastfulness was yet another charge leveled against de Vere by his enemies, and in the play, the tribune Junius Brutus accuses Coriolanus of "topping all others in boasting" (II.i.20). Coriolanus confirms this accusation in the climactic finale by proclaiming, "If you have writ your annals true, 'tis there that, like an eagle in a dove-cote, I [flutter'd] your Volscians in Coriloes. Alone I did it. 'Boy'!" (V.v.113–115). Among de Vere's more memorable claims for himself (at least, according to Charles Arundel) was that while in Italy he had been "reputed for his eloquence another Cicero and for his conduct a Caesar."[17] Perhaps de Vere reminded Shakespeare the writer of Plutarch's difficult and disagreeable nobleman.

Coriolanus is a tragic figure because his many faults lead to the downfall of a man otherwise admirable for his military prowess and devotion to family. Plutarch expressly notes that the true source of these failings was lack of education, and that the proper role of the humanities is to soften and curb such emotional extremes. Shakespeare picks up on this idea in Act I, scene iii, when Volumnia and Virgilia have the following exchange regarding Coriolanus' son, the young Martius:

> VOLUMNIA: "He [young Martius] had rather see the swords and hear a drum than look
> upon his schoolmaster."
> VIRGILIA: "A' my word, the father's son." (I.iii.56–57)

Both father and son prefer war to education. As a young man, the highly educated Edward de Vere had written to his guardian Lord Burghley expressing a desire to see military service,[18] and this wish was soon afterward fulfilled when he was allowed to join the Earl of Sussex during his Scottish campaign of 1570. Although a superb education apparently never succeeded in curbing de Vere's impetuosity, it is safe to say that without this education he surely would have been worse. Perhaps he even realized this. One of the great contradictions of de Vere's biography is the unusually high regard that other writers and artists seemed to have for him, despite his poor reputation in most other things.

As a furious and banished Coriolanus departs from Rome, he bitterly remarks that "There is a world elsewhere" (III.iii.135). These are the words of a man fully cognizant of other countries beyond his own native land and not afraid to venture there. De Vere, of course, had done precisely that on more than one occasion. As for Will Shakspere, we know that he left (or was banished from?)[19] his native Warwickshire during the 1580s, and to him London probably seemed like "a world elsewhere." Compared to de Vere's continental Grand Tour, however, Shakspere's relocation was a stroll around the block. Furthermore, although Will Shakspere may have been banished from Stratford, he eventually returned in triumph—a more fitting subject for him from Plutarch would have been the life of Camillus.[20] De Vere, on the other hand, remained in disgrace, although his Italian travels would have given him firsthand exposure to the ancient artifacts and lore that had inspired Plutarch and would later do the same for Shakespeare. As to why the Bard was fascinated by Coriolanus and Alcibiades in particular, among the entire galaxy of outstanding Roman and Greek personalities that were immortalized by Plutarch, one must turn to the authorship question in order to find answers.

ᔒ 29 ᔑ

Titus Andronicus

Play-Poets and common Actors (the Divels chiefest Factors) rake earth and hell it selfe;
... they travell over Sea and Land; over all Histories, poems, countries, times and ages
for unparalled villanies, that so they may pollute the Theater.
—William Prynne, *Histrio-Mastix:*
The Players Scourge, or, Actors Tragaedie [1633][1]

Titus Andronicus was the first Shakespeare play quarto published, albeit anonymously, in 1594. Two more anonymous quartos of *Titus* were published in 1600 and 1611 before the work was officially attached to the name of William Shakespeare in the First Folio of 1623. Previously, the only indication that it belonged to Shakespeare was an honorable mention among the Bard's works by Francis Meres in 1598. *Titus* was obviously a popular hit, going through three published editions, cited by Meres, and acted by at least three different companies; yet it was too hot a potato for anyone to take credit as author.[2] Modern commentators sometimes seem embarrassed by the play as well, and three different views have developed: namely, that Shakespeare did not really write *Titus* (despite attributions); or that Shakespeare collaborated with other lesser playwrights; or that Shakespeare wrote it, but as a very early work for which he should be excused.[3] Only with recent revival productions have scholars begun abandoning the notion that *Titus* is not worthy of the Bard's genius. In the words of Geoffrey Bullough, "Could any other dramatist but Shakespeare have written this *tour de force?*"[4]

Henslowe's diary recorded the first known performance of *Titus* in 1594, which referred to the play as being new.[5] Many scholars, however, have been suspicious on this last item. Edmund Chambers cautioned: "Moreover, there is some reason to suppose that *Titus Andronicus* was not altogether new in 1594."[6] Bullough was more specific: "it [*Titus*] may have been a revision of an earlier play written by Shakespeare or (more probably) by someone else."[7] By "someone else" Bullough meant someone other than the traditional Shakespeare, which leaves the door open for an alternative Shakespeare (de Vere), possibly revising his own earlier work. One reason for widespread critical doubt is that Ben Jonson, in 1614, without mentioning Shakespeare by name, scoffed at *Titus* (another indication of its popularity), irritably observing the play had held the stage for some 25 to 30 years.[8] If Honest Ben was being straight with us, then *Titus* had been around since 1584–1589. In 1584, the 20-year-old Will Shakspere was still in Stratford-upon-Avon begetting twins and possibly getting into trouble with the authorities over deer poaching. The idea of Shakespeare revising an Ur-*Titus* is similar to the widely accepted notion of the

Bard rewriting an Ur-*Hamlet*; in fact, one could take this to its logical conclusion by postulating an Ur-Shakespeare, thus explaining many lost and anonymous play titles that were performed at court during this earlier period and sound remarkably like Shakespeare's titles.

In February of 1577, a lost and anonymous play titled *The Historye of Titus and Gisippus* was performed at Whitehall Palace by the Children of St. Paul's. Some Oxfordians have claimed that "Titus and Gisippus" may have been a phonetically mistranscribed version of "Titus Andronicus"; however, surely this was an adaptation of the Boccaccio tale later translated by Thomas Elyot with the same title and a source for Shakespeare's *The Two Gentlemen of Verona*.[9] This was less than a year after de Vere had returned from Italy and concurrent with construction of the first two English public playhouses in Shoreditch by the Burbage family. Although *Titus and Gisippus* was not the Ur-*Titus* that Chambers and Bullough suspected, de Vere's theatrical and literary activities during this same period are documented, such as two years later (in 1579), when he was recorded as acting in a production at court.[10]

Regarding performance history, the 1594 frontispiece specified three acting companies, each sponsored by members of the nobility—the Earls of Pembroke, Derby, and Sussex. Although de Vere's own troupe (Oxford's Men) did not have a performance record with *Titus* or any other Shakespeare play, de Vere himself had personal connections with each of the three earls who did. Thomas Radcliffe, brother and uncle (respectively)[11] of the Fourth (d. 1593) and Fifth (d. 1629) Earls of Sussex, had been de Vere's mentor as a young man, as well as Lord Chamberlain to the acting company that would later become Shakespeare's. William Stanley, brother to the Fifth (d. 1594) Earl of Derby, would become de Vere's son-in-law in 1595. Philip Herbert, son of the Second (d. 1601) Earl of Pembroke, would also become de Vere's son-in-law in 1604.

As to Shakespeare's storyline, the plot has little or nothing to do with actual history. *Titus* is set during what appears to be the late Roman Imperial era, with the Empire fending off fierce Gothic invaders despite a weak and corrupt emperor. Both Romans and Goths, however, had been Christianized by that time, and the characters in *Titus* are decidedly pagan in their religious outlook. Furthermore, the character names are not to be found in the chronicles of this period, nor are specific events. An authentic but anonymous chapbook (i.e., a small book of tales), claiming Italian origins and probably dating from the 16th century, has a concise synopsis of *Titus*,[12] but whether Shakespeare utilized this or vice-versa is a typical chicken-and-egg type of problem routinely confronted by Elizabethan scholars.

More certain is that Shakespeare was heavily indebted to Book VI of Ovid's *Metamorphoses*, in which the maiden Philomela is savagely raped and mutilated by Tereus, but avenged when her sister Procne serves him their own son as a banquet. It is worth repeated mention that the first English translation of the *Metamorphoses* in 1567 (often named as the single most influential work on the Bard) was written by de Vere's maternal uncle Arthur Golding. De Vere was at that time 17 years old, with his mother Margery Golding dying the following year (in 1568). In the play, the young Lucius informs Titus: "Grandsire, 'tis Ovid's *Metamorphoses*, my mother gave it to me" (IV.i.42–43). It is not too hard to imagine that this volume may have been given to de Vere as a keepsake from his mother (written by her brother, his uncle), even if de Vere was not in fact Shakespeare and had no involvement with his Puritan uncle's salacious translation. Golding did take the trouble, however, to dedicate several books to his young nephew, including *The Histories of Trogus Pompeius* in 1564 and John Calvin's commentaries on *The Psalms of David* in 1571.[13]

Another ancient Roman writer whose shadow hangs over *Titus* (and other tragedies by Shakespeare) is Seneca. The term "Senecan" is synonymous with the almost cartoonish, hyper-violence frequently employed by the Bard, most notably in this play. Seneca's *Thyestes*, in particular, has a gruesome banquet finale of which *Titus* is reminiscent,[14] and Seneca is quoted at the key moment in which Chiron and Demetrius are identified as Livinia's assailants (IV.i.81–82). In 1589 (within Ben Jonson's range for the origins of *Titus*), the playwright Thomas Nashe both praised and spoofed an "English Seneca" for his eloquent but long-winded speeches.[15] That same year, *The Arte of English Poesie* would proclaim the 39-year-old de Vere[16] "best for comedy" (as would Francis Meres in 1598), although no works under his own name have come down to us. While *Titus* is far from being a comedy, comedic elements have long been acknowledged,[17] and one of the Bard's patented trademarks was his lack of inhibition at blending opposing genres together into a single unified whole.

Although the story of *Titus* is fictional, the Greco-Roman historian Plutarch seemed to be presiding over Shakespeare's creative process, as he certainly did in the other "Roman" plays. Bullough noted in particular Plutarch's comparative lives for Coriolanus and Alcibiades, who make character appearances in two other Shakespearean tragedies. Both (like Titus) were treated ungratefully by their countries after rendering heroic services, and then acted in a vengeful manner with tragic consequences.[18] In between receiving book dedications from his uncle Arthur, de Vere in 1569 (at the age of 19) purchased a copy of Plutarch in the French translation by Bishop Amyot (on which the later English version by Thomas North would be based).[19] Thus de Vere had documented and multiple connections with Ovid and Plutarch, two major sources for Shakespeare's play. While de Vere's connections with Nashe's "English Seneca" remain unsubstantiated,[20] his claim to this moniker is much stronger than Will Shakspere's, given their respective ages and reputations (or lack thereof) at the time.

Titus, like *Macbeth*, was surely influenced by the barbarity of the Wars of Religion during the late 16th century. Two horrendous atrocities were the Paris St. Bartholomew's Day Massacre of 1572 (French Catholics against French Protestants) and the Spanish Fury of Antwerp in 1576 (Spanish Catholics against Dutch Protestants). In Act I, scene i, of the play, Titus cold-bloodedly offers up Alarbus as a human sacrifice to the gods, prompting Tamora's anguished cry "O cruel, irreligious piety!" (I.i.130). This deed sets off the chain of murderous events. Thus, the otherwise despicable Tamora has an understandable motive for wreaking havoc against the family of Titus. Either Will Shakspere or Edward de Vere could have concocted this scenario, but de Vere had the added advantage of having recently traveled to Italy, as well as to Paris, only three years after the mass murders in France that had been committed in the name of religion. Earlier, in a 1572 letter to his father-in-law Lord Burghley, de Vere lamented the fate of French Huguenot refugees in the wake of St. Bartholomew's Day.[21]

One of the curiosities of this play includes its multiple allusions to the island of Sicily. For example, Titus' brother Marcus proclaims "Now let hot Aetna cool in Sicily" (III.i.242). References are later made to the obscure Typhon and Enceladus, mythological creatures confined beneath Mount Aetna (IV.ii.93–94). Shakespeare's memorable villain Aaron[22] is suggestive of Sicily as well, since the Moors were intermittent marauders in this region; yet, in the play, Aaron is confederate with the Gothic tribes of northern Europe. The setting of Rome, itself a southern city (at least to the Italians), gives the entire drama a distinctly Mediterranean flavor. Admittedly, a voracious reader like Shakespeare could have picked all this up via classical literature (with Hellenic Sicily as one of its focal points). On the other hand, we know that the nephew of Ovid's English translator had supplemented his reading by visiting Sicily.[23]

That de Vere's uncle was a strict Puritan who dedicated John Calvin's commentaries to his wayward nephew is interesting, and Shakespeare the writer was certainly no Puritan, based on the canon. The Puritans reciprocated by being fanatical and mortal enemies of the playhouses from day one. It is likely that *Titus* was an entertainment that upset them, not so much because of its horrific violence, but rather due to the very bad behavior of the characters in general. In many ways, *Titus* is a subtle pie in the face to the Calvinist worldview, with its blurry notions of good and evil, not to mention skeptical attitude toward the ultimate triumph of good over evil. It would have been natural for the politically ascendant Puritans to point a finger at *Titus* as an amoral corruptor of impressionable minds.

Half a century of Puritan diatribes against the playhouses climaxed in 1633 with the publication of *Histrio-Mastix: The Players Scourge, or, Actors Tragaedie* by William Prynne.[24] Prynne began work on his thousand-page *magnum opus* in 1624 and appears to have been inspired (if that is the right word) by the appearance of the First Folio in 1623. Although promptly imprisoned for this extraordinary tome—extraordinary even by Calvinist standards—Prynne was later viewed as a popular hero.[25] *Histrio-Mastix* makes instructive reading for anyone doubting the absolute ferocity of the Puritan attack on the English stage. Plays are described as "the chief delight of the Devil" and playhouses as "Devil's chapels." As for playgoers, "they that frequent Plays are damned."[26] Then Prynne complains, "Shackspeers Plaies are printed in the best Crowne paper, far better than most Bibles."[27] It would have been interesting hear what Prynne had to say if he had suspected "Shackspeer" was the morally suspect Earl of Oxford.

Regarding foreign actresses who had recently made appearances on the London stage, Prynne had plenty to say. He equates all "Woman-Actors" with "notorious whores," noting that "some French women, or Monsters rather, on Michaelmass Terme 1629, attempted to act a French Play, at the Play-House in Black-friers: an impudent, shamefull, unwomanish, graceless, if not more than whorish attempt."[28] Unfortunately for Prynne, these last remarks drew the attention of Queen Henrietta Maria, who enjoyed performing in court masques. As a result, William Prynne was arrested, brought to trial and condemned as follows: life imprisonment (although this was later commuted by Lord Protector Cromwell), a fine of £5,000, confiscation of all copies of his book to be burned before his eyes, revocation of his degree from Oxford and, his license to practice law from Lincoln's Inn, and last but not least, *his ears were publicly chopped off at the pillory.*[29] Then for good measure, King Charles had a new edition of his father's *Book of Sports* republished.[30] A contemporary cartoon depicted Archbishop William Laud (the Great Satan in the eyes of the Puritans) being served on a platter the severed ears of William Prynne, like something out of *Titus Andronicus.*[31] This was in 1641, one year before civil war broke out, and shows the intense feelings prevalent by that time. Our point is that the English Civil War did not happen overnight. It was the culmination of things that had been building for the entire previous generation, including the publication of the First Folio. Thus the same forces that caused the civil war probably had a direct bearing on the Folio, including its permanent attribution of authorship.

The year before the Folio (in 1622), *The Compleat Gentleman*, written by the distinguished Jacobean educator Henry Peacham,[32] was published. While a student at Cambridge in 1595, Peacham sketched a scene from *Titus*, believed to be the earliest surviving rendering of a scene from a Shakespeare play.[33] In *The Compleat Gentleman*, Peacham listed Elizabethan poets who made that era a "golden age,"[34] including Edmund Spenser and Philip Sidney, among others. First among Peacham's list, however, was "Edward Earl of Oxford." As for William Shakespeare, there is absolutely no mention of him, nor was this omission corrected in the multiple, subsequent editions that were published long after the First Folio had appeared.[35]

❧ 30 ❧

Romeo and Juliet

Arguably Shakespeare's most popular play, *Romeo and Juliet* has an enigmatic but rarely discussed publication history. Basic, fundamental questions are often ignored. For example, how it was written? How was it inspired? What kind of person created it? Anyone not interested in these questions needs to check their own pulse. According to playwright Tom Stoppard, *Shakespeare in Love* provides one scenario. Now there is nothing wrong with a good yarn, but we are fairly confident that is not how it really happened. Scholars of all authorship persuasions agree that *Romeo and Juliet* was a very old and well-known story that Shakespeare took with most of the details intact and then applied his own brand of wit and poetry. He did not—and this is important—*did not* just make it all up, genius though he was. As it turns out, the true story behind the work is probably far more interesting than the one told in the movie.

The first reference to Shakespeare's play is the initial publication, known as the "bad" quarto, printed by John Danter in 1597. The frontispiece advertised that it had "been often (with great applause) plaid publiquely, by the right Honourable the L. of Hunsdon his Servants."[1] Because there was a brief period (1596–1597) during which Shakespeare's acting company, the Lord Chamberlain's Men, was known as Lord Hunsdon's Men, it has been plausibly suggested that this was the same time frame for the public performances cited on the frontispiece.[2] This publication is anonymous with no mention of the name William Shakespeare.[3]

Two years later (in 1599) the second "good" quarto appeared, printed by Thomas Creede for the publisher Cuthbert Burby. The frontispiece advertises "Newly corrected, augmented and amended," but once again, there is absolutely no mention of William Shakespeare. Two more quarto versions of *Romeo and Juliet* later came out in 1609 and 1622(?), but these, too, were anonymous.[4] It is possible that because the Globe Theater opened in 1599, all parties involved felt they could profit from an updated version of this successful work. The absence of Shakespeare's name, however, is odd for several reasons. For one, Shakespeare was already the acknowledged author of two best-selling poems. For another, the previous year (in 1598), the very same publisher (Burby) had put out the first quarto of *Love's Labor's Lost* by "W. Shakespere," as well as *Palladis Tamia* by Francis Meres, who names Shakespeare as the greatest English playwright and gives *Romeo and Juliet* as an example of his work.[5] One is almost forced to conclude that Shakespeare told Burby to stop using his name, either because of some outside pressure or because of the special nature of this particular work. None of this jives very well with the conventional image of Shakespeare as a savvy businessman.[6] Finally, in the First Folio of 1623, the play was explicitly and permanently credited to William Shakespeare.

　　Romeo and Juliet is perhaps the Bard's most exuberantly amorous work. This applies not only to the intense teenage passion of the two lovers, but also to its foil—the jarringly crude street humor coming from the mouths of the other characters. The Puritans probably hated this play more than any other. Traditional biographer Marchette Chute wrote:

> nothing was better calculated to kindle the fire of inordinate lust in the tender minds of the young than to let them go to stage plays, and the Puritan opposition to the stage eventually became implacable.[7]

Add to this the civil unrest between feuding families that is so effectively dramatized, and it may well have been that the author was hesitant to be personally associated with this incendiary work. If "Shakespeare" was in reality a nobleman with a shady moral reputation (like de Vere), then there would have been doubly good reasons not be publicly associated. Although the Puritans had become politically more powerful than ever by 1623, perhaps by then everyone knew that "William Shakespeare" was the author and further pointless discretion was outweighed by a desire to unequivocally claim this great work under the Bard's name.

　　The first definite performances are those referred to by the 1597 quarto. In 1598, John Marston made an allusion to a performance at the Curtain,[8] one of the two original Burbage theaters built in Shoreditch during the late 1570s. This was a neighborhood around which de Vere is known to have resided most of his adult life. There is also a tradition that *Romeo and Juliet* was performed at Blackfriars,[9] although like the Curtain production, no dates are given. Blackfriars was probably the most controversial of the Elizabethan playhouses, repeatedly being opened and then shut down due to public (read: Puritan) pressure. It was also a theater that de Vere was associated with during the 1580s, both as a lessee and sublessor to his servant and secretary, the playwright John Lyly.[10] As a performance side note, in 1600—one year after the second quarto of *Romeo and Juliet*— the same printer (Creede) issued an anonymous play titled *The Weakest Goeth to the Wall*. The title also appears as a line in *Romeo and Juliet* (I.i.13–14), and, as advertised on the frontispiece, had been performed by Oxford's own acting company. While proving nothing in and of itself, this publication is intriguingly suggestive with respect to the possible connections between de Vere and Shakespeare's plays.

　　Oxfordian Charlton Ogburn, Jr., wrote that de Vere (if in fact Shakespeare the writer) could rightfully claim credit for helping to bring the Italian Renaissance back to England, and the source materials for *Romeo and Juliet* illustrate this point. The books and events that shaped Shakespeare's vision emerged from northern Italy during the 15th and 16th centuries, particularly from Tuscany and the Veneto, regions that were the focal point of de Vere's Grand Tour during the mid–1570s. Ogburn notes that if the Oxfordian theory is correct, then de Vere's continental travels may have been the most precipitous event in the history of world literature.[11]

　　Although elements of the story go back to ancient times, events very similar were retold by Masuccio di Salerno in his *Il Novellino*, published in 1476. These events occurred not in Verona, but in Tuscan Siena (a city visited by de Vere). According to Masuccio, two young lovers married secretly with the help of a friar, but the boy was banished from

Siena after killing someone in a street brawl. The girl was then pressured to marry someone else, and instead took a sleeping potion to feign death. The friar sent a message to her exiled husband to come and steal her back, but he first heard that she was dead and then got himself killed out of desperation. The girl awoke, learned of her husband's death, and retired to a convent where she reputedly died of a broken heart.[12]

In 1530, another book appeared, elegantly titled *Istoria Novellamente Ritrovata di due Nobili Amanti* by Luigi da Porto of Vicenza, located near Verona. He tells the tragic story of Romeo and Giuletta, using most of the same names that Shakespeare uses, and sets the story in Verona and Mantua. DaPorto acknowledges that he received the tale from a Veronese soldier named Peregrino. DaPorto also uses the names Montecchi and Cappelletti, which were probably taken from Dante's *Purgatorio*, in which both families are mentioned.[13]

In 1554, a third version of the story was published, this time in Tuscany (Lucca, to be exact). This was the famous *Novella* by Matteo Bandello, and now we are starting to get very close to Shakespeare. Most everyone agrees that Bandello was a major influence on the Bard, probably through the French translation by Pierre Boiastuau, published in 1559. This translation was part of the library of de Vere's guardian (and later father-in-law) Lord Burghley, and de Vere was known to have been fluent in both French and Italian. The book was very popular and Bandello, though himself a Tuscan, kept the Verona-Mantua settings and character names. He, too, names Peregrino of Verona as his source, but makes no mention of DaPorto.[14] In effect, Bandello was willing to give credit to an oral Veronese tradition, but not to an author from Vicenza. The stage was now set for the first English translation.

In 1562, *The Tragical History of Romeus and Juliet* by Arthur Brooke was published, a poem universally acknowledged as Shakespeare's primary source material.[15] On the frontispiece, Brooke credited Bandello as his source and noted that he had witnessed a stage play on this subject. Also generally undisputed is the dullness of Brooke's long, moralistic poem, but Shakespeare used all the details. Geoffrey Bullough wrote that "Brooke's poem is a leaden work which Shakespeare transmuted to gold" and marveled that "The surprising thing is that Shakespeare preserved so much of his source in vitalizing its dead stuff."[16] Posterity knows little about Arthur Brooke, although a few facts are verifiable. Brooke was an older contemporary of de Vere who died in 1567 when his transport ship sank in the English Channel after he had volunteered for overseas military service. Brooke was subsequently eulogized by George Turberville, who praised Brooke's youthful, poetic talents, associating these talents (curiously enough) with the Roman spear-shaker goddess Minerva. Brooke was also second cousin to William Brooke, Lord Cobham,[17] who is believed to have caused such a ruckus over Shakespeare's creation of Falstaff (see Chapter 20). This occurred about the same time that *Romeo and Juliet* was being written.

Among other things, Shakespeare took a cue from Brooke's advanced development of Mercutio as a character.[18] It is the death of Mercutio (Act III, scene i), caused by his craziness and reckless behavior, that signals the beginning of tragic events in the play. Mercutio, as a mercurial character type, is the flip side of Romeo's melancholic, self-absorbed personality. More than one commentator has suggested that that there may be more to the relationship between Romeo and Mercutio than conventional male friendship. This has even been the subject of an award-winning play by Joe Calarco, titled *Shakespeare's R & J.*

Romeo and Juliet begins with a sonnet prologue, and many scholars believe the play was written at approximately the same time as Shakespeare's towering sonnet cycle.[19] The distinctive English sonnet structure had been earlier pioneered by Oxford's uncle, Henry Howard, Earl of Surrey,[20] and the young de Vere is credited with writing in the sonnet form as well.[21] Regarding poetic style, the father of the Oxfordian theory, John Thomas Looney, noted striking similarities between the so-called "Echo" poem generally attributed to the young de Vere, and Juliet's speech (II.ii.160–163) in which she imagines calling Romeo's name into a cave and listening to the echo effect.[22]

To repeat, de Vere traveled to Italy during the mid–1570s and probably had firsthand experience with the settings of Shakespeare's play. Although there has been no hard evidence to date of his presence in either Verona or Mantua, the likelihood is great, given that these cities were directly on the canal route between Padua and Milan, where his presence is documented.[23] In addition, Verona has one of the most spectacular and best-preserved ancient outdoor theaters in the world—the Teatro Romano—which today is (fittingly enough) the venue for the Verona Shakespeare Festival. It is hard for any tourist to miss this landmark, which provides a graphic reminder of how the Italian Renaissance gave natural birth to modern drama in imitation of ancient models.

The play contains references to a Verona earthquake (I.iii.23) and Mantua plague (V.ii.10). The Nurse recalls that Juliet was born 11 years after the earthquake, and the Verona region did in fact experience one in 1570,[24] five years before de Vere's Grand Tour. The city of London also experienced an earthquake in 1580, which Puritans quickly attributed to divine wrath over the success of new public playhouses.[25] Both Oxfordians and traditionalists have expended large amounts of ink in order to precisely date events in the play to 1581 and 1591, respectively, but as Edmund Chambers skeptically noted, "This is pressing the Nurse's interest in chronology—and Shakespeare's—rather hard."[26] Both Will Shakspere and Edward de Vere could claim firsthand experience with these calamities, although de Vere could have taken it one better, having likely seen the aftereffects in Verona firsthand. More impressive is de Vere's experience with the plague, which ravaged Italy concurrent with his continental travels.[27] A letter dated September 1575 from de Vere in Venice to his father-in-law Lord Burghley complained that letters sent earlier had been returned due to imposed quarantines. This is precisely what happens to Friar Lawrence when he tries to send a letter to Romeo in Act V, scene ii, leading to Romeo's fatal misunderstanding.

Oxfordians see in Juliet (one of Shakespeare's many guileless, tragic heroines) a representation of Anne Cecil, Lord Burghley's daughter and de Vere's first wife. Similar to Juliet, who is portrayed by Shakespeare as 13 years old (I.iii.13), Anne Cecil was betrothed to de Vere when she was 14 and married when she was 15.[28] This is not in any of Shakespeare's sources; in fact, Juliet had previously been older.[29] Moreover, de Vere's mother-in-law Lady Burghley had no use for him,[30] similar to Lady Capulet in the play, who is cold toward Romeo, to put it lightly. Perhaps by coincidence, Lord Burghley died in 1598, the same year that William Shakespeare first appeared in print as a playwright and is praised by Francis Meres.

Like Romeo in the play, de Vere (in 1582) was involved in a sword fight against a formidable antagonist. Unlike Romeo, this was not a fight to avenge the death of Mercutio, nor did he vanquish his opponent. The altercation occurred because de Vere had dumped his former mistress (after she had a child by him) and returned to his wife Anne Cecil, from whom he had been separated.[31] The abandoned mistress in this case was Anne Vavasor, lady-in-waiting to the queen. Doubly unfortunate for de Vere, his mistress had an uncle who was an expert swordsman—Thomas Knyvet. De Vere was a good fencer as well, and this probably saved his life. Both combatants were wounded, although de Vere reportedly got the worst of it, and one of his servants was killed.[32]

The followers of both men later fought intermittently in the streets, which is very reminiscent of the brawls in *Romeo and Juliet*. Some of this fighting took place in the vicinity of Blackfriars Theater,[33] and there appear to be a number of parallels between these events and gang violence depicted in the play. Blackfriars, in addition to the playhouse, had space that was leased to London's premier fencing school, operated by the Italian master Rocco Bonetti. This, incidentally, was the same space that had originally been leased to de Vere and later subleased to John Lyly.[34] Act II seems to contain a number of fencing allusions by Mercutio, specifically in reference to Tybalt. Mercutio rants against "their bones, their bones" (II.iv.36), which has been interpreted as a pun on Bonetti's name.[35] Oxfordians view the irascible Tybalt (Juliet's cousin) as a rough anagram for Thomas Knyvet,[36] in addition to being recognizable Elizabethan slang for a vicious tomcat.[37]

Taken as a whole—the performance tradition of *Romeo and Juliet* at Blackfrairs, the presence of Bonetti's fencing school, Tybalt's resemblance to Thomas Knyvet, and de Vere's own connections to the theater, including the street fighting involving Knyvet—the cumulative weight of this data has impressed even orthodox scholars such as Irwin Smith, who admitted there may be a connection between these events and Shakespeare's play in terms of topographical allusions, if nothing else.[38] Will Shakspere is known to have co-leased Blackfriars in 1608 and co-purchased the Blackfriars Gatehouse in 1613,[39] but these events occurred more than 9–10 years after the first two quartos of the play had already appeared in print.

Juliet ponders "What's in a name?" (II.ii.43) and this question could well apply to the Shakespeare authorship question. Whether the true author was Will Shakspere or Edward de Vere, the mystery remains as to why Shakespeare's name was conspicuously omitted from the first four editions of this blockbuster drama through 1622. At least three good reasons, however, are suggested by external factors, and all apply regardless of who wrote the work. The first is that the original English source for this story (Arthur Brooke) was a kinsman to the same William Brooke recently scandalized by Shakespeare's dramatization of Falstaff.[40] Just as the Bard had transformed Brooke's Puritan martyr ancestor (Sir John Oldcastle) into the buffoonish Falstaff, he reworked Arthur Brooke's highly moralistic and cautionary tale for young lovers into the ultimate paean in praise of youthful hormonal ecstasy. Second, the play may have taken too close an aim at Sir Thomas Knyvet (as Tybalt), a well-respected man who received considerable favor from both Queen Elizabeth and King James.[41] Third, the gang violence associated with Blackfriars may have been too vividly evoked by staged mayhem on the streets of Verona. These associations would have been even more inconvenient for the author given the Puritans' aggressive and ongoing campaign to shut down all the theaters in general and Blackfriars in particular. All of this may have been a little too much for Will Shakspere to have taken credit for, whether he was the true author or merely a front man. In fact, one marvels that anyone was able to get away with writing it, especially in wake of the Falstaff-Cobham debacle. If de Vere was the true author, then his reputation as a degenerate spendthrift nobleman living off the largess of the monarchy would have been more reason to distance himself from this work, if not the entire canon. What's in a name?—One could say Puritan politics, among other things.

❧ 31 ❧

Timon of Athens

To expect stability from our life in this world is a waste of time—indeed, it seems to me things tend to go around in circles, and around and around.... But our human life runs giddily out, long before time does, and there is no hope for renewal except in the next world, which is eternal and without any end. Or so says Sidi Hamid, Muhammadan philosopher, for there are many who, without the light of true faith to show it to them, nevertheless fully comprehend the fickleness and instability of this mortal life, and the endless reach of eternity toward which it looks—though what our author is talking about, here, when he refers to the speed with which things come to an end, and are consumed, and lie totally undone, is how Sancho's governorship vanished into shadows and smoke.
—Cervantes, Don Quixote [1615][1]

Critical commentary (or lack thereof) on *Timon of Athens* is a living monument to the brute-stubborn stupidity of the orthodox Shakespeare academic establishment. In its sources and uses the play is intimately connected with Edward de Vere at every single turn; yet the very whisper of a possibility that the Bard perhaps had de Vere in mind while writing is viewed as absolute heresy. For most of these so-called scholars, it is far easier to remind us that Shakespeare probably did not have full involvement in the creation of *Timon* and therefore the play is not worthy of our full attention. Moreover, few have shared the epiphany of G. Wilson Knight that *Timon* is of "central importance to the interpretation of Shakespeare."[2] Oxfordians, however, tend to agree with Knight's adamancy on this point.

Timon of Athens saw its initial publication in the First Folio of 1623,[3] without which no one would have a clue of its existence. There are no recorded period performances; isolated, scattered references to Timon the Misanthrope in Elizabethan literature only prove that everyone was reading Plutarch and Lucian—that is, everyone who could read. Even the play's inclusion in the First Folio seems to have been an afterthought, with *Timon* late in the day supplanting *Troilus and Cressida*, which in turn was re-inserted at the last minute.[4] This was all of course years after the true author (whoever he was) had died. Edmund Chambers offered one plausible explanation: "I do not doubt that it was left unfinished by Shakespeare...."[5] With respect to dating, an occasional voice of honesty is heard, such as Frank Kermode, who openly admitted that "The date of the play is very uncertain."[6] The majority of commentators, however, are more comfortable ignoring the work altogether.

Stylistic grounds point to an approximate date of composition sometime during the early years of the 17th century. Some Oxfordians have argued that the anonymous, lost

179

play titled *The Historie of the Solitarie Knight*, performed on February 17, 1577, at White-hall Palace may have been an early version; however, this was far more likely to have been an adaptation of Chaucer's tale by the same name, which also influenced Shakespeare's *A Midsummer Night's Dream* and *The Two Noble Kinsmen*.[7] The entertainment was performed by the Lord Howard's Men, sponsored by Lord Charles Howard of Effingham, who until 1583 acted as deputy for the Lord Chamberlain, Thomas Radcliffe, Earl of Sussex.[8] Rad-cliffe during this time was Edward de Vere's mentor, as the latter became involved in a wide variety of literary and dramatic activities upon his return from the continent in 1576.

Shakespeare's starting point for this bitter tale of profligacy and hatred was Plutarch's life of Antony,[9] with additional suggestions taken from the lives of Alcibiades and Cori-olanus. Plutarch's younger contemporary Lucian expanded upon this tale for his play *Timon, or the Misanthrope*.[10] Both of these ancient authors were widely read during the Renaissance and several updated dramatic treatments were produced. Some of these the Bard may have known, such as the 15th-century Italian play *Timone*, written by the noble-man playwright Count Matteo Maria Boiardo.[11] Keeping things in perspective, however, Geoffrey Bullough reminded us that it was Plutarch who was Shakespeare's "primary source"[12]; with the life of Antony holding special fascination for him as the direct source of two separate plays.

During Shakespeare's time one did not just go to the nearest local public library and pick up a copy of Plutarch or Lucian. Books were rare and expensive, analogous today to the most expensive computer hardware and technology. There was limited access (and capa-bility of use) by a very small group of people. For Will Shakspere, we must assume that he was among the privileged few of his background who had both the wherewithal and contacts to take advantage of these treasures. Unfortunately, there is no evidence (even anecdotal) that he ever read, let alone owned a book; the best we can do is assume that he did. For de Vere, on the other hand, not only do we know that he owned and had direct access to books, but better yet, the books associated with de Vere appear to match those favored by Shakespeare as source materials. At age 19, de Vere purchased a copy of the seminal French Amyot translation of Plutarch (upon which the English translation was later based).[13] As a fallback, though, de Vere could always tap into the libraries of his guardian Lord Burghley or his tutor Thomas Smith, both of whom owned copies of Plutarch. Burghley's library also had copies of Lucian.[14] Perhaps Will Shakspere was bor-rowing his books from Edward de Vere.[15] As for possible minor sources such as the Bioardo play, the Italian-speaking de Vere may have witnessed a performance during his extended tour in Italy. After all, Oxfordians (like traditionalists) should be entitled to a few suppo-sitions such as this.

Regarding de Vere's personal connections to the story of *Timon*, it is not an over-statement to say that Shakespeare's play tells the story of de Vere's life. As the late Anglo-Oxfordian critic Edward Holmes succinctly put it, "The play is closest to autobiography."[16] If Will Shakspere dared to write anything so close to home regarding a peer of the realm, then we can only assume that he afterward realized it would get him into a heap of trou-ble (even after de Vere's death); therefore, he put it into a drawer where it stayed until 1623. On the other hand, if the Oxfordian theory is on target, then we are looking at a catharsis, a purging of demons. Edward Holmes again:

> *Timon* is too raw, too real for comfort. It was begun too close to the catastrophe which prompted it. That must be why it was left artistically undigested, incomplete.[17]

Under this scenario, Shakespeare the writer (de Vere) was writing *Timon* because he had to emotionally and certainly not for commercial gain. According to the Oxfordian view, this was a driven author who perhaps could not finish what he started.

The beginnings of Timon's downfall, apparent from Act I, scene i, are his spend-thrift ways. This immediately suggests de Vere, who could in all fairness be described as the biggest wastrel of his epoch, quite a distinction for that era and one for which he was legendary. In the words of Oxfordian author Joseph Sobran, de Vere's "only sense of money was that it existed to be spent and given away without limit."[18] De Vere, like Timon, lavishly patronized poets, painters, jewelers, and merchants, among others.[19] To catalogue his conspicuous consumption would constitute a study in and of itself; however, for pur-poses of this chapter, one selected example will suffice. De Vere owned a basin and ewer given to him by the queen; in the play, Timon's servant Flaminius entreats the flattering and two-faced Lucullus to loan his master money after presenting him with a "silver basin and ew'r" (III.i.6) as a gift.[20] As the cynical Apemantus observed earlier, however, "He that loves to be flattered is worthy o' the flatterer" (I.i.226), and Lucullus declines, declar-ing Flaminius "a fool, fit for thy master" (III.i.49) after he refuses to accept hush money. Shakespeare's Timon, like Plutarch's Antony, has a great weakness for flattery and his profligacy is fueled by it.

Timon also loves to entertain in first-class style. Music and dance are his passions. While female ballerinas amuse Timon and his guests, Apemantus sourly observes: "I should fear those that dance before me now / Would one day stamp upon me" (I.ii.143–144). Timon, highly pleased with himself, proudly notes that the musicians "Enter-tain'd me with my own device" (I.ii.1450).[21] Once again, keeping an image of de Vere out of one's head is possible only for those ignorant of his biography. In addition to patron-izing musicians and composers, de Vere was himself repeatedly praised by contemporaries as both an accomplished musician and dancer. During the first two acts of the play, one has trouble separating Shakespeare's portrait of Timon, whose rarified artistic tastes are not found in Plutarch, with one of de Vere during the 1570s. Speaking for the audience, the faithful steward Flavius asks, "What will this come to?" (I.ii.191). What it eventually "comes to" is bankruptcy for Timon and rank ingratitude on the part of his fair-weather friends. De Vere could have related. Flavius sums up the disaster in retrospect: "We have seen better days" (IV.ii.27).

When reality finally strikes home, Timon instructs Flavius, "Let all my land be sold" (II.ii.145), but is immediately informed that these have already been mortgaged to the hilt. For de Vere, reality came home to stay during his unbelievably expensive continental tour of 1575–1576. Writing to his father-in-law Lord Burghley from Siena on January 3, 1576, the 25-year-old earl vented for the first time financial woes that were to plague him for the duration of his life. De Vere complained of "dishonorable" consequences resulting from the "greediness" and "defamations" of his creditors, instructing that his lands be sold in order to satisfy them. He concludes the depressing missive with a note of defiance: "I have no help but of myne owne, and mine is made to serve me, and myself not mine."[22] For the 17th Earl of Oxford, this was no time to be discussing competing theories of husbandry;

personal honor was at stake, as it was for Timon in the play (II.ii.38). For someone with the anachronistic worldview of a feudal lord such as de Vere (or for that matter, Shakespeare's Timon or Antony), personal honor counted for everything to the exclusion of all else. Whether de Vere's directed fire sale was in fact a sound fiscal move is another matter beyond the scope of this study.

Standing opposite to Timon's old-fashioned, outmoded (and ultimately doomed) feudal ideals are the creditors and money lenders of Athens. When the bankrupt Timon is surrounded by his tormentors he cries out for them to "cleave me to the girdle!... cut his heart in sums ... tell out of my blood ... five thousand drops pays that.... Tear me...." (III.iv.89–98), and so forth. Recall that Shakespeare also explored the barbarous "pound of flesh" legal concept in *The Merchant of Venice*. This was a theme that apparently resonated with the Bard. After his precipitous fall and withdrawal from society, Timon gives the banished Alcibiades some of his newly discovered gold, instructing him to kill all of the Athenians, including "honor'd age" because "He is a usurer" (IV.iii.113). This was written by someone who understood the helpless fury of a debtor. If the upwardly mobile Will Shakspere was the true author, was he warning his own patrons not to be so generous? More plausibly, was he remembering his own destitute father John Shakspere (who by 1598 had his own coat of arms, thanks to his son), or was he merely engaging in a bit of self-flagellation?

Admittedly, Shakespeare's Athenians are not the most likeable of people. We admire Timon's generous spirit (before his hideous transformation), the devotion of his servants, the perceptive contrarianism of Apemantus, and the blunt candor of Alcibiades, but these individual exceptions are surrounded on all sides by vicious predators. We are introduced to the Athenian government by a Senator who proclaims that "Nothing emboldens sin so much as mercy" (III.v.3). Later, the Senate condemns an unnamed soldier to death for immorality despite pleas for mercy from Alcibiades, who is then promptly banished for his pains (III.v.97). It was again Edward Holmes who observed that the unnamed soldier's transgressions—sexual perversion, drunkenness, disturbing the peace—sound like similar charges leveled against de Vere.[23] This may be yet another one of the Bard's angry rebukes against the Jacobean Puritans who would later take over the country and demolish the playhouses. Timon's jackal creditors, merchants, and money lenders all have a distinctly pious air about them, while the only speaking female roles in the play are the two prostitute companions of Alcibiades.

About the only thing in *Timon of Athens* that is not autobiographical in relation to de Vere is the Athenian setting, although his son-in-law William Stanley reportedly traveled to Greece as part of his own continental tour. Then again, *Timon*, unlike Shakespeare's Italian and French plays, is not rich in topographical detail. Shakespeare's "Greek" plays also have a tendency to mix in Latin reference points, such as the "Senate" and "Senators" of Athens, along with the mostly Roman character names, excepting Timon, Apemantus, Alcibiades, and a few minor roles. Most of the exchanges in the last two acts take place in Timon's secluded wood—Shakespeare's idyllic "green world" turned on its head. If recent research by Oxfordian Christopher Paul is correct, then de Vere masqueraded his own death in 1604 to escape from creditors, possibly spending his remaining three (?) years of life in the Forest of Essex, which had been granted to him by King James.[24] James probably would have been glad to get rid of the 17th Earl's £1,000 annuity payment in return for a relatively small land grant. Maybe de Vere, like Timon, ended up secluded in the woods by choice. Alcibiades reads the epitaph on Timon's tomb in the final speech of the play, but it is Apemantus who earlier pronounces the true epitaph of Timon to his face, probably quite fitting for de Vere as well: "The middle of humanity thou never knewest, but the extremity of both ends" (IV.iii.300–301).

✦ 32 ✦

Julius Caesar

In the year 42 B.C., the largest assembly of Roman legions seen by the world up until that time[1] mustered near the city of Philippi in Macedonia. This was less than two years after the assassination of the dictator Gaius Julius Caesar in Rome, and the surviving assassins Brutus and Cassius led Republican forces facing off against the triumvirs Antony and Octavius. In two separate engagements over the course of three weeks, Brutus routed Octavius (who barely escaped with his life), while Antony simultaneously beat Cassius; then after both sides regrouped, Antony overpowered Brutus. Brutus and Cassius promptly committed suicide after their defeats, and with their deaths ended what was left of the Roman Republic. Military historians generally agree that Philippi was one of the most decisive and important land battles in history, and events before and after served as inspiration for Shakespeare's two great Roman tragedies, *Julius Caesar* and its sequel *Antony and Cleopatra*. The tragic hero of *Julius Caesar* is Brutus rather than the title character, who is assassinated in the middle of Act III. Although Caesar's Ghost subsequently appears to Brutus (Act IV, scene iii), it is the latter who remains the focal point of our attention throughout the play. Despite his upright personal virtue and high-minded political views, Brutus in the end is too impractical and idealistic to cope with the pragmatic and savvy Mark Antony.

The play did not appear in print until the First Folio of 1623, and was not identified with Shakespeare's name before then, at least as far as the record shows. The first definite recorded production took place on September 21, 1599, at the recently opened Globe Theater.[2] How similar that performed version of the play was to the printed edition 24 years later is anyone's guess. That same year (1599), Ben Jonson, in his own play *Every Man Out of His Humour*,[3] spoofed a line from *Julius Caesar*, "O judgment! Thou [art] fled to brutish beasts, and men have lost their reason" (III.ii.104–105)[4] with "Reason long since has fled to animals, you know" (V.vi.79).

Scholars agree that Shakespeare's primary source was Plutarch, and that the Thomas North English translation of 1569 was based upon the 1559 French translation by Bishop Jacques Amyot. Geoffrey Bullough added that the French was "the important translation," and that Amyot had earlier translated other books influential on the Bard, including Heliodorus' *Aethiopica* in 1546 and *Daphnis and Chloe* by Longus in 1559.[5] It is documented that the young Edward de Vere purchased the Amyot Plutarch[6] about the same time that Thomas Underdowne was dedicating his English translation of Heliodorus to Oxford in 1569.[7] De Vere also had associations with Longus through his secretary Angel

Day, who translated *Daphnis and Chloe* in 1587,[8] after dedicating his *English Secretarie* to Oxford in 1586 and praising his patron as "ever sacred to the Muses."[9]

Bullough noted that "although Shakespeare's main source was Plutarch, he seems to have dipped into other sources."[10] Other authorities have agreed, and one of these secondary sources appears to have been Cicero's *Philippics*.[11] Cicero is yet another author that the 19-year-old de Vere purchased about the same time he acquired his French Plutarch[12]— it seems as though one cannot escape de Vere when examining the Bard's favorite source material. If this were not enough, Frank Kermode, in his introduction for *Riverside*, identifies *De Republica Anglorum*, by the Cambridge don Thomas Smith and written in 1565, as another possible source for *Julius Caesar*.[13] Smith, as most Oxfordians know, was de Vere's personal childhood tutor,[14] and the 14-year-old earl graduated from Cambridge in 1564, the year before Smith wrote his work.[15] Also in 1564, de Vere was the dedicatee of *The Histories of Trogus Pompeius*, written by his uncle Arthur Golding, who attributed to his nephew an interest in ancient history.[16] In addition, Golding was the first English translator of Ovid, yet another influence on *Julius Caesar*, as cited by Bullough.[17]

One of the most famous lines in the play occurs when Caesar recognizes Brutus among the assassins and admonishes him in Latin with "*Et tu, Brute?*"[You too, Brutus?] (III.i.77). This is not from Plutarch, but a similar phrase is found in *The Twelve Caesars* by Suetonius (Plutarch's contemporary) who more precisely wrote, "You too, my child?"[18] Suetonius was not translated into English until 1606 (by Philemon Holland) and the only known use of the phrase in an English work before *Julius Caesar* is found in the anonymous play titled *The True Tragedy of Richard Duke of York*, printed in 1595. This later became *Henry VI, Part III*, but by that time, the line "*Et tu, Brute?*" had been omitted,[19] strongly suggesting that Shakespeare preferred to use it for *Julius Caesar*. This leads straight into the issue of the Bard's familiarity with the Latin and Greek languages which, contrary to popular perception, appears to have been considerable. Bullough was typical of the more modern orthodox view, maintaining that "Recent enquiries show that Shakespeare could certainly read Latin and both remembered much of what he had read at school and kept up some study of it."[20]

All of this seems to contradict what Ben Jonson wrote about Shakespeare's "small Latine, and lesse Greeke" in the prefatory material of the First Folio, but this tribute is highly equivocal for those who take the trouble to reflect. "And though thou hadst small Latine, and lesse Greeke" could have more than one meaning. The phrase "And though thou hadst" could mean "although you had" (the more modern sense of the phrase), or it could mean "even if you had"; in other words, Shakespeare would have been great *even if* he had small Latin and less Greek, which in fact was not the case.[21] For a similar usage of the word "though," the King James Bible of 1611 provides one example (see 1 Corinthians 13:1–3). Jonson's characterization of Shakespeare as "Sweet Swan of Avon" is also ambiguous. There are several Avon River Valleys in England, at least two of which (in Warwickshire and Wiltshire) had associations with Edward de Vere as well.[22] Less quoted from Jonson's tribute is his assertion that "For a good Poet's made, as well as borne. And such were thou." Assuming the true author was Will Shakspere, one might conclude that the Bard was "made" at Stratford Grammar School combined with on-the-job training in London, where he became proficient in the Latin classics, not to mention French, Italian, English, and perhaps Greek as well. In the play, Casca jokes that Cicero's multilingual skills are "Greek to me" (I.ii.284), but Casca is not a sympathetic character. Furthermore, Shakespeare's familiarity with the Greek language and source material has been intriguingly explored by Oxfordian scholar Andrew Werth.[23] Whether de Vere had any expertise in Greek is unknown; however, it is difficult to dispute his knowledge of Latin. In addition to his schooling, de Vere's Latin skills were attested to the Inquisition by Orazio Cuoco upon his return to Italy,[24] and some of de Vere's published poetry and prose were written in Latin as well.

Another myth that deserves thorough debunking is Jonson's purported steadfast affability toward Shakespeare—a myth based mostly upon apocryphal sources dating from the 18th century (or later), combined with Honest Ben's tribute in the First Folio. One example relating directly to *Julius Caesar* is that Jonson, in his *Timber, or Discoveries*, posthumously published in 1640, mixes both criticism and praise for the Bard, attributing to him the "ridiculous" line of "Caesar never did wrong, but with just cause...."[25] In point of fact, the First Folio text reads, "Know, Caesar doth not wrong, nor without cause will he be satisfied" (III.i.47). Whether the original had been subsequently altered and whether the alleged quote is in fact ridiculous were sensibly discussed by Samuel Schoenbaum,[26] who, unlike many commentators, saw the only real issue being Jonson's attitude toward Shakespeare, which he concluded was "ambivalent."[27] Schoenbaum noted that "The tradition of Jonson's malevolence derives from the scattered aspersions in his writings."[28]

Careful readers of Shakespeare's play have recognized that, while heavily utilizing Plutarch and perhaps other sources, the Bard made many subtle changes in characters and situations. These changes have the net effect of emphasizing personal relationships over complex political issues,[29] a not-too-surprising approach given that the groundlings at Elizabethan theaters lived in what today would be considered a police state, ruled by a near-absolute monarchy in cooperation with a small, elite peerage. The image of Brutus as a Republican liberator could not be pushed too far in this context without a backlash of government censorship. One reason why a work such as Smith's *De Republica* is viewed as a possible influence is that it emphasized distinctions between monarchy and tyranny. Therefore, for Smith (and presumably Shakespeare as well), the ideal form of government was a benevolent monarchy, as opposed to the potentially tyrannical dictatorship of a Caesar. In a very real sense, Shakespeare's source Plutarch faced the same dilemma, writing during the time of the Emperor Trajan—the high tide of Roman Imperialism—while extolling the virtues of an earlier Roman Republic. Contemporaries of Shakespeare such as Montaigne noted that although Plutarch was careful to condemn Caesar's assassins, this seems to have been mere political correctness on the part of the author.[30] In the case of Shakespeare, the same constraints applied except that the Bard overall seems to have had far less sympathy for governments without kings than Plutarch. Such an attitude would be somewhat surprising coming from anyone who was not a nobleman, since one generation later the English, after the upheavals of civil war, would experiment with pure parliamentary rule.

The second step in Shakespeare's process of skillfully altering his source material involved smoothing over the personal faults of the historical Brutus,[31] presumably to better emphasize his tragic flaws—impractical idealism characterized by over-bookishness and over-detachment from political realities. There are several good examples of this but one in particular involves the motivation of Brutus. Plutarch and Suetonius drew attention to Caesar's belief that Brutus may have been his natural son, but Shakespeare is careful to avoid any hint of this. "You too, my child?" is changed to "You too, Brutus?" and there is no mention of Caesar's past relations with Brutus' mother Servilia. Instead, Shakespeare's Brutus is driven purely by political idealism, declaring with respect to Caesar that "for my part, I know no personal cause to spurn at him" (II.i.10–11). In a similar manner, the purely personal grudge of Cassius against Caesar is somewhat of a departure from Plutarch, who emphasized that Cassius hated all tyrants, beginning with Sulla during his childhood. By taking the edge off the historical Brutus' militant Republicanism and implied personal enmity against Caesar, the Bard allowed his audience to focus on one aspect of this character, while at the same time avoiding trouble with the Elizabethan authorities—perhaps even venting his own personal political views in the process, if in fact Shakespeare was a nobleman himself.

Taking this one step further, Shakespeare's Roman and Greek tragedies may represent the author's attempts at exploring his personal failings within the dramatic context of ancient political backdrops. Even if the true author was de Vere, he probably would not have been allowed to do this in the history plays, for obvious reasons. Special privileges would not have included a license to glorify oneself or one's own lineage as part of the national epic and at the expense of other peers. Needless to say, if the true author was Will Shakspere, such decisions would not even have been part of the equation. If, on the other hand, de Vere was the true hand behind these works, then Shakespeare's ancient tragic heroes may represent different aspects of de Vere's highly flawed personal character: impracticality (Brutus), sensuality (Antony), arrogance (Coriolanus), profligacy (Timon), and so on. Was Shakespeare the writer merely looking at the human condition or was he examining his own human condition as well?

That de Vere was impractical is one of the few things that most historians can agree upon regarding this controversial personality. Apart from complete ineptitude with money,[32] de Vere's management of property and personnel appears to have been one disaster followed by another. For example, de Vere's attempt to establish a grammar school in Earls Colne was a near-complete fiasco, at least according to his most recent biography.[33] A further symptom of this impracticality—the cause some would say—was de Vere's acute bookishness (also one of Brutus' traits), as noted by contemporaries, even in their literary dedications to him. Perhaps the most notable of these admonishments came from Gabriel Harvey in 1578 while addressing the court in Latin at Audley End, who urged de Vere to "put away your feeble pen" while praising him in connection with Minerva, the Roman spear-shaker goddess of wisdom and warfare.[34]

Other parallels between de Vere and Brutus are easily identified. Like Brutus and his wife Portia, de Vere seems to have had an unusual relationship with his first wife, Anne Cecil. Just as Portia was the daughter of the esteemed Cato the Younger, Anne was the daughter of William Cecil, Lord Burghley, the queen's chief minister and de Vere's guardian, among other things. Anne died in June 1588, shortly before the invasion of the Spanish Armada in July, and it appears that de Vere was not present at her death or funeral, possibly making his own preparations for the imminent invasion. This would be similar to Brutus, who learns of Portia's death while on campaign, and reacts with cold, stoic detachment upon being told of her death a second time (IV.iii.188). Some commentators have seen in this passage a contradictory repetition that should be edited, but another possibility is that Brutus, like de Vere in June 1588, had little time for grief.

Superstition abounds in *Julius Caesar* (and in Plutarch), beginning with portents preceding the assassination and ending with Caesar's Ghost before the decisive struggle at Philippi. Early in the play, the soothsayer warns Caesar to "Beware the Ides of March" (I.ii.18) and his wife Calpurnia desperately tries to prevent his leaving the house with "The heavens themselves blaze forth the death of princes" (II.ii.30). As for de Vere, his enemies reported that he claimed to have seen his dead mother, who prophesied the future to him, as well as his dead stepfather holding a whip. Incidents such as this plus de Vere's known patronage of astrologers all seem to indicate that he had a substantial interest in the occult.[35] De Vere's fascination fits in well with Shakespeare's dramatic use of the supernatural in *Julius Caesar* and other plays.

On a more earthly level, the impractical idealism of Brutus makes a sharp contrast to the ruthless pragmatism of Antony. To make matters worse for Brutus, he fails to see the threat that Antony represents before it is too late for himself and the Republican cause. Cassius, on the other hand, sees Antony for what he is and tries to warn his partner, but to no avail. Brutus then makes two crucial mistakes in quick succession: first he prevents Antony from being killed during the assassination (II.i) and then allows him to speak during Caesar's funeral (III.i).

Before Antony's famous funeral oration in which he incites the mob against Caesar's assassins, Brutus justifies himself to the crowd with initial success. Plutarch noted, however, that Brutus had a laconic style of oratory that could be less than inspiring. The speech that Shakespeare puts into his mouth becomes almost a parody of ineffectual public speaking as Brutus tries to reason with the mob and pledges with chilling irony: "as I slew my best lover for the good of Rome, I have the same dagger for myself, when it shall please my country to need my death" (III.ii.44–47). This is followed by the skillful demagoguery of Antony, beginning with "Friends, Romans, countrymen, lend me your ears!" (III.ii.73). In this respect, de Vere definitely seemed to have more in common with the delivery of Antony, whose harangue is a masterpiece of inflaming passions. De Vere, after returning from Italy, was reported to have boasted that he was "reputed for his eloquence another Cicero and for his conduct a Caesar."[36] Antony, after deviously planting the seeds of violence with suggestions such as "if I were dispos'd to stir your hearts and minds to mutiny and rage" (III.ii.121–122), highlights his target with "This was the most unkindest cut of all" (III.ii.183).[37] Yet, after defeating Brutus at Philippi, Antony can still eulogize him as "the noblest Roman of them all" (V.v.68). With the death of Brutus, Shakespeare now seems to inhabit the character of Antony, whose own tragedy will be the theme of the sequel to come.

$$\text{\textit{ß}\,} 33 \text{\,\textit{Ω}}$$

Macbeth

"The Scottish Play" has been a bane to both actors and scholars, in part because of its deceptively simple origins combined with dark subject matter. The initial publication appeared in the First Folio of 1623[1]; therefore, we are yet again looking at a text printed years after the death of the author, whoever he may have been. The earliest known performance in 1611 at the Globe Theater was among those recorded in the diary of astrologer Simon Forman.[2] Thus *Macbeth*, like *The Tempest*, is noted on the stage circa 1611 and is first printed in the Folio. Unlike *The Tempest*, *Macbeth* is one of the Bard's most disturbing works, as well as his most compressed, shorter in length than any play except *The Comedy of Errors*.[3] Most scholars believe it was a relatively late creation, although many Oxfordians and some orthodox critics (such as Dover Wilson) have suggested that an earlier, Elizabethan version existed that was later revised.[4] In 1568, an anonymous lost play titled *The Tragedie of the Kinge of Scottes* had been performed in London by the Children of the Queen's Chapel.[5] The previous year (1567) presumably this same work was mentioned in a letter by William Drury, Governor of Berwick, to William Cecil. Drury refers to a boys' interlude presented in Stirling that dramatized the recent murder of the presumptive king of Scotland, Henry Stuart, Lord Darnley.[6] At that time, Edward de Vere was 17 years old and a law student at Gray's Inn. Will Shakspere was three years old and in Stratford.

The oft-repeated view that *Macbeth* was written as a compliment to King James deserves a closer look. There is no record of the play ever being acted at court, and this is in contrast to *The Tempest*, which is known to have been performed at least twice at Whitehall. Moreover, common sense would seem to reject the idea of a royal compliment. Portraying one's countrymen on the public stage with a homicidal lust for power and nihilistic worldview (plus insanity and suicide tossed in for good measure), particularly when both of King James' parents had been involved with murderous scandals and rumors, does not seem very complimentary. In fact, it could have been viewed as downright insulting to the new king, not to mention dangerous for the author, like attempting to flatter an Italian-American by writing *The Sopranos*.[7] *Macbeth* also contains a clear subliminal message: that the Scots are a violent people, especially Scottish kings. This hardly would have been appropriate material for making royal compliments. Such a story comes across more like a backhanded compliment (if not a slap in the face) to anyone of Scottish descent. At best, it could have been seen as a highly ambivalent attitude toward the Stuart succession. Indeed, the playwrights Ben Jonson and George Chapman were imprisoned for satirizing the Scots in their 1605 play *Eastward Hoe!*[8]

Macbeth and The Tempest are also similar in that isolated elements in both are often cited in attempts to prove that Edward de Vere died too soon in 1604 to be the true author. In the case of Macbeth, the so-called Porter scene (iii) of Act II, in which the Porter refers to the art of equivocation no fewer than five times, is typically regurgitated for this purpose. The repetitive view among orthodox scholars is that this scene is an allusion to the trial of Jesuit priest Henry Garnett in wake of the Gunpowder Plot of 1605; hence, Shakespeare must have written the play soon afterward. Assuming the Porter scene is not a later insert—a big assumption given that many believe Macbeth contains a number of such inserts[9]—there are more serious problems with this line of reasoning. For one, highly visible public trials involving the issue of equivocation had occurred several times during Queen Elizabeth's reign. One had been the celebrated case of Jesuit priest and poet Robert Southwell in 1595.[10] As early as 1581, however, another Jesuit priest and Catholic martyr, Edmund Campion, had been executed after a sensational trial in which the doctrine of equivocation received high profile.[11] In fact, given the very public history of this issue during indictments of Catholic priests beginning in 1581, it would not seem surprising if the former Catholic turned Anglican, Ben Jonson, himself resorted to this art for the famed prefatory poem of the First Folio.

As a side note, Edmund Campion and Edward de Vere seemed to keep close physical proximity to one another, either by coincidence or by design. Both graduated from Oxford in 1566, both were in Italy during the mid–1570s, and both were imprisoned in the Tower of London at different times during 1581. This is not necessarily to say the two were in cahoots; on the other hand, it is unlikely they would have missed each other. Perhaps most telling, de Vere's servant, the playwright Anthony Munday, was a chief witness against Campion during his trial and wrote numerous pamphlets around this same time portraying the Jesuits as traitors and insurgents.[12]

Getting back to Macbeth, the play ostensibly deals with quasi-historical events in Scotland and England during the 11th century, immediately prior to the Norman conquest. Shakespeare's main source was probably Raphael Holinshed's Chronicles, the first edition of which was dedicated to Holinshed's patron William Cecil, Lord Burghley (de Vere's guardian and later father-in-law), in 1577. Earlier in 1567, Holinshed had been a member of the jury that found de Vere innocent of murder in the Thomas Bricknell affair.[13] This was, perhaps by coincidence, two months after the letter of William Drury to Cecil mentioning the interlude at Stirling that depicted the murder of a Scottish king.

Macbeth abounds in the supernatural, beginning with the three witches or Weird Sisters, who speak the first lines in the play, then prophesy to Macbeth and Banquo in Act I, scene iii. Later in Act III (scene iv), Macbeth is tormented and taunted by the ghost of Banquo, whom he has just had murdered. Perhaps the most spectacular example, however, is in Act IV, scene i, where the witches conjure up for Macbeth a procession of eight kings, springing from the line of the murdered Banquo. The likely source is a 1578 Latin treatise written by Bishop John Leslie in passionate defense of the Stuarts' royal legitimacy. This book graphically illustrates the succession of eight Scottish kings descended from Banquo and his son Fleance, culminating with the son of Mary Stuart, King James VI of Scotland, later to become King James I of England.[14] Assuming the eighth king is James, commentators of all authorship persuasions have been troubled by Shakespeare's portrayal of a living monarch on stage, which was illegal at that time. This supposed flouting of the rules, however, is somewhat less perplexing if the play is viewed through the Oxfordian lens. In the first place, Shakespeare the writer does not appear to have been especially concerned about sanctions of law. Take, for example, his portrayal of an anointed English monarch being deposed in *Richard II*. Furthermore, if we entertain the possibility that an earlier, Elizabethan version existed, then Macbeth's vision does not yet represent a living English monarch.

One thing that King James and Edward de Vere had in common was a keen interest in the supernatural. James personally presided over witch trials and published in 1597 a book on the subject titled *Daemonology*,[15] prompting Henry the Great of France to dub him "the wisest fool in Christendom."[16] As for de Vere, he appears to have been an enthusiastic student of the occult. The leading astrologer of the day, John Dee, listed de Vere among his patrons, and lesser-known practitioners such as Nicholas Hill associated with Oxford as well.[17] De Vere's enemies claimed that he boasted of having conversed with the recently deceased and noted court musician Robert Parsons at Greenwich; of having seen his dead stepfather (brandishing a whip, no less) and dead mother, who then prophesied the future to him; of having copulated with female spirits; and of having conference with the devil, whom he had personally conjured up. Macbeth's famous line "Sleep no more!" (II.ii.32) could well have applied. Interestingly, many of these nightmare visions allegedly occurred shortly after de Vere returned home from active military duty in Scotland. Most remarkable, however, was de Vere's claim to have authored an illustrated book of prophecies, inspired by his supernatural encounter with Robert Parsons. The only person who admitted ever having seen this book, Charles Arundel, testified that one of the pictures depicted a male child crowned as royal successor to a queen.[18] At the time of this alleged prophecy, James was a minor, although in the play (Act IV, scene i) the vision of a crowned child is used to represent the usurper Malcolm.

Much has been written concerning the relationship between the unusual violence and treachery depicted in *Macbeth* to atrocities committed in France, such as the infamous St. Bartholomew's Day Massacre of 1572.[19] The savagery of the Wars of Religion unquestionably influenced the writing of *Macbeth* (as well as *Titus Andronicus*); however, contemporary events in Scotland and England were surely utmost in everyone's mind. Mary Stuart had been the child bride (and later widow) of Francis II of France, hence the daughter-in-law of Catherine de Medici, whom many historians view as the true architect of the St. Bartholomew's Day atrocities. De Vere got a firsthand look at the French court three years after the massacre, with most of the perpetrators still alive and thriving.

De Vere was entwined with these events his entire life, but perhaps the key formative experience of his early adulthood was his active participation in the military campaign of 1570 led by Thomas Radcliffe, Earl of Sussex, directed against English Catholic earls of the north and their Scottish rebel allies. In addition to being one of Elizabeth's best generals, Radcliffe was an adolescent mentor and surrogate father figure to de Vere,[20] and a future Lord Chamberlain and patron of the same acting company that eventually became associated with Shakespeare's plays.[21] Yet another future Lord Chamberlain, Henry Carey, Lord Hunsdon, also participated in this campaign.[22] Thus, not even counting de Vere, the Scottish campaign of 1570 was an assembly of future patrons for what later became known as Shakespeare's acting company and later still the King's Men of the Jacobean court.

Radcliffe's forces, who invaded Scotland like Malcolm's avenging Anglocentric army in *Macbeth*, did not play patty-cake with the rebels. In terms of sheer brutality toward innocent civilians and cold, calculated destruction of property, his punitive strike through southeastern Scotland would have been comparable to (if not worse than) Sherman's march to the sea through Georgia during the American Civil War.[23] Partly in response to this brutality, Pope Pius V excommunicated Elizabeth later that same year. De Vere spent his 20th birthday amidst the carnage and mayhem, presumably as a member of Radcliffe's staff,[24] and the likely impact it had on his subsequent worldview should not be underestimated. Yes, he had killed a man by the time he was 17, but that would have been little compared to what transpired in Scotland and probably surpassed anything he would ever see again in terms of human destruction and waste. A witness to these things could well have written that human life was "a walking shadow" (V.v.24) and "a tale told by an idiot, full of sound and fury, signifying nothing" (V.v.26–28).

This writer has never experienced war personally, but several near relatives have. One is an uncle who, at 18 years of age, was a member of the U.S. Fourth Marine Division that assaulted the Japanese island of Iwo Jima during World War II. Although this uncle served with distinction, emerging physically unscathed and going on to live a relatively productive and happy life, this same uncle is nevertheless (60 years later) haunted by that island because of the things he witnessed. He experienced the same thing millions of other young men have when exposed to the horrors of war—they remember and never forget. We believe that the author of *Macbeth* may have been such a person as well, as the play reflects the bleak mindset of one who had seen the degradations of war and human behavior at its worst, just as de Vere surely had in Scotland when he was a young man in the year 1570.

The Northern Rebellion had been sparked in 1569 by rumors of a pending Catholic marriage between Mary Stuart, the deposed Queen of Scots, and de Vere's first cousin, Thomas Howard, Duke of Norfolk, who would then allegedly supplant Elizabeth as reigning English monarchs.[25] Although the success of Radcliffe's expedition was swift and decisive, the Northern Rebellion and subsequent Ridolfi Plot did not finally collapse until three years later with the execution of Norfolk in 1572, followed in 1573 with the capture of Edinburgh Castle by the aforementioned William Drury. The prelude to the Northern Rebellion had been the murder in 1567 of the presumptive king of Scotland, Henry Stuart, Lord Darnley. His wife Mary Stuart had been implicated in this crime along with her lover, James Hepburn, Earl of Bothwell. Hepburn himself may have inspired the character of Macbeth. He was a talented, fiery, and ultimately tragic figure who died exiled and imprisoned in Denmark, home of still another bigger-than-life Shakespearean tragic hero.

The mother of Darnley (and King James' grandmother) was Margaret Douglas, Lady Lennox. By 1573, Lady Lennox was living at King's Place in Hackney, suburban London,[26] the very same house that later became the final residence of Edward de Vere. Oxfordians (such as Richard Whalen in his comprehensive article on *Macbeth*) have hypothesized that the library at King's Place was as likely a location as any for the so-called Stewart Chronicle manuscript to have been housed, probably by Lady Lennox herself.[27] This document was an early 16th-century manuscript (not printed until the mid–19th century) and is believed by some commentators to have been used by Shakespeare as a secondary source for details not found in Holinshed.[28] In the play, Shakespeare also gives small roles to Lord and Lady Lennox, though neither are mentioned by Holinshed, and we know that de Vere moved in the same company as the Douglases.[29] Lady Lennox died in 1578, under suspicious circumstances and shortly after having dinner with the notorious Robert Dudley, Earl of Leicester.[30] De Vere's mentor Thomas Radcliffe then died in a similar manner in 1583.[31] In fact, there appears to be a long list of people who had a fatal case of indigestion shortly after having dinner with the Earl of Leicester. Several of these possible victims—Margaret Douglas, Thomas Radcliffe, Nicholas Throckmorton—had been involved in Scottish politics and all were perceived as Leicester's rivals or enemies.[32] As for King's Place, it may have been the reputed sanctuary in Hackney provided by Lord William Vaux for the Jesuit "equivocators" Henry Garnett, Robert Southwell, and Edmund Campion.[33]

As most students of history know, these events came to a head in 1586 with the treason trial of Mary Stuart, at which de Vere himself sat in judgment as a juror,[34] just as Holinshed had sat in judgment of de Vere 19 years earlier. After Mary's execution in 1587, England withstood the onslaught of the Spanish Armada in 1588 and emerged as the most powerful nation-state in the world. Modern historians pretty much agree that while Mary may have been a vain and foolish schemer, she was certainly no Lady Macbeth, although at the time many perceived her that way. Mary's son James was later very sensitive about this whole affair, strenuously maintaining his mother's innocence. Historians also mostly agree that James' succession of Elizabeth was largely engineered by Robert Cecil, son of Lord Burghley and formerly de Vere's brother-in-law. De Vere had a proverbial ringside seat to observe the Stuart succession, largely through his ties with the Cecils, beginning with his wardship in Burghley House as a teenager and ending with his relationship to Robert Cecil, who was probably the earl's sole conduit to the power centers of the Jacobean court.

Shakespeare's apparent ambivalence toward the Scots in *Macbeth* was earlier noted, and de Vere was known to have displayed just such an attitude toward the accession of King James. In fact, we know that he appears to have been initially opposed to it outright. In 1603, shortly before the queen's death, recorded testimony reveals that Henry Clinton, Earl of Lincoln, had been lavishly entertained by de Vere at King's Place for the purpose of sounding out opposition to the Stuart succession.[35] Clinton demurred, however, and de Vere eventually came around himself, participating in the coronation ceremony of James, just as his father had participated in Elizabeth's.[36] In return he was awarded by James the continuance of his prodigious annuity, along with other favors.[37] This was all in spite of the fact that de Vere was about the last person in the world whose political support was needed by the new theater-loving monarch. De Vere, after all, had done a hatchet job on James' mother, literally and perhaps figuratively as well: literally, by voting in favor of her execution as a juror, and figuratively, if indeed he was Shakespeare, by turning her into Lady Macbeth, who is sort of an updated version of Medea. No wonder he was ambivalent toward the Stuarts.

Summing up, we began by commenting on the inappropriateness of *Macbeth* as a royal compliment to a Scottish monarch such as King James. Regardless of who wrote the play, the author probably did not write it as a straightforward compliment; whoever wrote it had definite mixed feelings toward the Scots in general and the Stuart succession in particular, just as Edward de Vere was known to have had. Nor is it outlandish to suggest that a work like *Macbeth* was *not* written by a normal, healthy, and well-adjusted person. On the contrary, it is very plausible that this dark and gloomy Scottish tragedy was the creation of a rather twisted and tormented soul, someone who was literally being driven by demons or at least believed that he was.

↜ 34 ↝

Hamlet

Shakespeare's longest play (nearly 4,000 lines, four hours in performance, uncut) was entered with the Stationers' Register in 1602 by the printer James Roberts. This first "bad" quarto, however, was published by "N.L. [Nicholas Ling] and John Trundell" in 1603 as *The Tragicall Historie of Hamlet* by "William Shake-speare." The first quarto is a much shorter version of the play, deviating considerably from later editions. The frontispiece reads "As it hath beene diverse times acted by his Highnesse servants in the Cittie of London: as also in the two Universities of Cambridge and Oxford, and elsewhere."[1] The reference to the King's Men acting company, successor to the Lord Chamberlain's Men, clues us in that this was after King James came to the throne, following the death of Queen Elizabeth in 1603. As for Cambridge and Oxford, both were the alma maters of Edward de Vere. Moreover, the phrase "and elsewhere" suggests that the play had been widely performed before its first publication. The majority view is that Shakespeare wrote his masterpiece right around the turn of the 16th century, although Edmund Chambers added rather honestly that "There is not much evidence as to the precise date of *Hamlet*."[2] In essence, the basis for the year 1600 is that this is when most orthodox scholars *want* to believe the play was written. The thought of anyone younger than Will Shakspere in the year 1600[3] writing this towering monument is a little too much even for those who claim that pure genius (without the wisdom of life experience) can accomplish absolutely anything.[4]

In 1589, over a decade before the conventional dating, Thomas Nashe, in his Epistle to Robert Greene's *Menaphon*, referred to an "English Seneca" who wrote "whole Hamlets, I should say handfuls of Tragical speeches."[5] Later, in 1594, the Henslowe diary logged in a performance. Then in 1596, Thomas Lodge in *Wit's Miserie* made yet another allusion to *Hamlet*. So how can scholars say it was written in 1600? Because, they explain, this was not Shakespeare's play—it was the so-called Ur-*Hamlet*, an earlier dramatic adaptation that the Bard used as source material. In 1589, Will Shakspere was 25 years old. De Vere was 39.

In 1604, one year after the first quarto, the second "good" quarto was published, again by Nicholas Ling, but this time printed by the original applicant, "J.R." or James Roberts. Edward de Vere purportedly died[6] in June that same year and Oxfordians view this play and *The Tempest* as swan songs. The frontispiece reads, "*The Tragicall Historie of Hamlet, Prince of Denmarke* By William Shakespeare. Newly imprinted and enlarged to almost as much againe as it was, according to the true and perfect Coppie."[7] The name

195

"Shakespeare" no longer had a hyphen, either because the traditional author insisted on the newer, correct spelling or because someone else became deadly serious regarding the use of a pseudonym. Roberts, incidentally, owned the predecessor firm that was eventually acquired by the Jaggard family, printers of the First Folio.

The Norse[8] legend of "Amleth" was first written down in its entirety during the 13th century by the Danish historian Saxo Grammaticus (in his *Historiae Danicae*, first printed in 1514). This story is profoundly different from the Bard's version. The original is a very violent and primitive tale that Shakespeare tones down quite a bit, if you can believe it. Noteworthy is the original "happy" ending—Hamlet kills everyone and becomes king.[9] Same thing in *King Lear*—the original had a happy ending. Shakespeare turned these into tragedies, arguably the two greatest tragedies ever written. The playwright must have believed a pile of bodies was better box office and/or had intensely personal and artistic reasons for doing so.

Saxo Grammaticus was translated into French by François Belleforest in his *Histoires Tragiques*, with the 1576 edition believed to have been most influential on the Bard.[10] Belleforest was a Catholic propagandist subsidized by King Henry III of France; earlier he had written a book criticizing middle-class English Protestants for increasing their political power through marriages with the old English nobility. This is precisely what Lord Burghley did by having his daughter Anne Cecil marry Edward de Vere, and Belleforest identifies them all by name.[11] Copies of both Saxo Grammaticus (in Latin) and Belleforest (in French) were in the library of de Vere's father-in-law.[12]

De Vere's ability to draw upon French sources cannot be ruled out, given that he was corresponding in French by age 13.[13] An example of de Vere's comfort level with Latin can be found in his lengthy and elegant preface for Bartholomew Clerke's 1572 Latin translation of *The Courtier* by Baldessare Castiglione.[14] Earlier in 1561, Castiglione had been translated into English by Burghley's brother-in-law Thomas Hoby. The influence of *The Courtier* on *Hamlet* has been widely acknowledged, including Geoffrey Bullough, who goes further by suggesting a connection between Castiglione and Shakespeare's play within the play, titled *The Murder of Gonzago* or "mousetrap" sequence in Act III, scene ii. According to Bullough, the victim the Bard may have had in mind was Francesco Maria della Rovere, Duke of Urbino, who was rumored to have been poisoned through the ear (exactly like Hamlet's father and Gonzago in the mousetrap) in 1538. Urbino, a man of great ability who was known personally by Castiglione, appears as one of the characters in *The Courtier*. Thus, the historical "Gonzago" [*sic*] was the alleged perpetrator, rather than the victim of the crime.[15] Before his death, Urbino was painted by Titian, and this portrait seems to resemble the ghost of Hamlet's father in every detail.[16] De Vere may have had an opportunity to see this portrait during his Grand Tour. He certainly would have known of the duke, given Castiglione's flattering portrayal in a book for which Oxford wrote a preface.

De Vere, himself a preeminent figure at court, would have been anxious to emulate, or at least appear to emulate, the ideals espoused in one of the most famous and popular books of the time—a publication that he had personally been involved with, to boot. Book I of *The Courtier* begins with an obligatory statement that the chief profession of the courtier is arms, then digresses into an extraordinary and extended discussion on the courtier's other role as a provider of princely entertainment. This includes emphasis on the courtier's abilities as a speaker, writer, musician, dancer, and even as a painter and sculptor. Castiglione writes, in the words of his character Canossa:

> I would have him more than passably learned in letters, at least in those studies we call the humanities.... Let him be versed in the poets, as well as in the orators and historians, and let him be practiced also in writing verse and prose.

The character Bembo takes it one step further:

> I do not see why you insist that this Courtier ... should regard everything as an ornament of arms, and not arms and the rest as an ornament of letters; which, without any other accompaniment, are as superior to arms in worth as the soul is to the body.[17]

Soldiering versus the humanities: which should be the nobleman's first goal? This was a serious debate during the Renaissance, and most of the great writers touch upon it.

Assuming Shakespeare's portrayal of the relationship between Hamlet and the players is accurate, one can easily postulate a similar dynamic between de Vere and the actors he was known to patronize. Did his role (like Hamlet's) include giving advice, writing parts, and mounting special productions? Given that contemporaries praise him as a playwright,[18] such active participation would not be total fantasy, even if de Vere were not in fact Shakespeare. In similar fashion, given that de Vere grew up in a household with actors, a Hamlet-Yorick type of relationship (Act V, scene i) would not have been out of the question.

"To be, or not to be, that is the question...." (III.i.55) may be the most famous speech in stage history. Did Shakespeare just make this up? Well, yes and no. Numerous orthodox scholars such as Joseph Hunter, Lily Campbell, Hardin Craig, and others have noticed that Hamlet's soliloquy draws upon and paraphrases another well-known work, even referring to it as "Hamlet's book" which he holds while feigning madness to Polonius. The book in question, *De Consolatione*, had been written by the Italian physician, philosopher and astrologer Girolamo Cardano, and included meditations on life, suffering, suicide and death.[19] Cardano, like Hamlet, compares death to sleep, dreaming, and foreign travel.[20] In 1573, the 23-year-old de Vere personally sponsored the first English translation by Thomas Bedingfield, known as *Cardanus Comforte*. This work was dedicated to Oxford, who wrote another lengthy introduction and prefatory poem,[21] both filled with Shakespearean turns of phrase.

The list goes on. Myriad literary sources identified for *Hamlet* include books that had either been written or translated by de Vere's family and servants, dedicated to and/or prefaced by Oxford, owned by him, or accessible to him through the libraries of his tutors and guardian. While de Vere did not have a monopoly on Elizabethan books, he did appear to have a monopoly on those influential for Shakespeare and *Hamlet* in particular. For example, in the case of John Lyly's *Euphues*, both the author and the book were associated with Oxford.[22] Another example is de Vere's personal copy of the Geneva Bible, today in the Folger Library, which has an isolated verse from Ezekiel (16:49) marked, including the unusual phrase "Pride, fulness of bread, and abundance of idleness"—almost identical in both sense and wording to Hamlet's lament that death "took my father grossly, full of bread" (III.iii.80).[23]

On a more esoteric level, *Hamlet* is thought to contain a cosmic allegory on the Elizabethan worldview, then shifting away from the ancient Ptolemaic perspective to the modern

Copernican outlook. This allegory, first fully expounded by Dr. Peter Usher, Professor Emeritus of Astronomy and Astrophysics at Penn State University, appears to have been worked out by Shakespeare in elaborate detail. King Claudius [Ptolemy's first name] represents the old world order, while Fortinbras, arriving in Denmark via Poland (home of Copernicus), symbolizes the new. The most famous astronomer of Shakespeare's day was the Danish stargazer Tycho Brahe, who worked out of Elsinore. Brahe proposed a compromise, tentatively accepted by the Vatican, in which all the planets revolved around the sun, *except* for the earth. One year before Nashe's reference to the Ur-Hamlet, a 1588 frontispiece depicts Brahe conspicuously surrounded by ancestral names on his family tree, two of which are Rosencrantz and Guildenstern. In the play, these two subtle villains (who pose as Hamlet's friends) are disposed of, just as the Tychonic worldview sank into oblivion after Shakespeare's time.[24] There is no known evidence of Will Shakspere's interest in astronomy; but for de Vere there are a number of examples. One was his patronage of John Dee,[25] a leading expert in Elizabethan England, and known to have Copernican leanings.

As critics are fond of reminding us ad nauseam, Will Shakspere had a young son named Hamnet who died in 1596.[26] Hamnet Shakspere had been named, not for the hero of Saxo Grammaticus, but after his father's Stratford friend and neighbor Hamnet Sadler, who in turn named his son William.[27] Making an imaginative leap from the sad, premature death of a Warwickshire 11-year-old to the high-powered Senecan revenge tragedy and Cardanian philosophical musings of Shakespeare's hero is comparable to walking up the 110 flights of stairs at the Sears Tower. Possible?—Yes. Likely?—Only for those doing it in the name of charity. If *Hamlet* dealt with innocent child mortality or the guilt-ridden grief of an absent parent, then this would make sense; but this is not what the play is about. In a similar fashion, other hypothesized links between Will Shakspere and *Hamlet*, such as the drowning of one Katherine Hamlett in the Avon River (reminiscent of Ophelia?), or the actor Will Kemp's visit to Elsinore, are often cited, but how these could have inspired the visionary reveries of the play remains a profound mystery. Slightly more persuasive is that Will Shakspere's destitute father John Shakspere died in 1601,[28] one year before *Hamlet* was registered. The ghost of Hamlet's father[29] crying out for revenge has somewhat more biographical resonance under this scenario. Furthermore, given that this is a Catholic ghost speaking from Purgatory, combined with John Shakspere's rumored Catholic religious beliefs, a minimum plausibility is achieved.[30]

Geoffrey Bullough sensibly observed that Shakespeare's treatment of the story (possibly via the Ur-Hamlet) was probably influenced by contemporary political events in Scotland—specifically, the scandals and rumors surrounding the murder of Mary Stuart's second husband, Henry Stuart, followed in rapid haste by her marriage to the ambitious James Hepburn, Earl of Bothwell.[31] Mary, according to malicious gossip, also had her first husband, Francis II of France, poisoned through the ear. As for Bothwell, he later died insane and imprisoned in Denmark. Under this scenario, Fortinbras obviously represents King James in the play. Will Shakspere, like everyone else in England, would have been aware of these events. De Vere, however, would have had a proverbial front-row seat, as discussed in Chapter 33 (on *Macbeth*).

What exactly attracted Shakespeare the writer to the Amleth legend? If we consider the possibility that Shakespeare may have been de Vere, then this question can be easily answered by any bright adolescent. When de Vere was 12 years old, his father died suddenly and his mother hastily remarried, then both his mother and stepfather died a few years later. The boy immediately became a royal ward and never lived with his family again.[32] Thus, every time we see a performance of *Hamlet* we may be witnessing the reenactment of a domestic tragedy played out at Castle Hedingham over 400 years ago. This single aspect has convinced many, such as Sigmund Freud, that de Vere was Shakespeare the writer, based on the psychological traits displayed by the author of *Hamlet*.[33] De Vere's childhood and teenage family experiences taken in isolation eclipse anything ever discovered about Will Shakspere that relate directly to this or any other play. This one imposing point, however, is only the tip of the Oxfordian iceberg.

Over the years, commentators such as Edmund Chambers have noticed that the character of Ophelia's father, Polonius, appears at least partially modeled on William Cecil, Lord Burghley. In addition to being a chief royal minister (like Polonius in the play), Burghley was de Vere's guardian and later his father-in-law (thus in real life, Hamlet married Ophelia). Panic-stricken[34] orthodox scholars have tried to deny this similarity, but have only sounded silly in the process. Anne Cecil (who, like Ophelia, became involved with a nobleman) was subjected to mental cruelty by de Vere and predeceased him in 1588 (again, one year before the Ur-*Hamlet*), just as Ophelia is verbally roughed up by Hamlet, preceding her insanity and death. Like Polonius, Burghley was originally of lower birth and rose to his position. Like Polonius, Burghley was ridiculed for his rambling letters and speech (II.ii.86–95), and was noted for his protectionism favoring the English fishing industry—hence, Hamlet taunts him as a "fishmonger" (II.ii.174). Like Polonius, Burghley sent his wayward son Thomas to Paris and then had him spied upon. In fact, a surviving copy of Burghley's precepts to his son Robert are nearly identical to those given by Polonius to Laertes (I.iii.58–80). The first quarto of Shakespeare's play gives the name of the character not as Polonius, but rather "Corambis," a devastating play on Burghley's Latin family motto *Cor unum via una*.[35] These similarities continue, but perhaps most impressive of all is that precious little of the Polonius-Ophelia-Laertes subplot is found in any of Shakespeare's known source material.[36] All of this, however, is unacceptably obvious to much of traditional academia. Interestingly, the name "William Shakespeare" first officially appears as a playwright in 1598, the same year as Burghley's death.[37]

Parallels between de Vere's relatives and *Hamlet* extend beyond his parents and first wife's family. In the play, Hamlet's confidant is Horatio, and the soldier Francisco is given a gratuitous role. In life, de Vere seems to have been on good terms with his two cousins, the English military heroes Horace and Francis Vere (the "Fighting Veres"). To the latter, Oxford entrusted part of his estate after death. As for Horace Vere, he appears to have been a mentor for Oxford's son Henry (the 18th Earl) during the Thirty Years' War on the continent.[38] And what about Denmark? Did de Vere ever travel there? No, but his brother-in-law, Peregrine Bertie, Lord Willoughby, did. He had been the English ambassador to Elsinore during the early 1580s.[39]

As for de Vere personally, there are no shortage of parallels. Like Hamlet, he was once captured by pirates on the English Channel.[40] Polonius' line on "falling out at tennis" (II.i.57) sounds suspiciously like de Vere's infamous tennis court spat with rival poet and courtier Philip Sidney, as noted by Edmund Chambers and others.[41] Like Hamlet, de Vere was involved with acting companies. At the end of the play, Hamlet dies at approximately age 30. This was de Vere's age in 1580, the year of his great fall from favor and from which he never recovered. Lack of space, rather than lack of material, prevents us from cataloguing the seemingly endless similarities between de Vere's biography and Shakespeare's storyline.

It is remarkable (at least, to any newcomer) how de Vere's life and the Oxfordian theory have become the great unmentionables among orthodox scholars. For example, Sigmund Freud's influence on modern Shakespearean performance is routinely discussed without any hint that his authorship beliefs were Oxfordian. Two famous 20th-century Hamlets were, like Freud, deeply impressed by the merits of the Oxfordian theory; and yet, biographers of John Gielgud and Leslie Howard tend to steer away from this crucial point.[42] A fine evasion, as the Bard would say.

Audiences hear a lot from critics about Hamlet's indecision and how it leads to his undoing, but this is a secondary theme in the play. The indecisive "To be, or not to be" speech is merely an interlude. *Hamlet* is primarily a *revenge* tragedy that dramatizes the consequences of revenge on both the innocent and guilty alike. Hamlet's tragic flaw is not his indecision but rather his willing obedience to the demands of his father's ghost for vengeance. This ties in with the play's ancient origins and leads us directly back to the authorship question. The influence of Seneca (inventor of the revenge tragedy genre) on the creation of *Hamlet* is a universal given: the five-act structure, the motivating ghost, the spectacular violence, the long and meditative soliloquies in blank verse, etc. English Seneca, indeed. In 1592, three years after alluding to "English Seneca" and the Ur-*Hamlet*, Thomas Nashe in his *Strange News* referred to a colleague named "Will Monox" who apparently was with Nashe and Robert Greene the night that Greene fatally overindulged in "pickled herring and Rhenish wine."[43] Were Nashe's Will Monox and English Seneca and Oxford all one and the same individual? Leaving aside (for the moment) whether de Vere was Shakespeare the writer, we are still waiting to hear a good reason why not.

✄ 35 ✆

King Lear

King Lear by "M. William Shak-speare" was entered with the Stationers' Register in 1607 and printed in quarto the following year. The 1608 quarto is somewhat different from the later First Folio version, and today a combination of the two texts is usually performed. The quarto frontispiece advertised that the play had been staged by the King's Men at the Globe Theater and Whitehall Palace on St. Stephen's Day (December 26), 1605. Most orthodox scholars date the writing to about 1605 (one year after de Vere's purported death),[1] based on alleged internal references. Edmund Chambers, however, asserted that "It is difficult to fix the date of *Lear* with precision." An example of these difficulties can be seen in Gloucester's allusions to lunar and solar eclipses (I.ii.103), often assumed to be references to historical events of 1605; yet many commentators (including Chambers) have noted that similar eclipses occurred throughout the reign of Queen Elizabeth, including in 1601, three years before de Vere's supposed passing.[2] Ultimately, the conventional 1605 dating rests on a conjecture that the play was written approximately two years before its initial registration.

Like that other twin pillar of Shakespearean tragedy, *Hamlet*, the traditional Lear story had a happy ending until the Bard reworked it.[3] It first appeared during the 12th century in Geoffrey of Monmouth's *Historia Regum Britanniae*, or "History of the Kings of Britain."[4] More famously, the King Arthur legend derives from Geoffrey, who also made an early mention of Stonehenge, both of which have minor associations with *Lear*. One of Geoffrey's favorite themes was the conflict between free will and predestination in human affairs, and Shakespeare picks up on this same idea. King Lear is presented by Geoffrey as prehistoric British history, but no one knows for certain how much is fact and fiction.[5] This pre–Christian setting may explain Lear's nihilistic response to the question of Cordelia's resurrection by repeating the word "never" five times (V.iii.309), although Shakespeare's personal religious beliefs are likely to be debated until doomsday.

The tale of Lear was widely reprinted during the Elizabethan era. Two of the better-known versions, assumed to have been read by Shakespeare, are found in Holinshed's *Chronicles* (first edition, 1577), and Edmund Spenser's *The Faerie Queene* (first edition, 1590).[6] The former is dedicated to Holinshed's benefactor and de Vere's father-in-law, William Cecil, Lord Burghley. Holinshed was also among the jurors who absolved de Vere of a murder charge in 1567.[7] The later work by Spenser contains a tributary sonnet addressed to Oxford, characterizing him as "most dear" to the "Heliconian imps" (i.e., the Muses). This phrase echoes similar praise lavished on de Vere in another dedication by Angel Day in 1586.[8]

Most agree, however, that Shakespeare's primary source was the anonymous play titled *The True Chronicle History of King Leir*,[9] not published until 1605 but first performed no later than 1594.[10] This "by no means contemptible play" (Geoffrey Bullough) still retained the happy ending and did not include the subplot of Gloucester and his two sons.[11] Even so, the "heavy influence" (Edmund Chambers) of this drama on Shakespeare is widely acknowledged.[12] Is it so outlandish to suggest that the author may have been de Vere, who was repeatedly praised by his contemporaries as a playwright, yet left no examples of his work? Oxfordians are naturally inclined to believe that Shakespeare's *King Lear* is a late revision by de Vere from the early 17th century of his own earlier play, which included adding the Gloucester subplot and tragic ending, as well as the mind-boggling poetry associated with the later quarto and First Folio versions.

The subplot of Gloucester and his two sons is thought to have been borrowed from *The Countess of Pembroke's Arcadia* by Philip Sidney (first edition, 1593).[13] Critics often speak of how Sidney influenced Shakespeare, but they rarely talk about who influenced Sidney. Those who have agree that Sidney probably derived his story of the gullible father entangled in a deadly feud between his two sons from the Greek romance titled *An Aethiopian Historie* by Heliodorus, first translated into English by Thomas Underdowne and published in 1569.[14] Remarkably, this earlier work was lavishly dedicated to the 19-year-old Edward de Vere, whom Underdowne repeatedly praises for his great learning.[15] Coming full circle, de Vere's daughter Susan would later wed one of Philip Sidney's nephews, to whom Shakespeare's First Folio would be dedicated in 1623.

Other acknowledged sources for Shakespeare's *Lear* include the Geneva Bible translations of the books of Job and Revelations.[16] Today, the Folger Library retains de Vere's personal copy of the Geneva Bible, complete with extensive marginalia, which became the subject of the first Oxfordian thesis awarded a doctorate, awarded at the University of Massachusetts in 2000.[17] Montaigne's *Essays* are also seen as an influence with their concerns over aging, senility, and insanity.[18] While there are no known direct connections between Montaigne and de Vere, it does seem that de Vere was a Francophile who owned at least one French book,[19] and in any event Montaigne's *Essays* had been translated into English by John Florio in 1603.

Perhaps the most colorful source for *King Lear* was a book with the wonderful title *A Declaration of Egregious Popish Impostures*, written by Anglican cleric Samuel Harsnett and published in 1603.[20] This virulent anti–Catholic treatise included a detailed description of the outrageous exorcism ceremonies performed by Jesuit priests in England during the Elizabethan period. Harsnett graphically lays out how these bogus exorcisms were dramatized in so-called miracle plays and performed in the great houses of pro–Catholic English nobility. The fantastical names of demons catalogued in *Popish Impostures* are identical to those rattled off by Edgar as he feigns insanity. Where did these events reputedly transpire? The Reverend Harsnett tells us—repeatedly. He states that the phony miracle plays were performed at the house of Lord Vaux in Hackney, suburban London—generally assumed to be King's Place.[21] After Lord Vaux's death, King's Place was acquired in 1597 by none other than Edward de Vere, who spent the last (?) seven years of his life there in relative retirement and seclusion.[22] Later during the 17th century, King's Place became a mental institution, and after it was damaged during the London Blitz, demolished in 1955. Thus the site has eerie associations with *King Lear* and its dominant theme of insanity, regardless of who in fact was the author.

In 1605 (the alleged date of composition), Will Shakspere was 41 years old and sup-posedly at the top of his game as a playwright and businessman. According to the tradi-tional biography, it would be another seven years before he retired. *King Lear*'s prominent themes of aging, senility, insanity, and loss of control (not to mention property) are some-what surprising coming from a man in his position, although 41 years of age was, granted, older then than now. Furthermore, familial relations between Shakspere, his wife, two daughters, and parents were probably not all that they could have been. As for loss of property, Shakspere accumulated rather than lost, although the example of his destitute father may have sufficed. A contemporary lawsuit involved property and competency dis-putes between a father and his two eldest daughters, while the third, youngest daughter, whose name was "Cordell," remained loyal to the father.[23] In any event, Shakespeare's concerns are certainly universal and can be appreciated by anyone with experience in life.

The biography of Edward de Vere, on the other hand, fits comfortably with *King Lear*, eclipsing all other comparisons, at least for anyone with a shred of impartiality. Like Lear, de Vere was a widower with three daughters. Like Lear, he turned over ownership of his ancestral estate at Castle Hedingham in trust to his daughters many years before his death, as part of the legal settlement with his father-in-law, Lord Burghley.[24] By the twilight of his life, de Vere had seen his two eldest daughters affluently married (like Goneril and Regan), and marriage of the youngest daughter had become a pressing mat-ter. If this were not enough, de Vere, like Gloucester, had two sons, one legitimate (by his second wife) and one illegitimate. While it would be grossly inaccurate to say that the three daughters and two sons in Shakespeare's play represent snapshot images of de Vere's own children, these cursory similarities should be enough to consider plausible the notion that the author at least had de Vere in mind when writing the play.

Characters in *King Lear* spend a lot of time talking about astrology, which many edu-cated people during Shakespeare's time subscribed to. This ties right in with the age-old question of free will, which concerned both Shakespeare and Geoffrey of Monmouth. Lear, Gloucester, and Kent (the good guys) all express profound belief in predestination. Their notable foil is the villain Edmund, who disses astrology in his chilling and justly famous soliloquy (I.ii.118–133), after proclaiming "Thou, Nature, art my goddess" (I.ii.1). Shake-speare spells "Nature" with a capital "N," meaning Nature in its sinister, Hobbesian sense of the word. Edgar probably knows he is hitting a nerve when he teases Edmund about being a "sectary astronomical" (I.ii.150), that is, an astrology expert. Edmund, however, with his dying breath pays tribute to the proverbial wheel of fortune (V.iii.175) and tries to save Cordelia. Other characters in the play tend to sound silly whenever they give astrol-ogy credence. This seemingly conflicting attitude has led to questions on Shakespeare's relative belief in astrology, and to what extent the Bard was a man of his times.[25] Given Shakespeare's concerns with astronomy and astrology in a play that is set in prehistoric Britain, an image of Stonehenge naturally comes to mind. At least one well-known pro-duction of *King Lear*, the Laurence Olivier film version of 1984, went so far as to set the action at Stonehenge.

While nothing is known of Will Shakspere's interests beyond his commercial enter-prises, there can be little doubt that Edward de Vere had a keen interest in astrology. The most successful astrologer in England, John Dee, listed Oxford among his patrons, and de Vere was known to have subsidized other minor figures such as Nicholas Hill.[26] The

1584 collection titled *Pandora* by John Southern is dedicated to Oxford and contains a poem in which the earl is praised for his knowledge of languages, music, history, and astrology.[27] Earlier in 1573, the 23-year-old de Vere was the dedicatee and sponsor of Thomas Bedingfield's English translation of *De Consolatione* by Girolamo Cardano, perhaps the most famous astrologer in Europe. De Vere also wrote an introduction and poem for *Cardanus Comforte*, both very Shakespearean in style.[28]

As a side note, both Edward de Vere (b. April 12) and Will Shakspere (b. April 23?) had Taurus as their birth sign—a sign gratuitously evoked by Shakespeare in several plays, along with the seven sisters or Pleiades that form the back of the bull's neck in the zodiac constellation. Toward the end of Act I, the Fool tries to cheer up Lear by telling jokes and quips, "the reason why the seven stars are no more than seven is a pretty reason" (I.v.34–36). During the same speech, the Fool repeatedly compares Lear's evil daughter Regan to a crab (I.v.15, 18), and (perhaps by coincidence) the famous Crab Nebula forms part of the Taurus zodiac, near the tip of the lower horn. Perhaps by now this stream of consciousness association has worn thin, but *King Lear* nevertheless demonstrates the author's preoccupation with (and expertise in) astronomy and astrology. This is an argument that can be used in favor of either Edward de Vere or Will Shakspere, although in the case of de Vere this expertise is at least documented.

After the Fool is done chattering, Lear exclaims, "O, let me not be mad, not mad, sweet heaven!" (I.v.46). Mental illness is another major riff in the play, and an important theme in all of Shakespeare. Lear is not the only character with issues. The Fool is certifiable and hence a court jester. Kent often goes crazy with rage, and Edgar pretends to be insane (like Hamlet) in his disguise as Tom of Bedlam, the generic name for a crazy street person or someone possessed by evil spirits. The word "Bedlam" is derived from "Bethlehem"; more specifically, from St. Mary of Bethlehem Hospital, the first (and most famous) lunatic asylum in Shakespeare's London. This institution was located just outside the north city walls on Bishopsgate Street, and close to London's original theater district in the Shoreditch neighborhood. Also in this same area, just down and across the street from the asylum, was a large house known as Fisher's Folly, the official residence of Edward de Vere during the middle 1580s. His later domiciles at Stoke Newington and King's Place in Hackney were located just a little further north. Thus for most of his later adult life, de Vere lived in and around the Shoreditch theater district and the environs of the Bethlehem asylum. Will Shakspere surely haunted this area as well, but we do not know even approximately where he resided during this same period.

As in *Hamlet*, family relations parallel to the storyline in *King Lear* perhaps constitute de Vere's most impressive connection to the play. These parallels begin with the character of Edmund, who is the bastard both literally and figuratively, and one of Shakespeare's most memorable villains. According to John Bartlett's *A Complete Concordance to Shakespeare*, the Bard uses variations of the word "bastard" in an astonishing 27 out of 37 plays (over two-thirds). Beyond mere word usage, Edmund is a prime example of Shakespeare's keen interest in the very idea of illegitimacy. To repeat, Edward de Vere had two sons, one of whom, Sir Edward Vere (1581–1629), was Oxford's illegitimate son by Anne Vavasor, lady-in-waiting to the queen.[29] In the play, the mad Lear emphatically maintains that adultery is not a capital offense (IV.vi.110–116). This truly sounds like the personal opinion of the author—perhaps as a retort to the Puritans, who during

Shakespeare's time were the rising political power in England and viewed virtually every infraction as a capital offense. As for Henry de Vere (1593–1625), Oxford's legitimate son and heir by his second marriage, he was only 11 years old at the time of his father's assumed death. Tragically, both of Oxford's sons died on the continent during the Thirty Years' War.

De Vere himself had firsthand experience with bastardy. The year after his father's death in 1562, the 13-year-old Oxford had his title challenged by the husband of his half-sister, based on the 16th Earl's somewhat irregular marriage to de Vere's mother, Margery Golding.[30] Ultimately, de Vere's title was legally sustained by the courts, but he was known to have been touchy about this affair for the rest of his life. For instance, he was reportedly not amused when the queen teased him about it.[31] In addition, de Vere had at one time questioned the paternity of his eldest daughter, Elizabeth Vere. When Lear asks his eldest child, Goneril, "Are you our daughter?" (I.iv.218), the question has troubling overtones for Oxfordians. Given the Bard's preoccupation with legitimacy of birth and his memorable bastard characters such as Edmund in *King Lear* and Faulconbridge from *King John*, de Vere's family history could have provided convenient inspiration for the playwright.

In terms of family relations, however, de Vere's associations with his three daughters by his first marriage are even more striking, particularly with his youngest daughter Susan Vere, who would marry Philip Herbert six months after her father's presumed death in 1604. Philip was the younger son of Mary Sidney Herbert, the nephew of Philip Sidney (to whom Shakespeare's Gloucester subplot is usually credited), and a co-dedicatee of Shakespeare's First Folio. As for Susan, she appears to have been somewhat a chip off the old block. She is known to have acted in the court masques of Ben Jonson (just as her father was a noted playwright) and was sketched in costume by Inigo Jones shortly after her wedding.[32] These, combined with her marriage to one of the First Folio's "Incomparable Brethren" and her known patronage of the Jaggard family (the Folio printers), all suggest more than a passing interest in the liberal arts.[33]

At Wilton House, the family seat of the Pembrokes, is a well-known Van Dyck portrait of Philip Herbert and his family circa 1635. By this time, Susan Vere had been dead six years and Herbert had remarried. Art historians are divided, however, on which of Herbert's wives is portrayed in the painting.[34] Some believe it to be a posthumous portrait of Susan Vere for several reasons. First, Herbert had become bitterly estranged from his second wife by this time. Second, the seated, folded-arm posture of the woman (who is clad in black) is a classical Roman funereal position. Third, all of the children in the portrait are Susan Vere's issue, and they have similar hair color and complexion to Herbert's portrayed wife. Fourth, another portrait of his second wife, Anne Clifford, does not resemble the woman in the painting. If in fact the portrait depicts Susan Vere Herbert, then Van Dyck's painting is the only known formal portrait of the woman Oxfordians believe may have inspired Shakespeare's Cordelia from *King Lear*.

Earlier we mentioned *Lear*'s associations with Stonehenge, which is physically located not far from Wilton House. In the play, Kent, while uttering threats against Oswald, warns him, "Goose [smile], and I had you on the Sarum plain, I'ld drive ye cackling home to Camelot" (II.ii.82–83). In other words, Kent will wipe the smile off Oswald's face by driving him all the way across the Sarum plain to Camelot. Geographically, that makes perfect sense because the "Sarum plain" was the Salisbury plain near the town of Old Sarum, also near Stonehenge and Wilton House. As for Camelot, no one knows exactly where it was, but many believe it to have been located in Somerset, immediately west of the Salisbury plain. With Lear, Camelot, and Stonehenge, we thus come back to Shakespeare's original source, Geoffrey of Monmouth.

It is attractive to speculate that in late 1603, de Vere visited Wilton House to discuss the future marriage of his daughter Susan with Mary Sidney's son Philip, and while there began to revise his old play of *King Leir* into the Shakespearean version we know today. Much of the action seems to be right in that neighborhood. When Mary lured King James to Wilton during that same season, she reportedly claimed to have "the man Shakespeare" staying with them.[35] Was this in reality a joking reference to Edward de Vere as "Shakespeare"? The King's Men (presumably with Will Shakspere in tow) did in fact perform at Wilton House for King James, who was said to have been fascinated with Stonehenge during the same excursion.[36] Perhaps Mary Sidney's reference to "the man Shakespeare" had humorous double meaning.

ᔥ 36 ᔥ

Othello

Shakespeare's cautionary tale against the "green-ey'd monster" (III.iii.166) has no publication history before 1622, when the first quarto was printed by Thomas Walkley.[1] Frank Kermode, in his introduction for *Riverside*, added that "*Othello* presents the editor with an intractable textual problem...."[2] The gist of this "intractable" dilemma is that the texts for the quarto and First Folio are substantially different, underscoring the likelihood that Shakespeare's plays were works in constant progress, undergoing revision by the author or authors, actors, and editors. It is possible that Walkley was given access to the first quarto for the purpose of beating the 1623 Jaggard-Blount Folio to the press and/or lighting a fire under the authorized publishers, since the project seemed to be lagging with delays.

Walkley entered the first quarto of *Othello* with the Stationers' Register in London on October 6, 1621.[3] In an interesting coincidence, Mary Sidney Herbert, Dowager Countess of Pembroke, passed away two weeks earlier in London on September 25, 1621.[4] Despite living in an era that did not recognize female intellectual accomplishments, Mary (along with her family) was arguably the most sought-after literary patron of her time.[5] In addition to being one of the best-educated women of her generation, she was the sister of courtier poet Philip Sidney, as well as his literary executor, editing posthumous works and seeing these through to publication. Two years after her death, Shakespeare's First Folio would be dedicated to Mary's two sons, the "Incomparable Brethren" William and Philip Herbert.[6] Mary's elder son William was Lord Chamberlain under King James and had once negotiated to marry Edward de Vere's daughter Bridget. Her younger son Philip had married de Vere's youngest daughter Susan. Mary was herself a poet and playwright, and a recent school of thought maintains that she may have been Shakespeare's literary executor as well, if not the true Shakespeare in fact.[7] It is tempting to believe that there was some connection between the passing of this great literary figure and the genesis of the First Folio (along with the first quarto of *Othello*) in 1621–1623.

The first recorded performance of *Othello* (by the King's Men) took place at Whitehall Palace on November 1, 1604.[8] The main social event at court during that holiday season of 1604–1605 was the wedding of Mary Sidney's son Philip Herbert to de Vere's daughter Susan, and *Othello* would be one of many Shakespeare plays performed for these celebrations over the course of several weeks. *Othello* would continue to be produced at court, as well as the Globe and Blackfriars Theaters, according to the advertisement on the first quarto[9]; yet publication of this towering masterpiece was withheld until

1622–1623. The precise reasons for this delay will probably always remain a hidden mystery.

Connections between Will Shakspere and the origins of *Othello* also remain hidden. The acknowledged source material adapted by Shakespeare was the Venetian book titled *Hecatommithi*, written by Giovanni Battista Giraldi (a.k.a. "Cinthio") and published in 1565.[10] Cinthio had drawn upon supposed historical events dating from the early 16th century and involving scandals surrounding the Oteli del Moro family of Venice.[11] How much of Cinthio's legend was fact and how much fiction is not known.[12] What is certain, however, is that this Italian book was not translated into English until long after Shakespeare's time. The Bard either had to have read the original Italian or a French translation.[13]

In contrast to the blank record concerning Will Shakspere, Edward de Vere once again appears to have been in the right place at the right time, having toured Italy (and making Venice his base of operations) in 1575–1576. De Vere spoke Italian and French, and Cinthio's book (in Italian) belonged to the library of de Vere's guardian and later father-in-law, William Cecil, Lord Burghley.[14] The historical backdrop of de Vere's stay in Venice is suggestive as well. Four years prior to his visit, the Venetian Republic island-outpost of Cyprus (the other setting in the play) was captured by the Ottoman Turks, who shortly afterward were defeated by a Venetian-led coalition fleet at the epic Battle of Lepanto in 1571.[15] At the time of de Vere's tour, Venice was the most cosmopolitan city in Europe (as well as a center for literature), and would have offered any Englishman an eyeful of ethnic and racial diversity, including Italians, Jews, and Moors, among others. The Venetians themselves were overbearingly conscious of their lofty status in Christendom, even among other Italian city-states. Shakespeare the writer demonstrated his awareness of this in *Othello* when the Clown (who is a Venetian) gratuitously makes fun of the Neapolitan accent (III.i.4). De Vere was likely to have witnessed this regional snobbery, along with everything else, firsthand.

Aside from direct access to source material, de Vere's personal connections to the story of *Othello* appear so immediate as to suggest biographical illuminated character studies within Shakespeare's drama. These apply not only to de Vere himself, but also to those who had the misfortune of being too close to him in his personal life. Among Othello's last words are "Speak of me as I am; nothing extenuate, nor set down aught in malice" (V.ii.342–343). Assuming that we are hearing the author's testament in this speech, we shall do our best in the foregoing analysis to comply with his last wishes.

Who are these people? Othello, invincible in war but a pushover in matters of the heart, judges himself as "one that lov'd not wisely but too well" (V.ii.344) and "one not easily jealous, but, being wrought, perplex'd in the extreme"(V.i.345–346). The Moor is not a character we think of as loving too well and not easily made jealous; nevertheless, we seem to be hearing the voice of experience. De Vere, it can never be forgotten, falsely accused his wife Anne Cecil of infidelity after returning to England from Italy in 1576. The issue was whether their eldest daughter, born during the absence, had been conceived before his departure for the continent. De Vere was initially persuaded that she was not, and lived apart from his wife for five years before apparently changing his mind over the affair and reconciling with Anne.

Desdemona is another one of Shakespeare's guileless heroines who may be a memorial to de Vere's first wife. After bearing him two more daughters who survived infancy,

Anne died in 1588. Even after their reconciliation, de Vere was far from a model husband, being plagued by bad investments, spendthrift personal habits, and addiction to a bohemian lifestyle. Anne, for her part, was known as a "second Grissel" for her patience.[16] In the play, Desdemona remains loyal to Othello as well, beginning with the deception of her own father. Brabantio in turn accuses his daughter of duplicity (I.iii.293), thus sowing the first seeds of doubt into the mind of Othello. This makes an interesting contrast to Ophelia in *Hamlet*, who earns the Dane's mistrust while trying to obey her father Polonius. Whatever the truth may have been for Anne Cecil, there can be no doubt that she was caught in a difficult position between her hot-headed spouse and powerful spymaster father. In both *Othello* and *Hamlet*, there are no parental machinations pushing the lovers together; in fact, both Brabantio and Polonius are obstacles. This seems to go against a frequent notion that de Vere and Anne were somehow tricked or maneuvered into wedlock by her scheming father.

Desdemona's lady-in-waiting is Iago's wife Emilia,[17] who confronts Desdemona's grief in Act IV, urging her to be more gay and carefree. Emilia suggests to her mistress that women should not be constricted by social mores, and that the misdeeds of men are often to blame for female shortcomings. As she puts it, "The ills we do, their ills instruct us so" (IV.iii.102). This liberated attitude brings to mind one of Shakespeare's contemporaries, the Jacobean poetess Aemilia Bassano Lanyer (1569–1645), put forth by orthodox scholar A.L. Rowse as a candidate for Shakespeare's "Dark Lady" of the sonnets. Aemilia's father, Elizabethan court musician Baptista Bassano, originally hailed from the Veneto region of Italy (as do the characters in Shakespeare's play). In addition to being one of the few published female English writers during that era, Aemilia Bassano Lanyer (like Shakespeare's Emilia) was known for her feisty and defiant independence.[18]

The main drama revolves around Othello's evil Ensign Iago, one of the greatest, if not *the* greatest of Shakespeare's villains.[19] One question that has lingered with many commentators (including this one) is that Iago's alleged motive—anger at being passed over for promotion—seems a small reason in relation to the havoc he wreaks and the trouble he goes to in order to accomplish it.[20] Furthermore, if this diabolical genius only wants promotion, then why does he not simply go after Cassio? Indeed, Iago achieves his stated objective when Othello unexpectedly promotes him (III.iii.479), but still proceeds with his murderous deception, presumably because the initial hurt cannot be remedied except by Othello's total destruction.

Another hypothesis is that Iago is himself infatuated with Othello and strikes back when, in short order, Othello marries Desdemona and promotes Cassio over him. This is not as ridiculous as it may seem. In Shakespeare's source, the unnamed, evil Ensign is really after Desdemona himself, and when rejected by her, embarks on his terrible vengeance. Shakespeare takes the trouble to remove Iago's interest in Othello's wife, which leaves a dramatic shortfall in terms of motivation. Iago, in spite of his professed hatred, says to Rodrigo (perhaps with double meaning), "In following him [Othello], I follow but myself" (I.i.58) and to Othello, "I am your own forever" (III.iii.480).[21] Geoffrey Bullough correctly observed that "Perhaps Shakespeare was attracted to Cinthio's tale because it would let him show (more fully, credibly and tragically than in *Much Ado*) an intriguer of even greater malevolence initiating and carrying out his plot to the end."[22] This, however, still does not answer the question "why?" as to Iago's motives.

One thing that most critics can agree upon is Iago's frightening ability to identify weaknesses in others and to prey upon these effectively. More than one has observed that Iago, who is from Florence, may represent the Bard doing a number on the Florentine playwright-turned-cynical political philosopher Niccolò Machiavelli (1467–1527). In contrast to Baldessare Castiglione's *The Courtier* (which Shakespeare seems to have admired), the chilling belief system of Machiavelli's *The Prince* may be receiving a rebuke as Iago's schemes (combined with Othello's frailties) destroy everything that is good around them.

Among the retainers accompanying de Vere upon his return from the continent in 1576 was the disreputable Rowland Yorke, English soldier of fortune and Spanish double agent.[23] This was the man who was at de Vere's side when he broke with his wife. Bypassing Anne and his Cecil in-laws who came out to welcome him home, de Vere elected instead to stay at the house of Yorke's brother before making his separation indefinite. Four years earlier (in 1572), Yorke had been present in de Vere's house when Anne was reportedly barred from rooms in which Yorke, de Vere and others engaged in reckless debauchery.[24] Limited space here cannot do full justice to Yorke's infamy,[25] but de Vere's biographer Professor Alan Nelson described Yorke's character as Machiavellian,[26] just as critics have often labeled Shakespeare's Iago. Elizabethan spelling sometimes substituted the letter *y* for *i*[27]; hence, the name "Iago"—a name that Shakespeare made up—may represent shorthand for "Rowland Yorke."

As unsavory a character as Yorke appears to have been, Oxfordians tend to lay the blame for de Vere's marital estrangement jointly with the 17th Earl's first cousin, Henry Howard. Howard, whom de Vere later described as "the worst villain that lived in this earth"[28]—a real distinction if de Vere was the true Bard—was also closely involved in the machinations following his cousin's return from Italy. It was Howard who passed along de Vere's claim that the child born to Anne could not be his, and it was he who worked to drive his cousin out of the English Protestant camp (i.e., de Vere's marriage into the Cecil family) and into a growing sphere of potential English Catholic insurgents. This effort would crumble in 1580–1581 after de Vere's renunciation of Catholicism and reconciliation with his wife, although the wily Howard would survive by laying low and convincing everyone that he was harmless. Many Oxfordians believe that Shakespeare's Iago represents an amalgamation of the brilliant but devious and two-faced Henry Howard with the audacious henchman-for-hire, Rowland Yorke.

In the play, Othello and Desdemona are not the only victims of Iago's malice. Michael Cassio, Iago's fellow Florentine whose promotion becomes the excuse for the tragedy that follows, is his first victim, although he survives to tell the tale. Cassio's weaknesses (other than good-natured gullibility) are wine and women. Iago uses the former to get Cassio cashiered, and then the latter (via Cassio's liasons with Bianca) to gradually convince Othello that Desdemona is the real object of his former lieutenant's sexual adventures. Deviously, as Iago coaxes Cassio into intoxication, he downplays their indulgence by singing an English drinking song—the English being (as he claims) the biggest drunks in Europe (II.iii.76–88). De Vere was known for his drunkenness, too, especially among the enemies whom he turned against in 1580–1581.[29]

Opposite to Cassio is Iago's lecherous and venal sidekick Rodrigo, who hopes to acquire Desdemona for himself. Iago succeeds not only in duping the dim-witted Rodrigo, but in getting him to finance his own foolish behavior as well. In an extraordinary sequence from Act I, Iago repeatedly advises his desperate associate to "Put money in thy purse" (I.iii.339). This has been often (and incorrectly) interpreted to mean that Iago values money above everything else and tells Rodrigo to do the same. Aside from not being in keeping with Machiavellian principles,[30] this shallow reading goes against the context of Shakespeare's drama. Iago is manipulating a fool, and does so effectively by telling him to focus on money.

The attitudes of the characters (and of Shakespeare the writer) in *Othello* toward money and reputation become dominant motifs that seem to lead us to the crux of the authorship question. Othello reveals his priorities by upbraiding Montano for his recklessness with "name" and "reputation" following the former governor's drunken brawl with Cassio (II.iii.194–195). Then, after being disciplined by his commander, Cassio launches into a lament as if his entire world has come to an end, by repeating the word "reputation" six times (II.iii.262–265). Later, as Iago plays on Othello's insecurities, he explains that reputation is far more important than wealth, contradicting what he previously told Rodrigo about money. This time Iago is speaking to a higher-minded person:

> Good name in man and woman, dear my lord,
> Is the immediate jewel of their souls.
> Who steals my purse steals trash; 'tis something, nothing;
> 'Twas mine, 'tis his, and has been slave to thousands;
> But he that filches from me my good name,
> Robs me of that which not enriches him,
> And makes me poor indeed. [III.iii.155–161]

Good name and reputation are more valuable than money. We suspect that de Vere and Shakspere would have agreed, although a closer look at their lives reveals several paradoxes.

For the traditional author, the childhood trauma of witnessing his father's decline both in fortune and reputation surely left its mark. Will Shakspere's meteoric rise in London was no doubt partly motivated by these unhappy memories; nor was his triumphant return to Stratford in 1597 likely to have erased these, given that his father was still alive. For traditionalists, the answer is straightforward: Will Shakspere valued both his reputation and his purse, and he was good on his word. Nevertheless, one must ask why such a supposedly brilliant person chose the lowly acting profession[31] as a vehicle of escape from poverty, unless there were absolutely no other options. More pointedly, how could a man who so valued affluence repeatedly write with conviction lines like "Who steals my purse steals trash...."?

In the case of Edward de Vere, a similar question could be asked: namely, if he valued his reputation so much, then why did he live such a scandalous life? One response is that de Vere probably valued his reputation more, even to the point of obsession (as Shakespeare seems to have), after he had completely lost it. As the song goes, you don't miss your water until your well runs dry. Regarding money and financial security, we have no difficulties reconciling Shakespeare the writer with de Vere. Like the Bard, de Vere apparently valued money little except as something to be spent, and was therefore chronically short of funds. He was good on his word, too, one could say.

A final enigma is the character of the Moor himself. As his belief in Desdemona's faithfulness disintegrates in Act II, Othello launches into the famous but curious speech, "Farwell the tranquil mind!" (III.iii.348). On the surface, Othello seems to be saying that everything in life rings hollow now that he believes Desdemona has been untrue. He does not, however, bemoan the loss of his marital relationship or reputation, but rather the supposed loss of his profession. Why would his wife's presumed unfaithfulness diminish his value as a soldier? Othello's lengthy farewell to the "Pride, pomp, and circumstance of glorious war" (III.iii.354) ends with the bitter coda, "Othello's occupation is gone" (III.iii.357). Like Cassio's regret over lost reputation, Othello's agony over pending unemployment seems a bit misplaced.

As with many other puzzling situations in the canon, de Vere's biography offers a satisfying explanation that is otherwise unavailable. When de Vere wed Anne Cecil in 1571, he had a promising future ahead of him as a soldier in the family tradition, but this military career was derailed when he became a domestic-bound courtier—for him (ultimately) the wrong choice. Unlike his admired cousins Horatio and Francis Vere (known to history as the "Fighting Veres"), the 17th Earl's future name would be associated with scandal, profligacy, and disgrace. Thus Othello's profuse regrets over a lost profession take on new and urgent resonance when viewed through the Oxfordian lens.

Even more tragic is the case of Anne Cecil, when compared to the fate of Desdemona in the play. Emilia in exasperation exclaims, "Hath she [Desdemona] forsook so many noble matches?" (IV.ii.125) Should Desdemona have married someone else? The question is provocative. In real life, before her marriage to de Vere, Anne's main competing suitor had been none other than Philip Sidney, brother to Mary Sidney.[32] Thus we return to Mary Sidney's conjectured role in the mysterious publication of this work. Maybe in hindsight, everyone (including de Vere?) realized that a Sidney-Cecil union would have been better for all involved. When these two families finally did unite one generation later at the wedding of Philip Herbert and Susan Vere (with *Othello* performed a few weeks before), it was therefore understandably an occasion of celebration. Of course, had Philip Sidney married Anne Cecil back in 1571, it is possible that de Vere, rather than Sidney, would have died on the battlefield of Zutphen. Had that happened, we ponder whether posterity would have been deprived of Shakespeare's works.

⁊ 37 ⌘

Antony and Cleopatra

One of the things most pleasant to a virtuous and distinguished man is to see himself, while he is still alive, go out among the nations and languages of the world, printed and bound, and bearing a good reputation. "A good reputation," I say, because, should it be the opposite, no death can be worse.

—Cervantes, *Don Quixote* [1615][1]

So vivid is Shakespeare's portrayal of Roman history that we tend to think of his version of events as an actual record of the past rather than that presented in the source material.[2] For example, Plutarch informs us that Cleopatra outlived Antony for some time and committed suicide only after protracted negotiations with Octavius broke down; yet Shakespeare would have us believe (and we tend to believe) that she and Antony died within hours of each other. Paradoxically, Shakespeare was able to achieve this illusion because more often than not he was faithful to his sources. Plutarch also tells us, as does Shakespeare, that at the naval battle of Actium[3] in 31 B.C., Antony disregarded his superiority on land to risk everything on a sea engagement—similar to Brutus, who earlier (in 42 B.C.) had wasted his naval superiority to stake all on a land battle at Philippi. Taken together with casual, offhand, and invariably accurate topographical details, this frequent and rather surprising fidelity to historical sources enabled the Bard to give free reign to his imagination whenever deemed necessary for dramatic purposes.

Antony and Cleopatra was entered with the Stationers' Register in 1608 but not published until the First Folio of 1623.[4] The year 1607 is favored as the date of composition among orthodox scholars, although the grounds for this estimate are shaky. Samuel Daniel's revised version of his own play titled *Cleopatra* was published in 1607, and shows signs of having been influenced by Shakespeare.[5] This, however, only establishes that the play was written sometime between 1599 (when its prequel *Julius Caesar* was performed at the Globe) and 1607. Although de Vere is previously thought to have died in June of 1604, recent research by Oxfordian Christopher Paul indicates that he may have lived at least until 1607, based on surviving letters that refer to de Vere in the present tense as if he were still alive.[6] Even assuming de Vere did in fact die in 1604, there appears to be no logical reason why the play could not have been written before then.

Cleopatra was a popular subject among Renaissance humanists, and Shakespeare had a wealth of material to draw upon. Modern scholars have been surprisingly uniform in their views as to which of these sources Shakespeare used, beginning with Plutarch's life of Antony, whom almost all agree provided the Bard with his starting point.[7] The only variance in opinion, if it can be described as such, is that more astute orthodox critics (such as Geoffrey Bullough) recognized that the 1569 translation of Plutarch by Thomas North was in fact based on the 1559 French translation by Jacques Amyot. This latter edition was acquired by the young, multi lingual Edward de Vere at about the same time he purchased his famous Geneva Bible and other books.[8] As we shall see, it was a French dramatist (following an Italian) who seems to have picked up on the Cleopatra theme before it was later embraced by the English.

Even before the French translation of Plutarch, however, the Italian author Giovanni Battista Giraldi (a.k.a. "Cinthio") wrote in 1542 a play titled *Cleopatra* that bears some similarity to Shakespeare's treatment. Shakespeare also drew upon Cinthio for *Othello* and *Measure for Measure*, two more of his later works; thus he appears to have taken an interest in this author toward the end of his career. Cinthio's play in turn appears to have influenced the French playwright Robert Garnier in his tragedy *Marc Antoine*, published in 1578.[9] De Vere, it should always be remembered, toured Italy and France in 1575–1576 when the works of Cinthio and Garnier were in circulation.

The story of Cleopatra and Antony finally received an English dramatic treatment in 1590 with Mary Sidney Herbert's free translation of the Garnier play, titled *The Tragedie of Antonie*.[10] Mary's biographer G.F. Waller noted that "She was deliberately taking up the matter of raising literary standards in a form which was becoming increasingly popular— the drama." In this she seems to have temporarily succeeded, with *Antonie* going through five editions in 15 years beginning in 1592.[11] Waller added that "the Countess' play is certainly the pioneer, and also one of the better products."[12] Two years later (in 1594), Samuel Daniel dedicated to Mary Sidney[13] the first edition of his *Cleopatra*, intended as a companion piece to her *Antonie*[14] and growing out of his associations with the Sidney literary circle at Wilton House, along with their enthusiasm for the French neo–Senecans.[15]

De Vere's family later became a part of this same circle in early 1604 with the marriage between de Vere's youngest daughter Susan and Mary's younger son Philip Herbert. Earlier, Mary's elder son William Herbert had negotiated to marry de Vere's daughter Bridget but this match did not materialize. As for de Vere, his infamous rivalry with Mary's brother Philip Sidney during the 1570s and 1580s made the later union between the two families a welcome event for King James, and the Herbert brothers would go on to become political allies with de Vere's son and the dedicatees of Shakespeare's First Folio. Mary, in addition to being an important literary patron (along with her sons) for Daniel, Edmund Spenser and others, was herself an accomplished poet and literary executor for her brother Philip. Could she have performed a similar role for Shakespeare? She certainly seems to have been in the thick of things regarding Shakespeare's source material for *Antony and Cleopatra*.

Waller recorded that Mary's "*Antonie* was the first attempt in England to act upon [Philip] Sidney's urgent cry for the establishment of a drama dignified by the 'noble morralitie' and 'stately speeches' of the French neo–Senecans."[16] He emphasized that *Antonie* is not as good as Shakespeare, but was still an important work showcasing the talent of its translator.[17] Especially noteworthy was Mary's "peculiarly favorable view of Cleopatra," almost in a pre-feminist manner. "In the Countess' translation," Waller explained, "although lacking Shakespeare's complexity, the same polarities operate...."[18] Essentially in the play, Roman virtue is corrupted by eastern vice, but Antony is still partly to blame and Cleopatra is not without her good points. This was a more subtle view of the story than had previously been dramatized. In spite of this hint of ambiguity, however, Mary Sidney's *Antonie* maintains a high moral tone, as advocated by the Aristotelian views of her brother and the French neo–Senecans.[19]

Shakespeare, on the other hand, completely freed the story from the narrow moralistic shackles that the rising tide of Puritanism was attempting to impose on everything at the time. Audiences do not pass judgment on Shakespeare's lovers so much as they become involved in their tragedies. Perhaps Mary and Philip Sidney's concerns for moralistic theater were misguided attempts to accommodate the irresistible political trends of the times. Shakespeare, fortunately for posterity, made no such accommodations; he dramatized moral dilemmas rather than neatly resolve them. It is provocative, however, that in 1589—about the same time Mary Sidney was translating the French neo–Senecan work— Thomas Nashe, in his Epistle to Robert Greene's *Menaphon*, both praised and spoofed one "English Seneca" who wrote "whole Hamlets, I should say handfuls of Tragical speeches."[20] In 1589, Will Shakspere was 25 years old and, in the judgment of most Bardolators, too young to write anything like *Antony and Cleopatra*, let alone *Hamlet*. De Vere was at the ripe age of 39.

Shakespeare's play, in addition to steering away from easy moral answers, rises above its predecessors with unforgettable characters and rapid—indeed, revolutionary for the times—episodic movement and scene changes. These changes violate every unity of time and place known to Aristotle but wildly succeed in engaging an attentive audience, especially modern ones that are more used to such rapidity and younger ones who demand it. Shakespeare compresses 10 years of history into what seems like a few months, and jumps around the Mediterranean world between Alexandria, Rome, Messina, Micenum, Syria, Athens, and Actium. Such previously unheard-of motion (almost cinematic in scope) would have more likely come from the imagination of a world traveler like de Vere who, although he did not visit Egypt, Greece, or Syria, did tour Italy and the Mediterranean (including Sicily), while his son-in-law William Stanley[21] was reputed to have traveled just about everywhere, including the Middle East. Admittedly, any homebody can have a sweeping imagination, but it may have been that Shakespeare's exotic scenery and scene changes, which are (to repeat) invariably both casual and accurate, were substantially aided by de Vere's personal travels and acquaintances. Orthodox critic Frank Harris noted that *Antony and Cleopatra* is special in this regard, with no recorded performances until the 18th century, presumably due to its challenging sweep and highly episodic structure.[22]

Returning to Shakespeare's unique characterizations, Mark Antony represents yet another one of the Bard's tragic heroes—perhaps the epitome—whose public reputation plummets during the course of the events. Even Macbeth, who only loses the kingdom of Scotland, does not fall as far as Anthony, whose enslavement to his own sensuality is skillfully exploited by Cleopatra. This is manifest from the very beginning as Philo tags him "The triple pillar of the world transform'd into a strumpet's fool" (I.i.12–13). After defeat at Actium, Anthony is painfully aware of his own decline in reputation as he declares, "Hark, the land bids me tread no more upon't, it is ashamed to bear me" (III.xi.1–2). This reputation loss is partially redeemed by his end: "Not Caesar's valor hath o'erthrown Antony but Antony's hath triumphed on itself" (IV.xv.14–15). Cleopatra responds by comforting him with, "So it should be, that none but Antony should conquer Antony, but woe 'tis so!" (IV.xv.16–17). This preoccupation with honor and public reputation extends to secondary characters in the play as well. Antony's former lieutenant Enobarbus, remorseful over his defection to Octavius, laments that "I am alone the villain of the earth, and feel I am so most" (IV.vi.29–30). Bottom line: among Shakespeare's Roman characters, reputation counts for all—money not excluded. This is a curious attitude, assuming it was sincere, coming from an Elizabethan playwright whose profession would have been viewed by that society as slightly more respectable than that of a street hustler. Perhaps Will Shakspere (if he was the true author) fully appreciated public reputation only after he realized that he had in fact little. On the other hand, at least he died solvent.

Plutarch's life of Antony contains a lengthy digression on Timon of Athens, subject of another Shakespearean tragedy, and to whom Antony compares himself after his downfall. The Bard obviously read this section of Plutarch with great interest. Although Timon's fall is caused by profligacy rather than military defeat, Antony is also a reckless spender and shares Timon's misanthropic loathing for humanity after his false friends begin to desert him. At the beginning of the play, Anthony informs Cleopatra that "There's beggary in the love that can be reckoned" (I.i.14). She is only too willing to comply. Antony maintains this principle even in the face of adversity by forwarding the treasure of Enobarbus to him after he learns of his defection (Act IV, scene v). This grand gesture prompts Enobarbus to repent his desertion and wish for his own death (Act V, scene vi), which follows shortly.

Plutarch notes that Antony's liberality sustained him long after a thousand follies were hastening his overthrow. A similar phenomenon seems to have occurred with de Vere. By 1581 he was a ruined man, both in reputation and finances; in spite of this, he not only managed to survive at least another 23 years, but at some points even seemed to prosper. In addition to his enormous royal annuity granted in 1586, de Vere was allowed to remarry a lady-in-waiting and received additional favors from both Elizabeth and James, despite apparent ambiguous relationships with both monarchs. Simultaneously, he continued to receive flattering literary dedications and praise as a poet-playwright. One is prompted to query what exactly the wayward earl was doing to deserve these handouts when many of his noblemen peers were being incarcerated (or worse) on the mere suspicion of misbehavior.

De Vere's military reputation, such as it was, had also bottomed out by the end of the 1580s. After participating in the ruthless Scottish campaign of 1570 led by the Earl of Sussex and gaining notoriety as a jousting champion, de Vere failed to do anything extraordinary. His 1584 cavalry command in the Low Countries was quickly superceded by the Earl of Leicester and Leicester's nephew Philip Sidney,[23] the latter dying in the field and becoming a national hero, while during the Armada invasion of 1588 de Vere was mainly noted for insubordination rather than any feats of valor.[24] We suspect that de Vere, like Antony in the play, had a sense of personal honor that was more exasperating than admirable to his contemporaries. When Antony sends a personal challenge to Octavius, Enobarbus doubts his sanity (III.xiii.194–200), and Octavius cleverly responds with "Let the old ruffian know I have many other ways to die" (IV.i.4–5). De Vere himself once declined a challenge issued in the wake of his messy affair with Anne Vavasor.[25]

While the pathos of Antony strongly suggests the life of de Vere, the charms (and manipulations) of Cleopatra defy any straightforward, cut-and-dry associations. Then again, real-life character amalgamations are the stock and trade of great dramatists. Along with Falstaff, Antony's "serpent of old Nile" (I.v.25) is one of the Bard's richest creations. Frank Kermode, in his introduction for *Riverside*, wrote that "Cleopatra deserves to be called the greatest of Shakespeare's female characterizations."[26]

If nothing else, Shakespeare's Queen of Egypt is one of the Bard's most impressive dramatic foils, standing in direct contrast and opposition to the stern Roman (read: Calvinist-Puritan) morality of Octavius. She expresses frustration whenever Antony tries to do his duty, to anyone other than her, that is: "He was dispos'd to mirth, but on the sudden a Roman thought hath struck him" (I.ii.82–83). As for her own past indiscretions, such as having a child by Julius Caesar, these are easily excused as "My salad days, when I was green in judgment, cold in blood" (I.v.73–75). Anyone crossing her gets pretty much the same treatment as the hapless messenger who announces that Antony has married Octavia. After responding to his verbal hedging with "I do not like 'but yet'" (II.v.50), she beats him and pulls a knife before he flees in terror. Later, though, the very same messenger learns to denigrate Octavia for the Queen's amusement, who compliments him with "I find thee most fit for business" (III.iv.36). Cleopatra is no novice in the arts of flattery herself. Plutarch related that Plato identified four kinds of flattery but Cleopatra knew a thousand, and that Antony was very susceptible. In the play, Enobarbus pays tribute to the Queen of Egypt with "Age cannot wither her, nor custom stale her infinite variety" (II.ii.234–235). This is only one small example of the Bard's adeptness at filling in a canvas only vaguely suggested by his source material.

Some commentators, including Oxfordians such as Eva Turner Clark, have noted a number of similarities between Shakespeare's Cleopatra and the reported changeable moods and autocratic personality of Queen Elizabeth. In particular, Clark believed the stormy and ultimately futile courtship of Elizabeth by the French Duke of Alençon, François de Valois, in 1579–1581 suggested many of the details found in the play.[27] Regardless of whether the true author of *Antony and Cleopatra* was Will Shakspere or Edward de Vere, one must question the prudence of dramatizing the human frailties of one's own monarch for the public (?) stage, although coming from a senior earl such a thing may have been less an obstacle. In any event, most agree that this particular work did not hit the boards until after Elizabeth's death in 1603, perhaps not until long after.

To repeat, in these situations, real-life character amalgamations are the fallback of the sensible dramatist. While portraying Queen Elizabeth I as Cleopatra would have been a risky venture, others have noticed similarities between Shakespeare's Queen of Egypt and his anonymous "Dark Lady" of the sonnets. This scenario is much easier to accept in terms of avoiding potential censorship problems. Commentators ranging from orthodox critic Alfred Leslie Rowse to Oxfordian scholar Stephanie Hopkins Hughes have seized upon this resemblance, and with good reason. Better yet, Rowse and Hughes identified who this individual may have been, whether the true author was Shakspere or de Vere, although this (for obvious reasons) is a much more controversial surmise than simply noting the kinship between Shakespeare's Dark Lady and Cleopatra in the play.[28]

In 1609, one year after *Antony and Cleopatra* was entered with the Stationers' Register (and two years after Daniel's revised version of his play), *Shake-speares Sonnets* were published, apparently without the cooperation of the author. The following year (1610) saw the publication of *Salve Deus Rex Judæorum*, written by the Jacobean poetess Aemilia Bassano Lanyer.

Proponents of Aemilia as Shakespeare's Dark Lady believe that *Salve Deus* was issued partly as an immediate response to Shakespeare's less than idealized portrayal of his mistress in the sonnets, and perhaps of Cleopatra as well. Aemilia in her book several times cited the relationship between Cleopatra and Antony as an example of profane love that led to greater evils in society,[29] and one in which there was joint responsibility for the adultery, as opposed to being solely the fault of the temptress. Bear in mind that by 1610, the Age of Milton was being ushered in by pious works such as this and that the bawdiness of Shakespeare's public stage was becoming less and less tolerable for those who controlled Parliament.

One of the co-dedicatees of *Salve Deus* was none other than Mary Sidney Herbert, Countess of Pembroke, whose high-minded and original translation of *Antonie* had some 20 years earlier begun to leave its influential mark, including with Shakespeare the writer. Thus Aemilia Bassano Lanyer, though herself not of high birth, appears to have belonged to (or at least aspired to be part of) the same aristocratic literary circle that nurtured Sidney, Spenser, Daniel, and (we would wager) Shakespeare as well. Shakespeare's immortal but highly ambiguous view of the feminine mystique may have required some clarification from whom it was inspired. Mary Sidney herself may have encouraged such a response. In the sonnets, the reader seems to meet a Dark Lady who is a Cleopatra without a crown, and a humbled narrator-poet no less befuddled than Mark Antony himself. Moreover, *Antony and Cleopatra*'s special place as the last play in the First Folio (along with *Othello*) may be the result of connections to Cinthio and Mary Sidney.

❧ 38 ℭ

Venus and Adonis

Nothing definite is known of Will Shakspere's first 29 years beyond birth and marriage records in Stratford, with the possible exception of indirect references made in *Greene's Groatsworth of Wit* from 1592. No one seemed to notice the young Will Shakspere except that he was born, married, and had children. Then in 1593, at age 29—boom, *Venus and Adonis*. Some critics have tried to belittle this work as a flawed, tentative assay by the young Bard, or a type of detour that one would expect from a budding poet-playwright still trying to realize his own potential. Those who take the trouble to read and appreciate this nearly 1,200-line poem, however, are more likely to come to the same conclusion as Mark Twain, who admired *Venus and Adonis* as "that graceful and polished and flawless and beautiful poem."[1] The work is indeed highly polished and sophisticated, chock full of easy, confident allusions to classical literature and, remarkably (it appears), Renaissance Italian art as well.

The name "William Shakespeare" made its first printed appearance in history on the dedication page of *Venus and Adonis*. The recipient was Henry Wriothesley, Third Earl of Southampton (1573–1624), viewed by many as the "Fair Youth" of the sonnets. In the dedication, Shakespeare refers to his poem as "the first heir of my invention," which has been the subject of some debate. Most agree that Shakespeare (whoever he was) had written plays by now, and some maintain that the phrase meant "first serious work," because plays were not considered respectable literature, while others feel it simply meant "first published work" under the name "William Shakespeare."

The top emblem of the frontispiece depicts Juno, the Roman goddess of marriage, flanked by peacocks, her symbolic bird. These were appropriate images given that Wriothesley was at that time engaged (by his guardian, Lord Burghley) to Elizabeth Vere, eldest daughter of Edward de Vere.[2] Wriothesley later went on to become close political allies with de Vere's son, Henry de Vere, during the Jacobean era.[3] Apart from a 23-year age difference, other commonalities between the two earls are numerous. Both lost their fathers young and became wards under Lord Burghley. Both were graduates of Cambridge and Gray's Inn. Both were patrons of literature and theater. Both were royal favorites as young men. Both were spendthrifts and fell out of favor with the queen for indiscretions with ladies-in-waiting. Both did time in the Tower of London. Both were shown later favor by King James, and so on.

The Latin inscription on the frontispiece, a quote from Ovid, translates: "Let base-conceited wits admire vile things / Fair Phoebus lead me to the Muses' springs."[4] This aspiration is not altogether surprising given Will Shakspere's upwardly mobile ambitions, but even less surprising if addressed from one haughty nobleman to another. This may have been a response to the "base-minded men" (i.e., playwrights) taunt from *Groatsworth*,[5] and gives notice of the higher plane being sought in this work, published at a time when the playhouses were shuttered due to the plague.

The publisher was the prominent London printer Richard Field, who originally hailed from Stratford-upon-Avon.[6] It is rightfully assumed that Will Shakspere probably had a connection with his fellow Stratfordian townsman. Less discussed is Field's connection with Edward de Vere in that he published several books associated with Oxford. For example, in 1589, four years before *Venus and Adonis*, Field printed *The Arte of English Poesie*,[7] an anonymous work generally attributed to George Puttenham, Lord Lumley. This book underscored that many of England's best writers were noblemen who suppressed publication of their works or refused to have these published under their own names because of perceived social stigma. First among these anonymous nobleman poet-playwrights, according to Puttenham, was Edward de Vere, 17th Earl of Oxford.[8]

The source for *Venus and Adonis* was Book X of Ovid's *Metamorphoses*, one of the most popular books of the Renaissance, and widely considered Shakespeare's most profound influence.[9] The *Metamorphoses* was first translated into the English language by de Vere's maternal uncle, Arthur Golding, during the mid–1560s when de Vere was a teenager. The first complete edition of this work in 1567 was dedicated to Robert Dudley, Earl of Leicester, the queen's longtime favorite.

In Shakespeare's poem, Adonis is killed by a wild boar while hunting, and so for that matter was Oxford's ancestor, the odious Robert de Vere, Ninth Earl of Oxford and dissolute favorite of King Richard II. In contrast, de Vere's father, the 16th Earl, single-handedly killed a wild boar with his sword in France when his hunting party was suddenly attacked. Reportedly, John de Vere shrugged it off to his impressed hosts and said that any boy from his country would have done the same.[10] Thus de Vere's family associations with wild boars went beyond the pictorial representation on his coat of arms. Furthermore, de Vere himself was once unfavorably compared to a boar in a letter by his rival Christopher Hatton.[11]

For his poem, Shakespeare takes liberties with Ovid in a variety of details. Startling similarities, however, between Shakespeare's departures and the famous series of paintings by the Venetian artist Titian have been remarked upon by both literary and art critics.[12] For example, the most idiosyncratic of Titian's five versions on the subject depicts Adonis wearing a hat, not mentioned by Ovid but repeatedly referred to by Shakespeare (lines 351 and 1,087–1,089). This particular version of the painting (today in the Palazzo Barberini in Rome) is thought to have been on display in Titian's house during de Vere's visit to Venice in 1575–1576. Moreover, Titian's house in the Venetian Ghetto was a popular party spot for the nobility of that era.[13]

Titian was criticized by his contemporaries for these departures from Ovid, and one may speculate on the motivations of the artist.[14] Recall that 16th-century Venice was renowned for, among other things, its tolerant acceptance of the courtesan profession. This acceptance was so prevalent that construction of the Venetian Arsenal was reportedly financed by a special tax on prostitution.[15] Perhaps Titian was representing the young men of Venice, in the allegorical person of Adonis, as being distracted by these courtesans, in the allegorical character of Venus, when they should have been focused on going off to fight the Turks. In any event, it is certainly plausible that the model for Venus may have been a Venetian courtesan.

When the 25-year-old de Vere arrived in Venice, the most famous courtesan of them all was at the height of her fame, both as a courtesan and as a published poet—the ubiquitous Veronica Franco (1546–1591).[16] Franco's best-known volume of poetry, *Terze Rime*, was published in 1575, a year which saw Venice a center for both writers and the book publishing industry—not only for Italy, but for all of Europe. Franco's patron was the retired Venetian Senator Domenico Venier, whose palazzo was one of the most prestigious literary salons on the continent, especially for poets interested in the Petrarchan sonnet form, as well as themes inspired by Ovid.[17] Some of the notable poets known to frequent this salon included Franco, Bernardo and Torquato Tasso, Pietro Arentino, Venier's nephews Marco and Maffio, and of course, Domenico himself.

While Venice circa 1575 would have been a likely destination for Shakespeare the writer had he traveled to Italy, Edward de Vere was, in fact, staying in the city at that very moment in time. Previously, Oxford had been involved in the publication and translation of Italian authors in England, such as Castiglione (in Latin) and Cardano (in English): reputedly spoke fluent Italian[18]: and upon his return to England was lampooned for Italianate manners and dress.[19] His uncle, Henry Howard, Earl of Surrey, had helped to pioneer the sonnet form in English, and (to repeat) his uncle Arthur Golding is credited with the first English translation of Ovid. De Vere could have been easily attracted to Venier's salon for its literary sophistication, not to mention hedonistic lifestyle.

As for Veronica Franco, in 1574 she had been chosen to entertain the visiting King Henry III of France, to whom she subsequently dedicated some of her poems. Six years later, in 1580, she sought out Montaigne, who was in Venice, to give him a copy of one of her books, which Montaigne then kept for his famous library in Bordeaux.[20] Could she also have met de Vere? Even if not, it is unlikely a visiting foreigner such as de Vere would have failed to notice or be influenced by the courtesan culture of 16th-century Venice. These experiences (including a possible encounter with Titian's painting) may have provided the initial inspiration for *Venus and Adonis.*

While we have no evidence that de Vere met Titian or Franco, we do know something of his whereabouts. Immediately adjacent to and southeast of the Cannaregio district (location of Titian's house and the Ghetto setting for *The Merchant of Venice*) is the Castello district, home of two churches noteworthy for Oxfordians. The first is the Church of San Giorgio dei Greci, where de Vere attended mass.[21] That he elected to attend a Byzantine, orthodox church in the Venetian "Greektown" should not surprise us. This non-–Catholic, non–Italian venue named after the patron saint of England would have been the politically correct choice.

Also in Castello is the Church of Santa Maria Formosa, about a five-minute walk from the Piazza San Marco, where de Vere met the choirboy Orazio Cuoco.[22] Santa Maria Formosa was also the parish church for Veronica Franco, as well as her patron Domenico Venier, whose palazzo (and literary salon) faced the church at 6129 Campo Santa Maria Formosa.[23] Unfortunately, Franco's exact whereabouts in 1575–1576 are not known; there is some indication she temporarily left Venice to escape the plague.[24] De Vere apparently bolted early from the pre–Lenten carnival of 1576 for similar reasons, taking Orazio Cuoco with him back to England as a page.[25]

De Vere did become involved with at least one Venetian courtesan, Virginia "Padoana," who lived off the Campo Santa Geremia[26] (again, not far from the Ghetto setting of *The Merchant of Venice*). While it has been suggested that de Vere contracted a sexually transmitted disease as a result of this liason, based on lines from a 1606 poem by Nathaniel Baxter, this claim has been subsequently refuted.[27] Margaret Rosenthal has noted that about one generation earlier (in 1543), one Lucieta Padovana had been absolved of charges she had flouted Venetian laws restricting the circulation of courtesans within church premises.[28] Whether she was related to the Virginia "Padoana" known by de Vere some 32 years later is uncertain.

Interestingly, the Jacobean poet Aemilia Bassano Lanyer (1569–1645), one of the leading candidates for Shakespeare's "Dark Lady" of the sonnets, also had Venetian roots. Her father, the court musician Baptista Bassano, came to England from the Veneto. In her younger days, Aemilia had been the mistress of Henry Carey, Lord Hunsdon (and Lord Chamberlain). She appears to have been, at least on her father's side, a product of the same culture that produced Veronica Franco.[29] Both women had to endure later in life a religious backlash from societies grown intolerant of their former way of life, although there would have been obvious and profound differences between Bassano's Puritan England of the early 1600s and Franco's Venetian Republic of the late 16th century.[30] Nevertheless, both women are credited with excellent poetic descriptions of country houses, where each nostalgically recalled happier times.[31]

During this period, Italy (unlike England) not only allowed women such as Franco to be published writers, but permitted women to act on stage as well—phenomena that likely caught de Vere's attention. As for Shakespeare's poem, we suspect that the origins of *Venus and Adonis* are to be found in the Venetian leg of de Vere's Grand Tour. The poem was considered very risqué for its time, and may have also been influenced by the permissive poetic license then in fashion among Italian poets.[32] This is in keeping with what is known of de Vere's mercurial temperament, not to mention his personal ties with the sources and storyline of the poem. As for Will Shakspere, all we know for certain is that his name resembles the one used in the dedication—and that, like Titian's Adonis, he was involved, perhaps reluctantly, with an older woman, Anne Hathaway.

ℬꝱ 39 ℭ℟

The Rape of Lucrece

In 1594, one year after *Venus and Adonis*, Shakespeare's second narrative poem, *The Rape of Lucrece*, was published by Richard Field in London. Like its predecessor companion work, *Lucrece* has a frontispiece adorned with the Roman goddess of marriage and features a dedication to the 21-year-old Henry Wriothesley[1] from "William Shakespeare." While the dedication in *Adonis* was remarkably warm, the one in *Lucrece* was absolutely unprecedented in its personal, intimate tone, beginning, "The love I dedicate to your Lordship is without end" Similarities between this dedication and the sonnets have led more than one scholar to equate Wriothesley with Shakespeare's "Fair Youth."[2] One then naturally queries how a commoner born and raised in provincial Warwickshire had the boldness, in his two very first published works, to address in print with such language the socially stratospheric Earl of Southampton.

In any event, both of these highly erudite poems were very popular and widely praised by contemporaries. *Lucrece* is typically viewed as more serious and heroic—probably the "graver labor" promised to Wriothesley by Shakespeare in the dedication to *Venus and Adonis*. Among Elizabethans who lauded both was the Cambridge divine William Covell, who in his *Polimanteia* of 1595 cites Shakespeare and his two narrative poems as among the outstanding literary productions from contemporary English writers who were (it is implied) university graduates. Either Covell was mistaken about Shakespeare's university credentials or was listing the Bard as an exception—or perhaps unwittingly knew something that most other people did not.[3]

Shakespeare's acknowledged sources for *Lucrece* were Ovid's *Fasti* and the Roman historian Livy,[4] of which copies of the latter are known to have been in the library of de Vere's guardian, Lord Burghley.[5] An earlier, Elizabethan English version of the story could also be found in William Painter's *Palace of Pleasure* (1567). A secondary source for Lucrece's 200+ line digression (lines 1,366–1,568) on the Trojan War appears to have been Book II of Virgil's *Aeneid*, first translated into English by none other than de Vere's uncle, Henry Howard, Earl of Surrey, who also pioneered the English sonnet form.[6]

Shakespeare, however, seems to have done more than simply read Virgil. Lucrece, in her grief and distraction, contemplates a series of paintings depicting the fall of Troy (an allegory for her own situation). During the 19th century, it was noticed by scholars that a series of paintings more or less corresponding to those portrayed by Shakespeare did in fact exist in Mantua.[7] These are the spectacular frescoes by Giulio Romano[8] in the Trojan Apartments of the Palazzo Ducale, the second largest palace in Italy after the Vatican.

In general, Shakespeare the writer seems to have had Mantua on the brain, as the city is mentioned or alluded to in a great number of his works, including, we believe, *Lucrece*.

Many famous people have come from Mantua, several very important to Shakespeare and beginning with the poet Virgil himself, whose work likely inspired Romano's Trojan paintings. According to legend, Mantua (like Rome) had been originally founded by Trojan refugees. Another famous Mantuan was Baldessare Castiglione, noted Renaissance man and author of *Il Cortegiano* ("The Courtier"), a book influential on the Bard, especially in the creation of characters such as Hamlet.[9] Castiglione was instrumental in recruiting Giulio Romano from Rome into the service of the ruling Gonzaga family of Mantua, for whom he would do his most memorable work. De Vere, three years before traveling to Italy, wrote a lengthy preface to Bartholomew Clerke's 1572 Latin translation of Castiglione's esteemed book.[10]

We have no definite proof that de Vere was in Mantua, possibly because archives were destroyed when the city was brutally sacked by the Imperial Army during the Thirty Years War. His presence there would seem likely, however, given that he is known to have been in Venice, Padua and Milan.[11] Mantua, along with Verona (two more inland port cities), were at the time of Oxford's Grand Tour located directly on the canal route between the three aforementioned places.[12] Furthermore, it is known that the Gonzagas enjoyed showing off the artistic treasures of the Trojan Apartments to visiting foreign noblemen, who were frequently offered lodging within these apartments as well.[13] In addition to the fall of Troy, the Trojan Apartments contain a faded fresco by Romano depicting *The Rape of Lucrece*.[14]

The centerpiece of the Trojan frescoes shows the deployment of the Trojan Horse by the Greeks, who are being personally directed by their benefactor Minerva, the "spearshaker" goddess of wisdom and warfare. The wooden horse depicted by Romano in this fresco—at least to this untrained eye—is one of the most dramatic and realistic Trojan Horses ever painted, a skill for which Romano was particularly noted. The Palazzo Ducale at one time contained a series of Romano's equestrian paintings (since destroyed) noted for their impressive realism. These have recently been proposed by Dr. Noemi Magri as a possible source for an episode of Shakespeare's *Venus and Adonis*, in which the poet describes at length the beauty of a painted horse (lines 289–306).[15]

Another series of well-known equestrian frescoes by Romano did survive, however, and can be found in the aptly named Room of the Horses at the Palazzo Te in Mantua, located a short walking distance from the Palazzo Ducale.[16] The Palazzo Te is in many ways a more awe-inspiring experience than the Palazzo Ducale, because every detail—painting, sculpture and architecture—was conceived and executed by Romano and his assistants. In addition to the Room of the Horses, this edifice houses massive frescoes depicting scenes inspired by Ovid, including a group of bas-reliefs, one of which portrays *The Rape of Lucrece*.[17] Shakespeare the writer would have loved it, to be certain.

In the poem, when not giving pictorial descriptions, Shakespeare spends a lot of time inside the heads of his characters, particularly the rapist Tarquin and his victim, Lucrece. Tarquin's vacillations and rationalizations before the crime, combined with shame and flight afterward, have a realism and plausibility that are a tribute to the Bard's genius for this sort of thing. Even more stunningly, Shakespeare gives us a lengthy exposition of Lucrece's anguished and bitter thoughts after the fact. One may well ask whether anyone has any business delving into the thoughts and feelings of a rape victim, even for the sake of poetic drama; yet Shakespeare takes the reader right into the psyche of the heroine in a manner that is compelling, to say the least. No one can ever accuse the Bard of not having been in touch with his feminine side; his female characters are memorable like few others during that era and still retain their power today.

Lucrece is despondent at having lost her honor and reputation. This is a theme in the canon repeatedly struck by Shakespeare, and this particular poem represents only one of many examples. One is naturally curious how a man like Will Shakspere, whose life was one long success story, could have known such feelings. Perhaps the memory of his insolvent father or some other unknown childhood embarrassment provides the answer. The life of Edward de Vere, on the other hand, presents us with a tragic case study in how far one person can fall in a single lifetime. Moreover, as great as de Vere's financial losses were (he died in debt), these were certainly exceeded by his losses in public reputation and esteem. In the poem, between Tarquin's inglorious exit and Lucrece's reflections on the fall of Troy, the reader can only marvel at over 600 lines of lamentation, including the victim's unforgettable refrain cursing the perpetrator, "Let him have time" to rave, despair, and so forth (lines 981–994). It is difficult to believe that such outpourings could have been written by someone who did not have personal experience with these emotions.

Disturbingly, de Vere himself stood accused of rape. This accusation came in the aftermath of the scandalous events from 1580, during which he first charged his former cohorts Charles Arundel, Henry Howard (de Vere's first cousin and son of the poet), and Robert Southwell with treason. These men, particularly Arundel, then turned on Oxford, accusing him of every imaginable crime. Especially repulsive was the allegation that de Vere had forced himself upon several boy servants.[18] Although Oxford was not arraigned or punished as a result of these specific charges (while Arundel went to jail and later exile), these nevertheless stuck in the mind of public opinion, and have remained there to this very day.[19] De Vere would soon later be incarcerated in the Tower of London for getting one of the queen's ladies-in-waiting pregnant, about the same time he was losing what was left of his inherited fortune. Afterward, his father-in-law Lord Burghley accurately wrote in 1583 that Oxford's reputation had been ruined.[20] Even in today's permissive and scandal-dominated world, such a soiled reputation would be enough to discredit any literary production from an author so tainted. Four hundred years ago, this problem surely would have been more aggravated, especially during the Puritan political ascendancy of those times. In retrospect, it is remarkable that de Vere managed to survive at all, given that homosexuality in Elizabethan England was a capital crime and that other nobility had lost (and would continue to lose) their heads for doing far less. His marriage to a Cecil would have shielded de Vere only up to a point, especially in light of the many perceived wrongs he had committed against Burghley's daughter.

The troubling issues raised by *Lucrece* lead us directly into the even thornier problems of the sonnets. Edward de Vere may have been in no position to preach sermons on morality, but one can easily imagine him offering poetic cautionary tales to a younger, up-and-coming colleague such as the Earl of Southampton. This seems far less of a stretch than Henry Wriothesley receiving such fare from the 30-year-old Will Shakspere, no matter how much the young earl may have admired his talent. One must, however, eventually ask whether these challenging works were the brainchild of a self-made entrepreneur from Warwickshire, or a disgraced and degenerate renegade nobleman. Either way, it is certainly hard to fathom that these poems were anything but the anguished musings of a soul in torment. For the time being, perhaps we should save the final word for Shakespeare's Lucrece: "Time's glory is to calm contending kings, to unmask falsehood and bring truth to light" (lines 939–940).

ℰ 40 ℭ

The Sonnets

Of Man I can believe nothing less easily than invariability: nothing more easily than variability. Whoever would judge a man in his detail, piece by piece, separately, would hit on the truth more often.
　　　　　　　　　—Montaigne, *On the Inconstancy of Our Actions* [1592][1]

A few years ago this commentator attended a book-signing event for Pulitzer Prize–winning author David McCullough.[2] After a short but illuminating presentation, McCullough fielded questions from a large audience. Frankly, most of these questions were not very good and one could detect that the distinguished guest was beginning to get tired, if not a little bored. Then suddenly, someone (not yours truly) raised their hand and asked McCullough if he had ever begun a book project and then later regretted it. He immediately perked up and in animated fashion said that, yes, he had always wanted to write a biography of the artist Pablo Picasso, and then one day got the chance to do so. Unfortunately, as McCullough did his research, he learned that Picasso was not, shall we say, an admirable human being—a great artist, yes—but not worthy of praise beyond his work. McCullough then said that he had to abandon the project in midstream because he had fallen so out of sympathy with his subject matter. We share this story due to our concern that Shakespeare the writer may have been a similar paradox: great artist and great SOB as well. If this proves to be true, then we would be well-advised to follow the maxim of D.H. Lawrence—no saint himself—to trust the tale and not the teller.

Regarding the sonnets of William Shakespeare, Edmund Chambers qualified his own remarks by commenting acerbically that "More folly has been written about the sonnets than about any other Shakespearean topic."[3] The reasons for this will be explored presently, but before we possibly add our own name to the list of those who have written foolishly on the subject, readers would do well to remember that the sonnets were probably never intended by Shakespeare for publication. As a result, we are likely catching a glimpse of the Bard's most unguarded and personal manner, at least to the extent that he allowed his intimate friends to see it. Thus the sonnets stand apart from the rest of the canon, even more so than his two great narrative poems.

Shake-speares Sonnets,[4] telling of amorous relations between at least four people, three of whom appear to have been male, were first published in 1609.[5] Samuel Schoenbaum represented the overwhelming majority view among scholars in his belief that this edition was printed without the authorization of the author.[6] It was quickly suppressed and surviving first editions are rare—13 total are known to exist.[7] Publisher Thomas Thorpe ("T.T.") dedicated the work to "the onlie begetter of these insuing sonnets Mr. W.H." The true identity of "Mr. W.H." alone has inspired mountains of literature. Nobleman candidates such as William Herbert, Earl of Pembroke, and Henry Wriothesley (with the initials reversed), Earl of Southampton, have been very popular among both traditionalists and Oxfordians. Dissenters have pointed out that for Thorpe to have addressed a peer of the realm as "Mr. [Master]" plus initials would have been viewed as bald-faced insolence, unless it was the nobleman's own idea. Taking this further, if the supposed nobleman "Mr. W.H." wanted his identity partially or entirely hidden, then why not use a pseudonym or simply stay anonymous, as others did?[8] And why would a nobleman even cooperate in such a venture?

Our own favorite candidate for "Mr. W.H." is the notorious stationer pirate and London man-about-town William Hall,[9] first proposed by orthodox biographer Sidney Lee[10] during the 19th century and later adopted by some Oxfordians, beginning with Bernard M. Ward. Hall offers many credentials and no drawbacks that have been brought to our attention. For starters (as noted by Schoenbaum and others), the words following "Mr. W.H." in Thorpe's acrostic dedication are "ALL HAPPINESSE," thus reading "Mr. W.H. ALL" or "Mr. W. Hall."[11] From the Oxfordian point of view, Hall is a nice fit as well, since he was apparently living in Hackney, suburban London, at the same time the Countess of Oxford sold King's Place in 1608, along with no doubt some of its contents, which may have included manuscripts.[12]

Another curiosity in the Sonnets' dedication is a respectful salute to the author as "our ever-living poet"—curious because the phrase "ever-living" was always and without exception used to describe someone who was dead, and Will Shakspere was still very much alive in 1609.[13] Edward de Vere was of course certainly dead by 1609, although the exact date of his demise between 1604 and 1608 has been lately disputed.[14] One example of the phrase "ever-living" being used in this sense is by Shakespeare himself, who in *Henry VI, Part I* makes a reference to the deceased King Henry V as "ever-living" (IV.iii.51).[15] In any event, after the initial publication of the sonnets had been suppressed, it would be another 31 years before these again appeared in print (by "Wil. Shake-speare"),[16] albeit with gender changes in the text to eliminate the controversial perception of bisexuality. This would be in 1640, two years before civil war broke out; an edition faithful to the original would not appear until the 18th century, and had it not been for the piracy of Thomas Thorpe and William Hall (?), these treasures may well have been lost to posterity.[17]

Prior to the unauthorized publication of 1609, the sonnets had first been mentioned by Francis Meres in 1598, who cited Shakespeare's "sugred [sic] sonnets among his private friends"; then in 1599, two of the 26 "Dark Lady" sonnets (138 and 144) were published in the collection titled *The Passionate Pilgrim*.[18] This was immediately followed in 1600 with "sonnetes by W.S." being entered with the Stationers' Register, possibly to prevent further unauthorized publication of the sort that had occurred the previous year. These were re-registered in 1609 prior to the first complete edition.[19] Critics (not surprisingly) disagree sharply over when the poems were written, but most favor composition over a period of several years, beginning in the early 1590s. Chambers, like many others, noted an affinity of style and mood with Shakespeare's two narrative poems published in 1593–1594:

> The chronological inferences appear to be that the sonnets began as a continuation of the lyrical impulse represented by *Venus and Adonis* and *Lucrece*, in the former of which the invitation to marriage theme is already, rather inappropriately, found; that the three-years' range of civ was probably 1593–6; that the bulk of the sonnets belong to this period....[20]

Recall that the dedicatee of these two narrative poems was Henry Wriothesley, Earl of Southampton, who had been engaged to de Vere's daughter Elizabeth before breaking it off sometime during 1594 (see Chapters 38 and 39).[21] To this point we shall return.

A proper overview of the sources for Shakespeare's sonnets should include a brief history of the sonnet form itself. The art of 14-line iambic pentameter poetry first gained popularity during the 13th century at the royal court of Frederick II in Palermo, Sicily.[22] Though Sicily was under German rule at this time, Frederick's mother was a Norman, and it was in the wake of the earlier Norman conquest that Sicilian culture revived and flourished. De Vere's family, it should be remembered, was also of Norman descent. Later during the 14th century, the sonnet form was further developed and indeed became synonymous with the name of the Italian poet Francesco Petrarca, better known as Petrarch. This popularity continued through the 16th century; one of the leading Petrarchan circles could be found at the Venetian literary salon of the Venier family, frequented by personages such as Arentino, Tasso, and the courtesan poetess Veronica Franco (see Chapter 38). Curiously, de Vere is known to have attended the Church of Santa Maria Formosa that stood opposite the Venier salon during his stay in Venice. So far, then, we have established that de Vere had remote ethnic and travel connections to the Italian origins of sonnet poetry, but this is a mere prelude to the even more remarkable series of coincidences between the 17th Earl and Shakespeare's most elusive works.

The first writers to pioneer sonnet-writing in English during the early 16th century were two noblemen courtier poets, Sir Thomas Wyatt (1503?–1542) and Henry Howard, Earl of Surrey (1517?–1547). Wyatt, the elder of the two, wrote first and in strict imitation of the Italian Petrarchan model, with some later variations of his own. His younger disciple Howard, on the other hand, created his own style. Whereas the Italian sonnet typically began with an eight-line octave followed by a six-line sestet, Howard developed an original form in which three quatrains were capped off by a rhymed couplet. This structure was later adopted by the Bard and is now rightfully known as the Shakespearean sonnet form.[23] And oh yes, Howard was de Vere's uncle.

Among the English courtier poets, the sonnet achieved its height of popularity during the early 1590s but then quickly fell out of favor. Among the leaders were Philip Sidney, whose posthumous *Astrophel and Stella* cycle was published in 1591, and others attached to the Sidney-Pembroke circle, such as Edmund Spenser, whose *Amoretti* were published in 1595. De Vere had associations with both of these poets, being Sidney's arch-rival at court during the 1570s and 1580s, and Spenser dedicating a tributary sonnet to de Vere in the first edition of *The Faerie Queene* in 1590.[24] The Vere and Sidney families would also eventually intermarry in 1604 with the wedding between de Vere's daughter Susan and Sidney's nephew Philip Herbert. More belonging to the Elizabethan avant-garde was the poet Richard Barnfield, whose homoerotic works included *Certain Sonnets*, published in 1595. Barnfield, who insofar as we know was never punished for his writings, infused his poems with the pagan sensuality of Ovid and Virgil, both of whom had first been translated into English by de Vere's uncles. This was in polar opposite to his more pious contemporaries in the Sidney-Pembroke circle, and Barnfield's originality has been more appreciated during modern times. Lastly, it should be noted that most of these English sonneteers more or less followed Wyatt's example by imitating the Italian model or devising their own distinctive structures. Few imitated Howard's example, except for Shakespeare and a few others.

Another courtier poet is known to have written in the sonnet form—Edward de Vere. De Vere's sonnet titled *Love Thy Choice*, beginning with the line "Who taught thee first to sigh, alas, my heart?" was probably written when he was a young man. Professor Steven W. May believed that no poem attributed to de Vere dated any later than 1593 (the year the name "William Shakespeare" first appeared in print), a stunning admission that de Vere's biographer Alan Nelson did not contest.[25] Moreover, de Vere's sonnet is written in exactly the same form that was invented by his uncle Henry Howard, and later adapted by the Bard.[26] If this were not enough, another early poem by de Vere titled *The Lyvely Larke Stretcht Forth Her Wynge* has fairly overt same-sex overtones, as noted by Professor Nelson and others.[27]

De Vere's published prose also suggests, if nothing else, an influence on Shakespeare's sonnets. His lengthy poetic epistle attached to the Thomas Bedingfield translation of *Cardanus Comforte*, published in 1573 when de Vere was 23 years old, reads like a condensed digest of thoughts and feelings later molded into the distinctive Surrey sonnet form by Shakespeare. Limited space allows for only one of many examples. In his letter, de Vere declares that by publishing Bedingfield's book he "shall erect you such a monument that, as I say, in your lifetime you shall see how noble a shadow of your virtuous life shall hereafter remain when you are dead and gone."[28] In the sonnets, Shakespeare rather immodestly assures the Fair Youth in a similar manner that:

> Not marble, nor the gilded monuments
> Of princes, shall outlive this powerful rime;
> But you shall shine more bright in these contents
> Than unswept stone, besmear'd with sluttish time. [#55]

Then again in Sonnet 109: "And thou in this shalt find thy monument, / When tyrants' crests and tombs of brass are spent...." To repeat, this is only one example.[29] De Vere's prefatory letter to *Cardanus Comforte*, an unprecedented, published endorsement from a nobleman circa 1573, reads like a great harbinger of the Shakespearean canon that would begin to appear in print some 20 years later. Then again, de Vere seems to have hovered around most of the influences that would later leave their mark on Shakespeare's work.

At this point we need to pause and remember that the sonnets stand in a class by themselves. To look for consistent Shakespearean quality in anyone other than Shakespeare would be foolish. The sonnets tend to eclipse other contemporary poetry, and there are reasons for this, given their extraordinary emotional intensity and intellectual inventiveness. This is why they are considered among the greatest poetry ever written. It was appropriate that the 20th-century American songwriter Cole Porter wrote the song lyric "You're the top, you're a Shakespeare sonnet" for his classic 1934 musical *Anything Goes*. Porter, like many other outstanding personalities throughout history, was known to have been bisexual; although he was relatively unknown until age 28,[30] few geniuses came better prepared to do their life's work.

Suffice it to say that all readers of the sonnets face three interpretive options. The first is that the sonnets are completely non-biographical and strictly a poetic convention; hence Shakespeare was just pretending and did not really mean the things he wrote.[31] This is a good stance for aspiring academics who are worried about offending anyone. The second option is that the sonnets are semi-autobiographical. This is the most popular view because one can pick and choose what is autobiographical and what is not, depending on one's own personal preferences; unfortunately, this method is also the most subjective. The third option, originally favored, later disregarded and now making a comeback, is that the sonnets are autobiographical, plain and simple—Shakespeare's poetic diary, if you will. We lean toward the last view, although there could have been a wide gap between what was real and what the Poet believed to be real; in this sense, the second option has some merit as well. The first option is pure evasive nonsense, but then again, as Oxfordian Joseph Sobran has written, "Rescuing Shakespeare from his own obvious meaning became a kind of duty in the age of Bardolatry."[32]

While de Vere's poetry and letters offer surprising parallels with the sonnets, his biography truly gives one pause in that Shakespeare seems to be obliquely telling the story of the 17th Earl's last 10–15 years. The sonnets themselves speak mostly of the Poet's troubled and troubling relationship with a younger Fair Youth, and to a lesser extent, the Poet's affair with a mysterious Dark Lady. The Youth also appears to have relations with the Dark Lady, as well as with a Rival Poet. This basic outline of a "plot" has been recognized by everyone from traditional scholars such as Chambers[33] to more recent Oxfordian commentators such as Joseph Sobran. In fact, among Oxfordians, little if anything can be added to Sobran's incisiveness.[34]

During the course of 154 sonnets, a number of specific personal traits for the author are detected, or rather revealed by the Sonneteer himself. For starters, he appears to be old, lame, tired of life, and obsessed with death. These are very basic observations that have been made by the most conservative of orthodox critics.[35] For example, in Sonnet 37 the Poet ruefully contrasts his own run-down physical condition with the vigor and virtue of the Fair Youth:

> As a decrepit father takes delight
> To see his active child do deeds of youth,
> So I, made lame by fortune's dearest spite,
> Take all my comfort of thy worth and truth.

De Vere by 1593 was no spring chicken. He was 43 years old and probably looked and felt older. His fortune and reputation were gone. He appears to have been lame, of which he was complaining openly by 1597. His health was reportedly not good and rumors of his death were circulating as early as 1595.[36] Will Shakspere, on the other hand, was 29 years old in 1593 and, according to the traditional biography, rapidly approaching the summit of his successful career. Taken within the context of the orthodox view, it might make some sense after all to claim that the author of the sonnets was purely making everything up as he wrote.

Another point on which even the most subjective of readers can usually agree is that the Poet feels a strong sense of disgrace and unworthiness, with a tainted brand upon his name.[37] This mood is established early in the cycle, for example, in Sonnet 29: "When in disgrace with fortune and men's eyes / I alone beweep my outcast state"—perhaps Will Shakspere was beginning to realize that acting and playwriting were not the most respectable professions in Elizabethan England. Later the same sentiment intensifies in Sonnet 71, as the Poet advises the Youth: "No longer mourn for me when I am dead"— a bleak outlook to be sure. Nothing, however, prepares us for Sonnet 72, in which the Poet laments "After my death dear love forget me quite / For you in me can nothing worthy prove"; then comes the finale:

> My name be buried where my body is,
> And live no more to shame nor me nor you.
> For I am shamed by that which I bring forth,
> And so should you to love things nothing worth.

The Poet is so ashamed of himself (for whatever reason) that he does not want his name to survive, and chides the Youth for his affection—insincerely perhaps, but highly effective in the poetic scheme of things. Oxfordians interpret this to mean that de Vere knew his name would end up in obscurity, and may have even been grateful for it. Traditionalists can only shrug and say that Will Shakspere was having a bad day.

De Vere was acquainted with public disgrace his entire life, beginning with a challenge to his legitimacy at age 13, continuing with rumors surrounding the birth of his first child while he was traveling, and reaching a fever pitch following his extramarital affair with Anne Vavasor in 1581. Concurrent with the latter scandal were public accusations against him for treason and pederasty. Despite de Vere's release after a short prison stint, all of these charges stuck in public opinion and his father-in-law Lord Burghley wrote privately and accurately in 1583 that de Vere's reputation had been ruined.[38] Early on, de Vere wrote poetry about these experiences, and his *Loss of Good Name* (first published in 1576) was described by Professor May as "a defiant lyric without precedent in English Renaissance verse."[39]

More subtle but apparent nevertheless is the Poet's indication of his own considerable social rank. Chambers and others have noted that the Poet appears to be of a lower status than the Fair Youth,[40] but this is not the same as being a commoner. By the 1590s, and despite his earldom, de Vere was in political reality a nobody, and younger courtiers such as Southampton and Essex carried far more influence. Still, the Poet is conscious of his own position (however ritualistic) when he writes in Sonnet 125: "Were't aught to me I bore the canopy," an allusion that the *Riverside* editors concede is a reference to the ceremonial canopy carried over a royal personage.[41] Earlier, in Sonnet 91, the Poet tells the Youth: "Thy love is [better] than high birth to me." This matter-of-fact statement can be taken for its obvious meaning, or if one frantically clings to the traditional biography, alternative readings must be devised. One could interpret it to mean that the Poet is telling the Youth (who is of high birth?) that the Poet loves him not because of his rank but because of him personally; or perhaps the Poet is telling the Youth that if he could trade love for high birth, he would not do it. Thus it becomes a question of choosing the first obvious meaning or creating other meanings that get around the first impression, which is that the Poet himself is of noble birth.

The identity of the Fair Youth has been the subject of a major literary manhunt. This is understandable given that 126 sonnets (82 percent of the total) are addressed to him. It would appear that the Youth was *the* love of Shakespeare's life. Somewhat surprising is that, unlike the Dark Lady (and unlike the Poet himself, for that matter), the number of real-life candidates proposed for the Fair Youth has been relatively small; in fact, two young men in particular probably account for 99 percent of Bardolatry opinion, at least for those who think the Youth was a real person. These two are Henry Wriothesley, Earl of Southampton (the majority view), and to a lesser extent, William Herbert, Earl of Pembroke.[42] Although both Wriothesley and Herbert were undeniably close to Shakespeare the writer, we tend to favor the former due mainly to his overt connection with the two narrative poems. Either way, both men were connected with de Vere; in the case of Herbert, he negotiated marriage with de Vere's daughter Bridget while his brother Philip ended up marrying Bridget's sister Susan Vere.

"From fairest creatures we desire increase"—thus begins the cycle with the so-called "procreation" Sonnets 1–17, in which the Poet urges the Youth to marry and have children. As mentioned before, Wriothesley's claim to the Youth's identity is strongly supported by the dedication of Shakespeare's two narrative poems to the young earl in 1593–1594, at a time when Wriothesley was engaged to de Vere's daughter Elizabeth. Although no one recorded having seen de Vere and Wriothesley (who was 23 years younger) associating with each other, a number of interesting similarities between the two earls are documented. Aside from the marriage negotiations (which were eventually broken off), both became royal wards under Burghley at a young age after their fathers had died, both attended Cambridge and Gray's Inn, both were interested in theater and patronized writers, both received initial favor from Queen Elizabeth, both married ladies-in-waiting to the queen, both fell out of favor with the queen and were imprisoned, and both later received favor from King James. De Vere was part of the tribunal in 1601 that found Wriothesley guilty of treason by association with the Earl of Essex, but Oxford's former brother-in-law Robert Cecil reputedly had Wriothesley's sentence commuted to life until the Queen died in 1603.[43] Later during the Jacobean era, Wriothesley became close political allies with de Vere's son Henry, the 18th Earl of Oxford. In complete contrast to this extensive laundry list, absolutely no documented connections have been discovered between Wriothesley and Will Shakspere. As eloquently surmised by Oxfordian author Richard Whalen, "Conventional biographies ignore the cumulative weight, or cumulative absence, of evidence."[44]

The first real shock comes in Sonnet 18 with "Shall I compare thee to a summer's day?" written from one man to another. The next 109 sonnets continue in this vein. By Sonnet 20, many would-be Bardolators are running for cover: "A woman's face with Nature's own hand painted / Hast thou, the master mistress of my passion" and concluding with "But since she [Nature] prick'd thee out for woman's pleasure, / Mine be thy love, and thy love's use their treasure."[45] Thus the Poet, who three sonnets earlier was urging the Youth to marry and have children, is now infatuated with the Youth himself. At this point in the canon, all readers must unavoidably decide for themselves whether or not the Bard was bisexual.

During the late 20th century, the answer to the above question increasingly became "How could he not have been?" Leading the charge was orthodox scholar Professor Joseph Pequigney, whose ground-breaking 1985 study of the sonnets, along with the 1991 follow-up work of Pequigney's disciple Professor Bruce R. Smith, remain basic required reading for anyone attempting to tackle this problem. Pequigney and Smith joined a growing number of critics, including G.P.V. Akrigg, Leslie Fiedler, G. Wilson Knight, Kenneth Muir, and others, who realized that to skirt around this issue only diminishes the Bard's greatness. As Harold Bloom wrote:

> The human endowment, Shakespeare keeps intimating, is bisexual: after all, we have both mothers and fathers. Whether we "forget" either the heterosexual or homosexual component in our desire, or "remember" both, is in the Sonnets and the plays not a question of choice, and only rarely a matter for anguish.[46]

In defense of his reading, Pequigney extensively cited the theories of Sigmund Freud with respect to human bisexuality.[47] This was appropriate since Freud himself was a great Bardolator, but Pequigney forgot to mention that Freud was also an Oxfordian in his authorship beliefs and in his own humorous words, "a follower of" Looney.[48]

By now, many readers choose to retreat into the aforementioned first and second options of interpretation: Shakespeare was just kidding or not communicating well and really meant something other than what he seems to have meant. Among all authorship persuasions, a host of non-bisexual readings have been concocted, some of which even have a sort of internal logic. At the end of the day, however, these come across like someone trying to avoid a bad neighborhood by driving half way around town—or the world, for that matter. Oftentimes, just driving directly through the "bad neighborhood" does not turn out to be nearly as bad as one imagined.

In Sonnets 40–42, the Youth appears to steal the Poet's mistress, but is forgiven as the Poet assures him that "we must not be foes" (#42). The idea of Will Shakspere offering such assurance to the Earl of Southampton is truly a smiler. Be that as it may, in 1594 (during the initial burst of Shakespeare's sonnet creativity), an anonymous work mysteriously titled *Willobie His Avisa* was published, in which one "W.S." advises "H.W." or "Henry Willobego" how to seduce a married and virtuous lady named Avisa.[49] Traditionalists have discovered that an actual person named Henrie Willobie had a brother who married the sister of a woman who married one of the overseers of Will Shakspere's estate (got that?). This seems to approach something like plausibility until we consider other possibilities. One is that *Willobie His Avisa* may have been an elaborate allegorical spoof of courtiers such Wriothesley and his disreputable buddy "Shakespeare" who were continually seeking the queen's favor.[50]

Sonnets 78–86 introduce a Rival Poet for the Youth's affection. The Sonneteer wonders whether it "Was it the proud full sail of his great verse, / Bound for the prize of all too precious you" (#86) that drew the Youth away from him. Assuming Wriothesley was the Fair Youth, we would conjecture that the Rival Poet was Robert Devereux, Earl of Essex, to whom Wriothesley attached his fortunes about this time. Essex was not only a prominent courtier poet, but according to Professor May, wrote poetry of a highly utilitarian nature geared toward his own political advancement.[51]

The last sonnet addressed to the Youth in the cycle (#126) consists of six rhymed couplets as the Poet bids him adieu. It concludes with poetic legalisms: "Her [Time's] audit (though delay'd) answered must be, / And her quietus is to render thee." As in many other works (*The Merchant of Venice*, *Measure for Measure*, etc.), Shakespeare poetically employs legal terminology with effortless grace. If de Vere was writing about Wriothesley, then it seems a natural farewell from one Gray's Inn alumnus to another.

Sonnets 127–152 are addressed to the Poet's mistress,[52] popularly known as the Dark Lady. Sonnet 127 begins with the qualification "In the old age black was not counted fair," followed by one back-handed compliment after another. In Sonnet 130, the Poet praises her beauty by informing us that "My mistress' eyes are nothing like the sun" but eventually condemns her in Sonnet 147: "For I have sworn thee fair, and thought thee bright, / Who art black as hell, as dark as night." This is pretty strong stuff and could not have been taken kindly by the lady in question.

Fans of the orthodox biography love to harp on Sonnet 145, especially the line "'I hate from hate away she threw, / And sav'd my life, saying 'not you.'" They insist that "hate away" is a pun on the name of Will Shakspere's wife Anne Hathaway, thus identifying her with the Dark Lady. Apart from being rather far-fetched, these same partisans then forget to read Sonnet 152 in which the Poet declares "In loving thee thou know'st I am forsworn." Responsible editors agree this means the Poet is admitting that he and the Dark Lady are committing adultery.[53] In charity it can be said that most Bardolators at one time or another are guilty of obsessing over a single line while ignoring the balance of the text.

Among the countless candidates that have been proposed for Shakespeare's Dark Lady, our favorite is Jacobean poetess Aemilia Bassano Lanyer, daughter of the Venetian-imported court musician, Baptista Bassano. Aemilia was first proposed by orthodox scholar and Oxfordian nemesis Alfred Leslie Rowse; later she was splendidly incorporated into the Oxfordian theory by researcher Stephanie Hopkins Hughes.[54] The discovery of Aemilia was probably Rowse's finest moment as a scholar, for which of course he has been vilified. We remained intrigued. In 1610—one year after *Shake-speares Sonnets* appeared in print— was published Aemilia's own *Salve Deus Rex Judæorum*, a passionate, poetic defense of feminine virtue made within the context of holy scripture. Aemilia's supporters view this work as a direct response to Shakespeare's sonnets. *Salve Deus* was dedicated to various noble women patrons, including Mary Sidney Herbert, by then mother-in-law to de Vere's daughter Susan. Among the many other attractive qualifications of Aemilia as the Bard's dark, amoral temptress, one was her presumed musicality, as she hailed from one of the most distinguished musical families in Renaissance Italy and England.

De Vere, as we have seen in other chapters, was musical as well. Memorably in 1601, as Queen Elizabeth performed at court on the virginals, word came that the Earl of Essex had been executed; de Vere whispered something in reference to Walter Raleigh that made bystanders chuckle. The Queen demanded it repeated and de Vere quipped, "when Jacks went up, heads went down." This startling pun on the word "Jacks" referred both to the plucking mechanism of the virginals and to Raleigh's humble origins.[55] Perhaps de Vere had been reading Shakespeare's Sonnet 128: "Do I envy those jacks that nimble leap.... Since saucy jacks so happy are in this...." We would gladly welcome any other known examples of a similar pun on the word "Jacks" in Elizabethan literature, that is, besides by William Shakespeare and Edward de Vere.

Lastly, we come to the famous "Will" sonnets, 135–136, in which the Poet jokingly uses the words "Will," "will," "wills," and "wilst" 19 times over the course of 20 lines. There is no need to repeat here the exhaustive analysis these poems have received by others, but within the context of the authorship question, Shakespeare's twentieth variation of the word in the final phrase of Sonnet 136, "for my name is *Will*," deserves brief comment.

For true believers, this may be the ultimate proof that Shakespeare was Shakespeare. For the rest of us, the two "Will" sonnets, like most other things, suggest ambiguity rather than clear-cut, definitive answers. For the Poet who wanted his name "buried where my body is" (#72), to then turn around and make it into a joke for his mistress, is a quite a mood-swing. Possible?—certainly. Probable?—only if we refuse to consider other scenarios. One is that "Will" was an alias. Would, say, Mark Twain have been more likely to make a literary joke about Mark Twain or Samuel Clemens? We allow readers to judge for themselves.

Stepping back even further, in 1609 Jacobean England, who in their right mind would attach their name to such poetry? Never mind that homosexuality was a capital offense, the Puritans (among others) would have gone ballistic. Some commentators have queried why Shakespeare was not more overt in his homoeroticism (like Barnfield, for example), but it may well have been that a certain amount of equivocal window dressing was thrown in for self-protection, and to leave possible future readers guessing as well. Professor Smith noted that while draconian sodomy statutes were officially on the books, these laws were rarely (if ever) enforced, except in cases for which there were ulterior motives (read: political expediency) for doing so.[56]

Most of us can agree that Shakespeare the writer rejected the Aristotelian view of poetry as adopted by Philip Sidney and his subsequent followers—namely, that poetry must have a specific moral purpose. On the other hand, Shakespeare in his sonnets—indeed, in the entire canon—achieved a moral purpose in spite of himself. This is similar to Cervantes' Don Quixote who, after all of his adventures and delusions, changes the world for the better in ways he never imagined or anticipated. Shakespeare succeeded in acquainting the rest of us with our own feelings and those of others. It's all about getting to know human emotions. What de Vere felt, no one can say, but if he felt anything, Shakespeare certainly wrote about it. The same applies for the rest of us.

Conclusion

*So I guarantee you nothing for certain, except my making known what point I have so
far reached in my knowledge of it.*

                                                 –Montaigne, *On Books* [1580][1]

Everyone has their own Shakespeare. We all believe in the inexplicable miracle of
genius; yet most of us still want to know as much as we can about it. In a sense, traditional Shakespearean biography is a perfect vehicle for our self-indulgence. We have the
canon, we have the text. It is a blank canvas that our imaginations can fill in any way we
want to—and most of us do. This can be fun, but also misleading—it is certainly better
to try and know what the process actually was. Anyone with a healthy curiosity wants to
know the truth, as opposed to merely imagining it. For example, if we are interested in
architecture, we not only want to see the finished building, we want to know about the
entire design and construction process, step by step. The danger with imagination is that
we risk getting it wrong, and if we cannot even imagine the process, we might give up, as
students have been known to do on occasion. The same thing applies to creative writing,
and this is what the Oxfordian theory attempts to facilitate. It examines a body of knowledge about Edward de Vere in order to try and have a tiny bit of insight into Shakespeare's
creative world. By doing so, we hope to have a better understanding not only of Shakespeare's writings, but of our culture and of ourselves.

Anyone involved with this topic for more than a few minutes knows that Oxfordians
and all questioners of the traditional biography[2] are routinely accused of snobbery and
"conspiracy" obsessions. This response takes on many guises but our favorite is the one
in which doubters are blatantly psychoanalyzed by opponents. Oxfordians must either be
genuine believers in the superiority of the English aristocracy or, worse, deprived souls
who desperately need their humdrum lives spiced up with a little bit of romance and
intrigue. This latter indictment has actually been leveled against people like Mark Twain
and Sigmund Freud—posthumously, of course. Rather than directly respond to this frequent allegation, let us just note for the record that psychoanalysis can be a two-way street.
Furthermore, objections such as de Vere died too soon, or his early poetry is not good
enough, or that he was a bad person—these arguments hold water only for those whose
minds are made up to begin with. The truth of the matter is that lame and lazy responses
to innocent questions have probably created more authorship skeptics by traditionalists
than all authorship literature combined.

One sure sign of the infantile level to which this debate often sinks is that genuinely valid and challenging rebuttals to the Oxfordian theory are often ignored. After all, why bother to discuss real issues when one can get away with superficiality? As noted in the Introduction, "why?" and "how?" remain central and complex questions that have yet to receive conclusive answers. In this study, on a play by play basis, we have attempted (but not necessarily succeeded) to demonstrate how the political realities of Shakespeare's England would have made it very awkward—if not self-defeating—for a wayward, subsidized peer of the realm such as de Vere to have taken public credit for these works. This was not merely due to the traditional social stigma against noblemen poets and playwrights which was, admittedly, beginning to break down. More importantly, the primarily propagandistic function of the plays, combined with the growing importance of an English Parliament in staunch opposition to the monarchy, made most of canon political dynamite. Even Will Shakspere, either as front man or true author, declined to take credit for much of the canon during his own lifetime.

To be fair to the Puritans, they were hostile toward a skewed and lopsided social system that would have easily facilitated an authorship ruse, if in fact there was one. The Puritans may have motivated the government to conceal Shakespeare's authorship, but it was the latter who would have committed the act, aided and abetted by a status quo eventually swept away by the English Civil War, 19 years after publication of the First Folio. The symbol of this tension would be the greatest literary figure of the following generation, John Milton, who began life as a political and religious conservative before falling under the spell of education and the classics. These, along with a troubled marriage that instructed him to be charitable toward those in a similar plight, eventually transformed this mighty religious poet, whose writings are often confused with holy scripture, into an outcast among his own Calvinist community, but to the inestimable benefit of future readers. Would it be so very strange if his forerunner Shakespeare in reality had been a public *persona non grata* who elected to be hidden from the public eye? Would it be so improbable that such a hoax was intentionally perpetuated after the death of the author by a defensive-minded monarchy, one to be overthrown by its subjects in less than 20 years? Would it be so unlikely in view of a new government that would outlaw and demolish the playhouses?

One important aspect of this problem that we have treated in (at best) cursory fashion is the possibility of group authorship for Shakespeare's works. The possibility that de Vere belonged to a succession of authors involved in the writing process must be acknowledged, although he would have been the logical group leader, if not founder of such a coterie. In addition to his son-in-law William Stanley, other peers such as Roger Manners, Earl of Rutland, were well-placed to lend a hand.[3] Our main objections to the original nobleman alternative, Francis Bacon, is that his biography and writing style seem very un–Shakespearean in comparison to de Vere's; plus he was so heavily involved in affairs of state (unlike the outcast and misanthropic Oxford) that it is hard to see how he would have found the time. Even so, who can say who definitely did or did not have a hand in the process? Maybe the traditional author chipped in after all. Actors, producers, patrons, editors, and printers were surely involved, as were perhaps university wits such as Marlowe. We rule out Ben Jonson only because he was so scrupulously careful in making sure that he received credit for his work. Above all, we are struck by the fact that nearly half the canon did not see print until 1623. Most of the other half seems to have existed in some earlier primitive form varying considerably from the text eventually published in the First Folio. Under these circumstances, to inflexibly argue that so-and-so definitely wrote this or that is just silly.

Even if the Oxfordian theory one day proves to be incorrect, at least the debate will hopefully spur professional academics and performers to talk intelligently about the authorship issue, which is something they have largely failed to do thus far. Orthodox apologists complain that the question "has already been resolved" but "just won't go away," presumably due to the elitist conspiracy nuts that keep it alive. In reality, the Oxfordian theory would quickly fade into oblivion if these same apologists would just roll up their sleeves (for a change) and establish basic, comparative facts. For one, we often hear that other Elizabethan noblemen have biographical parallels to the canon rivaling de Vere's, but when pressed for specific examples, defenders of orthodoxy suddenly find it more convenient to attack one's motives for asking questions in the first place. It would be refreshing to see a serious quantitative study in which, say, two hundred biographical parallels with de Vere also apply to another single personage. For example, was anybody else known to have been involved with bed-tricks? The same applies for Shakespeare's source material. Did anyone besides de Vere go out as a teenager and buy Plutarch in French? A book smaller than this volume showing similar connections between the Bard's favorite works and another Elizabethan personality would do considerable damage to the Oxfordian movement. Then we could all stop being heretics and go back to normal. Is it such an unreasonable thing to request?

Let us pretend for a moment that it was proven beyond a reasonable doubt that Shakespeare the writer was Will Shakspere of Stratford-upon-Avon. Perhaps a manuscript is discovered or something like that. The next question that should naturally arise in everyone's mind is *why was Shakespeare thinking of de Vere's life in almost every single work?* Did they know each other? One would think. Was license for this given? Either that or Will Shakspere was receiving big-time protection from someone. Even if we assume that Will Shakspere was the true author or main author, the questions regarding de Vere's extensive connections to the canon must still be addressed. Specifically, we should know whether these were purely coincidental or not. In a similar manner, if the Oxfordian theory were to be suddenly and unexpectedly proven correct, how could one still ignore the role of Will Shakspere?

It may be that even greater pitfalls attach to a widespread acceptance of the Oxfordian theory. Bardolators may choose to replace one myth with another, in which case the initial effort would have been wasted. If one cannot replace a myth with something superior then it is better not to bother. For example, writing in regard to the early growth of Christianity (in some respects, a good analogy),[4] British historian Edward Gibbon noted that the early church often found it more feasible to adapt pagan superstitions to its own use, rather than completely disregard them:

> The decline of ancient prejudice exposed a very numerous portion of human kind to the danger of a painful and comfortless situation. A state of skepticism and suspense may amuse a few inquisitive minds. But the practice of superstition is so congenial to the multitude that, if they are forcibly awakened, they still regret the loss of their pleasing vision.... So urgent on the vulgar is the necessity of believing that the fall of any system

of mythology will most probably be succeeded by the introduction of some other mode
of superstition.[5]

Apart from Gibbon's snooty reference to "the vulgar," this same principle applies to the
Shakespeare authorship question. Even if de Vere were widely accepted as the true Bard,
this might entail glossing over his unattractive qualities or worse, deterring newcomers
from reading Shakespeare because the true author was such a loose canon. The net result
would be that students of Shakespeare are left with yet another misinterpretation of the
text and more distortions, perhaps even worse that the current paradigms. The purpose
of literary biography, after all, is to enhance our understanding and appreciation of the
works, not to soothe our own prejudices.

If forced to look into our crystal ball, our forecast would be cautiously optimistic
from an Oxfordian point of view. Barring any sensational documentary discoveries that
would settle the authorship issue once and forever (unlikely to occur with limited fund-
ing), we would wager that interest in this topic will continue to grow at a slow but steady
pace. Among those who love Shakespeare's works, the number of skeptics (and within
that subset, Oxfordians) will probably increase. Opposed to this group will be orthodox
academics and other traditionalists who fiercely need a Bard that is a sympathetic voice
of the common man and an uplifting role model for aspiring mediocrity everywhere. On
the other hand, we could do a lot worse: people could stop reading and enjoying Shakespeare altogether. Besides, even if the Oxfordian theory is correct, this does not signal
the demise of all human sympathy found within the canon. The text is the text—if anything, it makes us appreciate this quality even more. As Lear goes mad upon the heath,
he cries out in anguish, "O, I have ta'en too little care of this!" (III.iv.32), meaning those
less fortunate than himself. The 17th Earl of Oxford, in spite of his innumerable personal
failings, saw fit to mingle with writers and artists who were way below his own social status, for which they were expressly and repeatedly grateful. As one recent Oxfordian convert told us, de Vere makes a lousy poster boy for snobs.

> *"By my faith as a knight errant," replied Don Quixote, "when I saw this cart I thought
> I was about to have some grand adventure, but now I must say that a man needs to touch
> mere appearances with his hand, to keep from being deceived. Go with God, good folk,
> and put on your play, and keep in mind that, should there be anything useful I can do
> for you, please command me and I will do it most willingly, for I have been all my life a
> devoted play-goer, and indeed as a young man I was particularly fascinated by everything
> theatrical."*
>
> —Cervantes, *Don Quixote* [1615][6]

Notes

Introduction

1. Montaigne, p. 605.
2. Greenwood, *Is There a Shakespeare Problem?*, p. 291. A few pages later, Greenwood sardonically added, "But let us not use the word [genius] as a magic wand or cabalistic sign, just to save us the trouble of thinking further" (p. 297).
3. See "Carmel Hosts SOS Conference," *Shakespeare Oxford Newsletter* (Shakespeare Oxford Society), Fall 2001, pp. 1, 3. Dr. Shuttleworth belongs to a small but growing number of openly Oxfordian university professors in this country.
4. Reminiscent of Winston Churchill's sly response when offered a copy of *"Shakespeare" Identified*: "I don't like to have my myths tampered with." See Ogburn, p. 162.
5. Take for example the 20th century American songwriting genius Cole Porter, who, despite having perhaps the most sophisticated background ever brought to bear on popular culture, was always (and wisely) at pains to cultivate his false public image as an unaffected country boy from Indiana.
6. This was Grant's first major literary effort, written at an advanced age as he was dying of cancer.
7. The proposed candidacy of Francis Bacon, which reached its zenith during the late 19th century, has been gradually if not totally eclipsed by the Oxfordian theory, first proposed in 1920.
8. Twain, p. 422.
9. This is the very first definite, printed mention of Shakespeare as a playwright, with three play quartos expressly credited to his name appearing that same year.
10. Schoenbaum, *Compact Life*, pp. 49, 74.
11. From Greenwood's *The Shakespeare Problem Restated* as quoted by Twain, p. 436.
12. By this time Will Shakspere appears to have made a lot of money, buying New Place, the second largest house in Stratford, to which he would later retire and dabble in various non-theatrical investment activities.
13. The frequently hyphenated form of the name William "Shake-speare" from that era has also suggested a pseudonym to many readers.
14. Nelson, p. 190. See also Ward, p. 163.
15. Schoenbaum, *Compact Life*, pp. 200–201. See also Ogburn, pp. 104–105.
16. Schoenbaum, *Compact Life*, pp. 306–313.
17. Chambers, *William Shakespeare*, Vol. II, pp. 504–506.
18. No one has ever disputed Will Shakspere's business acumen. It is typically assumed that the triple threat of playwright, actor, and theater shareholder, combined with frugality and shrewd investments, made him a

wealthy man. The problem with this would-be reassuring thought is that the arithmetic does not work (see Schoenbaum, *Compact Life*, pp. 211–212). Typical wages for these then-fledgling professions do not even begin to approach Shakespeare's later affluence. Additional patronage is the only reasonable explanation. Once again, there are no records, although there is a fascinating legend that Shakspere received £1,000 from the Earl of Southampton (see Schoenbaum, *Compact Life*, pp. 178–179) an extraordinary sum and equal to the annuity granted Edward de Vere by Queen Elizabeth in 1586.
19. Schoenbaum, *Compact Life*, pp. 291–292. See also Ogburn, pp. 117–118.
20. Some rumors of Shakespeare's lost papers finally began to surface during the 18th century, approximately 100 years after his death. See Schoenbaum, *Compact Life*, pp. 305–306.
21. Schoenbaum, *Compact Life*, pp. 237–239. Schoenbaum flatly states the letter was never sent (p. 238).
22. Montaigne, p. 368.
23. For "Sweet Swan of Avon," see Chapter 32. For Shakespeare's "Stratford monument," see Chapter 18.
24. Schoenbaum, *Lives*, p. 57. Schoenbaum (p. 127) was rightfully perplexed by Basse's title "*One* [emphasis added] Mr. Wm. Shakespeare." See also Ogburn, pp. 40–41, 231.
25. Ramón Jiménez, "Camden, Drayton, Greene, Hall, and Cooke: Five Eyewitnesses Who Saw Nothing," *Shakespeare Oxford Newsletter* (Shakespeare Oxford Society), Fall 2002, pp. 1, 12–16.
26. For the period 1605–1612, arguable and fragmentary references to Will Shakspere in London are restricted to the testimony of others given years after his death. For example, his leasehold interest in Blackfriar's Theatre circa 1608 (assuming this necessitated his physical presence there) is based on legal testimony recorded in 1619. Chambers, *William Shakespeare*, Vol. II, p. 52.
27. If Will Shakspere was in Stratford-upon-Avon during this period, we are at a loss to give another example of a commercially successful playwright (or commercially successful anything) so far removed from his base of operations in a time and place in which horse, foot, and boat were the only travel options.
28. Whalen (quoting Schoenbaum), p. 12.
29. This scarcity is exacerbated if posthumous records and recollections are discounted.
30. Montaigne, p. 280.
31. James also refered to the traditional Shakespeare as a "fraud." See Ogburn, pp. 54, 152.
32. Merilee Karr, "Semiotics and the Shakespeare Authorship Debate," *Shakespeare Oxford Newsletter* (Shakespeare Oxford Society), Winter 2001, p. 13.

33. Joe Sharkey, "On the Road: A Retro Look at Flying and a Ghostwriter's Ruse," *The New York Times* (May 13, 2003).

34. Nevertheless, England was in many ways more progressive than the rest of Europe.

35. For example, it is now well known that much of the popular movie *Ben-Hur* (1959) was written by Gore Vidal, reportedly well paid for his services yet never receiving any official credit.

36. Shakespeare's biography is usually ignored when studying his works, but to study drama by a modern playwright such as Eugene O'Neill or Tennessee Williams without any reference to the life of the author is considered absurd.

37. This is evidenced during the Elizabethan and Jacobean periods by the frequent use of phonetically spelled prefixes to the name, such as "Shak-," "Shack-," "Shag-," "Shax-," etc.

38. Richard Whalen, author of *Shakespeare: Who Was He?*, has eloquently stressed the need for this distinction (p. xvi).

39. Schoenbaum, *Compact Life*, p. 25.

40. Price, pp. 301–305.

Chapter 1

1. Wilson discussed by Chambers, *William Shakespeare*, Vol. I, p. 492.

2. *Riverside*, p. 1656.

3. De Vere, too, experienced the loss of an only son in 1583—a victim of infant mortality. See Nelson (pp. 289–290) and Ward (p. 232).

4. John Thomas Looney, father of the Oxfordian theory, went to great lengths to explain why he thought *The Tempest* had not been written by Edward de Vere. See Looney, pp. 429–453. This, however, has always been an isolated view among Oxfordians.

5. Matus, pp. 158–160.

6. Joseph Hunter, *A Disquisition on the Scene, Origin, Date, etc. etc. of Shakespeare's* Tempest (London: C. Whittingham, 1839), pp. 32–53. See also Price, pp. 281–285.

7. Nelson, p. 10. See also Ward, p. 11.

8. *DNB*, Vol. X, p. 27.

9. Karl Elze, "The Date of *The Tempest*," from *Essays on Shakespeare*, translated by L. Dora Schmitz (London: MacMillan and Co., 1874), pp. 6–9.

10. Bullough, Vol. VIII, pp. 248–249.

11. Bullough, Vol. VIII, pp. 245–248.

12. Munday's Euphuistic works, also influential on Shakespeare, were associated with de Vere as well.

13. Ward, pp. 200–202.

14. Chambers, *William Shakespeare*, Vol. I, pp. 493–494.

15. Bullough, Vol. VIII, pp. 249–250.

16. Nelson, p. 53.

17. Montaigne, p. 7.

18. Ward, pp. 20–21, 101. See also Ogburn, pp. 540, 741–742.

19. Clark, pp. 592–593.

20. Bullough, Vol. VIII, pp. 253–255. See also Nelson, p. 383.

21. Ward, pp. 164–177. See also Nelson (pp. 195–200) and Ward (pp. 300–301).

22. Palmer, p.187.

23. Nelson, p. 369. See also Ward, p. 330.

24. Clark, p. 589.

25. Ogburn, p. 740.

26. Otto J. Scott, *James I* (New York: Mason/Charter, 1976), p. 276.

27. Recently, the date of de Vere's death in the year 1604 has come into legitimate question. See Paul, *Monument Without a Tomb*.

28. Ogburn, p. 742.

29. "put away your feeble pen" (translated from Latin), Nelson, p. 181. See also Ward, p. 157.

30. Ogburn, pp. 221–222.

31. Edmund Malone, *Plays and Poems of William Shakespeare*, Vol. XV (London: C. Baldwin, 1821), p. 3.

32. Joseph Hunter, *Disquisition*, pp. 17–18. See also Ogburn, p. 388.

33. David Riggs, *Ben Jonson: A Life* (Cambridge: Harvard University Press, 1989), p. xi ("Sites associated with Jonson's life") and p. 10. See also E.H. Sugden, *A Topological Dictionary to the Works of Shakespeare and His Fellow Dramatists* (Manchester: Manchester University Press, 1925), p. 58.

34. Ogburn, p. 389.

35. Paul H. Altrocchi, "Aeolian Stinking Pitch: Tempestuous Shipwreck on the Island of Vulcano," *The Shakespeare Oxford Newsletter* (Shakespeare Oxford Society), Summer 2003, pp. 3, 18–20.

36. Hunter, *Disquisition* p. 18.

37. This book belonged to Burghley's library. See Jolly, "Burghley's Library," pp. 11–12.

38. Ward, pp. 340–342. See also Nelson, p. 419.

39. Ogburn, p. 783.

Chapter 2

1. Cervantes, p. 326.

2. Bloom, pp. 36–40.

3. See Chambers (Vol. I, pp. 329–330) and Bullough (Vol. I, p. 203).

4. Chambers, *William Shakespeare*, Vol. I, p. 330.

5. *Riverside*, p. 178. Curiously, Cervantes also adapted a version of this tale for his story of Cardenio in *Don Quixote*. See also Chambers (*William Shakespeare*, Vol. I, p. 331) and Bullough (Vol. I, p. 206).

6. Ogburn (quoting Chambers), pp. 661–662.

7. According to Francis Meres and George Puttenham, presumed author of *The Arte of English Poesie*.

8. One of the earliest to recognize this was John Thomas Looney, father of the Oxfordian theory (Looney, p. 223). See also Chambers (*William Shakespeare*, Vol. I, p. 331).

9. Yet a third, earlier, lost, and anonymous play, *A History of the Duke of Millayn and the Marques of Mantua*, was performed at Whitehall on December 26, 1579, and was viewed by Oxfordian Eva Turner Clark as a possible earlier version of *Two Gentlemen*. This was the same year (1579) that de Vere himself was recorded as acting in a court performance. *Duke of Millayn* was performed by the Lord Chamberlain's Men, later to become Shakespeare's principal acting company. At that time, the Lord Chamberlain was Thomas Radcliffe, Earl of Sussex, and de Vere's mentor (Clark, p. 298).

10. *Riverside*, p. 1995.

11. De Vere left Italy in 1576.

12. See Chambers (*William Shakespeare*, Vol. I, p. 331) and Bullough (Vol. I, p. 208).

13. Many of the Italian Renaissance playwrights who invented modern drama, such as Flaminio Scala, Luigi Pasqualigo, and Alessandro Piccolomini, were noblemen. That a similar phenomenon may have occurred in England (instigated by a contemporary of the Italians who may have even come into contact with them) is apparently too disagreeable a possibility for orthodox academics to contemplate.

14. Bullough, Vol. I, p. 208.

15. Bullough, Vol. I, p. 207.

16. *Riverside*, p. 178. See also Chambers (*William Shakespeare*, Vol. I, p. 331) and Bullough (Vol. I, pp. 204–206).

17. Launce is traveling west from Verona to Milan, while Padua is east of Verona; hence many editions (such as *Riverside*) change "Padua" to "Milan."

18. Ogburn (quoting Chambers), p. 302.

19. Ogburn (quoting Grillo), p. 302.

20. The Cole Porter song "We Open in Venice" from *Kiss Me, Kate* comes to mind.

21. Shakespeare also referred to Milan as a port city in *The Tempest* (I.ii.144–145).

22. The Brenta has been immortalized by many writers, including Goethe, Byron, and probably (though not by name) in Act V of Shakespeare's *The Merchant of Venice.*

23. Grillo, p. 142. Canals were obviously not the fastest way to travel but were more comfortable and secure from brigands than the highways.

24. Sir Eglamour seems to be a sort of forerunner (or homage?) to Cervante's Don Quixote.

25. This same illustration depicts mountains not far from Mantua, possibly those referred to by Shakespeare. When in Mantua this writer asked Dr. Noemi Magri if she thought it odd that the Bard wrote about traveling to Milan by boat and her reply was: "Do you think it odd traveling to Chicago by boat?"

26. Noemi Magri, "No Errors in Shakespeare: Historical Truth and *The Two Gentlemen of Verona,*" *De Vere Society Newsletter* (De Vere Society), May 1998. As for the Milanese canals, traffic was controlled by floodgates designed by Leonardo da Vinci. For a good discussion, see Lambin, pp. 429–448.

27. Braun and Hogenberg's *Civitates Orbis Terrarum* represents one of the great Renaissance achievements in cartography.

28. Among others, the author recommends *Milan and Turin*, Antony Shugaar, Translator (Milan: Touring Club of Italy, 1997).

29. Ogburn (quoting Karl Elze), p. 304.

30. Amy Freed's play *The Beard of Avon* is one example.

Chapter 3

1. The other one is *King Lear.*

2. Chambers, *William Shakespeare*, Vol. I, pp. 426–427.

3. Bullough, Vol. II, p. 3.

4. This was St. George's Day and Will Shakspere's (estimated) 33rd birthday.

5. *Riverside*, p. 320.

6. Bullough, Vol. II, p. 3.

7. See Chambers (*William Shakespeare*, Vol. I, p. 437) and Bullough (Vol. II, pp. 4–5).

8. Bullough, Vol. II, pp. 8–9.

9. Brazil, pp. 123–124. See also Bullough, Vol. II, pp. 17–18.

10. Brazil, pp. 119–120.

11. Stritmatter, pp. 102–103.

12. Bullough, Vol. II, p. 18.

13. Nelson, p. 239.

14. Brazil, pp. 120–122. See also Nelson, pp. 247–248.

15. Chambers, *William Shakespeare*, Vol. I, p. 3.

16. Schoenbaum, *Compact Life*, p. 97.

17. Schoenbaum, *Compact Life*, p. 101.

18. A detailed account of this legend is given by Schoenbaum (*Compact Life*, pp. 97–109), who loved it as much as we do. Chambers also discusses it at length (*William Shakespeare*, Vol. I, pp. 18–21). Today one can visit a deer park at Charlecote Place, the magnificent country estate of Sir Thomas Lucy and (along with Billesley Manor) one of the most worthwhile tourist sites in the vicinity of Stratford-upon-Avon.

19. At least one Warwickshire monument, however, has been identified in which Lucy's three heraldic luces have been quartered or multiplied times four, thus equaling the 12 luces alluded to in *Merry Wives.*

20. Brazil, p. 129.

21. Schoenbaum, *Compact Life*, pp. 100, 107.

22. Brazil, p. 129.

23. Ward, p. 192. See also Nelson, p. 84.

24. Nelson, pp. 84–86, 246, 391. De Vere's bear-related activities call to mind Slender's recollection in *Merry Wives* that he had witnessed "Sackerson" the bear perform on several occasions (I.i.295).

25. Brazil, pp. 125–128.

26. Brazil, p. 126.

27. Nelson, p. 367.

28. Brazil, p. 125.

29. Neslon, p. 319.

30. Ward (quoting Courthope), p. 175. A paraphrase of this line also concludes the libretto of Verdi's opera.

Chapter 4

1. Montaigne, p. 1216.

2. See Chambers (*William Shakespeare*, Vol. I, pp. 452–453) and Bullough (Vol. II, p. 399).

3. See Chambers (*William Shakespeare*, Vol. I, p. 453) and Bullough (Vol. II, p. 399).

4. Philip Herbert, along with his brother William, would later be the co-dedicatees of the First Folio.

5. Nelson, p. 429.

6. Chambers, *William Shakespeare*, Vol. II, p. 331.

7. *Riverside*, p. 579.

8. *Riverside*, p. 579.

9. The Geneva translation reads "and with what measure ye mete, it shall be measured unto you again." See *Riverside*, p. 579.

10. Asimov, Vol. I, p. 635.

11. See Chambers (*William Shakespeare*, Vol. I, p. 457) and Bullough (Vol. II, pp. 401–402).

12. For example, Shakespeare (like Cinthio and unlike other versions) introduces the idea of substituting a hardened criminal for execution in the place of Claudio (IV.ii).

13. Bullough, Vol. II, pp. 402–403.

14. Jolly, "Burghley's Library," p. 12.

15. See Chambers (*William Shakespeare*, Vol. I, pp. 454, 457) and Bullough (Vol. II, pp. 403–404).

16. For example, Lucio in the play mentions the legend of Pygmalion (III.ii.45) from Ovid's *Metamorphoses*, a book closely associated with de Vere's family through his uncle Arthur Golding.

17. Bullough, Vol. II, p. 406.

18. *DNB*, Vol. XX, pp. 1361–1362.

19. See Chambers (*William Shakespeare*, Vol. I, p. 457) and Bullough (Vol. II, p. 405).

20. E.N.S. Thompson considered Whetstone and Rankins as among the "insincere disputants" who loudly and piously criticized the theaters while simultaneously trying to write successful plays. See Thompson, pp. 87–88.

21. *DNB*, Vol. XX, pp. 1360–1362.

22. Tonart was then rescued on the scaffold by an angry mob and later pardoned by the king. This was also the same period when Montaigne was writing his *Essays.*

23. Holmes, pp. 17–25. See also Sobran, p. 186.

24. Holmes, pp. 17–25.

25. This information specifically came from letters to Walsingham by William Brooke, Lord Cobham, the Puritan sympathizer (see Lambin, p. 494), whose renowned ancestor Sir John Oldcastle would receive an outrageous send-up by the Bard as Sir John Falstaff.

26. One Englishman who did visit Vienna was Philip Sidney, whose nephew Philip Herbert was married to de Vere's daughter the day after the premiere of *Measure for Measure.* See *DNB*, Vol. XVIII, p. 222.

Cinthio had set the story in Innsbruck, Austria (see

Bullough Vol. II, p. 407), a city de Vere may have visited on his way to Italy, but Shakespeare moved the action to Vienna—a compliment to the bridegroom's family, perhaps?

27. Nelson, pp. 280–287. See also Ward, pp. 227–228.
28. *Riverside*, p. 580.
29. Ogburn, pp. 575–576.
30. It is sometimes argued that the "bed-trick" was a "common" plot device. Other than Shakespeare's occasional source Boccaccio (not translated into English during Shakespeare's time but belonging to Lord Burghley's library), we would welcome some other specific examples. Even if one or two other examples existed, however, that would not make it "common."
31. Alexander, p. 97.
32. Twain, p. 412.
33. De Vere served as a juror in the treason trials of Thomas Howard, Duke of Norfolk, in 1571, Mary Queen of Scots in 1586, and Robert Devereaux, Earl of Essex, in 1601, just to give a few examples.
34. Bullough, Vol. II, p. 416.
35. Bullough, Vol. II, p. 417.
36. *Riverside*, p. 585.
37. See Paul, pp. 37, 39, 41, 47, 49.
38. Chambers, *Elizabethan Stage*, Vol. I, p. 262. de Vere's son-in-law William Stanley is also recorded as having been involved with the Children of Paul's. See Nelson, p. 393. This was a descendent of the same acting troupe disbanded during Elizabeth's time for portraying the Puritan advocate Martin Marprelate on stage with a cock's comb, wolf's belly, and ape's face. See Thompson, p. 199.
39. Heinemann, p. 284.
40. *Riverside*, p. 581.
41. Among the seven Shakespeare plays performed during these festivities, three (*Measure for Measure*, *The Merchant of Venice*, and *The Comedy of Errors*) were expressly credited to "Shaxberd", while four others (*Othello*, *The Merry Wives of Windsor*, *Love's Labor's Lost*, and *Henry V*) listed no author of record. See Chambers, *William Shakespeare*, Vol. II, pp. 331–332.

Chapter 5

1. Montaigne, p. 461.
2. See Chambers (*William Shakespeare*, Vol. I, pp. 305, 307) and Bullough (Vol. I, p. 3). See also *Riverside*, p. 112.
3. Chambers, *William Shakespeare*, Vol. II, p. 194.
4. See Chambers (*William Shakespeare*, Vol. I, p. 310) and Bullough (Vol. I, p. 3). See also *Riverside*, pp. 111–112.
5. See Chambers (*William Shakespeare*, Vol. I, p. 308) and Bullough (Vol. I, p. 3). See also *Riverside* (pp. 111–112) and Clark (p. 151).
6. See Chambers (*William Shakespeare*, Vol. I, p. 311) and Bullough (Vol. I, pp. 3–4).
7. Chambers, *William Shakespeare*, Vol. I, p. 312.
8. *Riverside*, p. 111.
9. Jolly and O'Brien, p. 20.
10. See Chambers (*William Shakespeare*, Vol. I, p. 311) and Bullough (Vol. I, pp. 3–4). See also *Riverside*, p. 112.
11. Nelson, p. 157.
12. See Chambers (*William Shakespeare*, Vol. I, p. 311) and Bullough (Vol. I, pp. 10–11). See also *Riverside*, p. 11.
13. Nelson, p. 386.
14. Bullough, Vol. I, p. 9.
15. Schoenbaum, *Compact Life*, pp. 93–94.
16. Nelson, p. 41. Professor Nelson was skeptical because the uncle misstated de Vere's age and Mary was not mentioned in her father's legacies of 1552 and 1554 (pp. 23, 41).

17. See Staunton, Vol. I, p. 150.
18. Chambers, *William Shakespeare*, Vol. I, p. 310. See also Staunton, Vol. I, p. 112.
19. Nelson, p. 349. See also Ogburn, pp. 741–742.
20. *Riverside*, p. 113.
21. These names are intended to be confusing.
22. Nelson, p. 381.
23. Bullough, Vol. 1, pp. 9–10. Also recall that *The Historie of Error* was performed in 1577 by the Children of Paul's—an additional connection with this particular saint.
24. *Riverside*, p. 114.
25. See *The Poems of Shakespeare's Dark Lady*, introduction by A.L. Rowse.
26. *Riverside*, p. 112.
27. Nelson, p. 58, p. 62. See also Ward, pp. 49–50.
28. Bullough, Vol. 1, pp. 9–10.
29. Bullough, Vol. 1, pp. 9–10.
30. Bullough, Vol. I, p. 9.
31. Asimov, Vol. I, pp. 170–172.
32. Nelson, pp. 131, 137. See also Ward, pp. 111–112.
33. *Riverside*, p. 113.

Chapter 6

1. See Chambers (*William Shakespeare*, Vol. I, pp. 384–385) and Bullough (Vol. II, p. 61).
2. Chambers, *William Shakespeare*, p. 387.
3. Ogburn, p. 614.
4. See Chambers (*William Shakespeare*, Vol. I, p. 388) and Bullough (Vol. II, p. 68).
5. De Vere sponsored acting companies and playwrights, and was himself noted as an actor and playwright ("best for comedy," according to the *Arte of English Poesie* in 1589).
6. See Chambers (*William Shakespeare*, Vol. I, pp. 387–388) and Bullough (Vol. II, pp. 64–66).
7. See Chambers (*William Shakespeare*, Vol. I, p. 388) and Bullough (Vol. II, pp. 68–69, 134).
8. This was the same year that de Vere left Italy to return to England.
9. See Chambers (*William Shakespeare*, Vol. I, p. 388) and Bullough (Vol. II, pp. 63–64).
10. Nelson, p. 383. See also Ward, pp. 300–301.
11. Nelson, p. 287. See also Ward, pp. 194–197.
12. Ogburn, p. 661.
13. See Chambers (*William Shakespeare*, Vol. I, p. 388) and Bullough (Vol. II, pp. 78–79).
14. Nelson, p. 237. See also Ward, pp. 80–83.
15. Nelson, pp. 131, 137. See also Ward, pp. 111–112.
16. See "Shakespeare? He's One of Us, Say Italians," *The Times of London*, April 8, 2000.
17. Asimov, Vol. I, p. 548.
18. The monsters were allegories for the very real rocks and whirlpools that made the Straits of Messina a risky passage for ancient mariners.
19. Cervantes, p. 261.
20. See Lambin, p. 207.
21. Bullough, Vol. II, p. 81.
22. *Riverside*, pp. 364–365.
23. Price, pp. 68–77. See also Ogburn, pp. 74–75.
24. This is translated from the Latin *Non sans droit*. See Schoenbaum, *Compact Life*, pp. 227–232.
25. Chambers, *William Shakespeare*, Vol. I, p. 387. For a common-born playwright to portray a living nobleman on the public stage, no matter how flatteringly, especially in comic role, would certainly have been to risk imprisonment, at the very least.
26. Nelson, p. 266. See also Ogburn, pp. 646–647.
27. Looney/Miller, p. 562.
28. Ogburn, p. 661.

Chapter 7

1. Cervantes, p. 476.
2. See Chambers (*William Shakespeare*, Vol. I, pp. 331–332) and Bullough (Vol. I, p. 425). Also appearing in 1598 under Shakespeare's name were *Richard II* and *Richard III*.
3. *Riverside*, p. 1970.
4. Bullough, Vol. I, p. 425.
5. Londré (quoting Carroll), p. 5.
6. This was Jehande de Simier, who was soliciting the hand of Queen Elizabeth in marriage on behalf of his master François de Valois. Elizabeth, like the ladies in *Love's Labor's Lost*, eventually sent all of her suitors packing.
7. Clark, p. 214.
8. Londré, pp. 327–328. De Vere, according to a 17th-century *tirata*, once made a cameo appearance on stage in Italy as a jouster and was defeated in similar fashion by his leading lady. See Ogburn (pp. 549–550) and Nelson (p. 140).
9. Londré, p. 13.
10. Bullough, Vol. I, pp. 426–427.
11. Chambers, *William Shakespeare*, Vol. I, p. 338.
12. Marguerite's memoirs were not published until long after Shakespeare's play had appeared.
13. Londré, pp. 328–329. See also Chambers (*William Shakespeare*, Vol. I, pp. 337–338), Bullough (Vol. I, pp. 428–431), and *Riverside*, p. 209.
14. Two years after Lefranc proposed Stanley, the Oxfordian theory was put forth in 1920 by John Thomas Looney, advocating Stanley's father-in-law Edward de Vere as the true Bard. The historical Navarre connection to Shakespeare's play appears to be an example of a hypothesis made by an anti–Stratfordian that was later widely adopted by orthodox scholars.
15. Nelson, p. 349. See also Ogburn, pp. 741–742.
16. Bullough, Vol. I, p. 428.
17. Bullough, Vol. I, p. 434.
18. Nelson, p. 53. See also Ward, p. 33.
19. Londré, p. 6.
20. Ward, p. 187. See also Nelson, p. 239.
21. Ogburn, p. 627. See also Ward, p. 187.
22. Ogburn, p. 774. See also Nelson, p. 238.
23. Londré, p. 6.
24. Londré, p. 8.
25. Chambers, *William Shakespeare*, Vol. I, pp. 335–336. See also Londré, p. 328. Yet again, this is one year before the *Maske of Amasones* was performed at court.
26. Jiménez, pp. 141–142. See also Nelson (pp. 49, 238, 328–330) and Ward (pp. 28–30, 301–303).
27. See Chambers (*William Shakespeare*, Vol. I, p. 336) and Bullough (Vol. I, pp. 426–427).
28. Londré, pp. 333–334.
29. Mantua, a city that fascinated Shakespeare (based on the number of allusions), was located directly on the canal route between Venice and Milan, two cities in which de Vere's presence was documented.
30. Londré, pp. 330–331 (citing Looney, Vol. I, pp. 248–250).
31. See Chambers (*William Shakespeare*, Vol. I, p. 337) and Bullough (Vol. I, pp. 426–427).
32. De Vere's daughter Susan would marry Philip Sidney's nephew Philip Herbert. Part of these wedding celebrations included a revival performance of *Love's Labor's Lost*. See *Riverside*, p. 2010.
33. Ogburn, pp. 614–615.
34. Nelson, p. 190. See also Ward, p. 163. This was two months after the *Maske of Amasones*.
35. Chambers, *William Shakespeare*, Vol. I, pp. 334–335. See III.i.196–197.

36. Montaigne, *On Schoolmasters' Learning* (1580), pp. 150–151.
37. Chambers, *William Shakespeare*, Vol. I, pp. 335, 337. De Vere and Sidney are also probably represented in this work by the poetic rivals "Willie" and "Perigot," respectively. See Ogburn, pp. 622–623.
38. Looney, Vol. I, pp. 243–245. See also *DNB*, Vol. IX, p. 83.
39. The cumulative weight of events dating from 1578 to 1580 that relate to *Love's Labor's Lost* should appear impressive even to the most staunch authorship traditionalist.
40. Nelson, p. 181. See also Ward, pp. 156–158.
41. Nelson, pp. 225–226. See also Ward, pp. 189–190.
42. Nelson, pp. 225–226. See also Ward, pp. 189–190.
43. Londré, p. 332.
44. It has been observed that Shakespeare's Don Armado is more a precursor to Cervantes' Don Quixote than a descendent of the braggart-soldier or *capitano* in *commedia dell' arte*. See Asimov, Vol. I, p. 432.

Chapter 8

1. Montaigne, p. 197.
2. *Riverside*, p. 251.
3. This does not include the murky, ambiguous, and less-than-complimentary notice given in *Greene's Groatsworth of Wit* (1592).
4. Nelson, p. 386. See also Ward, p. 264.
5. See Chambers (*William Shakespeare*, Vol. I, pp. 356–363) and Bullough (Vol. I, p. 367).
6. Bullough, Vol. I, p. 367.
7. See Chambers (*William Shakespeare*, Vol. I, pp. 358–359) and Ward (citing Chambers), p. 318.
8. Chambers, *William Shakespeare*, Vol. I, p. 362.
9. Bullough, Vol. I, p. 368.
10. See Chambers (*William Shakespeare*, Vol. I, pp. 363) and Bullough (Vol. I, pp. 368–369).
11. Nelson, p. 53. See also Ward, p. 33.
12. Jolly and O'Brien, "Shakespeare's Sources," p. 20.
13. Chambers, *William Shakespeare*, Vol. I, pp. 531.
14. Chambers, *William Shakespeare*, Vol. I, pp. 528–529.
15. Bloom, p. 695.
16. Chambers, *William Shakespeare*, Vol. I, pp. 531–532.
17. Katherine Chiljan, "Oxford and *Palamon and Arcite*," *Shakespeare Oxford Newsletter* (Shakespeare-Oxford Society), Spring 1999, pp. 10–13.
18. Nelson, p. 78. See also Ward, p. 89.
19. See Paul, *Monument Without a Tomb*.
20. Nelson, p. 10. See also Ward, p. 11.
21. Bullough, Vol. I, p. 370.
22. *Riverside*, p. 251. De Vere, it should be added, was fluent in French.
23. Schoenbaum, *Compact Life*, p. 116.
24. Chambers, *William Shakespeare*, Vol. I, p. 358. Also, in *Twelfth Night* there is a reference to Arion on a dolphin's back (I.i.15), but he is not singing.
25. Chambers, *William Shakespeare*, Vol. I, p. 363.
26. Staunton, Vol. I, p. 339.
27. Ogburn, p. 719.
28. Bullough, Vol. VIII, pp. 253–255. See also Nelson, p. 383.
29. Ogburn, p. 622.
30. Titania, in wonderment, recollects, "Methought I was enamour'd of an ass" (IV.i.77).
31. Bullough, Vol. I, p. 371.
32. *DNB*, Vol. XVII, p. 1001.
33. Bullough, Vol. I, pp. 372–373.
34. Apuleius, *The Golden Ass*, William Adlington, translator with revisions by G. Gaselee (Cambridge, MA: Harvard University Press, 1971), p. viii.

35. See also *Much Ado About Nothing* (III.v.16). Dogberry is also sensitive about being called an ass (IV.ii.73–78).

36. *Riverside*, p. 251.

37. Bullough, Vol. I, p. 374.

38. Chambers, *William Shakespeare*, Vol. I, p. 360.

39. *Riverside*, p. 252.

40. Nelson, pp. 337, 345.

41. *DNB*, Vol. XV, p. 856.

Chapter 9

1. See Chambers (Vol. I, *William Shakespeare*, pp. 368–374) and Bullough (Vol. I, pp. 445–446).

2. These are probable references to Shylock and Portia's two unsuccessful suitors.

3. Clark, p. 331. See also Bullough, Vol. I, pp. 445–446.

4. Chambers believed that there had been "several probable intermediate handlings by various dramatists" and "a revision by Shakespeare in 1594" (*William Shakespeare*, Vol. I, p. 371). Bullough adds that "*The Jew* may have been Shakespeare's source" (Vol. I, p. 446).

5. These were Francis Meres in *Palladis Tamia* (1598) and the author (George Puttenham?) of *The Arte of English Poesie* (1589).

6. This is yet another relationship in the canon that seems to go beyond conventional male friendship.

7. See Chambers (*William Shakespeare*, Vol. I, p. 373) and Bullough (Vol. I, p. 446).

8. Price, p. 249. Another acknowledged source for the play, according to Chambers (*William Shakespeare*, Vol. I, p. 373) and Bullough (Vol. I, pp. 452–454), is *Zelauto* (1580), written by de Vere's servant Anthony Munday, who lavishly dedicated this work to Oxford. See also Nelson (p. 238) and Ward (p. 187).

9. John Paul Stevens, "The Shakespeare Canon of Statutory Construction" (Vol. 140, *University of Pennsylvania Law Review*, 1373), p. 1385 (1992). Justice Stevens, incidentally, is known for his Oxfordian authorship beliefs (Ogburn, p. 524).

10. Bloom, p. 171.

11. Edith Z. Friedler, "Shakespeare's Contribution to the Teaching of Comparative Law: Some Reflections on *The Merchant of Venice*" (Vol. 60, *Louisiana Law Review*, 1087), pp. 1091–1093 (2000).

12. Gibbon, Vol. II, p. 1472.

13. Friedler, "Shakespeare's Contribution," p. 1096.

14. Alexander, pp. 57–58.

15. Alexander, pp. 98–100.

16. See the comprehensive discussion by attorney Daniel Kornstein in *Kill All the Lawyers?* (Princeton University Press, 1994), pp. 230–238.

17. Similar training has been conjectured for Will Shakspere, but there is no evidence.

18. See Nelson (p. 46) and Ward (p. 27). Similar to Charles Dickens, de Vere was exposed to the law as a young man but did not become a lawyer. For legal education, Gray's Inn was perhaps the most prestigious institution of its time.

19. Whalen, pp. 106–107. See also Nelson (pp. 186–189) and Ward (pp. 236–243).

20. Holmes, pp. 105–106.

21. The most spectacular example of this was de Vere's £1,000 royal annuity grant of 1586.

22. This was the play that first suggested to John Thomas Looney, father of the Oxfordian theory, that the true Shakespeare was more likely to have been someone like Edward de Vere. See Looney, p. 2.

23. Magri, "Places in Shakespeare: Belmont and Thereabouts," *de Vere Society Newsletter* (de Vere Society), June 2003, pp. 6–14.

24. Ogburn (quoting Karl Elze), p. 303.

Chapter 10

1. *Riverside*, p. 400.

2. See Chambers (*William Shakespeare*, Vol. I, pp. 401–402) and Bullough (Vol. II, p. 1).

3. Ogburn, p. 712. Billesley Manor is today a luxury hotel and one of the more memorable tourist sites in the Stratford area.

4. Charlotte Carmichael Stopes, *Shakespeare's Warwickshire Contemporaries* (Stratford-upon-Avon: Shakespeare Head Press, 1897), pp. 210–213.

5. Schoenbaum, *Compact Life*, pp. 234–240.

6. Nelson, p. 10.

7. Chambers, *William Shakespeare*, Vol. II, p. 329.

8. Schoenbaum, *Compact Life*, p. 167.

9. This tradition was first recorded during the 18th century. Its credibility wavers under scrutiny, the second-hand source purportedly being Shakspere's own aged brother, variously described in the documents as "stricken in years," "memory so weakened in infirmity," and of "weak intellects." See Chambers, *William Shakespeare*, Vol. II, pp. 278, 289.

10. Schoenbaum, *Compact Life*, pp. 231–232.

11. Schoenbaum, *Compact Life*, pp. 250–251.

12. Garber, p. 449.

13. Ogburn, pp. 734–735, citing Bronson Feldman from the *Shakespeare Fellowship Quarterly*, VIII, No. 3, Autumn 1947.

14. Bullough, Vol. II, p. 1.

15. Bullough, Vol. II, p. 158.

16. Furthermore, if the name "Shake-speare" itself was in fact a pseudonym, then one could not have chosen a more flattering name for a poet-playwright.

17. Londré, p. 6.

18. *DNB*, Vol. XII, pp. 63–64.

19. Asimov, Vol. I, p. 562.

20. Bullough, Vol. I, p. 145.

21. Ogburn, pp. 713–714.

22. *Riverside*, p. 400.

23. *Riverside*, p. 402.

24. Garber, p. 438.

25. Garber, p. 438.

26. Nelson, p. 78. See also Ward, p. 89.

27. This allusion could have also applied to de Vere, who found himself hemmed in by financial difficulties later in life, and may well have experienced a claustrophobic "reckoning" with his powerful benefactors.

28. Sobran, p. 104.

29. Christopher Paul, "This Strange Eventful History," *Shakespeare Oxford Newsletter* (Shakespeare Oxford Society), Summer 2002, pp. 1, 12–15, 24.

30. Clark, pp. 526, 528. See also Bullough, Vol. II, p. 155.

31. Collinson, p. 441.

32. Collinson, pp. 391–392.

33. Collinson, p. 295.

34. See the discussion by Anne Barton in her introduction for *Riverside*, p. 402.

35. A term coined by Northrop Frye.

36. *Riverside*, p. 400.

37. Bullough, Vol. II, p. 143.

38. These included family members and legal adversaries.

39. See Paul, *Monument Without a Tomb*.

40. This is also where de Vere's Trussell great-grandfather had come from, near Warwickshire.

41. Elizabeth had been at court at least since 1582, where she had been described in a letter as the "fair" Mistress Trentham. See Nelson (p. 336) and Ward (p. 307).

42. Nelson, pp. 336, 343. See also Ward, pp. 307, 313.
43. Nelson, pp. 336–337, 408. See also Ward, p. 307.

Chapter 11

1. Cervantes, p. 554.
2. A Wagnerian musical term approximately translating as "art encompassing all of the arts."
3. See Chambers (*William Shakespeare*, Vol. I, p. 328) and Bullough (Vol. I, p. 60). Chambers also informs us that a Stephen Sly was a ditch-digger in Stratford-upon-Avon for Shakspere's disreputable friend John Combe. During their abortive attempt to enclose public lands in 1615, Sly and Combe were confronted by the local magistrates, whom Combe contemptuously referred to as "puritan knaves" (Chambers, *William Shakespeare*, Vol. II, p. 144).
4. A conflation of William the Conqueror with his descendent Richard the Lion-Hearted.
5. Ogburn, pp. 746–747.
6. These themes would be further explored by Shakespeare in the comedies *Love's Labor's Lost, Much Ado About Nothing, Twelfth Night,* and *As You Like It.*
7. See Chambers (*William Shakespeare*, Vol. I, p. 322) and Bullough (Vol. I, p. 57).
8. Chambers, *William Shakespeare*, Vol. I, pp. 325, 328.
9. See Chambers (*William Shakespeare*, Vol. I, pp. 322–323) and Bullough (Vol. I, p. 57).
10. Bullough, Vol. I, p. 38.
11. Chambers, William Shakespeare, Vol. I, 324.
12. Bullough, Vol. I, p. 57.
13. Bullough, Vol. I, p. 38.
14. Chambers, *William Shakespeare*, Vol. I, p. 327. The sons of the Earl of Pembroke would later become the dedicatees of the First Folio, and one would marry de Vere's youngest daughter.
15. Clark, pp. 102, 107–108.
16. Two months later, in March 1579, de Vere himself acted in a production at court. See Nelson (p. 190) and Ward (p. 163).
17. Sobran, p. 5.
18. Bullough, Vol. I, p. 38.
19. Bullough, Vol. I, p. 38.
20. Nelson, p. 386.
21. Nelson, pp. 44–45.
22. *A Hundreth Sundrie Flowres*, p. 23.
23. *DNB*, Vol. VI, p. 543.
24. *A Hundreth Sundrie Flowres*, pp. 23, 50.
25. See Chambers (*William Shakespeare*, Vol. I, p. 328) and Bullough (Vol. I, p. 66).
26. *A Hundreth Sundrie Flowres*, p. 14.
27. See comprehensive discussion by Ward, pp. 130–144.
28. Bullough, Vol. I, pp. 61–62.
29. Reminiscent of Shakespeare's "Will" sonnets.
30. Bullough, Vol. I, p. 63.
31. Nelson, pp. 129–131. See also Ward, pp. 107–109.
32. Ogburn, p. 547.
33. Grillo, p. 125.
34. Nelson, p. 157.
35. Grillo, p. 141.
36. These two wives included Anne Cecil (in 1571) and Elizabeth Trentham (in 1591).
37. To give only one example, Henry Wriothesley, Earl of Southampton, effectively derailed his political career by prompting the queen's rage at his affair with and marriage to Elizabeth Vernon.
38. Nelson, pp. 40–41. See also Ward, pp. 7–8.
39. Nelson, p. 134.
40. See Ogburn (pp. 591–594) and Clark (pp. 102–104).

41. Nelson, p. 179. See also Ward, p. 154.
42. Nelson, p. 176. See also Ward, pp. 153–154.
43. Ogburn, p. 635. See also Clark, pp. 367–369.
44. Nelson, p. 180. See also Ward, p. 154.
45. Nelson, pp. 281–282. See also Ogburn, p. 651.
46. *Riverside*, p. 140.

Chapter 12

1. Chambers, *William Shakespeare*, Vol. I, p. 450. This is one of 12 Shakespeare plays named by Meres in *Palladus Tamia.*
2. *Riverside*, p. 536.
3. Chambers, *William Shakespeare*, Vol. I, p. 450.
4. Chambers, *William Shakespeare*, Vol. I, p. 450.
5. The "first Helen" was Helen of Troy, a connection made in Shakespeare's play (I.iii.69–79).
6. Ogburn, p. 617.
7. It is sometimes claimed that this is a typical Elizabethan plot device. Beyond Shakespeare and his source material, we believe this to be an overstatement.
8. *OED*, Vol. XIII, p. 186. The Elizabethans loved punning and multiple word meanings, unlike modern audiences who are, more often than not, annoyed by such things.
9. Ogburn, pp. 773–777.
10. Staunton, Vol. II, p. 3.
11. *DNB*, Vol. VII, p. 769.
12. See Chambers (*William Shakespeare*, Vol. I, p. 452) and Bullough (Vol. II, pp. 376–377).
13. Bullough, Vol. II, p. 376.
14. Jolly, "Burghley's Library," p. 12.
15. Chambers, *William Shakespeare*, Vol. I, p. 452.
16. This is also a line from *Romeo and Juliet* (I.i.13–14).
17. See Chambers (*William Shakespeare*, Vol. I, p. 450) and Bullough (Vol. II, p. 375). The First Folio uses the word "lustique."
18. Nelson, pp. 246–247, 391–392. During this same period, recent Stratford family man Will Shakspere is believed to have acquired a traveling jones. See Schoenbaum, *Compact Life*, Chapter 8.
19. Clark, pp. 120–121, citing Georges Lambin.
20. Nelson, p. 167. See also Ward, pp. 207–209.
21. This is a quote from Henry IV (i.e., "the Great"), who converted to raise the siege of Paris in 1593.
22. Nelson, p. 121. See also Ward, p. 101.
23. Ward, p. 21.
24. Clark, pp. 131–132. See also Nelson (p. 349) and Ogburn (pp. 741–742).
25. *Si pigliano per gli orecchi.* See Grillo, p. 98.
26. Nelson, p. 204.
27. See Chambers (*William Shakespeare*, Vol. I, p. 452) and Bullough (Vol. II, p. 377).
28. Gossip-monger John Aubrey recorded that de Vere, who was a reckless spendthrift, while in Florence lived in greater splendor than Duke Francesco. See Holmes, pp. 6–7.
29. Nelson, p. 205. See also Holmes, pp. 6–7.
30. Bullough, Vol. II, p. 385.
31. Clark, p. 115.
32. See discussion by Whalen, pp. 104–106.
33. Bullough, Vol. II, p. 381.
34. Clark, p. 122, citing Georges Lambin.
35. Similar to Gonzalo in *The Tempest* and Camillo in *The Winter's Tale.* In Act V, scene iii, a match between Bertram and Lafew's daughter is proposed; in real life, de Vere married Burghley's daughter. Although not Lafew's daughter in the play, Helena (Oxfordians believe) was modeled on Anne Cecil.
36. Bullough, Vol. II, p. 386.
37. Bullough, Vol. II, p. 387.

38. *Riverside*, p. 540.
39. De Vere himself appears to have been accused (by Gabriel Harvey) of "valorous" words and "womanish" works. See Nelson (pp. 225–226) and Ward (pp. 189–190).
40. Nelson, p. 252. See also Ward, p. 117.
41. Ogburn, pp. 575–576.

Chapter 13

1. Chambers, *William Shakespeare*, Vol. I, p. 404.
2. See Chambers (*William Shakespeare*, Vol. I, p. 405) and Bullough (Vol. II, p. 269). Leslie Hotson's theory that the play was performed on Twelfth Night, 1601, for the visiting Don Orsino Virginio, Duke of Bracciano, has found some support (see *Riverside*, p. 437), but Bullough wryly observed that "it is doubtful whether the Duke of Bracciano would approve of having the sentimental hero [Orsino] named after him" (p. 269).
3. Schoenbaum, *Compact Life*, pp. 137–140. Schoenbaum believed that Shakespeare may have had connections with the Swan.
4. Clark, p. 364. See also Frank Davis, "Revisiting the Dating of *Twelfth Night*," *Shakespeare Oxford Newsletter* (Shakespeare Oxford Society), Fall 2002.
5. In the First Folio, the alternative title is ... *or, What You Will*, perhaps a reference to this multiplicity.
6. Bullough, Vol. II, p. 271. See also Introduction in *Five Italian Renaissance Comedies*, Bruce Penman, Editor (New York: Penguin Books, 1978). Siena, like many other northern Italian city-states, had its own academy for the performing arts, helping give rise to modern drama during the Renaissance.
7. Bullough, Vol. II, p. 270.
8. Bullough, Vol. II, pp. 270–275. See also Radcliff-Umstead, p. 273.
9. Radcliff-Umstead, pp. 196–197.
10. *Riverside*, p. 438.
11. Feste, Sir Toby, Maria, and Sir Andrew engage in this kind of behavior, although Sir Toby gets it wrong (as in other things) when he croons, "O' the twelf day of December" (II.iii.84).
12. The frontispiece reads, "Il Sacrificio, Comedia de gli Intronati, celebrato ne i giuochi d'un carnovale in Siena." Other editions have similar advertisements.
13. Nelson, p. 132. See also Ward, p. 110.
14. Radcliff-Umstead, p. 201. It would have been natural for the Sienese nobility to roll out the red carpet for de Vere, as a visiting English nobleman with rumored Catholic sympathies.
15. Bullough, Vol. II, pp. 277–278.
16. Chambers, Vol. I, p. 407.
17. Bullough, Vol. II, 271.
18. *Riverside*, p. 470. See also Nelson (pp. 236–237) and Ward (pp. 30–31).
19. Jolly, "Shakespeare's Sources," p. 20.
20. Nelson, p. 96. See also Ward, pp. 74–75.
21. Nelson, pp. 187–189. See also Ward, pp. 236–241.
22. Nelson, pp. 228–229. See also Ward, pp. 192–194.
23. If the true author was Will Shakspere, such a skewering would have been a bold move, to put it lightly. Numerous similarities between Malvolio and Hatton are summarized by Ogburn (pp. 633–634).
24. For an excellent background discussion, see Chambers, "Humanism and Puritanism" (Chapter 8), *Elizabethan Stage*, Vol. I, pp. 236–268.
25. Chute, pp. 34–35.
26. Nelson, p. 246.
27. Actors are described as "fiends that are crept into the world by stealth" and "sent from their great captain Satan (under whose banner they bear arms) to deceive the world, to lead people with enticing shows to the Devil." See Chute, p. 54 (footnote).
28. *DNB*, Vol. XVI, p. 735.
29. One generation later, the Vere and Sidney families would intermarry.
30. Nelson, p. 41. Professor Nelson, however, believes Mary was several years younger than her brother because her uncle misstated his age and she is not mentioned in her father's legacies of 1552 and 1554 (pp. 23, 41).
31. Nelson, p. 134.
32. In both plays, these couples wed. See Ogburn (pp. 593–594) and Clark (pp. 102–103).
33. Ogburn, p. 635, quoting Clark (pp. 367–369).
34. *The Taming of the Shrew* (II.i.290).
35. Nelson, p. 176. See also Ward, pp. 153–154.
36. Nelson, p. 180. See also Ward, p. 154.
37. Nelson, pp. 281–282. See also Ogburn, p. 651.
38. Whoever controlled this area had a piece of the eastern trade routes. Shakespeare may have felt that the Balkan States made a better setting for the contentious military backdrop of the story. De Vere, who traveled in Venetian galleys, would surely have been familiar with this area.
39. Clark/Miller, pp. 378–379. Aleppo is directly mentioned in *Othello* (V.ii.352) and *Macbeth* (I.iii.7).
40. Clark/Miller, p. 380. In *Macbeth*, the First Witch specifically says that the *Tiger* had gone to Aleppo (I.iii.7).
41. Clark, p. 820.
42. Nelson, p. 4.
43. Chambers, *William Shakespeare*, Vol. I, p. 405.
44. Ward, pp. 203–204.
45. Nelson, pp. 165, 381–382.
46. Mosher, pp. 43–44.
47. Nelson, p. 207. See also Ward, p. 213.
48. Nelson, pp. 37, 95. See also Ward, pp. 20, 78.
49. Nelson, p. 181. See also Ward, p. 161.
50. Nelson, pp. 155, 248.

Chapter 14

1. *Riverside*, p. 1612. For a detailed discussion, see "Note on the Text" (*Riverside*, p. 1652).
2. *Riverside*, p. 1612. Hallet Smith, author of the introduction, admitted, "How much earlier than its first known performance *The Winter's Tale* was written is a matter of surmise...."
3. Ogburn, p. 386.
4. See *The Poems of Shakespeare's Dark Lady*, introduction by A.L. Rowse. Rowse's theory has been attacked over the years for various reasons; we remain fascinated.
5. Bullough, Vol. VIII, pp. 127–128. See also *Riverside*, p. 1615.
6. Nelson, p. 391. This was at Coventry.
7. *Riverside*, p. 1612. Orthodox scholars, with a few exceptions (e.g., Isaac Asimov), are surprisingly slow to defend Shakespeare's very plausible choice of location.
8. Dennis P. Hupchick and Harold E. Cox, *The Palgrave Concise Historical Atlas of Eastern Europe* (New York: Palgrave Publishers, Ltd., 2001), Map #20. National boundaries on the Dalmatian coast have been in flux throughout the ages.
9. *New Encyclopedia Britannica*, Vol. XVI, pp. 904–905.
10. Hupchick and Cox, *Palgrave Atlas*, Map #20. Prague's political influence extended well beyond the physical boundaries of Bohemia.
11. Hupchick and Cox, *Concise Historical Atlas*, Map #27.
12. Bullough, Vol. VIII, pp. 117–118. See also Ian Barnes and Robert Hudson, *The History Atlas of Europe* (New York: Macmillan, 1998), p. 89.

13. Bullough, Vol. VIII, p. 150. Bullough conceded that Romano made gesso reliefs in addition to paintings.

14. Bullough, Vol. VIII, p. 150, quoting Vasari's *Lives of the Painters*.

15. Bullough, Vol. VIII, p. 118.

16. *Riverside*, p. 1612.

17. *DNB*, Vol. VIII, p. 509.

18. Nelson, p. 381. See also Ogburn, p. 675.

19. Ogburn, pp. 56–64. See also Whalen, pp. 42–44, 137–139.

20. Bullough, Vol. VIII, pp. 126–127.

21. Bullough, Vol. VIII, pp. 126–127.

22. Bullough, Vol. VIII, p. 118.

23. Eddi Jolly, "Burghley's Library," p. 12.

24. Nelson, p. 53. See also Ward, p. 33.

25. Bullough, Vol. VIII, p. 124.

26. Nelson, p. 53. See also Ward, p. 33.

27. *Riverside*, p. 1797.

28. Bullough, Vol. VIII, p. 134.

29. Bullough, Vol. VIII, p. 121.

30. Nelson, pp. 236–237. See also Ward, pp. 30–31.

31. Ogburn, pp. 688, 718. Spenser wrote (in reference to de Vere), "the love which thou dost bear to th'Heliconian imps, and they to thee; they unto thee, and thou to them, most dear."

32. Bullough, Vol. VIII, p. 126.

33. Sobran, p. 122.

34. Herrick, p. 225.

35. Nelson, pp. 289–290. See also Sobran, pp. 187–188.

36. Sobran, p. 122.

37. Nelson, pp. 308–311, 321–322. See also Ward, p. 262.

38. Nelson, pp. 308–311. See also Ward, p. 288.

39. Regarding Baptista's daughter Katherina, Petruchio predicts, "For patience she will prove a second Grissel," *The Taming of the Shrew* (II.i.295).

40. Sobran, p. 122. Sobran, like many other Oxfordians, believes de Vere may have been originally motivated by a list of grievances against his Cecil in-laws.

Chapter 15

1. Chambers (*William Shakespeare*, Vol. I, p. 484) and Bullough (Vol. VIII, p. 3).

2. Clark (quoting J.M. Robertson and Coleridge), p. 79. Critics such as Hallet Smith, writing the introduction for *Riverside*, also labeled Cymbeline's Queen as the "cruel stepmother" (p. 1567).

3. Bullough, Vol. VIII, p. 3.

4. Clark, p. 79.

5. Several another anonymous plays from this earlier period, the texts of which have survived, are often viewed as being minor influences on Shakespeare's *Cymbeline*. Foremost among these is *The Rare Triumphs of Love and Fortune*, published in 1589 and premiered at court no later than 1584. See Chambers (*William Shakespeare*, Vol. I, p. 487) and Bullough (Vol. VIII, pp. 21–23). Given that these plays were performed for exclusive court audiences while Will Shakspere was still in Stratford-upon-Avon, we are struck by orthodox scholarship's reluctance to attribute these anonymous works to de Vere, who was a noted playwright but left no surviving examples of his work, at least under his own name.

6. Chambers (*William Shakespeare*, Vol. I, pp. 486–487) and Bullough (Vol. VIII, pp. 13–14).

7. Jolly, "Burghley's Library," p. 12.

8. Chambers (*William Shakespeare*, Vol. I, p. 487) and Bullough (Vol. VIII, p. 25).

9. *Access: Florence, Venice & Milan*, 3rd Ed. Lois Spritzer, Editor (New York: Access Press, 1996), p. 178. See also Magri (*Venetian Inquisition*, p. 6) and Rosenthal (pp. 66, 89).

10. Chambers (*William Shakespeare*, Vol. I, p. 487) and Bullough (Vol. VIII, pp. 10–11).

11. Chambers, *William Shakespeare*, Vol. I, p. 486. Bullough agreed (see Vol. VIII, p. 12).

12. Clark, p. 79.

13. Bullough, Vol. VIII, pp. 23–24.

14. Jachimo makes a pass at Imogen in Act I, scene vi, but only does this for the sake of his wager.

15. Bandello was another writer whose works were to be found in Lord Burghley's library. See Jolly, "Burghley's Library," p. 12.

16. Bullough, Vol. VIII, pp. 20, 87.

17. Nelson, p. 237.

18. Chambers (*William Shakespeare*, Vol. I, p. 485) and Bullough (Vol. VIII, p. 3).

19. Nelson, p. 381. See also Ogburn, p. 675.

20. Chambers (*William Shakespeare*, Vol. I, p. 487) and Bullough (Vol. VIII, p. 16).

21. Apulieus, *The Golden Ass*, William Adlington, translator with revisions by G. Gaselee (Cambridge, MA: Harvard University Press, 1971), p. viii.

22. Nelson, pp. 236–237. See also Ward, pp. 30–31.

23. Clark/Miller, p. 98, quoting from *Cymbeline*: The Arden Edition, J.M. Nosworthy, Editor (London: Methuen and Co. Ltd., 1955), p. 197.

24. Bullough, Vol. VIII, p. 7.

25. The answer is none during his lifetime, in sharp contrast to his contemporaries. See Price, pp. 302–305. While it should be noted that book dedications tended to be directed toward noblemen, commendatory verses among fellow writers were common. A highly debatable exception may be "To our English Terence Mr. William Shake-speare" by John Davies of Hereford, published in 1611, but this epigram can also be easily interpreted to mean that the "Shake-speare," the "English Terence," was a pseudonym with a front man (Price, pp. 62–67).

26. Imogen is reading of Terseus and Philomela, also used by Shakespeare in *Titus Andronicus*.

27. Nelson, p. 10. See also Ward, p. 11.

28. Translated from the Latin. See Nelson, p. 45. This praise of de Vere in relation to the Muses would later be repeated by Angel Day in 1586 and Edmund Spenser in 1590.

29. Nelson, p. 48.

30. Due to their natural father's waywardness (and death), both sons essentially fell under the tutelage of other older men, as do Cymbeline's sons in the play.

31. Ogburn, p. 410.

32. Nelson, p. 78. See also Ward, p. 89.

33. Nelson, pp. 58, 62. See also Ward, pp. 49–50.

34. Nelson, p. 143. See also Ward, pp. 116–118.

35. De Vere seems to have gotten off scot-free until his affair with Anne Vavasor was revealed.

36. Nelson, p. 367.

37. *DNB*, Vol. II, pp. 1331–1332.

38. *DNB*, Vol. II, 1330.

39. Nelson, p. 369. See also Ward, pp. 329–330. Bridget Vere negotiated to marry William Herbert, future Earl of Pembroke, Lord Chamberlain, and along with his brother Philip, co-dedicatee of Shakespeare's First Folio. Philip, however, would later marry Bridget's sister Susan Vere in 1605.

40. Son of Peregrine Bertie, Lord Willoughby, and Mary Vere, de Vere's sister.

41. Asimov, Vol. II, p. 56.

42. *DNB*, Vol. XIV, pp. 565, 569.

Chapter 16

1. The play was registered by Edward Blount but printed by William White for Henry Gosson. See Chambers, *William Shakespeare*, Vol. I, p. 518.

2. One of these performances was witnessed by the Venetian ambassador sometime after his arrival in May 1606. See *Riverside*, p. 1527.

3. See Chambers (*William Shakespeare*, Vol. I, pp. 518–520) and Bullough (Vol. VI, p. 349).

4. Chambers, *William Shakespeare*, Vol. II, p. 210.

5. Chambers, *William Shakespeare*, Vol. I, pp. 521–522.

6. *Riverside*, p. 1527.

7. Chambers, *William Shakespeare*, Vol. I, pp. 526–527.

8. Chambers, *William Shakespeare*, Vol. I, pp. 526.

9. Bullough, Vol. VI, p. 354–355.

10. Bullough, Vol. VI, p. 373.

11. Bullough, Vol. VI, p. 373.

12. *Riverside*, p. 1527.

13. *Riverside*, p. 1528.

14. For *The Comedy of Errors*, Gower is viewed by orthodox scholars as a secondary source. The primary source was Plautus.

15. See Nelson (p. 237) and Ward (pp. 84–85). See also *DNB*, Vol. IXX, pp. 1330–1331.

16. See Chambers (*William Shakespeare*, Vol. I, p. 527) and Bullough (Vol. VI, pp. 355–356). Sidney's Pyrocles, Prince of Macedon, is a similar figure to Apollonius of Tyre and may have been modeled after him. Bullough noted that Shakespeare adopts the spelling for the Pericles found in Plutarch, and that this character seems to embody many of the traits found in Plutarch's Pericles of Athens (p. 356). De Vere, it should be remembered, owned a copy of Plutarch, which he purchased as a young man. See Nelson (p. 53) and Ward (p. 33).

17. Philip Herbert was one of the "Incomparable Brethren" to whom Shakespeare's First Folio would be dedicated in 1623.

18. Nelson, pp. 69–70, 131, 261–265, 277–278. See also Ward, pp. 56–61, 112.

19. Ogburn, pp. 549–550. See also Nelson, p. 140.

20. Nelson, pp. 135–137. See also Ward, p. 118.

21. Ward, pp. 203–204.

22. Mosher, pp. 43–44.

23. Nelson, pp. 37, 95. See also Ward, pp. 20, 78. De Vere, for his part, had the gumption to criticize the queen's singing voice. See Nelson (p. 207) and Ward (p. 213).

24. Ogburn, pp. 142–144. Two years later (in 1920) *"Shakespeare" Identified* by John Thomas Looney was published, proposing Stanley's father-in-law, Edward de Vere.

25. Nelson, pp. 393, 482. Fenner, like many of his contemporaries, found Stanley's hobby contemptible.

26. Nelson, p. 359.

27. Ogburn, p. 386.

Chapter 17

1. *Riverside*, p. 805.

2. Chambers, *William Shakespeare*, Vol. I, pp. 366.

3. Bullough, Vol. IV, p. 1.

4. *Riverside*, p. 805.

5. Chambers, *William Shakespeare*, Vol. I, pp. 364–365.

6. *Riverside*, p. 805.

7. Chambers, *William Shakespeare*, Vol. I, pp. 367. See also Bullough, Vol. IV, p. 367.

8. One should not rule out the possibility that Francis Meres in 1598 was referring *to the earlier work* as being written by Shakespeare.

9. Bullough, Vol. IV, p. 3.

10. Bullough, Vol. IV, p. 3.

11. Nelson, p. 29. See also Ward, pp.12–13.

12. Jesse W. Harris, *John Bale* (Urbana, IL: University of Illinois Press, 1940), pp. 24, 100.

13. Bullough, Vol. IV, p. 9.

14. Chambers, *William Shakespeare*, Vol. I, p. 364.

15. Schoenbaum, *Compact Life*, p. 117.

16. Ogburn (quoting Edmund Chambers), pp. 661–662.

17. Bullough, Vol. IV, p. 25.

18. Nelson, p. 301. See also Ward, pp. 355–358.

19. Among the internal disputes, perhaps more dangerous to national security than divisions between the Protestant majority and Catholic minority were rising tensions among the Protestants themselves, specifically between Anglicans and Presbyterians (and Puritans). For the generation after Shakespeare, these tensions would help to trigger the English Civil War.

20. The title of Faulconbridge was associated with the Belasius family, itself of Norman origins. During Shakespeare's time, this family belonged to the same social circle as de Vere's guardian, Lord Burghley. See comments by E.A.J. Honigmann in his introduction to the play for the *Arden Shakespeare*, Fourth Edition (London: Methuen & Company, Ltd., 1973), p. xxiv.

21. This story was recorded in the diary of John Manningham. See Schoenbaum, *Compact Life*, pp. 205–206. We assume in this case that "William Shakespeare" was Will Shakspere, rather than a moniker for someone else, although the latter scenario is possible as well.

22. *Riverside*, p. 805.

23. Nelson, pp. 289–290.

24. Ogburn, p. 419.

25. Making fun of Lord Cobham's ancestor Sir John Oldcastle (as Falstaff) was apparently okay for Shakespeare as well, at least initially.

26. Ogburn (quoting Holinshed), pp. 419–420.

27. Aside from receiving a passing mention in Holinshed, Faulconbridge appears to have been the Bard's original creation. See discussion by E.A.J. Honigmann in his introduction to the play for the *Arden Shakespeare*, pp. xxii–xxv.

28. In *Henry V*, Shakespeare's French Duke of Britain snarls, "Normans, but bastard Normans, Norman bastards!" (III.v.9–10). If Shakespeare the writer was in fact of Norman descent, then many of these associations (Faulconbridge = Norman = bastard = de Vere = Shakespeare) come into sharper focus.

29. The question was whether the marriage of de Vere's father to his mother was bigamous.

30. See Nelson (pp. 40–41, 206) and Ward (p. 124). Elizabeth was the daughter of Anne Boleyn, whose marriage to Henry VIII was never recognized by the Catholic Church and who was subsequently executed by order of the king himself.

31. For a good discussion, see Ren Draya, "Shakespeare's *King John*," *Shakespeare Oxford Newsletter* (Shakespeare Oxford Society), Spring 1999, pp. 1, 13–15.

Chapter 18

1. Chambers, *William Shakespeare*, Vol. I, p. 348.

2. See also *Love's Labor's Lost, Richard III*, and *Pallaius Tamia* by Francis Meres.

3. Ward, p. 89.

4. Bloom, p. 252.

5. Chambers, *William Shakespeare*, Vol. I, p. 351.

6. Nelson, pp. 349–350, 352–353, 359–361, 367–368. See also Ward, pp. 318–319.

7. *Riverside*, p. 852. See also Chambers, *William Shakespeare*, Vol. I, p. 351.

8. The inflammatory deposition scene, however, was not printed until after the queen's death. See Chambers, *William Shakespeare*, Vol. I, pp. 354–355.

9. Schoenbaum, *Compact Life*, p. 219. See also *Riverside*, pp. 845–846.

10. Nelson, p. 397. See also Ward, p. 336.

11. Peter W. Dickson, *Shakespeare Oxford Newsletter* (Shakespeare Oxford Society), Spring 1999, p. 8. See also Nelson (pp. 323, 349) and Ward (pp. 313–314, 318).

12. Chambers, *William Shakespeare*, Vol. I, p. 354.

13. Chambers, *William Shakespeare*, Vol. I, pp. 353–354.

14. Chambers, *William Shakespeare*, Vol. I, p. 356.

15. *Riverside*, p. 843.

16. Shakespeare's unique spelling of "Bolingbroke" bears a curious similarity to the name "Oxford (Ox/Bullford/brook)." This of course proves nothing but if the Oxfordian theory is correct, then it can be added to other examples demonstrating Shakespeare's Lancastrian sympathies in the history plays.

17. Probably the most famous modern stage portrayals of Gaunt and Richard have been by John Gielgud and Derek Jacobi, respectively, in the 1978 BBC production. Jacobi, like Gielgud before him, has expressed Oxfordian leanings in his authorship beliefs. See his interview with the *Washington Times*, April 25, 1997.

18. Geoffrey Chaucer, *Troilus and Cresyde* (New York: Penguin Books Ltd., 1982), cover art.

19. Edward III, Richard II, and Henry IV.

20. *Riverside*, p. 1732. This was one year after the previously mentioned events on Canon Row and one year before the first quarto of *Richard II*.

21. Both Edmund Chambers and Geoffrey Bullough judged it to be genuine. See Chambers (*William Shakespeare*, Vol. I, p. 352) and Bullough (Vol. III, p. 358).

22. Wright, "Vere-y Interesting," pp. 14–16.

23. Nelson, pp. 225–226. See also Ward, pp. 189–190.

24. Nelson, pp. 69–70, 131, 261–265, 277–278. See also Ward, pp. 56–61, 112.

25. Nelson, pp. 262–264.

26. Ogburn, pp. 549–550. See also Nelson, p. 140.

27. Ward, p. 192. See also Nelson, p. 84.

28. Nelson, p. 386. See also Ward, pp. 299, 321.

29. This is Ophelia's description of Hamlet (III.i.153).

30. Nelson, p. 301. See also Ward, pp. 355–358.

31. Thomas Jefferson immediately comes to mind, who, upon arriving in Stratford-upon-Avon (according to his companion John Adams), fell to his knees and kissed the ground in homage. Adams was less impressed. He wrote: "There is nothing preserved of this great genius ... which might inform us what education, what company, what accident turned his mind to letters and drama." See David McCullough, *John Adams* (New York: Simon & Schuster, 2001), p. 359.

32. See Nelson (p. 425) and Ward (pp. 370–371). Regarding Leonard Digges' First Folio tribute to Shakespeare's "Stratford monument," "Stratford" could mean Stratford-upon-Avon in Warwickshire or the London Borough of Stratford, nearest town proper to which de Vere was buried. See Ogburn (pp. 232, 235–236) and Whalen (pp. 55–58).

33. Ward, p. 89.

Chapter 19

1. See Chambers (*William Shakespeare*, Vol. I, pp. 375–376) and Bullough (Vol. IV, p. 155).

2. *Riverside*, pp. 1989, 1991.

3. There is a strong orthodox tradition that such a place did exist (during the Tudor era, at least) and was Shakespeare's intended setting, although the Bard does not specify the Boar's Head Tavern by name. See discussion by Looney, pp. 337–341.

4. Nelson, pp. 391–392. Whether this was the same Boar's Head Tavern traditionally associated with Shakespeare's Falstaff is uncertain.

5. See Nelson, Figure 13.

6. Nelson, p. 96. See also Ward, p. 75.

7. Hughes, "New Light on the Dark Lady," p. 11.

8. Nelson, pp. 343, 368. See also Ward, pp. 313, 319.

9. See Chambers (*William Shakespeare*, Vol. I, p. 383) and Bullough (Vol. IV, pp. 161, 180).

10. E.M.W. Tillyard, *Shakespeare's History Plays* (New York: Barnes & Noble, Inc., 1964), p. 101.

11. See Ramón Jiménez, "*The Famous Victories of Henry the Fifth*: Key to the Authorship Question?" *Shakespeare Oxford Newsletter* (Shakespeare Oxford Society), Summer 2001, pp. 7–10. Holinshed died in 1580, not long after the first edition of the *Chronicles* was published in 1577. The second edition of 1587 retained Holinshed's name but was augmented with new material by other writers.

12. Ward, p. 373.

13. Bullough, Vol. IV, p. 167.

14. See the series of articles by Ramón Jiménez in the *Shakespeare Oxford Newsletter* (Shakespeare Oxford Society), Summer 2001, Fall 2001, and Spring 2002.

15. The source materials only make a vague reference to this event and do not specify the place (Gads Hill) or the month (May). See Jiménez, "Famous Victories," p. 9.

16. Nelson, pp. 95–96. See also Ward, pp. 90–92.

17. Sobran, p. 193.

18. Nelson, p. 305. See also Ward, p. 286.

19. Wright, "Vere-y Interesting," pp. 16–19.

20. The "Henry IV" painting is now in the National Portrait Gallery of London. John Julius Norwich, author of *Shakespeare's Kings* (New York: Scribner, 1999), believed it was copied from a portrait of the French King Charles VI, with the artist then adding a beard, moustache, and red Lancastrian rose in the right hand, but leaving the French *fleur-de-lys* on the scepter (p. 162). Norwich does not name his source, but others have simply noted that this may be an Elizabethan "actor" in costume. As for the *fleur-de-lys*, we should remember that during the early 1400s, England controlled France. It was not until later, during the time of Henry VI and Joan of Arc, that France truly became an independent state. If nothing else, this portrait seems to have influenced the costuming and make-up for actor Jon Finch's portrayal of Henry IV in the BBC production of 1979.

21. Chambers, *William Shakespeare*, Vol. I, pp. 375–376.

22. Palmer and Palmer, p. 177.

23. Palmer and Palmer, p. 177.

24. Nelson, p. 337. See also Ward, p. 313.

25. Wriothesley was the dedicatee of Shakespeare's two narrative poems and (many believe) the "Fair Youth" of the sonnets.

26. From "*On Bad Means to a Good End*" (1592), in Montaigne, p. 776.

Chapter 20

1. Chute, p. 191.

2. A period portrait of William Brooke and his family by Hans Eworth (circa 1567) captures the very earnest and serious character of the man.

3. Chute, pp. 191–192. Edmund Chambers, in a rare flash of emotion, described this proclamation as a "very irritating document." See Chambers, *Elizabethan Stage*, Vol. I, p. 268.

4. Schoenbaum, *Compact Life*, pp. 207–209.

5. Chambers, *William Shakespeare*, Vol. I, p. 377. The billing order for *Part I* was King Henry IV, Hotspur, and Falstaff.

6. Chambers believed that "*Part II* must have followed pretty quickly." See Chambers, *William Shakespeare*, Vol. I, p. 383.

7. Chambers, *William Shakespeare*, Vol. I, p. 381.

8. Bullough, Vol. IV, pp. 169–170.

9. Bullough, Vol. IV, p. 170.

10. Holinshed, Vol. III, p. 62.

11. Holinshed, Vol. I, p. v.

12. See Chambers (*William Shakespeare*, Vol. I, p. 383) and Bullough (Vol. III, p. 161).

13. Nelson, p. 301. See also Ward, pp. 355–358.

14. Montaigne, p. 280 (footnote).

15. Price, p. 63.

16. From "On Educating Children" (1580), in Montaigne, p. 198.

17. Nelson, pp. 26, 422–423. See also Ward, p. 346.

18. Ogburn, pp. 636–637, citing Norman Ault, *Elizabethan Lyrics* (London: Longman's Green, 1925), p. 104.

19. This idea has been suggested by James Webster Sherwood, author of the novel *Shakespeare's Ghost* (New York: Opus Books, 2002).

20. See Chambers (*William Shakespeare*, Vol. I, pp. 383–384) and Bullough (Vol. IV, p. 167).

21. This is the same period in which Mary Stuart would be tried and executed (1586–1587), followed by the onslaught of the Spanish Armada in 1588.

22. See Ramón Jiménez, "Edward de Vere, Philip Sidney, and the Battle of Agincourt, '...in brawl ridiculous,'" *Shakespeare Oxford Newsletter* (Shakespeare Oxford Society), Spring 2002, p. 12.

23. The First Folio spells the name from *Henry VI, Part I* as "Falstaffe," the same as the character from the *Henry IV* plays and *The Merry Wives of Windsor*. The name of the historical character, however, was "Fastolfe," as often spelled in later editions.

24. Bullough, Vol. IV, pp. 170–171.

25. See Chambers (*William Shakespeare*, Vol. I, p. 383) and Bullough (Vol. IV, p. 156).

26. Nelson, p. 367.

27. *DNB*, Vol. II, p. 1331.

28. Nelson, p. 97. See also Ward, p. 330.

29. Nelson, p. 99. See also Ward, pp. 330–331.

30. Palmer, p. 24.

31. See William Hazlitt, *The Doubtful Plays of William Shakespeare* (London: George Routledge and Sons, 1887), p. 106. Some believe the 1600 "William Shakespeare" quarto is in fact a backdated publication from as late as 1619. See Chambers, Vol. I, pp. 533–534. All, however, agree that this came after the anonymous quarto of 1600.

32. *Sir John Old-castle* was included among Shakespeare's works in the Third Folio of 1664.

33. Schoenbaum, *Lives*, p. 86.

Chapter 21

1. Cervantes, p. 103.

2. In the Olivier film, before a line is spoken, the camera pans around the Globe Theater and we see a mysterious nobleman dressed in black, buying fruit, and carefully inspecting the premises. Olivier's subtle tribute to the authorship question perhaps? Though not professing Oxfordian beliefs (at least, not openly), Olivier was associated with others who did, including John Gielgud, Leslie Howard, and Sigmund Freud.

3. The Vere coat of arms featured the image of a mullet or star, so often invoked by Shakespeare.

4. The Branagh film featured as the Chorus Derek Jacobi, a professed Oxfordian in his authorship beliefs.

5. Saints Crispian and Crispinian ("Crispin Crispian" in the play), two brothers martyred during the third-century persecutions under the Emperor Diocletian. See Staunton, Vol. II, p. 119.

6. Asimov, Vol. II, p. 517.

7. See Chambers (*William Shakespeare*, Vol. I, pp. 388–390) and Bullough (Vol. IV, p. 347).

8. See Chambers (*William Shakespeare*, Vol. I, p. 395) and Bullough (Vol. IV, p. 376).

9. This was also the year that Mary Queen of Scots was executed.

10. Nelson, p. 48.

11. Bullough, Vol. IV, pp. 408, 430.

12. Jolly, "Burghley's Library," p. 12.

13. Bullough, Vol. IV, p. 167.

14. Jiménez, "Edward de Vere," pp. 1, 12–15.

15. Londré, p. 6.

16. Bullough, Vol. IV, p. 356.

17. Price, pp. 260–261.

18. Ward, pp. 164–177. See also Nelson, pp. 195–200.

19. Ramón Jiménez, "'Rebellion broached on his sword': New Evidence of an Early Date for *Henry V*," *Shakespeare Oxford Society* (Shakespeare Oxford Society), Fall 2001, pp. 8–11, 21.

20. Staunton, Vol. II, p. 118.

21. Schoenbaum, *Compact Life*, p. 264.

22. Nelson, p. 206.

23. Nelson, pp. 225–226. See also Ward, pp. 189–190.

24. See Jiménez, "Famous Victories," pp. 7–10.

25. De Vere may have come under heavy criticism from his peers for self-aggrandizement if he authored *Famous Victories*, or he may have just had second thoughts if he wrote *Henry V*. See Wright, "'Vere-y Interesting,'" p. 9.

26. Chambers (citing Wilson), *William Shakespeare*, Vol. I, p. 395. See also Charles Wisner Barrell, "Shakespeare's Fluellen Identified as a Retainer of the Earl of Oxford," *Shakespeare Oxford Newsletter* (Shakespeare Oxford Society), Summer 2001, pp. 16–17, 24.

27. In real life, Falstaff (a.k.a. Sir John Oldcastle) was burned at the stake by Henry V in 1417 as an outlaw and heretic.

28. Wright, pp. 196–197.

29. Wright, p. 211.

30. Wright, p. 216.

31. Wright, p. 221–222.

32. This is similar to Bardolph earlier breaking up a fight between Pistol and Nym (II.i.63–65).

Chapter 22

1. *Riverside*, p. 623.

2. See Chambers (*William Shakespeare*, Vol. I, p. 279) and Bullough (Vol. III, p. 23).

3. See Chambers (*William Shakespeare*, Vol. I, p. 292) and Bullough (Vol. III, p. 23).

4. Chambers, *William Shakespeare*, Vol. I, pp. 290, 293.

5. Bullough, Vol. III, pp. 24, 34, 40.

6. We agree with Bullough, however, in the sense that Shakespeare the writer deserves primary credit for authorship of this particular play and the *Henry VI* trilogy in general.

7. See Chambers (*William Shakespeare*, Vol. I, p. 289) and Bullough (Vol. III, p. 25). 1550 was also the year that de Vere was born.

8. Jolly and O'Brien, p. 20.

9. Nelson, p. 48.

10. Goldstein (quoting E.K. Chambers), p. 163.

11. Wright, "'Vere-y Interesting,'" pp. 16–19.
12. Nelson, pp. 300–302. See also Ward, pp. 355–357.
13. Collinson, pp. 392–393.
14. Ogburn, p. 716.
15. See Elizabeth Appleton, *An Anatomy of the Marprelate Controversy, 1588-1596* (Lewiston, NY: The Edwin Mellen Press, 2001).
16. Chambers, *William Shakespeare*, Vol. I, p. 33.
17. Bullough, Vol. III, p. 41.
18. Bullough, Vol. III, p. 35.
19. Ogburn, p. 453.
20. De Vere's office of Lord Great Chamberlain also involved a ceremonial staff. Thanks to James Webster Sherwood for pointing out this one.
21. *A Hundreth Sundrie Flowres*, pp. 24–25.

Chapter 23

1. Chambers, *William Shakespeare*, Vol. I, p. 293.
2. A second Battle of St. Albans was fought and won by Lancastrians in 1461.
3. See Chambers (*William Shakespeare*, Vol. I, pp. 277–279) and Bullough (Vol. III, p. 89).
4. See Chambers (*William Shakespeare*, Vol. I, p. 289) and Bullough (Vol. III, p. 90).
5. Neither Wriothesley nor Field had any documented connections to Will Shakspere, other than possibly the appearance of their names on publications bearing the authorship of "William Shakespeare."
6. De Vere's hostile biographer Alan Nelson characterized him as a "necromancer." See Nelson, p. 58.
7. Ogburn, p. 432.
8. *"Bona terra, mala gens"* (IV.vii.56) or "good land, bad people." See *Riverside*, p. 696.
9. De Vere's biographer Alan Nelson emphatically reminded us that the Earl's efforts in this direction produced more than one fiasco; on the other hand, he admits that the school "survived Oxford's interference and neglect, and survives today." See Nelson, pp. 339–342.
10. Several real-life models have been proposed as Shakespeare's inspiration, most of them French (such as Catherine de Medici), but none of these do full justice to Margaret's relentless ferocity of character.
11. Nelson, pp. 135–137. See also Ward, p. 556. Curiously, Shakespeare elects to give Suffolk a sympathetic demise because of his high birth and inherent nobility, despite the fact he is both a murderer and adulterer.
12. Bullough, Vol. III, p. 35. See also *Riverside*, p. 659.
13. Nelson, pp. 40–41. See also Ward, p. 124.
14. Nelson, p. 391.

Chapter 24

1. *Riverside*, p. 628.
2. A phrase taken in turn from an American Civil War soldier. See Geoffrey C. Ward (with Ric Burns and Ken Burns), *The Civil War: An Illustrated History* (New York: Alfred A. Knopf, Inc., 1990), p. 227.
3. A 1602 Stationers Register entry indicates the author of Parts I and II was "William Shakespeare." See Chambers, *William Shakespeare*, Vol. I, p. 279.
4. In the case of *Part II*, quartos advertise performances by Lord Strange's Men, who were sponsored by Ferdinando Stanley, brother to the William Stanley who later married de Vere's daughter Elizabeth.
5. See Chambers (*William Shakespeare*, Vol. I, pp. 277–279) and Bullough (Vol. III, p. 157).
6. See Chambers (*William Shakespeare*, Vol. I, p. 289) and Bullough (Vol. III, p. 158).
7. Bullough, Vol. III, p. 167.
8. Jolly and O'Brien, p. 20.
9. See Chambers (*William Shakespeare*, Vol. I, p. 287) and Bullough (Vol. III, p. 158).
10. Schoenbaum, *Compact Life*, pp. 153–158. See also Ogburn, pp. 58–64.
11. Schoenbaum, *Compact Life*, pp. 56–64.
12. Whalen, pp. 42–44, 137–139. See also Sobran, pp. 32–39.
13. Price, pp. 25–30.
14. Nelson, p. 381. See also Ogburn, p. 675.
15. According to Asimov, this was a greater number than had fallen during any single battle of the Hundred Years' War in France. See Asimov, Vol. II, pp. 645–646.
16. We cannot help but suspect that de Vere and his co-actors were inspired by the legendary military prowess of the historical Earl of Warwick, whether or not de Vere was in fact Shakespeare the writer.
17. Nelson, pp. 237–238.
18. Asimov, Vol. II, pp. 671–672.
19. Wright, "'Vere-y Interesting,'" pp. 16–19. See also Asimov, Vol. II, p. 674.
20. Ogburn (quoting Whitman), p. 260. See also Whalen (p. 66) and Sobran (p. 55).

Chapter 25

1. Cervantes, p. 376.
2. "Tudor propaganda" is an appropriate phrase used by Herschel Baker (among others) in his introduction to the play. See *Riverside*, p. 750.
3. President (and Southerner) Woodrow Wilson once described D.W. Griffith's racist movie *The Birth of a Nation* as akin to rewriting history with lightning bolts.
4. In the year 1598 the name William Shakespeare first appears in print as a playwright with quarto publications for *Love's Labor's Lost*, *Richard II*, and *Richard III*.
5. *Riverside*, p. 748. See also Chambers (*William Shakespeare*, Vol. I, pp. 294–296) and Bullough (Vol. III, p. 221).
6. Bullough, Vol. III, p. 224.
7. *Riverside*, p. 748.
8. Bullough, Vol. III, pp. 225–226. Edward de Vere was born during King Edward's reign in 1550, and was probably named after him.
9. See Chambers (*William Shakespeare*, Vol. I, p. 304) and Bullough (Vol. III, p. 227).
10. Nelson, p. 48.
11. Jiménez, "*The True Tragedy*," p. 132.
12. *Riverside*, p. 748.
13. Bullough, Vol. III, pp. 237–239.
14. Jiménez, "*The True Tragedy*," p. 128.
15. Jiménez, "*The True Tragedy*", p. 121.
16. Bullough, Vol. III, pp. 238–239.
17. Bullough, Vol. III, p. 232.
18. Jiménez, "*The True Tragedy*," pp. 141–142. See also Nelson (pp. 49, 238, 328–330) and Ward (pp. 28–30, 301–303).
19. Chambers, *William Shakespeare*, Vol. I, p. 53.
20. Clark, pp. 273–274.
21. Clark, pp. 252–255, 273–274. See also Nelson (p. 190) and Ward (p. 163). At that time, the Lord Chamberlain was de Vere's mentor, Thomas Radcliffe, Earl of Sussex.
22. Nelson, pp. 89–92.
23. Clark, p. 297. Of the numerous verbal similarities between *Arden of Feversham* and Shakespeare's plays noted by Clark, over half (55%) related to the first historical tetralogy: specifically, *Henry VI*, *Parts II* and *III* and *Richard III*.
24. Nelson, p. 174.
25. The surviving sister of these two princes, Elizabeth,

eventually became the grandmother of Queen Elizabeth I by marrying Henry Tudor (Henry VII). The mother of these three siblings was also a Queen Elizabeth, the widow of Edward IV (Richard's brother) before she not surprisingly joined forces with the Tudors after the murder of her sons. Thus the Yorkists and Lancastrians eventually united in opposition to Richard's tyranny.

26. Regardless of whether they were related, we would not be surprised if Charles' family had slightly changed the spelling of their last name (as well as the pronunciation) to avoid the stigma attached to the older name, thanks in no small part to the machinations of Tudor propaganda.

27. Nelson, p. 50.

28. Asimov, Vol. II, pp. 724–725.

29. Richard takes pride in this ability, observing, "And though I clothe my naked villainy / With odd old ends stol'n out of holy writ / And seem a saint when most I play a devil" (I.iii.335–337).

30. Nelson, pp. 58, 62. See also Ward, pp. 49–50.

31. Nelson, pp. 58, 62, 218–219.

32. This symbolism was brilliantly deployed in the 1995 film version starring Ian McKellan.

33. Ward, p. 96. See also Ward (p. 75) and Sobran (pp. 109–110).

34. Wright, "'Vere-y Interesting,'" p. 19.

35. For example, the author John Stubbes was condemned to have his right hand chopped off merely for suggesting that the popular Queen Elizabeth should not marry a French prince. See Ogburn (quoting G.M. Trevelyan), p. 607.

36. Nelson, p. 206.

37. Jiménez, "The True Tragedy," pp. 120, 144. De Vere occasionally signed his name with a crown figure indicating the number seven, as in "Edward VII," a conceit that he dropped upon King James' accession in 1603.

38. Asimov, Vol. II, p. 701.

Chapter 26

1. See Chambers (William Shakespeare, p. 495) and Bullough (Vol. VI, p. 435).

2. It is likely that Edward de Vere (b. 1550) was named after Henry's son and successor, King Edward VI, who reigned from 1547 to 1553. This was the same King Edward of Mark Twain's Prince and the Pauper fame.

3. Riverside, pp. 1023–1024, 1690. Fletcher is also favored as Shakspere's collaborator on The Two Noble Kinsmen and the now lost play Cardenio.

4. Only 18 Shakespeare plays appeared in print before 1623; furthermore, these earlier quarto versions often differ considerably from those in the First Folio.

5. Chambers, William Shakespeare, Vol. I, p. 497.

6. Some similarities with Samuel Rowley's 1605 play When You See Me have been identified, but these are too slight to provide the "earlier plot" that Chambers envisioned. See Bullough, Vol. VI, pp. 437–442.

7. Bullough, Vol. VI, p. 443.

8. Chambers, William Shakespeare, Vol. I, p. 495.

9. Among several contemporary accounts, that of Henry Wotton is perhaps the most vivid. Reading in between the lines, Sir Henry seemed to laugh at the whole affair with his noble cronies, describing one spectator who extinguished the flames on his pants by pouring a bottle of ale over himself. See Riverside, p. 1022.

10. Schoenbaum, Compact Life, p. 277.

11. Godfrey Davies, The Early Stuarts (Oxford: Clarendon Press, 1932), pp. 393–394. This is reminiscent of Bottom in A Midsummer Night's Dream.

12. In his famous autobiography, Malcolm X expressed astonishment on this point as well.

13. Nelson, p. 209.

14. Legitimacy of birth is also a theme in King Lear, King John, Richard III and Much Ado About Nothing.

15. Nelson, pp. 40–41, 206. See also Ward, p. 124.

16. Henry's own view (officially, at least) was that his marriage to Catherine (the widow of his brother) was never legal to begin with. Furthermore, their failure to produce a male heir was a sign of divine displeasure in a so-called "marriage" that needed to be annulled.

17. Cranmer was burned at the stake during Bloody Mary's reign in 1556, and was hailed as a Protestant martyr.

18. In the play, Griffith eulogizes Wolsey: "He was a scholar, and a ripe good one..." (IV.ii.51).

19. Chambers, William Shakespeare, Vol. I, p. 503.

20. See Chambers (William Shakespeare, Vol. I, p. 504) and Schoenbaum (Compact Life, p. 214). Chambers gives an exhaustive and comprehensive analysis, concluding that there is no good reason not to believe.

21. Surrey was married to the sister of de Vere's father. His sons Thomas and Henry would later figure prominently in the life of their cousin.

22. Joseph Sobran, "Oxford's Uncle Henry: Sir Thomas More Considered in Oxfordian Light," Shakespeare Oxford Newsletter (Shakespeare Oxford Society), Winter 2002, pp. 3, 6.

23. Nelson, p. 249. See also Ward, pp. 207–209.

24. Nelson, p. 343. See also Ward, p. 311.

Chapter 27

1. Staunton, Vol. III, p. 324.

2. This is the same year that Pericles and the sonnets were first published.

3. See Chambers (William Shakespeare, Vol. I, pp. 438–439) and Bullough (Vol. VI, p. 83).

4. Riverside, p. 526.

5. Oxfordians see this as a clear play on the name "E. Vere" or Edward de Vere.

6. The unapologetic elitism of the advertisement has led many to believe that the only previous (if any) performances of the play had been private or at the Inns of Court.

7. This insistence on the play as a comedy may be publisher hyperbole, reminding readers that many scenes are supposed to be funny.

8. By 1609, Edward de Vere was dead but Will Shakspere was still alive, apparently unconcerned with this piracy. Oxfordians argue that the publisher either did not know who the true author was and/or was referring to the diminishing supply of Shakespearean works, rather than the author himself.

9. Traditionalists maintain that the "grand possessors" refer to Shakespeare's acting company, the King's Men. Oxfordians take the word "grand" literally, as referring to noblemen sponsors.

10. See Chambers (William Shakespeare, Vol. I, pp. 441–442) and Bullough (Vol. VI, p. 84).

11. Bullough, Vol. VI (p. 100).

12. Riverside, p. ix. Were the editors being tongue-in-cheek?

13. This is not to say that Shakespeare the writer did not delight in seeing how far he could push the envelope in making a play both tragic and satiric.

14. Chambers, William Shakespeare, Vol. I, p. 444.

15. Bullough, Vol. VI, p. 84.

16. Riverside, p. 477.

17. Clark, p. 627. Even de Vere's skeptical and adamantly non–Oxfordian biographer Alan Nelson thought that de Vere may have possibly authored this earlier work. Professor Nelson implies that de Vere received

repeated praise as a playwright while in fact not writing any plays at all. See Nelson, p. 393.

18. See Chambers (*William Shakespeare*, Vol. I, p. 448) and Looney (Vol. I, pp. 261–265).

19. Nelson, pp. 245–246.

20. Homer is often compared to Shakespeare in that we know so little about him; Homer, on the other hand, was (according to legend) blind. This happens to jive with the poems attributed to Homer, which exhibit an obsessive concern with the physical sight of his characters. Thus even Homer's legendary biography can make more sense than the traditional biography for William Shakespeare.

21. See Chambers (*William Shakespeare*, Vol. I, p. 448) and Bullough (Vol. VI, p. 87).

22. Jolly, "Burghley's Library," p. 12.

23. Nelson, p. 126. See also Ward, p. 112.

24. *Riverside*, p. 459. See also Bullough, Vol. VI, p. 88.

25. De Vere is not known to have traveled to Asia Minor; however, his son-in-law William Stanley is believed to have gone there. In any event, *Troilus and Cressida*, unlike Shakespeare's Italian and French settings, is devoid of topographical detail.

26. Nelson, pp. 86–87. See also Ward, p. 71–72.

27. See Chambers (*William Shakespeare*, Vol. I, p. 447) and Bullough (Vol. VI, pp. 90–92, 95).

28. Jolly and O'Brien, p. 20.

29. Bullough, Vol. VI, p. 97.

30. Roughly translated "seriously seeking reward."

31. See *A Hundreth Sundrie Flowres*, pp. 13–48, 69–74.

32. The identification of Troilus with the author is not a controversial observation. In the case of de Vere, this parallel fits naturally with details in the play, such as Troilus' line "I am as true as truth's simplicity, / And simpler than the infancy of truth" (III.ii.169–170). The Vere family motto was *Vero nihil verius* ("Nothing truer than truth"), variations of which are found throughout the canon. See Sobran, p. 109.

33. Nelson, pp. 2, 252. See also Ward, p. 117.

34. Nelson, p. 249.

35. Ogburn (citing Charles Wisner Barrell), p. 611.

36. Garber, p. 553.

37. Garber, p. 557.

38. Garber, p. 562.

39. See *Hamlet* (II.ii.192).

40. Garber, p. 538.

41. Nelson, pp. 213–218.

42. Homosexuality was a capital offense. Either the allegations were completely discounted (an unlikely scenario) or de Vere was somehow considered to be of use to the government.

43. Asimov, Vol. I, pp. 94–96.

44. Furthermore, Shakespeare's occasional poetic comparisons of the sun to a chariot were likely influenced by classical literature, rather than by a Ptolemaic view of the cosmos. De Vere was noted to have been well-versed in astronomy by contemporaries such as John Southern, and patronized known Copernicans such as John Dee.

45. In one of his letters, de Vere quoted the Latin proverb *Finis coronat opus* ("The end crowns the work"). This line is also quoted by Shakespeare (in French) in *Henry VI, Part II* (V.i.27). See Sobran, p. 272.

Chapter 28

1. This writer once witnessed a gripping performance of perhaps Shakespeare's most testosterone-charged play by (surprisingly) an all-female troupe in Healdsburg, California.

2. See Chambers (*William Shakespeare*, Vol. I, pp. 478–479) and Bullough (Vol. V, pp. 453–454).

3. Nelson, p. 53. See also Ward, p. 33. Nelson states the book was purchased in 1570 but Ward gives the date of receipt as the first quarter between January 1569 and September 1570 (p. 32). In either event, this was 9–10 years before the English translation by North.

4. Jolly, "Burghley's Library," p. 12.

5. Two years later (in his *Britannia* of 1607), Camden then curiously neglects to mention Shakespeare in a comprehensive listing of famous people from Warwickshire. See Ramón Jiménez, "Camden, Drayton, Green, Hall, and Cooke: Five Eyewitnesses Who Saw Nothing," *Shakespeare Oxford Newsletter* (Shakespeare Oxford Society), Fall 2002, p. 1.

6. Staunton, Vol. III, pp. 125–126.

7. The "historical" Coriolanus dated from the early Republican period, although some scholars have questioned his very existence.

8. Nelson, p. 30. See also Ward, p. 14.

9. Nelson, p. 58.

10. The canon is also filled with wronged, innocent heroines.

11. *Riverside*, p. 1441.

12. *Riverside*, p. 1440.

13. *Riverside*, p. 1441.

14. Nelson, p. 249. See also Ward, pp. 207–209. We like to speculate that de Vere, in return for royal forgiveness of his lapse, was instructed to become the official propagandist for the English Reformation, via Shakespeare's history plays, a service for which he would be well paid.

15. Some commentators have suggested that de Vere spent a good part of his adult life as a double agent, a not entirely implausible scenario, especially given his reputed abilities (even among enemies) for subterfuge and putting on appearances.

16. Nelson, p. 425.

17. Nelson, p. 206.

18. Nelson, pp. 51–52. See also Ward, pp. 39–40.

19. One of our favorite unsubstantiated legends surrounding the traditional author is that, as a young man, he was forced to leave Stratford-upon-Avon for allegedly poaching deer and then composing satirical doggerel against the magistrate who ruled against him. See Schoenbaum, *Compact Life*, pp. 97–109.

20. Camillus was a Roman general recalled from banishment to defeat the Gauls, who had recently invaded Italy and sacked Rome.

Chapter 29

1. Thompson, p. 166.

2. See Chambers (*William Shakespeare*, Vol. I, pp. 312–314) and Bullough (Vol. VI, pp. 3–4). The frequent explanation that play authorship was not highly valued holds true only up to a point; by 1593, the name "William Shakespeare" was a recognized commodity with respect to poetry, and this had translated to play quartos (plus specific praise by Francis Meres) by 1598; yet anonymous Shakespeare quartos continued to be published afterward.

3. *Riverside*, p. 1066. In one sense, it is refreshing to hear commentators admit that Shakespeare the writer improved as he went along, rather than insisting the canon sprang fully mature from the genius of his mind like Minerva from the head of Jupiter.

4. Bullough, Vol. VI, p. 32.

5. *Riverside*, p. 1065.

6. Chambers, *William Shakespeare*, Vol. I, p. 318.

7. Bullough, Vol. VI, p. 6.

8. *Riverside*, p. 1066.

9. Noemi Magri, "No Errors in Shakespeare: Historical

Truth and *The Two Gentlemen of Verona*," *De Vere Society Newsletter* (De Vere Society), May 1998. See also Clark, p. 47.

10. Nelson, p. 190. See also Ward, p. 163.

11. *DNB*, Vol. XVI, p. 586.

12. Bullough, Vol. VI, p. 7.

13. Nelson, pp. 236–237. See also Ward, pp. 23–24, 77–78.

14. Bullough, Vol. VI, pp. 12–13.

15. This was from Nashe's Epistle to Robert Greene's *Menaphon*. See *Riverside* (p. 1184) and Bullough (Vol. VII, p. 15). According to Nashe, "English Seneca" was capable of writing "whole Hamlets, I should say handfuls of Tragical speeches."

16. Will Shakspere was 25 years old in 1589.

17. Julie Taymor's spectacular 2000 film version of *Titus* brought out these quasi-comedic elements in a very Fellini-esque manner.

18. Bullough, Vol. VI, pp. 23–24.

19. The receipt for this transaction still exists in the accounts of Lord Burghley. See Ward (p. 33) and Nelson (p. 53).

20. Nashe, in 1593, also referred to one "Will Monox" (= Oxford / Shakespeare?), who was apparently present at the banquet in which Robert Greene fatally overindulged himself. See Ogburn (quoting Thomas Nashe and Gabriel Harvey), pp. 725–726.

21. Nelson, p. 87. See also Ward, pp. 71–72.

22. Aaron's famous last words are "If one good deed in all my life I did, I do repent it from my very soul" (V.iii.189–190).

23. Ward, pp. 111–112. See also Nelson, pp. 131, 137.

24. Some believe Prynne to have been a literary forefather to Hawthorne's Hester Prynne.

25. *DNB*, Vol. XVI, pp. 432–433.

26. *The Revels History of Drama in English*, Lois Potter, Editor (New York: Methuen, 1981), pp. 15, 63.

27. Thompson, p. 170.

28. *The Revels History of Drama in English*, p. 14.

29. *DNB*, Vol. XVI, pp. 432–433.

30. *The Revels History of Drama in English*, p. 15. King James' *Book of Sports* (1618) was originally published as a royal rebuke to Puritan complaints about breaking the Sabbath, and specifically allowed various recreational activities on Sundays.

31. D.R. Watson, *The Life and Times of Charles I* (London: Weidenfeld and Nicolson, 1972), pp. 82–83.

32. For a recitation of Peacham's impressive accomplishments, see *DNB*, Vol. XV, pp. 578–580.

33. See Chambers, *William Shakespeare*, Vol. I, Plate XI.

34. *DNB* calls the list "a valuable survey ... of contemporary English efforts in science, art, and literature" (Vol. XV, p. 580).

35. Roger Stritmatter, "The Not-too-Hidden Key to *Minerva Britanna*," *Shakespeare Oxford Newsletter* (Shakespeare-Oxford Society), Summer 2000, p. 10. See also Ogburn (p. 767) and *DNB* (Vol. XV, p. 580).

Chapter 30

1. Chambers, *William Shakespeare*, Vol. I, pp. 338–339.

2. Staunton, Vol. I, p. 156.

3. Chambers, *William Shakespeare*, Vol. I, pp. 338–339.

4. A few copies of the fourth quarto read "Written by W. Shake-speare." Chambers, *William Shakespeare*, Vol. I, pp. 339–340.

5. Schoenbaum, *Compact Life*, p. 190.

6. Marchette Chute gives the following example:

"These pulpit attacks had a certain promotion value to a manager who was trying to fill a large theatre; for the London preachers depicted the sinful delights of that 'gorgeous playing place,' as they called it, with such fascinated horror that they must have supplied an excellent advertisement for the place. As the sober journal of Sir Roger Wilbraham indicates, the Elizabethan business man was well aware of the value of this kind of publicity. Wilbraham tells the case of a printer at the turn of the century who found himself loaded with unsold copies of a certain book. 'He caused a preacher in his sermon to inveigh against the vanity thereof; since which it hath been six times under press, so much it was in request.'" (pp. 32–33)

7. Chute, p. 33.

8. Chambers, *William Shakespeare*, Vol. II, pp. 195–196.

9. This tradition was first recorded during the Restoration period. Smith, p. 502.

10. Nelson, pp. 247–248. See also Ward, p. 280.

11. Ogburn, p. 539.

12. Bullough, Vol. I, pp. 269–270.

13. Chambers, *William Shakespeare*, Vol. I, p. 346. Dante, though a Florentine by birth, learned of his political banishment while in Siena and spent the latter part of his life as a wandering exile. He also spent a good deal of time in Verona, where he received protection and patronage.

14. Bullough, Vol. I, pp. 271–274.

15. Another English version of the story appeared in 1565–1567, from William Painter's *Palace of Pleasure*, but there is general agreement that Shakespeare relied on the earlier translation by Arthur Brooke. See Chambers (*William Shakespeare*, Vol. I, p. 346) and Bullough (Vol. I, pp. 272–273).

16. Bullough, Vol. I, pp. 277–278.

17. Green, "Who Was Arthur Brooke?," p. 65.

18. Bullough, Vol. I, pp. 279–280.

19. See Chambers (*William Shakespeare*, Vol. I, p. 346) and Bullough (Vol. I, p. 269).

20. Howard, like his nephew de Vere, was a jousting champion in addition to being a poet.

21. Nelson, p. 385. See also Ward, p. 196.

22. Looney, pp. 163–165.

23. Nelson, p. 123. See also Ward, p. 130.

24. Staunton, Vol. I, pp. 157, 214–215.

25. Chute, p. 32.

26. Chambers, *William Shakespeare*, Vol. I, p. 345.

27. Grun, p. 225.

28. Nelson, p. 71.

29. Staunton, Vol. I, p. 215, note 8.

30. Nelson, p. 147.

31. This is also similar to Romeo in the play, who falls for Juliet after rebounding from an infatuation with one Rosaline (= Anne Vavasor?), who does not appear in the play. De Vere returned to his wife after a five-year separation.

32. Nelson, pp. 280–287.

33. Nelson, p. 281.

34. Ward, pp. 268–269. See also Nelson, p. 287. De Vere reportedly feuded with Bonetti as well.

35. See Smith (pp. 156–157) and Staunton (Vol. I, pp. 216–217).

36. Clark, p. 466.

37. Asimov, Vol. I, p. 478.

38. Smith, pp. 156–157.

39. Schoenbaum, *Compact Life*, pp. 264–267, 272–275.

40. Arthur Brooke's poem was republished in 1587, the same year that the second edition of Holinshed's *Chronicles* was profusely dedicated to Lord Cobham. This

was indeed a banner year for the Brooke family in terms of literary prominence, and it is conceivable that de Vere, emboldened by his recent royal annuity grant in 1586, may have been provoked into delivering dramatic reprisals, literally speaking.

41. In an interesting by coincidence, Knyvet died in 1622, the estimated date of the fourth quarto and one year before the First Folio. *DNB*, Vol. XI, p. 340.

Chapter 31

1. Cervantes, p. 640.
2. *Riverside* (Frank Kermode citing Knight), p. 1489.
3. See Chambers (*William Shakespeare*, Vol. I, p. 480) and Bullough (Vol. VI, p. 225).
4. Chambers, *William Shakespeare*, Vol. I, pp. 480–481.
5. Chambers, *William Shakespeare*, Vol. I, p. 482.
6. *Riverside*, p. 1490.
7. On New Year's Day, 1577 (one month previous), a lost, anonymous play titled *The Historie of Error* was performed at Hampton Court, which Oxfordians and some orthodox scholars believe was an early version of *The Comedy of Errors*. See Clark, pp. 15, 30.
8. Clark, p. 30. Later Charles Howard would sponsor the Lord Admiral's Men.
9. After his defeat at Actium, Antony declares he wants to shun humankind like Timon of Athens, providing Plutarch with an opportunity for a short but memorable digression.
10. See Chambers (*William Shakespeare*, Vol. I, p. 482) and Bullough (Vol. VI, p. 227). This work had not been translated into English during Shakespeare's time.
11. See Chambers (*William Shakespeare*, Vol. I, p. 483) and Bullough (Vol. VI, pp. 229–230).
12. Bullough, Vol. VI, pp. 235–236.
13. Nelson, p. 53. See also Ward, p. 33.
14. See Jolly ("Burghley's Library," p. 12), and Jolly and O'Brien, p. 20.
15. Need we apologize to orthodox academia for the utterance of this horrible blasphemy?
16. Holmes, p. 237.
17. Holmes, p. 238.
18. Sobran, p. 112.
19. Clark, pp. 33–34.
20. Holmes, p. 246.
21. Holmes, p. 248.
22. Nelson, pp. 132–134. See also Ward, p. 110.
23. Holmes, p. 252.
24. See Paul, *Monument Without a Tomb*.

Chapter 32

1. This is according to Plutarch.
2. See Chambers (*William Shakespeare*, Vol. I, pp. 396–397) and Bullough (Vol. V, p. 3).
3. See Chambers, *William Shakespeare*, Vol. I, pp. 397–398, and Vol. II, pp. 210–211.
4. Antony, delivering his subtle condemnation of the assassins in the play, seems to be punning on the name of Brutus with "brutish beasts."
5. See Chambers (*William Shakespeare*, Vol. I, p. 401) and Bullough (Vol. V, p. 13).
6. Nelson, p. 53. See also Ward, p. 33.
7. Nelson, pp. 236–237. See also Ward, pp. 30–31.
8. Bullough, Vol. VIII, p. 121.
9. Nelson, p. 381. See also Ward, p. 199.
10. See Chambers (*William Shakespeare*, Vol. I, p. 401) and Bullough (Vol. V, p. 4).
11. See Chambers (*William Shakespeare*, Vol. I, p. 401) and Bullough (Vol. V, pp. 5–7).
12. Nelson, p. 53. See also Ward, p. 33.

13. *Riverside*, p. 1148. See also Hughes, pp. 29–30.
14. Nelson, p. 25. See also Ward, p. 10.
15. Nelson, pp. 42–43. See also Ward, p. 22.
16. Nelson, p. 43. See also Ward, pp. 23–24.
17. Bullough, Vol. V, p. 36.
18. See Chambers (*William Shakespeare*, Vol. I, p. 401) and Staunton (Vol. III, pp. 460–461).
19. Chambers, *William Shakespeare*, Vol. I, p. 401.
20. Bullough, Vol. V, p. 35.
21. Ogburn, pp. 232–233.
22. De Vere's theatrical connections to Warwickshire included his acting company touring Stratford-upon-Avon, as well as entertainments he sponsored in Coventry (bear-baiting) and at Warwick Castle (a mock battle). His Wiltshire connections include his daughter's marriage into the Herbert family.
23. Werth, "Shakespeare's 'Lesse Greek,'" pp. 11–29.
24. Nelson, p. 157.
25. *Riverside*, p. 1146.
26. Schoenbaum, *Compact Life*, pp. 258–259.
27. Schoenbaum, *Compact Life*, p. 256.
28. Schoenbaum, *Compact Life*, p. 258.
29. Bullough, Vol. V, pp. 54–57.
30. Montaigne, p. 464.
31. *Riverside*, p. 1147.
32. In the play, Brutus upbraids Cassius over bribery and extortion, and refers to money as "trash" twice in quick succession (IV.iii.26, 74), a surprising attitude coming from the presumed traditional author.
33. Nelson, pp. 339–342.
34. Translated from the Latin. See Nelson (p. 181) and Ward (p. 157).
35. Nelson, pp. 58, 62. See also Ward, pp. 49–50.
36. Nelson, p. 206.
37. Meaning Caesar's stab wound from Brutus.

Chapter 33

1. *Riverside*, p. 1355.
2. *Riverside*, p. 1356.
3. Chambers, *William Shakespeare*, Vol. I, p. 471.
4. *Riverside*, p. 1356.
5. Bullough, Vol. VII, p. 428.
6. Whalen, "Shakespeare in Scotland," p. 61.
7. There have in fact been several gangster film versions of *Macbeth*, the latest titled *Men of Respect* (1991), starring John Turturro, Stanley Tucci, and Dennis Farina. The latter plays the Banquo character or, as he is called in the movie, "Bankie."
8. Bullough, Vol. VII, p. 428.
9. *Riverside*, pp. 1355–1356.
10. Chambers, *William Shakespeare*, Vol. I, p. 474.
11. Gary Wills, *Witches and Jesuits: Shakespeare's* Macbeth (New York: Oxford University Press, 1995), pp. 94–95.
12. *Butler's Lives of the Saints*, Complete Edition, edited by Herbert J. Thurston and Donald Attwater (Allen, TX: Christian Classics, 1996), Vol. IV, pp. 466–469. See also Sarah Smith, "a Reattribution of Munday's 'The Paine of Pleasure,'" *The Oxfordian* (Shakespeare Oxford Society), Vol. V, 2002.
13. Nelson, p. 48.
14. Bullough, Vol. VII, p. 441.
15. *Riverside*, p. 1356.
16. Asimov, Vol. II, p. 151.
17. Nelson, pp. 58, 62. See also Ward, pp. 49–50.
18. Nelson, pp. 58, 62, 218–219.
19. Bullough, Vol. VII, pp. 444–446. 20. Ogburn, p. 666.
21. Ward, p. 373.
22. Ward, pp. 41–43, 373.
23. Ward, pp. 43–46. See also Nelson, p. 53.

24. Ward, p. 48.

25. Alison Weir, *Mary, Queen of Scots and the Murder of Lord Darnley* (New York: Ballantine Publishing Group, 2003), p. 550.

26. Whalen, *Shakespeare in Scotland*, p. 69.

27. Whalen, *Shakespeare in Scotland*, p. 68.

28. Bullough, Vol. VII, pp. 475–476.

29. Whalen, *Shakespeare in Scotland*, pp. 68–69.

30. Weir, *Mary, Queen of Scots*, p. 565.

31. Ogburn, p. 666.

32. *Leicester's Commonwealth*, an anonymous 1584 publication, lays out these accusations in detail. Opinion has always been deeply divided over its veracity.

33. Although Henry Carey, Lord Hunsdon, was the "official" resident of King's Place until 1583 (when he became Lord Chamberlain two years after Campion's trial and execution), Carey during this period was still heavily engaged in Scottish affairs and may well have rented his house to Lord Vaux, who resided there until his death in 1595. Vaux had been accused of sheltering Campion, Southwell, and Garnett at his house in Hackney. See Miller, pp. 235–236. See also *DNB*, Vol. III, p. 977, and Vol. XX, p. 196.

34. Ward, p. 283. See also Nelson, p. 303.

35. Nelson, pp. 414–415.

36. Nelson, pp. 26, 422–423. See also Ward, p. 344.

37. Nelson, p. 423. See also Ward, p. 344.

Chapter 34

1. Chambers, *William Shakespeare*, Vol. I, p. 408.

2. Chambers, *William Shakespeare*, Vol. I, p. 423.

3. Will Shakspere was 36. Edward de Vere was 50.

4. A notable exception is Harold Bloom, who opines that the young Will Shakspere may have written an earlier version of the play. See Bloom, p. 383.

5. *Riverside*, p. 1184. See also Bullough, Vol. VII, p. 15. One view among orthodox scholars is that Nashe implied "English Seneca" was the playwright Thomas Kyd, presumed author of *The Spanish Tragedy*, and to which Shakespeare's *Hamlet* bears some resemblance. Nashe's commentary, however, can more easily be interpreted to mean that "the Kid" (Nashe's own expression) was a pale imitator of "English Seneca."

6. See Paul, *Monument Without a Tomb*.

7. Chambers, *William Shakespeare*, Vol. I, p. 408.

8. This appears to be the only Norse material ever used by Shakespeare. De Vere may have taken an interest, being of Norman ancestry. The Normans were partially descended from the Norsemen of Scandinavia.

9. *Riverside*, pp. 1184–1185.

10. Bullough, Vol. VII, p. 11.

11. Jolly, *The Writing of* Hamlet, pp. 32–33.

12. Jolly, "Burghley's Library," p. 12.

13. Ward, pp. 20–21, 101. See also Ogburn, pp. 540, 741–742.

14. Nelson, p. 237. See also Ward, pp. 80–83.

15. Bullough, Vol. VII, pp. 29–33.

16. Bullough includes an illustration of an engraving based on Titian's painting, taken from a book that was also in Burghley's library. See Vol. VII, facing page 31. See also Jolly, *The Writing of* Hamlet, pp. 24–25.

17. Baldessare Castiglione, *The Book of the Courtier*, translated by Charles Singleton (New York: W.W. Norton, 2002), pp. 44–45.

18. Nelson, p. 386. See also Ward, pp. 299, 321.

19. Ogburn, p. 528. Cardano was still alive (however, under house arrest by the Inquisition) in Rome during de Vere's Grand Tour. There is no evidence the two ever met.

20. See passage quoted by Ogburn, p. 528.

21. Nelson, p. 237. See also Ward, pp. 86–90.

22. While *Euphues* was dedicated to Lord de la Warr, Lyly dedicated the sequel to his employer Oxford, who is generally associated with the Euphuist movement. See Nelson (p. 238) and Ward (pp. 184–187).

23. Jolly, *The Writing of* Hamlet, p. 29, quoting Stritmatter.

24. See Usher, "Advances in the Hamlet Cosmic Allegory" and "Shakespeare's Support for the New Astronomy."

25. Nelson, p. 58. See also Ward, pp. 49–50.

26. Schoenbaum, *Compact Life*, p. 224.

27. Schoenbaum, *Compact Life*, p. 94.

28. Schoenbaum, *Compact Life*, p. 240.

29. The ghost of Hamlet's father is one of only two roles that Shakespeare is said to have personally acted on stage (the other being Old Adam in *As You Like It*), according to tradition (see Schoenbaum, *Compact Life*, pp. 201–202); De Vere is also recorded as having acted in at least one court masque.

30. See Schoenbaum, "John Shakespeare's Spiritual Testament" (Chapter 5), from *Compact Life*. It should also be noted that de Vere and his father (the 16th Earl) had their own flirtations with Catholicism.

31. Bullough, Vol. VII, p. 18.

32. Nelson, pp. 29–39, 41–44, 49–50. See also Ward, pp. 14–22.

33. Whalen (quoting Freud), p. 69.

34. The notion of the Bard daring to caricature Burghley on stage is ludicrous unless one assumes that Shakespeare the writer was uniquely shielded among his contemporaries, or, alternatively, was perhaps the social equal of Burghley.

35. Translation: "One heart, one way." "Corambis" translates as "two-hearted." This was quickly changed to "Polonius" in the second quarto of 1604. See Ogburn, pp. 202–203, 369–370, 557–558. See also Whalen (pp. 108–110) and Sobran (pp. 192–195).

36. *Riverside*, pp. 1184–1185.

37. This was in the first quarto for *Love's Labor's Lost* and *Palladis Tamia* by Francis Meres.

38. Nelson, pp. 151, 425. See also Ward, pp. 126–127, 347.

39. Ward, pp. 234–235.

40. Nelson, pp. 135–137. See also Ogburn, p. 556.

41. Jolly, *The Writing of* Hamlet, p. 30.

42. See Ogburn (p. 152) and Sobran (p. 5). Howard and Gielgud simultaneously portrayed Hamlet at opposite ends of Broadway in 1936. Some still maintain that Gielgud was the greatest Hamlet ever to take the stage. Howard's production tanked despite a creative team that included director John Houseman, choreographer Agnes de Mille, and composer Virgil Thomson—probably due to competition from Gielgud down the street.

43. Ogburn, p. 725.

Chapter 35

1. See Paul, *Monument Without a Tomb*.

2. *Riverside*, pp. 1297–1298. See also Chambers, *William Shakespeare*, Vol. I, pp. 463–468.

3. Lear lives to see Cordelia defeat their enemies and become Queen of Britain.

4. Bullough, Vol. VII, p. 272.

5. *The New Arthurian Encyclopedia*, Norris J. Lacy, Editor (New York: Garland Publishing, Inc., 1991), pp. 179–182. See also John North, *Stonehenge* (New York: The Free Press, 1996), pp. 395–396.

6. *Riverside*, p. 1298.

7. Nelson, p. 48.

8. Nelson, p. 383.

9. Shakespeare was first to spell the name "L-E-A-R."

10. Bullough, Vol. VII, pp. 276–277. See also Chambers, *William Shakespeare*, Vol. I, p. 33.

11. Bullough, Vol. VII, p. 278.

12. Chambers, *William Shakespeare*, Vol. I, p. 469.

13. The Countess of Pembroke in question was Mary Sidney Herbert, Philip Sidney's famous sister who survived him, edited his material, and probably had a hand in writing portions of it. One naturally wonders whether she performed similar services for Shakespeare, since the First Folio was dedicated to her sons after her death.

14. See Gerald N. Sandy, *Heliodorus* (Boston: Twayne Publishers, 1982), pp. 103–104.

15. Nelson, pp. 236–237. See also Ward, pp. 30–31.

16. *Riverside*, p. 1301.

17. W. Boyle, "Paradigm Earthquake Strikes Amherst, Mass.," *Shakespeare Oxford Newsletter* (Shakespeare Oxford Society), Spring 2000, pp. 1, 8–9.

18. *Riverside*, p. 1299.

19. This was the Amyot translation of Plutarch. See Nelson (p. 53) and Ward (p. 33).

20. Bullough, Vol. VII, p. 269.

21. Ogburn, p. 385. See also Miller, pp. 235–243.

22. To be more exact, King's Place was purchased by de Vere's second wife, Elizabeth Trentham, and the widowed Lady Vaux continued to live with de Vere and his family. Earlier, King's Place had been the residence of Henry Carey, Lord Hunsdon and Lord Chamberlain of the acting company most associated with Shakespeare. During the Jacobean era, it became the home of Fulke Greville, Lord Brooke (hence, Brooke House, as it was known afterward) and close friend of Philip Sidney. See Ward, pp. 383–384.

23. Bullough, Vol. VII, p. 270.

24. Nelson, p. 335. See also Ward, p. 306.

25. See the collection of essays, *The King Lear Perplex*, Helmut Bonheim, Editor (Belmont, CA: Wadsworth Publishing Company, Inc., 1968).

26. Nelson, pp. 58, 62. See also Ward, pp. 49–50.

27. "For who marketh better than he the seven turning flames of the sky?"—i.e., the seven then-known planets of the moon, Mercury, Venus, the sun, Mars, Jupiter, and Saturn. See Nelson (pp. 59–60) and Ward (p. 50).

28. Ogburn, pp. 526–528.

29. Nelson, p. 266.

30. Nelson, pp. 40–41. See also Ward, p. 124.

31. The queen, who had her own experience in these matters, called de Vere a bastard.

32. Ogburn, p. 740.

33. Peter W. Dickson, "The Jaggard-Herbert-de Vere Connection (1619–1623)," *Shakespeare Oxford Newsletter* (Shakespeare Oxford Society), Winter 1999, pp. 14–15, 23. See also Ogburn, pp. 221–222.

34. Gerit Quealy, "The Temple in Lord Pembroke's Garden," *Shakespeare Oxford Newsletter* (Shakespeare Oxford Society), Summer 2003, p. 8.

35. Schoenbaum, *Compact Life*, p. 167.

36. One of the earliest illustrations of Stonehenge appeared in William Camden's *Britannia* (1575), which also suggested that excavations were taking place at about that time. See John North, *Stonehenge* (New York: The Free Press, 1996), pp. 395–396.

Chapter 36

1. Chambers, *William Shakespeare*, Vol. I, pp. 457–458.

2. *Riverside*, p. 1246.

3. Chambers, *William Shakespeare*, Vol. I, p. 457.

4. *New Encyclopedia Britannica*, Vol. IX, p. 252.

5. Their beneficiaries included Ben Jonson, author of the First Folio prefatory material, and William Jaggard, printer of the Folio project.

6. The Folio would include 18 plays not previously seeing the light of day.

7. This idea was most recently put forth by Ms. Robin Williams during the 2003 Shakespearean Authorship Trust Conference at the Globe Theater in London.

8. The author is listed as the poet "Shaxberd." See Chapter 4.

9. Chambers, *William Shakespeare*, Vol. I, pp. 457, 461.

10. See Chambers (*William Shakespeare*, Vol. I, p. 462) and Bullough (Vol. VII, p. 194).

11. Bullough, Vol. VII, p. 195. See also Holmes, p. 211.

12. To this day, one can see Venetian tourist attractions such as "Desdemona's House" on the Grand Canal.

13. Bullough, Vol. VII, p. 194.

14. Jolly, "Burghley's Library," p. 12.

15. Shakespeare's great contemporary Cervantes participated in this battle. Curiously, Cervantes' tale of Cardenio from *Don Quixote* also deals with the theme of sexual jealousy, but in a profoundly different manner.

16. Nelson, p. 310. See also Ward, p. 288.

17. Emilia is also the name of the lady-in-waiting for the falsely accused Hermoine in *The Winter's Tale*.

18. Bassano's patrons included Mary Sidney, among others. See Introduction to *The Poems of Shakespeare's Dark Lady* by A.L. Rowse.

19. His only real competition is Edmund from *King Lear*.

20. Iago intimates to the audience that rumors "abroad" have it Othello has cuckolded him, but in the same breath admits that he does not care (I.iii.387–390).

21. One must also question Shakespeare's need to transfer the Ensign's desire to a newly invented third party (Rodrigo).

22. Bullough, Vol. VII, p. 206.

23. Yorke died in the Low Countries in 1587, despised by the Dutch, as well as by the English and Spanish.

24. Nelson, p. 81.

25. For example, Mary Sidney's brother Philip Sidney was reportedly another victim of Yorke's duplicity at Zutphen. See Ogburn, p. 564.

26. Nelson, pp. 345–346.

27. Nelson, p. 63.

28. Ward, p. 117. Ward viewed Howard as Iago-like. See also Nelson, p. 252.

29. Nelson, p. 259.

30. Machiavelli valued power above all else, and viewed money merely as one means of achieving this.

31. Professional actors were considered barely one step above common vagabonds, especially in the eyes of the politically ascendant Puritans.

32. A previous engagement between Anne Cecil and Philip Sidney was broken off so she could marry de Vere. See Nelson (p. 71) and Ward (p. 61).

Chapter 37

1. Cervantes, p. 375.

2. Perhaps it is more accurate to say that Shakespeare overshadows his sources, to the extent these are historically accurate.

3. Located off the eastern coast of the Ionian Sea.

4. Chambers (*William Shakespeare*, Vol. I, p. 476) and Bullough (Vol. V, p. 215).

5. *Riverside*, p. 1391.

6. See Paul, *Monument without A Tomb*.

7. Chambers (*William Shakespeare*, Vol. I, p. 478) and Bullough (Vol. V, p. 218).

8. Nelson, p. 53. See also Ward, p. 33.

9. Bullough, Vol. V, p. 229.

10. Chambers (*William Shakespeare*, Vol. I, p. 478) and Bullough (Vol. V, p. 229).

11. Waller, pp. 107–108.
12. Waller, p. 111.
13. Chambers (*William Shakespeare*, Vol. I, p. 478) and Bullough (Vol. V, p. 215).
14. *DNB*, Vol. V, p. 470.
15. Waller, p. 66.
16. Waller (quoting Philip Sidney), p. 108.
17. Waller, pp. 120–121.
18. Waller, pp. 114–115.
19. Waller, p. 80.
20. *Riverside*, p. 1184. See also Bullough, Vol. VII, p. 15.
21. Stanley (the Sixth Earl of Derby) married de Vere's eldest daughter Elizabeth in 1595 and is another popular candidate for an alternative Shakespeare.
22. Ogburn, pp. 85–86.
23. Nelson, p. 297. See also Ward, pp. 254–255.
24. Nelson, pp. 317–318. See also Ward, p. 292.
25. Nelson, pp. 295–296. See also Ward, p. 229.
26. *Riverside*, p. 1391.
27. Clark, pp. 349–357.
28. Hughes, "New Light on the Dark Lady," pp. 1, 8–15.
29. Hughes, "New Light on the Dark Lady," p. 14.

Chapter 38

1. Twain, p. 420.
2. Shakespeare the sonneteer also urges the Fair Youth to marry. The projected union fell through, however, and Wriothesley eventually wed Elizabeth Vernon, lady-in-waiting to the queen, while Elizabeth Vere married William Stanley, Earl of Derby. See Nelson (pp. 323, 349) and Ward (pp. 313–314, 318).
3. See Peter W. Dickson, *Shakespeare Oxford Newsletter* (Shakespeare Oxford Society), Spring 1999, p. 8. There has been speculation that Henry Wriothesley was Henry de Vere's namesake.
4. *Riverside*, p. 1799.
5. Schoenbaum, *Compact Life*, p. 151.
6. Schoenbaum, *Compact Life*, p. 175.
7. Ben Jonson owned a copy of this book. See David Riggs, *Ben Jonson: A Life* (Cambridge: Harvard University Press, 1989), illustration.
8. Nelson, pp. 386–387. See also Ward, pp. 299–300.
9. *Riverside*, p. 1797.
10. Sobran, pp. 109–110.
11. Nelson, p. 96. See also Ward, p. 75.
12. Magri, *Influence of ... Works*, p. 2.
13. Proper protocol for visiting foreign noblemen required first paying respects to the Doge, then to the nearly 100-year-old Titian, by then the living embodiment of Venetian culture. See Magri, *Influence of ... Works*, pp. 3–4.
14. Magri, *Influence of ... Works*, pp. 3–4. Titian also painted *The Rape of Lucrece*.
15. A Renaissance example of a vice tax. See Rosenthal, p. 268, n. 44.
16. Franco was the literary subject of *The Honest Courtesan* (1992) by Margaret F. Rosenthal, as well as the major motion picture *Dangerous Beauty* (1998).
17. Rosenthal, pp. 5, 89, 177–178, 304–305, n. 102.
18. Magri, *Venetian Inquisition*, p. 7.
19. Ward, pp. 189–190.
20. Rosenthal, pp. 116, 119.
21. Magri, *Venetian Inquisition*, p. 7.
22. Magri, *Venetian Inquisition*, p. 6.
23. *Access: Florence, Venice & Milan*, Third Edition, Lois Spritzer, Editor (New York: Access Press, 1996), p. 178. This palazzo still exists. See also Rosenthal, pp. 66, 89.
24. Rosenthal, pp. 162, 209. Franco is believed to have retreated near Verona to Fumane, the country villa of Marcantonio Della Torre, another outstanding artistic and literary patron of the age. Fumane is praised as an artistic haven in Book XI of Matteo Bandello's *Novelle* (see Rosenthal, p. 346, n. 90), a major Shakespearean influence and a work probably known to de Vere.
25. Magri, *Venetian Inquisition*, pp. 5–7. Cuoco's parents were among the victims of the plague.
26. Nelson, pp. 5–7. This information comes from a 1587 letter by Stephen Powle from Venice.
27. For example, why would such a statement be made in a poem dedicated to de Vere's youngest daughter Susan? See Frank M. Davis, "'Her Warbling Sting'—Music Not Malady: Refuting Alan Nelson's Thesis on Nathaniel Baxter's 1606 Poem," *Shakespeare Oxford Newsletter* (Shakespeare Oxford Society), Summer 2001, pp. 3–4.
28. Rosenthal, pp. 71–72. Lucieta's successful defense did not deny that she was a courtesan, but asserted that the law was meant to apply only to common prostitutes and not to a married, professional woman such as herself. The court apparently ruled that courtesans were in fact subject to the same restrictions, but that Lucieta herself was exempt due to her married status. It is safe to say that de Vere, as an English tourist in Venice, would have encountered social mores quite different from those prevalent in England.
29. See *The Poems of Shakespeare's Dark Lady*, Introduction by A.L. Rowse. Like Franco, Bassano and Shakespeare's Dark Lady stood accused of promiscuity. Rowse's theory has been attacked over the years for various unpersuasive reasons. See also Hughes, "New Light on Shakespeare's Dark Lady."
30. Rosenthal, pp. 45–48, 162–163. Even at its most censorious, Venice would have been more tolerant than Puritan England. Franco was essentially a love poet; Lanyer, after marrying, became for the most part a religious poet.
31. Rosenthal, pp. 240–242. Franco praises Fumane; Lanyer, Cookeham. See also Rowse, pp. 137–143.
32. Rosenthal, pp. 18–19, 35–37. Some of this poetic license was directed toward Franco herself.

Chapter 39

1. Wriothesley at this point had presumably yet to break off his engagement to de Vere's daughter.
2. *Riverside*, p. 1814.
3. This is from the chapter titled "England to Her Three Daughters, Cambridge, Oxford, Innes of Court, and to All Her Inhabitants." Covell (in the margins) writes, "All praise worthy. Lucretia[,] Sweet Shak-speare ... Wanton Adonis." On the same page he lauds Spenser and Daniel, who both attended university.
4. *Riverside*, p. 1814.
5. Eddi Jolly, "Burghley's Library," p.12.
6. Sobran, p. 109.
7. John Hamill, "The Ten Restless Ghosts of Mantua," *Shakespeare Oxford Newsletter* (Shakespeare Oxford Society), Summer 2003, p. 13.
8. "[T]hat rare Italian master" as described by Shakespeare in *The Winter's Tale* (V.ii.98).
9. Ogburn, p. 499.
10. Nelson, p. 237. See also Ward, pp. 80–83.
11. Nelson, p. 130. See also Ward, pp. 106, 109.
12. In Shakespeare's *Two Gentlemen of Verona* the characters travel overland to Mantua en route between Verona and Milan.
13. Magri, *Italian Renaissance Art*, p. 10. See also *The Palazzo Ducale in Mantua*, Translator: David Stanton (Milan: Electa, 1992), p. 58.
14. *The Palazzo Ducale in Mantua*, p. 62.

15. Magri, *Influence of ... Works*, p. 7.
16. *Palazzo Te in Mantua*, Translator: Christopher Hugh Evans (Milan, Electa, 1994), p. 55.
17. This is found in the Room of the Candleholders.
18. Nelson, pp. 213–218. See also Sobran, pp. 125–126.
19. The recent biography of de Vere by Alan Nelson is titled *Monstrous Adversary*, the same phrase used by Charles Arundel to describe de Vere in his counter-charges.
20. Nelson, p. 286. See also Ward, p. 232.

Chapter 40

1. Montaigne, p. 374.
2. Among other notable works, McCullough wrote the foreword for Charlton Ogburn, Jr.'s landmark *The Mysterious William Shakespeare*. See Ogburn, p. x.
3. This was written around 1930; it remains truer than ever. Chambers, *William Shakespeare*, Vol. I, p. 561.
4. This is yet another example of Shakespeare's name being hyphenated, indicating that it may have been understood as a pseudonym.
5. Another poem attributed to Shakespeare, titled *A Lover's Complaint*, was included in the 1609 publication. *Riverside*, p. 1875.
6. Schoenbaum, *Compact Life*, p. 268.
7. Pequigney, p. 2.
8. Staunton, Vol. III, p. 759.
9. At the risk of adding to the "folly" of previous writers, we will not shrink from attempting to identify all the actors connected to the sonnets with historical people.
10. Chambers, *William Shakespeare*, Vol. I, pp. 565–566.
11. Schoenbaum (citing Sidney Lee), *Compact Life*, p. 270.
12. Looney/Miller, Vol. II, pp. 207–211, 215–221.
13. Ogburn, p. 206.
14. See Paul, *Monument Without a Tomb*.
15. Price, pp. 145–146.
16. The publisher was one John Benson.
17. *Riverside*, pp. 1841–1842. See also Chambers, *William Shakespeare*, Vol. I, pp. 556–557.
18. Chambers, *William Shakespeare*, Vol. I, p. 559.
19. Chambers, *William Shakespeare*, Vol. I, pp. 555–556.
20. Chambers, *William Shakespeare*, Vol. I, pp. 564–565.
21. Nelson, p. 323. See also Ward, p. 314.
22. De Vere is recorded as having visited Palermo during his Grand Tour.
23. *Riverside*, p. 1840.
24. Nelson, p. 383. See also Ward, pp. 300–301.
25. Nelson (citing May), p. 385.
26. Samuel Daniel and Michael Drayton, whose sonnets were published during the early 1590s, also utilized the English form. De Vere's sonnet predates these by almost 20 years. See Looney, pp. 386–387. A few anonymous and pseudonymous sonnets were written in the English form as well, such as the "Phaeton Sonnet." See Joseph Sobran, "Before He Was Shakespeare," *Shakespeare Oxford Newsletter* (Shakespeare Oxford Society), Winter 2005, pp. 1, 13–16.
27. Nelson, p. 161.
28. Ward, p. 89.
29. Sobran, p. 203. The analysis of Sobran in this respect is comprehensive.
30. This was the same age as Will Shakspere at the time *Greene's Groatsworth of Wit* was published.
31. Skeptical of this view, Chambers once again cut to the chase: "But the use of a convention is not inconsistent with the expression of personal feeling." See Chambers, *William Shakespeare*, Vol. I, p. 561.

32. Sobran, p. 98.
33. Chambers, *William Shakespeare*, Vol. I, p. 560.
34. The first Oxfordian interpreter of the sonnets was John Thomas Looney, and Sobran's observations are a logical extension of Looney's pioneering work.
35. Chambers, *William Shakespeare*, Vol. I, p. 560.
36. Nelson, pp. 367, 354.
37. Chambers, *William Shakespeare*, Vol. I, p. 560.
38. Nelson, p. 286. See also Ward, p. 232. One marvels at de Vere's ability to have taken such hits and still survive. The benefits of being an earl and Burghley's son-in-law extended only so far. The queen not only pardoned de Vere, but three years later in 1586, while facing war with Spain, granted him a staggering annuity of £1,000. Something is missing from this picture.
39. May, p. 53.
40. Chambers, *William Shakespeare*, Vol. I, p. 560.
41. *Riverside*, p. 1866.
42. Chambers, *William Shakespeare*, Vol. I, pp. 565–567.
43. "The mortal moon hath her eclipse endur'd" from Sonnet 107 is widely interpreted as referring to Queen Elizabeth's death in 1603 and Wriothesley's subsequent release from prison by King James. See Chambers, *William Shakespeare*, Vol. I, p. 563.
44. Whalen, p. 27.
45. The word "prick'd" is not a misprint.
46. Bloom, p. 714.
47. Pequigney, pp. 81–82.
48. Ogburn (quoting Freud), p. 146.
49. Chambers, *William Shakespeare*, Vol. I, pp. 568–569.
50. Schoenbaum, *Compact Life*, pp. 180–182. See also Ogburn, pp. 736–740.
51. May, p. 125.
52. Sonnets 153–154, the last in the series, stand apart as an independent coda.
53. *Riverside*, p. 1871.
54. Hughes, "New Light on the Dark Lady," pp. 1, 8–15. See also *The Poems of Shakespeare's Dark Lady*, Introduction by A.L. Rowse. Rowse's book, incidentally, was dedicated to John Gielgud, who had Oxfordian sympathies in his authorship beliefs.
55. Nelson, p. 397. See also Ward, p. 336.
56. Smith, pp. 46–53.

Conclusion

1. Montaigne, pp. 457–458.
2. Marlovians (i.e., those who favor Christopher Marlowe as the true Bard) only have to deal with accusations of being obsessed with conspiracies. The "conspiracy nut" rap is the second-most frequent charge leveled against authorship skeptics.
3. The poem ascribed to William Shakespeare titled *The Phoenix and the Turtle* comes across almost as a tribute to Manners and his Countess. Manners himself has been proposed as the true Bard, most recently by the Russian critic Ilya Gililov.
4. Traditionalists would of course view the Oxfordian theory as a heretical attack on the true faith.
5. Gibbon, Vol. I, p. 389. Gibbon, though an outspoken critic, believed that the rise of early Christianity was a happy event in that it saved western civilization from other worse belief systems that could have easily filled the void left by the decline in Greco-Roman paganism. For Gibbon, change was inevitable: it was a question of whether that change would be good or bad—something Bardolators would do well to remember with respect to the authorship question.
6. Cervantes, p. 414.

Bibliography

Alexander, Mark André. "Shakespeare's Knowledge of the Law." *The Oxfordian* (Shakespeare Oxford Society), Vol. VI, 2001.

Anderson, Mark. *"Shakespeare" by Another Name: The Life of Edward de Vere, Earl of Oxford, The Man Who Was Shakespeare.* New York: Gotham Books / Penguin Group, 2005.

Asimov, Isaac. *Asimov's Guide to Shakespeare.* Vols. I–II. New York: Doubleday, 1978.

Bloom, Harold. *Shakespeare: The Invention of the Human.* New York: Riverhead Books, 1998.

Brazil, Robert. "Unpacking *The Merry Wives.*" *The Oxfordian* (Shakespeare Oxford Society), Vol. II, 1999.

Bullough, Geoffrey. *Narrative and Dramatic Sources of Shakespeare.* Vols. I–VIII. New York: Columbia University Press, 1975.

Cervantes, Miguel de. *Don Quixote.* translated by Burton Raffel. edited by Diana de Armas Wilson. New York: W.W. Norton, 1999.

Chambers, E.K. *The Elizabethan Stage.* Vols. I–IV Oxford: Clarendon, 1923.

_____. *William Shakespeare: A Study of Facts and Problems.* Vols. I–II Oxford: Clarendon, 1930.

Chute, Marchette. *Shakespeare of London.* New York: Dutton, 1949.

Clark, Eva Turner. *Hidden Allusions in Shakespeare's Plays.* Edited by Ruth Loyd Miller. 3rd Ed. Port Washington, NY: Kennikat, 1974.

Collinson, Patrick. *The Elizabethan Puritan Movement.* Oxford: Clarendon, 1967.

The Dictionary of National Biography. Vols. I–XXII. London: Oxford University Press, 1949–1950.

Garber, Marjorie. *Shakespeare After All.* New York: Pantheon, 2004.

Gibbon, Edward. *The Decline and Fall of the Roman Empire.* Vols. I–III. New York: Modern Library, 1995.

Goldstein, Gary. "Did Queen Elizabeth Use the Theater for Social and Political Propoganda?" *The Oxfordian* (Shakespeare Oxford Society), Vol. VII, 2004.

Green, Nina. "Who Was Arthur Brooke?" *The Oxfordian* (Shakespeare Oxford Society). Vol. III, 2000.

Greenwood, George. *Is There a Shakespeare Problem?* London: John Lane, 1916.

_____. *The Shakespeare Problem Restated.* London: John Lane, 1908.

Grillo, Ernesto. *Shakespeare and Italy.* Glasgow: Robert Maclehose/The University Press, 1949.

Grun, Bernard. *The Timetables of History.* 3rd ed. New York: Simon & Schuster/Touchstone, 1991.

Heinemann, Margot. *Puritanism and the Theatre.* Cambridge: Cambridge University Press, 1980.

Herrick, Marvin T. *Italian Comedy in the Renaissance.* Urbana: University of Illinois Press, 1966.

Holinshed, Raphael. *Holinshed's Chronicles: England, Scotland, and Ireland.* Vols. I–VI. New York: AMS, 1965.

Holmes, Edward. *Discovering Shakespeare.* County Durham: Mycroft, 2001.

Hughes, Stephanie Hopkins. "New Light on the Dark Lady." *Shakespeare Oxford Newsletter* (Shakespeare Oxford Society), Fall 2000.

_____. "Shakespeare's Tutor: Sir Thomas Smith (1513–1577)." *The Oxfordian* (Shakespeare Oxford Society), Vol. III, 2000.

A Hundreth Sundrie Flowers. From the original edition of 1573. Edited by Bernard M. Ward and Ruth Loyd Miller. 1926. Reprint, Port Washington, NY: Kennikat 1975.

Jiménez, Ramon. "*The True Tragedy of Richard the Third*: Another Early History Play by Edward de Vere." *The Oxfordian* (Shakespeare Oxford Society), Vol. VII, 2004.

Jolly, Eddi. "Dating Shakespeare's *Hamlet.*" *The Oxfordian* (Shakespeare Oxford Society), Vol. II, 1999.

_____. "'Shakespeare' and Burghley's Library." *The Oxfordian* (Shakespeare Oxford Society), Vol. III, 2000.

_____. "The Writing of *Hamlet*." *De Vere Society Newsletter* (De Vere Society), January 2001.

_____, and P. O'Brien. "Shakespeare's Sources and Sir Thomas Smith's Library." *De Vere Society Newsletter*, July 2001.

Lambin, George. *Travels of Shakespeare in France and Italy.* Edited and translated by W. Ron Hess. Lincoln, NE: Writers Club Press/iUniverse, 2002.

Londré, Felicia Hardison, Editor. *Love's Labor's Lost: Critical Essays.* New York: Routledge, 1997.

Looney, John Thomas. "*Shakespeare*" *Identified.* Vols. I–II. Edited by Ruth Loyd Miller. Port Washington, NY: Kennikat, 1975.

Magri, Noemi. "The Influence of Italian Renaissance Art on Shakespeare's Works." *De Vere Society Newsletter* (De Vere Society), January 2001.

_____. "Italian Renaissance Art in Shakespeare." *De Vere Society Newsletter* (De Vere Society), July 2000.

_____. "The Venetian Inquiry into Orazio Cuoco (1577)." *De Vere Society Newsletter* (De Vere Society), January / February 2002.

Malim, Richard, ed. *Great Oxford: Essays on the Life and Work of Edward de Vere, 17th Earl of Oxford, 1550–1604.* Tunbridge Wells, UK: Parapress, 2005.

Matus, Irvin Leigh. *Shakespeare, In Fact.* New York: Continuum, 1994.

May, Stephen W. *The Elizabethan Courtier Poets.* Asheville, NC: Pegasus, 1999.

Montaigne, Michel de. *The Complete Essays.* Translated and edited by M.A. Screech. New York: Penguin Putnam, 1991.

Mosher, Sally. "William Byrd's 'Battle' and the Earl of Oxford." *The Oxfordian* (Shakespeare Oxford Society), Vol. I, October 1998.

Nelson, Alan H. *Monstrous Adversary.* Liverpool: Liverpool University Press, 2003.

The New Encyclopedia Britannica. Chicago: Encyclopedia Britannica, 2002.

Ogburn, Charlton, Jr. *The Mysterious William Shakespeare.* 2nd Ed. McLean, VA: EPM, 1992.

Palmer, Alan, and Veronica Palmer. *Who's Who in Shakespeare's England.* New York: St. Martin's, 1999.

Paul, Christopher. "A Monument Without a Tomb: The Mystery of Oxford's Death." *The Oxfordian* (Shakespeare Oxford Society), Vol. VII, 2004.

Pequigney, Joseph. *Such Is My Love: A Study of Shakespeare's Sonnets.* University of Chicago Press, 1985.

Price, Diana. *Shakespeare's Unorthodox Biography.* Westport, CT: Greenwood, 2001.

Radcliff-Umstead, Douglas. *The Birth of Modern Comedy in Renaissance Italy.* University of Chicago Press, 1969.

Rosenthal, Margaret F. *The Honest Courtesan.* University of Chicago Press, 1992.

Rowse, A.L. Introduction to *The Poems of Shakespeare's Dark Lady: Salve Deus Rex Judæorum* by Emilia Lanier. New York: Clarkson N. Potter, 1979.

Schoenbaum, Samuel. *Shakespeare's Lives.* New York: Oxford University Press, 1970.

_____. *William Shakespeare: A Compact Documentary Life.* New York: Oxford University Press, 1987.

Shakespeare, William. *The Complete Illustrated Shakespeare.* Vols. I–III. Edited by Howard Staunton. New York: Park Lane, 1979.

_____. *The Riverside Shakespeare.* Edited by G. Blakemore Evans. 2nd Ed. Boston: Houghton Mifflin, 1997.

Smith, Bruce R. *Homosexual Desire in Shakespeare's England.* University of Chicago Press, 1991.

Sobran, Joseph. *Alias Shakespeare.* New York: Free Press, 1997.

Stritmatter, Roger A. *The Marginalia of Edward de Vere's Geneva Bible.* Doctoral Thesis (University of Massachusetts Amherst, Department of Comparative Literature), February 2001.

"Symposium: Who Wrote Shakespeare? An Evidentiary Puzzle." *Tennessee Law Review*, Vol. 72, no. 1, Fall 2004.

Thompson, Elbert N.S. *The Controversy Between the Puritans and the Stage.* New York: Russell and Russell, 1966.

Twain, Mark. "Is Shakespeare Dead?" from *The Complete Essays of Mark Twain.* Edited by Charles Neider. Garden City, NY: Doubleday, 1963.

Usher, Peter. "Advances in the Hamlet Cosmic Allegory." *The Oxfordian* (Shakespeare Oxford Society), Vol. IV, 2001.

_____. "Shakespeare's Support for the New Astronomy." *The Oxfordian* (Shakespeare Oxford Society), Vol. IV, 2001.

Waller, G.F. *Mary Sidney, Countess of Pembroke.* Edited by James Hogg. Universität Salzburg: Institut für Anglistik und Amerikanistik, 1979.

Ward, Bernard M. *The Seventeenth Earl of Oxford (1550–1604.)* London: John Murray, 1928.

Werth, Andrew "Shakespeare's 'Lesse Greek.'" *The Oxfordian* (Shakespeare Oxford Society), Vol. V, 2002.

Whalen, Richard. *Shakespeare: Who Was He?* Westport, CT: Praeger, 1994.

_____. "Shakespeare in Scotland." *The Oxfordian* (Shakespeare Oxford Society), Vol. VI, 2003.

Wright, Daniel L. *The Anglican Shakespeare: Elizabethan Orthodoxy in the Great Histories.* Vancouver, WA: Pacific-Columbia, 1993.

_____. "'Vere-y Interesting': Shakespeare's Treatment of the Earls of Oxford in the History Plays." *Shakespeare Oxford Newsletter* (Shakespeare Oxford Society), Spring 2000.

Index